WEBSTER'S
BAD SPELLERS'
DICTIONARY

WEBSTER'S
BAD SPELLERS'
DICTIONARY

Executive Editors:
Bud Wileman and Robin Wileman
Project Editor: Regina Roselli Coles

BARNES
&NOBLE
BOOKS
NEW YORK

Copyright © 1992, 1991, 1989, 1988, 1987, 1985
by Wileman Publications

This edition published by Barnes & Noble Inc.,
a division of Marboro Books Corp.,
by arrangement with Buddy William Neil Wileman
and Deborah Robin Wileman
1992 Barnes & Noble Books

Printed and bound in the United States of America

ISBN 0-88029-772-7

M 9 8 7

In gratitude
to all those children and adults
who helped with the spelling
in this dictionary

CONTENTS

Introduction

How To Find a Word

If possible, write down what you think is the spelling of the word you wish to find.
Decide what are the first two or three letters.

Find these in the dictionary by looking at the left-hand column. If you have the correct spelling you will find the word printed in **black**.

If you have the incorrect spelling you will find the word printed in **blue**, in the second left-hand column. You will then find the correct spelling in **black** in the right-hand column.

If you do not find the word, check any directions that may be given, e.g.,

> Look under **de-** if the word is not under **di**.

Proceed as above. Check how close you were to the correct spelling and if necessary learn the correct spelling.

How To Learn the Correct Spelling

Say the word and the letters.
Look at the word carefully.
Write the word three times.
Close your eyes and think of the word. **Write it down** with your eyes closed.
Check to see that you are correct.
Write the word in a sentence so that you will remember its meaning as well as its spelling.
Consult a standard dictionary if you are unsure of the meaning.

About the Dictionary

You will see that all the words, correct spellings, and incorrect spellings, are listed in alphabetical order.

Nouns

To form the plural of most nouns add "**s**" to the word.
  e.g., rabbit, rabbits
Where the plural may be difficult, you are given help.
  e.g., injury, -ries (for "injuries")
     goose, geese
     piano, pianos
You will find hints to help you with plurals on page xii.

Verbs

Verbs listed in the dictionary give the endings for the past tense, the past participle and the present participle. Most verbs have the same word for the past tense and the past participle.

    e.g., reach, -ed, -ing for reach, **reached, reaching**

Where difficulty could occur with the spelling, you are given further help.

    e.g., collide, -lided, -liding for collide, collided, colliding

            erase, erased, erasing

Where the past tense and the past participle are different, the full words are given.

    e.g., sing, sang, sung, singing

You will find hints to help you with verbs on page xi.

Adjectives

Where there may be difficulty in spelling the comparative and superlative forms further help is given.

    e.g., dizzy, dizzier, dizziest

Adverbs

Where the ending -**ly** is given, it is added to the word.

    e.g., mythical, -ly for "**mythically**"

Where there is a change in spelling, further help is given.

    e.g., haste, -tily for "**hastily**"

            palpable, -bly for "**palpably**"

SPELLING HINTS

Double the last letter of short (one syllable) words *that do not end in e* when adding -ed, -er or -ing; e.g., ban, banned; jog, jogger; fit, fitting.

Drop the **e** when -ed, -er or -ing are added, to short words *that end in e where the central vowel sound is said the same way as the letter name*; e.g., cope, coped; make, maker; bite, biting.

Short words keep the **e** when -ly is added; e.g., tame, tamely; time, timely.

Short words (one syllable) ending in **y**, preceded by a vowel, keep the **y** when -ed, -er or -ing are added; e.g., key, keyed; buy, buyer; toy, toying. If the **y** is preceded by a consonant, when -ed, or -er are added, the **y** is changed to **i**; e.g., try, tried; fly, flier.
The **y** is kept when adding -ing; e.g., try, trying.

Change the **y** to **i** when adding other parts to longer words ending in **y**; e.g., berry, berries; marry, marriage; happy, happiness; hurry, hurried; heavy, heavier and heaviest.
However, the **y** is kept when adding -ing; e.g., hurry, hurrying; bury, burying.

The vowels that can be doubled are: **e** (been), **o** (moon) and sometimes **u** (vacuum); **a** and **i** are not doubled in English words.

Letters that can be doubled in the middle of a word are: **b, d, f, g, m, n, r, s, t** and **z**.

F, l, s and **z** are doubled when found at the end of short words; e.g., cuff, doll, pass, buzz.

One **l** is dropped when **full** is added to the end of a word; e.g., helpful.

One **l** is dropped when **all-** or **well-** are added to the front of a word; e.g., already, welcome.

The **s** is not doubled when **dis-** and **mis-**, meaning "not," are placed in front of a word — e.g., disable, misbehave — unless the main word begins with **s**; e.g. disservice, misspell.

The **n** is not doubled when **un-** is placed in front of a word — e.g., unmade — unless the main word begins with **n**; e.g. unnecessary.

Similarly, when **in-** is placed in front of a word, the **n** is not doubled — e.g., insane — unless the main word begins with **n**; e.g., innumerable.

PLURALS

1. Most words ad **s** to form the plural; e.g., cat, cats; but words that end in a sibilant sound, (-s, -sh, -ss, -tch, -x), add **es**; e.g., gases, wishes, masses, catches, boxes.

2. Most words ending in **f** change the **f** to **v** and add **es**; e.g., thief, thieves. There are some exceptions, so check the word.

3. Most words ending in **o** add **es**; e.g., potato, potatoes. The exceptions are foreign words, so check the word if you are unsure.

4. Words ending in **y**, *preceded by a consonant*, change the **y** to **i** and add **es**; e.g., ferry, ferries; but words ending in **y**, *preceded by a vowel*, add **s**; e.g., day, days; monkey, monkeys.

5. Words ending in **-ful** usually put the **s** after the stem word; e.g., cupful, cupsful. However, the placement of **s** at the end of the word is now becoming acceptable; e.g., cupful, cupfuls.

6. Some words add **-en** or **-ren** to the stem word; e.g., ox, oxen; child, children.

7. Some foreign words change the ending and add **a**, **ae**, **i**; e.g., compendium, compendia; formula, formulae; bacillus, bacilli.

POSITION OF LETTERS

1. In "**ee**" sounding words, **c** is always followed by **ei**; e.g., receive, ceiling. Most others have **ie**; e.g., believe, priest. However, there are many exceptions, so check the word if you are unsure.

2. **q** is always followed by **u** in English words.

3. No English words end in **j** or **v**.

4. If **g** and **h** come together in a word, **g** is always before **h**; e.g., eight, enough.

5. **ck** never starts a word.

SOUND

1. If a long word (more than one syllable) ends in the sound, "**shun**," it can be spelled -tion, -sion or -cion.

2. **ti**, **si** and **ci** make the "**sh**" sound, but not at the beginning of a word.

3. A long word ending in the "**j**" sound could be spelled -age, -ege, -ige or -dge. Check the word if you are not sure.

4. A long word ending in the "**ree**" sound could be spelled -ary, -ery, -ory, -ury or -ry. Check if you are not sure.

5. Short words (one syllable) ending in **y** make the "**i**" sound as in sly, pry, sky.

6. Words ending in the "**ul**" sound could be spelled -ble, -al, -el, -il, -ol or -le. Check if you are not sure.

Aa

aback
abacus, abaci, abacuses

abait	abate
abakus	abacus

abalone

abalonie	abalone

abandon, -ed, -ing
abandonment
abase, abased, abasing
abasement
abashed
abate, abated, abating
abatement

abators	abattoirs

abattoirs

abatwaz	abattoirs
abayance	abeyance

abbess (nun)

abbess	abyss (hole)

abbey, -beys

abbie	abbey

abbot
abbreviate, -ated, -ating
abbreviation

abcence	absence
abdicasion	abdication
abdacate	abdicate

abdicate, -cated, -cating
abdication
abdomen

abducksion	abduction

abduct
abduction
abductor

abel	able
aberasion	aberration

aberrant
aberration

abet, abetted, abetting
abeyance

abeyense	abeyance

abhor, abhorred, abhorring

abhore	abhor
abhorent	abhorrent

abhorrent, -ly
abidance

abidanse	abidance

abide, abode, abided, abiding
ability, -ties

abillity	ability
abismal	abysmal
abiss	abyss

abject, -ly

abjective	objective
abjekt	abject

abjure, -jured, -juring
ablaze
able, abler, ablest
able-bodied

abligation	obligation
abliterate	obliterate
ablong	oblong

ablution

abnegasion	abnegation

abnegate, -gated, -gating
abnegation
abnormal, -ly
abnormality, -ties

abnoxious	obnoxious

aboard
abode
abolish
abolishment

abolision	abolition

abolitionary
abolitionist

abollish	abolish

A-bomb
abominable
abominably
abominate, -nated, -nating
abomination

abominible	abominable
abord	aboard

aboriginal

Aborigine
  aborsion — abortion
abort, -ed, -ing
abortion
abortive, -ly
abound, -ed, -ing
about
above
aboveboard
  abowt — about
abracadabra
abradant
abrade, abraded, abrading
abrasion
abrasive
abreast
  abrest — abreast
abridge, abridged, abridging
abridgment
  abrige — abridge
abroad
abrogate, -gated, -gating
abrupt, -ly
abruptness
  absail — abseil
abscess
abscond, -ed, -ing
absconder
abseil, -ed, -ing
absence
  absense — absence
absent, -ed, -ing
absentee
absenteeism
absent-minded
  absess — abscess
absinth
  absolusion — absolution
absolute, -ly
absolution
absolutism
absolutist
absolve, -solved, -solving
absorb, -ed, -ing
absorbency
  absorbensy — absorbency
absorbent

  absorbsion — absorption
absorption
absorptive
abstain, -ed, -ing
  abstane — abstain
abstemious, -ly
  abstemius — abstemious
  abstension — abstention
abstention
abstinence
  abstinense — abstinence
abstinent, -ly
abstract, -ed, -ing
abstraction
  abstrakt — abstract
  abstraktion — abstraction
abstruse, -ly
absurd, -ly
absurdity
abundance
abundant, -ly
  abundence — abundance
  abundent — abundant
  abusave — abusive
abuse, abused, abusing
abusive, -ly
abut, abutted, abutting
abuttal
abysmal, -ly
abyss (hole)
  abzorb — absorb
  abzurd — absurd
acacia
academic
academician
  academision — academician
academy, -mies
  accacia — acacia
  accademic — academic
  accademy — academy
accede, -ceded, -ceding (agree)
  accede — exceed (surpass)
accelerate, -rated, -rating
acceleration
accelerator
accent, -ed, -ing

accentual, -ly
accentuate, -ated, -ating
accept, -ed, -ing (receive)
  accept   except (omit)
acceptability
acceptable, -bly
acceptance
  acceptense   acceptance
  acceptible   acceptable
access (approach)
  access   excess (extra)
  accessable   accessible
accessary, -ries (crime)
accessibility
accessible, -bly
accession
accessory, -ries (extra)
accident
accidental, -ly
acclaim, -ed, -ing
acclamation
acclimatise, -tised, -tising
  acclusion   occlusion
accolade
accommodate, -dated, -dating
accommodation
  accomodation accommodation
accompaniment
accompanist
accompany, -nied, -nying
  accompanyment accompaniment
accomplice
accomplish, -ed, -ing
accomplishment
  accompliss   accomplice
accord, -ed, -ing
accordance
  accordanse   accordance
accordant, -ly
accordingly
accordion
accordionist
accost, -ed, -ing
account, -ed, -ing
accountability
accountable
accountably

accountancy
accountant
  accountible   accountable
  accoustic   acoustic
accredit, -ed, -ing
accreditation
  accresion   accretion
accretion
  accrew   accrue
  accross   across
accrual
accrue, -crued, -cruing
  accult   occult
  accumen   acumen
accumulate, -lated, -lating
accumulation
accumulative
accumulator
  accupational occupational
accuracy
  accurasy   accuracy
accurate, -ly, -ness
accursed
  accusasion   accusation
accusation
accuse, -cused, -cusing
accuser
accustom, -ed, -ing
  accute   acute
ace
  acelerate   accelerate
  acerage   acreage
  acerbait   acerbate
acerbate, -bated, -bating
acerbic
acerbity
  acerige   acreage
acetate
acetic (acid)
  acetic   ascetic (hermit)
  acetilene   acetylene
acetylene
ache, ached, aching
  acheivable   achievable
  acheive   achieve
achievable
achieve, achieved, achieving

achievement
achiever
  achievible   achievable
acid
acidic
acidify, -fied, -fying
acidity
ackers
acknowledge, -edged, -edging
  acknowlege   acknowledge
acknowledgment

| For other ack- words, look under ac- or acc-. |

  aclaim   acclaim
  aclamation   acclamation
acme
acne
  acolade   accolade
  acommodate   accommodate
  acommodasion   accommodation
  acompanist   accompanist
  acompany   accompany
  acomplice   accomplice
  acomplish   accomplish
  acord   accord
  acordion   accordion
acorn
  acost   accost
  acount   account
acoustic
acoustical, -ly
acouastics
acquaint, -ed, -ing
acquaintance
  acquaintence   acquaintance
acquiesce, -esced, -escing
acquiescence
acquiescent, -ly
  acquiesense   acquiescence
  acquiess   acquiesce
acquire, -quired, -quiring
acquisition
acquisitive, -ly
acquit, -quitted, -quitting
acquittal
acre

acreage
  acredit   accredit
acrid, -ly
acrimonious, -ly
acrimony, -nies
acrobat
acrobatic
acrobatically
acrobatics
  acrofobia   acrophobia
acrophobia
acropolis
across
acrylic
  acryllic   acrylic
act, -ed, -ing
  acter   actor
acting
action
actionable
  actionible   actionable
activate, -vated, -vating
active
activism
activist
activity, -ties
actor
actress
actual, -ly
actuality, -ties
actually
actuarial, -ly
actuary, -ries
actuate, -ated, -ating
actuity
acumen
acupuncture
acupuncturist
  acupunshur   acupuncture
  acuse   accuse
acute, -ly
acuteness
adage
adagio
  adajio   adagio
adamant
  adament   adamant

adapt, -ed, -ing (adjust)
  adapt   adept (expert)
adaptability
adaptable
  adaptasion   adaptation
adaptation
  adaptible   adaptable
adaption
adaptive, -ly
adaptor
  adda   adder
addendum, -da
adder
  addication   addiction
addict, -ed, -ing
addiction
addictive
  addision   addition
addition (add)
  addition   edition (book)
additional, -ly
additive
addled
address, -ed, -ing
  adducable   adducible
adduce, -duced, -ducing
adducible

> For other add- words,
> look under ad-.

adenoid
adept, -ly, -ness (expert)
  adept   adapt (adjust)
adequacy
  adequasy   adequacy
adequate, -ly
  adherant   adherent
adhere, -hered, -hering
adherence
  adherense   adherence
adherent, -ly
adhesion
adhesive, -ly
adjacent, -ly
  adjasent   adjacent
adjectival, -ly
adjective

  adjetival   adjectival
  adjetive   adjective
adjoin, -ed, -ing (abut)
adjourn, -ed, -ing (suspend)
adjournment
adjudicate, -cated, -cating
adjudication
adjudicative, -ly
adjudicator
adjunct
adjure, -jured, -juring
  adjurn   adjourn
  adjurnment   adjournment
adjust, -ed, -ing
adjustable, -bly
  adjustible   adjustable
adjustment
  admeral   admiral
administer, -ed, -ing
administrable
administrate, -trated, -trating
  administrater   administrator
administration
administrative, -ly
administrator
  administrible   administrable
admirable, -bly
admiral
admiralty, -ties
  admirasion   admiration
admiration
admire, -mired, -miring
admirer
  admirible   admirable
  admision   admission
  admissable   admissible
admissible, -ly
admission
admit, -mitted, -mitting
admittance
  admittanse   admittance
admittedly
admonish, -ed, -ing
  admonision   admonition
admonition
ad nauseam
  adnoid   adenoid

ado
adobe
adolescence
adolescent
  adolesense — adolescence
  adolesent — adolescent
  adopsion — adoption
adopt, -ed, -ing
adoption
adoptive, -ly
adorable
adorably
  adorasion — adoration
adoration
adore, adored, adoring
  adorible — adorable
adorn, -ed, -ing
adornment
  adorrable — adorable
  adorre — adore
adrenalin
  adress — address
adrift
adroit, -ly
  adroyt — adroit
adulate, -lated, -lating
adulation
adulatory
adult
  adultarate — adulterate
adulterate, -rated, -rating
adulteration
adulterer
adulteress
adulterous
adultery, -teries
adulthood
  adultry — adultery
  advacate — advocate
advance, -vanced, -vancing
advancement
  advanse — advance
  advansement — advancement
advantage, -taged, -taging
advantageous, -ly
  advantagious — advantageous
  advantaje — advantage

  advenshure — adventure
advent
adventure, -tured, -turing
  adventureous — adventurous
adventurer
adventuresome
adventurous, -ly
adverb
adverbial, -ly
adversary, -saries
adverse, -ly (against)
  adverse — averse (unwilling)
  adversery — adversary
adversity, -ties
advert, -ed, -ing
advertise, -tised, -tising
advertisement
advertiser
  advertisment — advertisement
  advertize — advertise
advice (opinion)
  advice — advise (give advice)
advisability
advisable, -bly
  advisary — advisory
advise, -vised, -vising (give advice)
  advise — advice (opinion)
advised, -ly
adviser
  advisery — advisory
  advisible — advisable
advisory
  advize — advise (give advice)
advocacy
  advocasy — advocacy
advocate, -cated, -cating
  advokate — advocate
adze
aegis
aeon
aerate, -rated, -rating
  aerater — aerator
aerator

aerial, -ly
aerie
aerobatics
aerobics
aerodynamics
aeronautical, -ly
aeronautics
  aeronortics   aeronautics
aerosol
aerospace
aesthetic
  afable   affable
  afadavit   affadavit
  afair   affair
afar
  afasia   aphasia
  afect   affect (pretend)
  afect   effect (result)
  afectation   affectation
  afected   affected
  afected   effected
  afection   affection
  afectionate   affectionate
  afective   affective
  afeild   afield
affability
affable, -bly, -ness
  affadavit   affidavit
affair
  affare   affair
  affecktion   affection
affect, -ed, -ing (pretend)
  affect   effect (result)
affectation
affection
affectionate, -ly
affective, -ly (emotion)
  affective   effective
                    (actual)
  affend   offend
  affible   affable
affidavit
affiliate, -ated, -ating
affiliation
  affilliation   affiliation
affinity, -ties
affirm, -ed, -ing

  affirmasion   affirmation
affirmation
affirmative, -ly
affix, -ed, -ing
  afflicktion   affliction
afflict, -ed, -ing
affliction
afflictive, -ly
affluence
  affluense   affluence
affluent, -ly
afford, -ed, -ing
affordable
  affordible   affordable
  affraid   afraid
affray
  affresh   afresh
affront, -ed, -ing
afield
  afinity   affinity
  afirm   affirm
  afirmative   affirmative
  afix   affix
  aflict   afflict
  aflicktion   affliction
afloat
  afluent   affluent
  aford   afford
afraid
  afray   affray
afresh
  afront   affront
aft
after
afterbirth
afterglow
afterlife
aftermath
afternoon
afterthought
afterward
again
against
agape
agate
age, aged, ageing or aging
ageism

agency, -cies		agraculture	agriculture
agenda, -das		agrarian	
agensy	agency	agravate	aggravate
agent		agravation	aggravation
agghast	aghast	agree, agreed, agreeing	
aggrandize, -dized, -dizing		agreeable, -bly, -ness	
aggrandizement		agreeible	agreeable
aggrandizer		agreement	
aggravate, -vated, -vating		agregate	aggregate
aggravater	aggravator	agression	aggression
aggravation		agressive	aggressive
aggravator		agresser	aggressor
aggregate, -gated, -gating		agribusiness, -es	
aggregation		agricultural, -ly	
aggregative		agriculturalist	
aggreived	aggrieved	agriculture	
aggresion	aggression	agrieved	aggrieved
aggresser	aggressor	agronomist	
aggression		agronomy	
aggressive, -ly		aground	
aggressor		ahead	
aggrevate	aggravate	ahed	ahead
aggrieved		ahoy	
aggrivate	aggravate	aid (help)	
agground	aground	aide (assistant)	
aghast		ail, -ed, -ing	
agile, -ly		ail	ale (beer)
agility		aileron	
agis	aegis	ailias	alias
agist, -ed, -ing		ailment	
agistment		aim, -ed, -ing	
agitate, -tated, -tating		aimless, -ly, -ness	
agitater	agitator	ain't (am not)	
agitation		aint	ain't
agitative		air, -ed, -ing (gas)	
agitator		air	hair (head)
agle	ogle	air	heir (inherit)
agnastic	agnostic	airate	aerate
agnostic		airborn	airborne
agnosticism		airborne	
ago		air brake	
agog		air break	air brake
agonize, -nized, -nizing		airbus	
agonizingly		air-condisioned	air-conditioned
agony, -nies		air-conditioned	
agorafobia	agoraphobia	air conditioning	
agoraphobia		aircraft, -craft	

airfeild	airfield	alas	
airfield		Alaska	
airforce		albatros	albatross
airgun		albatross, albatrosses	
airial	aerial	albeeit	albeit
airily		albeit	
airlift		albino, -nos	
airline		albinism	
airliner		album	
airlock		albumen (egg white)	
airmail		albumin (protein)	
airobatics	aerobatics	albuminous	
airobics	aerobics	albuminus	albuminous
airodynamics	aerodynamics	alcali	alkali
airosol	aerosol	alcaline	alkaline
airplane		alchemist	
air pocket		alchemy	
airport		alcohol	
air pressure		alcoholic	
airship		alcoholism	
airspace		alcove	
airspeed		alderman, -men	
airstrip		ale (beer)	
air terminal		ale	ail (ill)
airtight		alege	allege
airtite	airtight	alert, -ed, -ing	
airwaves		alfa	alpha
airy, airier, airiest		alfabet	alphabet
aisle (path)		alfalfa	
aisle	I'll (I will)	alfresco	
aisle	isle (island)	alga, -gae	
aitch		algebra	
ajar		algebraic, -ally	
ajis	aegis	alias, aliases	
akimbo		alibi, -bis	
akin		alien	
alabaster		alienate, -nated, -nating	
alabi	alibi	alienater	alienator
alacart	à la carte	alienation	
à la carte		alienator	
alackrity	alacrity	alight, alighted, alighting	
alacritous		align, -ed, -ing	
alacritus	alacritous	alignment	
alacrity		alike	
Alah	Allah	aliment (food)	
alarm, -ed, -ing		aliment	element (part)
alarmist		alimentary (food)	

alimentary	elementary
	(basic)
alimony	
alive	
alkaholic	alcoholic
alkali, -lis, -lies	
alkaline	
alkalinity	
alkeline	alkaline
alkohol	alcohol
alkoholic	alcoholic
alkoholism	alcoholism
alkove	alcove
all (every)	
all	awl (tool)
allabaster	alabaster
Allah	
all-American	
allay, -layed, -laying (calm)	
allay	alley (lane)
allay	ally (friend)
allbatross	albatross
alledge	allege
allegasion	allegation
allegation	
allege, -leged, -leging	
allegiance	
allegianse	allegiance
allegorical, -ly	
allegory, -ries	
allegro	
alleluia	
allergic	
allergy, -gies	
allert	alert
alleviate, -ated, -ating	
alleviation	
alleviater	alleviator
alleviator	
alley, alleys (lane)	
alley	allay (calm)
alley	ally (friend)
alliance	
allied	
alliense	alliance
allies	
alligater	alligator

alliterasion	alliteration
alliteration	
alliterative, -ly	
allmanac	almanac
allmost	almost
allocate, -cated, -cating	
allocation	
alloft	aloft
allone	alone
allot, -lotted, -lotting	
allotment	
allow, -ed, -ing	
allowable	
allowance	
allowense	allowance
allowible	allowable
alloy	
all right	
alright	all right
allso	also
all together	altogether
allude, -luded, -luding (refer)	
allude	elude (avoid)
allure, -lured, -luring	
allusion (reference)	
allusion	elusion (evade)
allusion	illusion (trick)
allusive, -ly (refer)	
allusive	elusive (avoid)
allusive	illusive (tricky)
alluvial	
ally, -lies (friend)	
ally, -lied, -lying	
ally	allay (calm)
ally	alley (lane)
almanac	
almighty, -tily, -tiness	
almond	
almoner	
almost	
alms (gifts)	
alocate	allocate
aloe	
aloft	
alone	
along	
alongside	

alood	allude
aloof	
alot	a lot (of)
alot	allot (give)
aloud (speak)	
aloud	allowed (permit)
alow	allow
alowable	allowable
alowance	allowance
aloy	alloy
alp	
alpaca	
alpacka	alpaca
alpha	
alphabet	
alphabetical, -ly	
alphebet	alphabet
alpine	
already	
alredy	already
Alsatian	
also	
altar (church)	
altatude	altitude
altenate	alternate
alter (change)	
alterable, -bly	
alterasion	alteration
alteration	
altercasion	altercation
altercation	
altercative	
alter ego	
alterior	alterior
alterible	alterable
alternate, -nated, -nating	
alternately	
alternater	alternator
alternation	
alternative, -ly	
alternator	
alterration	alteration
although	
altimeter	
altitude	
alto, -tos	
altogether	
altruism	
altruistic, -ally	
alturnate	alternate
alude	allude
alumina	
aluminum	
alumminum	aluminum
alumna, -nae	
alumnus, -ni	
alure	allure
alurt	alert
alushion	allusion
alusive	allusive
always	
amaize	amaze
amalgam	
amalgamate, -mated, -mating	
amalgamation	
amalgum	amalgam
amaretto	
amass, -ed, -ing	
amassable	
amassible	amassable
amatcher	amateur
amater	amateur
amateur	
amatory	
amaze, -mazed, -mazing	
amazement	
amazment	amazement
Amazon	
ambaguity	ambiguity
ambassader	ambassador
ambassador, -ial	
ambeance	ambiance
ambeance	ambience
ambel	amble
amber	
ambiance	ambience
ambiant	ambient
ambidexterity	
ambidextrous, -ly	
ambience	
ambiense	ambience
ambient	
ambiguity, -ties	

ambiguous, -ly
ambiguus — ambiguous
ambision — ambition
ambit
ambition
ambitious, -ly
ambitous — ambitious
ambivalence
ambivalense — ambivalence
ambivalent
ambile — amble
amble, -bled, -bling
ambulance
ambulanse — ambulance
ambush, -ed, -ing
ame — aim
ameanable — amenable
ameba — amoeba
amego — amigo
ameliorate, -rated, -rating
amelioration
amen
amenable, -bly
amend, -ed, -ing (change)
amend — emend (correct)
amendment
amends
amenible — amenable
amenity, -ties
America
ameter — ammeter
amethist — amethyst
amethyst

For amf- words, look
under **amph-**.

aimiable — amiable
amiability
amiable, -bly
amicability
amicable, -bly
amicible — amicable
amid
amidst
amigo
amiss
amity, -ties (friendship)

amity — enmity
(hostility)
ammeter
ammonia
ammunision — ammunition
ammunition

For other amm- words,
look under **am-**.

amnesia, -iac
amnesty, -ties
amnesty, -tied, -tying
amnezia — amnesia
amoeba, -bae, -bas
amoebic
amok
amond — almond
among
amongst
amoral, -ly
amorfous — amorphous
amorous, -ly
amorphism
amorphous, -ly
amorphus — amorphous
amortize, -tized, -tizing
amount, -ed, -ing
amownt — amount
ampair — ampere
ampel — ample
amperage
ampere
amphetamine
amphibian
amphibious, -ly
amphitheater
ample, -pler, -plest (enough)
amplefy — amplify
amplification
amplifier
amplify, -fied, -fying
amplitude
amply
ampoule (bottle)
ampul — ample (enough)
ampule (bottle)
amputate, -tated, -tating

amputation

amuck

  amuk — amok

  amuk — amuck

amulet

  amung — among

  amunision — ammunition

amuse, amused, amusing

amusement

anachronism

anachronistic

  anackronism — anachronism

  anackronistic — anachronistic

anaconda

anagram

  anaky — anarchy

anal

analgesia

analgesic

  analisis — analysis

  analist — analyst

  analitic — analytic

  analize — analyze

analog

analogous, -ly

analogue

analogy, -gies

analysis, -ses

analyst

analytic

analytical, -ly

analyze, -lyzed, -lyzing

anarchical, -ly

anarchism

anarchist

anarchy

  anatamy — anatomy

anathema, -mas

anatomical, -ly

anatomist

anatomy, -mies

  anceint — ancient

ancestor

ancestral, -ly

ancestry, -tries

anchor, -ed, -ing

anchorage

anchorman, -men

anchovy, -vies

ancient

ancillary, -aries

anecdotal

anecdote

anemia

anemic

anesthesia

anesthetic

anesthetist

anesthetize, -ized, -izing

aneurism

anew

  anewity — annuity

angel (spirit)

  angel — angle (fishing)

angelic

  angellic — angelic

anger, -ed, -ing

  angery — angry

angina

angle, angled, angling (fishing)

  angle — angel (spirit)

angler

Anglican

Anglicanism

Anglo-Catholic

  Anglo-Sacksen — Anglo-Saxon

Anglo-Saxon

angora

angrily

angry, angrier, angriest

  angsiety — anxiety

anguish, -ed, -ing

angular, -ity

  anguler — angular

  angwish — anguish

  anigma — enigma

  anihilate — annihilate

animal

  animasity — animosity

animate, -mated, -mating

animatedly

animation

  animel — animal

animosity, -ties

aniseed
aniversary	anniversary
anjel	angel
anjelic	angelic
anjina	angina
ankel	ankle
anker	anchor

ankle
anklet
annals
anneal, -ed, -ing
annex, -ed, -ing
annexation
| annialate | annihilate |

annihilate, -lated, -lating
anniversary, -ries
| annix | annex |

Anno Domini
annoint	anoint
annomaly	anomaly
annorexia	anorexia

annotate, -tated, -tating
annotation
announce, announced, announcing
announcement
annoy, annoyed, annoying
annual, -ly
annuity, -ties
annul, annulled, annulling
annulment
annulus, -li, -luses
annunciate, -ated, -ating
annunciation

> For other ann- words,
> look under an-.

anode
| anodine | anodyne |

anodyne
anoint, -ed, -ing
| anomaley | anomaly |

anomaly, -lies
anon
| anonimity | anonymity |
| anonimous | anonymous |

anonymity
anonymous, -ly

anorak
| anorecksia | anorexia |

anorexia
another
anoynt	anoint
anser	answer
anserable	answerable
ansestor	ancestor
ansestral	ancestral
ansestry	ancestry
ansilary	ancillary

answer, -ed, -ing
answerable, -bly
| answerible | answerable |

ant (insect)
| ant | aunt (relative) |

antacid
antagonism
antagonist
antagonistic, -ally
antagonize, -nized, -nizing
Antarctic
| antasid | antacid |

ante- (before)
| ante | anti- (against) |
| anteak | antique |

anteater
antecedent
antechamber
| anteclimax | anticlimax |
| antecyclone | anticyclone |

antedate, -dated, -dating
| antediloovian | antediluvian |

antediluvian
| anteek | antique |
| antefreeze | antifreeze |

antelope, antelopes
antemeridian (adjective)
ante meridiem (adverb)
| antena | antenna |

antenatal
| antenatel | antenatal |

antenna, -tennae, -tennas
anterior
anteroom
anthem
anthill

anthology, -gies			antiperspirant	
anthracite			antiphon	
anthracks	anthrax		antipodes	
anthrasite	anthracite		antipodies	antipodes
anthrax, -thraces			antiquarian	
anthropoid			antiquary, -quaries	
anthropologey	anthropology		antiquated	
anthropologist			antique (rare)	
anthropology			antique	antic (trick)
anti- (against)			antiquity, -quities	
anti	ante- (before)		antiroom	anteroom
antibiotic			anti-Semitic	
antibody, -bodies			anti-Semitism	
antic, -ticked, -ticking (trick)			antiseptic, -ally	
antic	antique (rare)		antisiclone	anticyclone
anticeptic	antiseptic		antisipation	anticipation
antichamber	antechamber		antisocial, -ly	
Antichrist			antithesis, -theses	
anticiclone	anticyclone		antithisis	antithesis
anticipasion	anticipation		antitoksic	antitoxic
anticipate, -pated, -pating			antitoksin	antitoxin
anticipation			antler	
anticipatory			antonim	antonym
anticlimacks	anticlimax		antonym	
anticlimactic			anus	
anticlimax			anuther	another
anticyclone			anvil	
anticyclonic			anvul	anvil
antidate	antedate		anxiety, -ties	
antidepressant			anxious, -ly	
antidepressent	antidepressant		any	
antidotal			anybody	
antidote			anyhow	
antifon	antiphon		anyone	
antifreeze			anything	
antigen			anyway	
antihisstamine	antihistamine		anywear	anywhere
antihistamine			anywere	anywhere
antikwarian	antiquarian		anywhere	
antikwated	antiquated		anziety	anxiety
antikwitey	antiquity		aorta, -tas, -tae	
antilope	antelope		apace	
antimony			Apache, Apache, Apache	
antinatal	antenatal		aparent	apparent
antinewklear	antinuclear		apart	
antinuclear			apartheid	
antipathy, -pathies			apartied	apartheid

apartite	apartheid
apartment	
apase	apace
apathetic, -ally	
apathy	
ape, aped, aping	
apeace	apiece
apease	apiece
apeice	apiece
apeks	apex
apercher	aperture
apergee	apogee
apergey	apogee
aperitif	
aperture	
apex, apexes, apices	
aphasia	
aphid	
aphorism	
aphrodisiac	
apiary, apiaries	
apiece	
apissul	epistle
apistle	epistle
aplom	aplomb
aplomb	
aply	apply
apocalipse	apocalypse
apocalypse	
apocalyptic	
apocrifal	apocryphal
apocryphal, -ly	
apogee	
apologetic, -ally	
apologey	apology
apologist	
apologize, -gized, -gizing	
apology, -gies	
apoplectic	
apoplexy	
aposle	apostle
apostasy, -sies	
apostle	
apostolate	
apostolic	
apostrofy	apostrophe
apostrophe	

aposul	apostle
apothecary, -ries	
apoynt	appoint

> For other ap- words,
> look under **app-**.

appal, -palled, -palling	
Appalachea	
Appaloosa	
apparatus, -tus, -tuses	
apparel	
apparent, -ly	
apparision	apparition
apparition	
appart	apart
appeal, -ed, -ing	
appealing, -ly	
appear, -ed, -ing	
appearance	
appearense	appearance
appease, -peased, -peasing	
appeasement	
appelant	appellant
appellant	
appellate	
appellation	
append, -ed, -ing	
appendacitis	appendicitis
appendage	
appendectomy, -mies	
appendicitis	
appendige	appendage
appendiks	appendix
apperatus	apparatus
apperel	apparel
appertain, -ed, -ing	
apperture	aperture
appetite	
appetizer	
applaud, -ed, -ing	
applause	
applawd	applaud
applaws	applause
apple	
appliance	
applianse	appliance
applicability	

applicable, -bly
applicant
   applicasion   application
application
   applie   apply
applied
applique
apply, -plied, -plying
appoint, -ed, -ing
appointment
   apporsion   apportion
apportion, -ed, -ing
apportionment
   apposishion   apposition
apposite, -ly (appropriate)
   apposite   opposite
                 (contrary)
apposition
appraisal
appraise, -praised, -praising (judge)
   appraise   apprize
               (inform)
   appraximate   approximate
   appreciabel   appreciable
appreciable, -bly
appreciate, -ated, -ating
appreciation
appreciative, -ly
apprehend, -ed, -ing
   apprehenshion apprehension
   apprehensibel   apprehensible
apprehensible
apprehension
apprehensive, -ly
apprentice
apprenticeship
   apprentise   apprentice
   appricot   apricot
apprize, -prized, -prizing (inform)
   apprize   appraise (judge)
approach, -ed, -ing
   approachabel approachable
approachable
approbation
   approch   approach
   approchible   approachable
   approove   approve

   appropos   apropos
appropriate, -ated, -ating
appropriation
approval
approve, -proved, -proving
   approvel   approval
approximate, -mated, -mating
approximately
approximation
apricot
April
apron
apropos
apt, -ly, -ness
aptitude
   aptley   aptly
aqualung
aquamarine
aquaplane
aquarium
Aquarius
aquatic
aqueduct
aqueous
aquiline
   aquaint   acquaint
   aquire   acquire
   aquit   acquit
   arabel   arable
   arabesk   arabesque
arabesque
Arabic numerals
arable
   araign   arraign
   arain   arraign
   arange   arrange
   aray   array
   arber   arbor
   arbitary   arbitrary
arbiter
arbitrary
arbitrate, -trated, -trating
arbitration
arbor
arboreal
arboricultural
arboriculture

arc, arced, arcing (curve)
| arc | ark (boat) |

arcade
arcane
arch
archaeological, -ly
archaeologist
archaeology
archaic
archaism
archangel
| archary | archery |

archbishop
archeology
archer
archerfish
archery
archetypal
archetype
archipelago, -gos, -goes
architect
architectural, -ly
architecture
architrave
archival
archives
archivist
arcipelago	archipelago
arcitect	architect
arcitectural	architectural
arcitecture	architecture
arcives	archives

arc light
arctic
Arctic Circle
ardent, -ly
| arder | ardor |

ardor
arduous, -ly, -ness
| arduus | arduous |

are
area
| arears | arrears |

arena
aren't
| arent | aren't |
| arest | arrest |

argent
| argew | argue |

argon
arguable, -bly
argue, -gued, -guing
| arguement | argument |
| arguible | arguable |

argument
argumentation
argumentative, -ly
argus
| arguw | argue |

argyle
aria (melody)
aria	area (piece)
arial	aerial
arible	arable

arid, -ly, -ness
aridity
Aries
| arina | arena |

arise, arose, arisen, arising
aristocracy, -cies
| aristocrasy | aristocracy |

aristocrat
aristocratic
arithmetic
arithmetical, -ly
arithmetician
| arival | arrival |
| arive | arrive |

ark (boat)
| ark | arc (curve) |

> For other ark- words,
> look under arc-.

arm
| armachure | armature |

armada
armadillo, -los
Armageddon
armament
| armastice | armistice |

armature
armchair
armed
| armer | armor |

armey	army	arrowroot	
armistice		arsenal	
armistise	armistice	arsenic	
armoner	almoner	arsenical	
armor		arsnic	arsenic
armored		arson	
armorer		art	
armory, -ries		artachoke	artichoke
armpit		artacle	article
arms (weapons)		artefact	
arms	alms (gifts)	arterial	
army, -mies		artery, -teries	
arogance	arrogance	artesian well	
aroganse	arrogance	artful, -ly	
arogant	arrogant	arthritic	
aroma		arthritis	
aromatic		articel	article
arora	aurora	artichoke	
arose		article, -cled, -cling	
around		articulate, -lated, -lating	
arousal		articulation	
arouse, aroused, arousing		artifact	
arow	arrow	artifice	
arownd	around	artificer	
arowroot	arrowroot	artificial, -ly	
arowse	arouse	artificiality	
arpeggio		artifise	artifice
arpejio	arpeggio	artifishial	artificial
arraign, -ed, -ing		artillery	
arraignment		artisan	
arrange, -ranged, -ranging		artist (painter)	
arrangement		artiste (actor)	
arrant, -ly (notorious)		artistic	
arrant	errand (trip)	artistry	
arrant	errant (diviate)	artizan	artisan
arras		artless, -ly	
array, -ed, -ing		arwry	awry
arrears		arye	awry
arrest, -ed, -ing		asailant	assailant
arrival		asbestos	
arrive, -rived, -riving		ascend, -ed, -ing	
arrogance		ascendancy	
arroganse	arrogance	ascendant	
arrogant, -ly		ascenshun	ascension
arrogate, -gated, -gating		ascension	
arrouse	arouse	ascent (upward)	
arrow		ascent	assent (agree)

ascertain, -ed, -ing		askew	
ascertainabel	ascertainable	askue	askew
ascertainable, -bly		asleep	
ascertainible	ascertainable	asma	asthma
ascertainment		asmatic	asthmatic
ascetic, -ally		asp	
asceticism		asparagus	
ascot		aspect	
ascribe, ascribed, ascribing		aspen	
ase	ace	aspersion	
asend	ascend	asphalt	
asendancy	ascendancy	asphyxia	
asendansy	ascendancy	asphyxiate, -ated, -ating	
asendant	ascendant	asphyxiation	
asenshion	ascension	aspic	
asent	ascent (upward)	aspirant	
asent	assent (agree)	aspirasion	aspiration
aseptic, -ally		aspirate, -rated, -rating	
asertain	ascertain	aspiration	
asertion	assertion	aspirator	
asetic	ascetic	aspirayte	aspirate
aseticism	asceticism	aspire, aspired, aspiring	
asexual, -ly		aspirin	
asfalt	asphalt	asprin	aspirin
asfelt	asphalt	ass, asses	
asfixia	asphyxia	assail, -ed, -ing	
asfixiate	asphyxiate	assailant	
ash		assassin	
ashamed, -ly		assassinate, -nated, -nating	
ashfelt	asphalt	assassination	
ashore (beach)		assault	
ashore	assure (certain)	assaulter	
aside		assay, -ed, -ing (analyze)	
asidity	acidity	assay	essay (try)
asign	assign	assayer	
asilum	asylum	assemblage	
asimetrical	asymmetrical	assemble, -bled, -bling	
asimetry	asymmetry	assembly, assemblies	
asine	assign	assend	ascend
asinement	assignment	assendancy	ascendancy
asinine, -ly		assendant	ascendant
asininity		assension	ascension
asistance	assistance	assent (agree)	
asitic	ascetic	assent	ascent (upward)
ask, -ed, -ing		assention	ascension
askance		assershion	assertion
askanse	askance	assert, -ed, -ing	

ssertion		aster	
ssertive, -ly		asterisk	
asses	assess	astern	
ssess, -ed, -ing		asteroid	
assessabel	assessable	asthma	
ssessable		asthmatic	
assesser	assessor	astigmatism	
assessible	assessable	astir	
ssessment		astonish, -ed, -ing	
ssessor		astonishment	
sset, assets		astound, -ed, -ing	
ssiduous, -ly		astownd	astound
ssign, -ed, -ing		astral	
ssignable, -bly		astray	
ssignation		astride	
ssignee		astringency	
ssignment		astringent, -ly	
ssimilate, -lated, -lating		astrologer	
ssimilation		astrological, -ly	
assine	assign	astrology	
assinment	assignment	astronaught	astronaut
ssist, -ed, -ing		astronaut	
ssistance		astronautics	
ssistant		astrul	astral
assistence	assistance	astur	astir
assistent	assistant	asturn	astern
ssociate, -ated, -ating		astute, -ly, -ness	
ssociation		asunder	
ssociative, -ly		asylum	
ssonance		asymetry	asymmetry
assonanse	assonance	asymmetric	
ssonant		asymmetrical, -ly	
ssort, -ed, -ing		asymmetry	
ssortment		ate (food)	
assosiate	associate	ate	eight (number)
ssuage, -suaged, -suaging		ateen	eighteen
ssume, -sumed, -suming		atey	eighty
ssumption		athaletic	athletic
assumsion	assumption	atheism	
ssurance (certainty)		atheist	
assurance	insurance	atheistic	
	(protection)	athiesm	atheism
ssure, -sured, -suring (certain)		athiest	atheist
assure	ashore (beach)	athiestic	atheistic
assure	insure	athleet	athlete
	(guarantee)	athlete	
ast	ask	athletic	

atlas
atmosfear — atmosphere
atmosferic — atmospheric
atmosphere
atmospheric
atol — atoll
atoll
atom
atomic
atomizer
atone, atoned, atoning
atonement
atrocious, -ly
atrocity, -ties
atrophy, -phied, -phying
atrosious — atrocious
attach, -ed, -ing (bind)
attaché (aide)
attachment
attack, -ed, -ing (assault)
attain, -ed, -ing
attainable
attainment
attempt, -ed, -ing
attend, -ed, -ing
attendance
attendant
attendent — attendant
attension — attention
attention
attentive, -ly, -ness
attenuate, -ated, -ating
attest, -ed, -ing
attic
attire, -tired, -tiring
attitude
attorney
attract, -ed, -ing
attraction
attractive, -ly, -ness
attribute, -uted, -uting
attrision — attrition
attrition
attune, -tuned, -tuning
atum — atom
atune — attune
aturney — attorney

For other **at-** words,
look under **att-**.

atypical, -ly
aubergine
auburn
aucksion — auction
auction, -ed, -ing
auctioneer
audable — audible
audacious, -ly
audacity
audasity — audacity
audeo — audio
audibility
audible
audibly
audience
audiense — audience
audio
audiometer
audiometric
audiometry
audiovisual
audision — audition
audit, -ed, -ing
audition
auditor
auditorium, -toriums, -toria
auditory
auditree — auditory
auditry — auditory
auger (tool)
auger — augur (foretell)
aught (any part)
aught — ought (should)
augment, -ed, -ing
augmentation
augur (foretell)
augur — auger (tool)
augural
august (majestic)
August
aukward — awkward
auning — awning
aunt
aura

aural, -ly (hearing)
aural   oral (spoken)
aureole
auricle
auricular
auriferous
auriole   aureole
aurora
auspice, auspices
auspicious, -ly
auspise   auspice
austairity   austerity
austeer   austere
austere, -ly
austerity, -ties
austral
Australia
Australian
australite
autagraph   autograph
autamatic   automatic
autamobile   automobile
authentic
authenticate, -cated, -cating
authentication
authenticity
authentisity   authenticity
author
authoratarian   authoritarian
authoress
authoritarian
authoritative, -ly
authority, -ties
authorizasion   authorization
authorization
authorize, -rized, -rizing
autism
auto
autobiographical, -ly
autobiography, -phies
autocracy
autocrasy   autocracy
autocrat
autocratic
autocue
autograf   autograph
autograph

automasion   automation
automatic
automation
automobile
automotive
autonomee   autonomy
autonomous, -ly
autonomus   autonomous
autonomy
autopilot
autopsy, -sies
autum   autumn
autumn
autumnal, -ly
auxiliary, -ries
avacado   avocado
avail, -ed, -ing
availability
available
availible   available
avalable   available
avalanch   avalanche
avalanche
avale   avail
avaliable   available
avant-garde
avarey   aviary
avarice
avaricious, -ly
avaricous   avaricious
avaris   avarice
avenew   avenue
avenge, avenged, avenging
avenger
avenue
aver, averred, averring
average, -raged, -raging
avericious   avaricious
averidge   average
averiss   avarice
averse, -ly (unwilling)
averse   adverse
                     (against)
aversion
aversive, -ly
avert, -ed, -ing
avery   aviary

avgas
aviary, aviaries
  aviasion — aviation
aviate, -ated, -ating
  aviater — aviator
aviation
aviator
aviatrix, -trixes, -trices
avid, -ly
  avinue — avenue
avionics
  avlanch — avalanche
avocado, avocados
avoid, -ed, -ing (evade)
  avoid — ovoid (egg)
avoidable, -ably
  avoidible — avoidable
avow, -ed, -ing
avowal
  avoyd — avoid
  avrage — average
  avud — avid
  avur — aver
  avurse — averse
  avursion — aversion
  avurt — avert
await, -ed, -ing
awake, awoke, awaking
awaken, -ed, -ing
award, -ed, -ing
aware
awareness
  awate — await
away
  awayte — await
  awb — orb
awe, awed, awing (fear)
  awe — oar (boat)
  awear — aware
awesome, -ly
awful, -ly
  awgy — orgy
  awksilary — auxiliary
awkward, -ly, -ness
  awkword — awkward
awl (tool)
  awl — all (every)

  awl — owl (bird)
awning
awoke
awry
ax, axes
axe, axes
axe, axed, axing
axial, -ly
  axident — accident
  axidental — accidental
axiom
axiomatic
axis, axes
axle
  axsede — accede
  axseed — accede
  axsel — axle
  axsellerate — accelerate
  axsent — accent
  axsentuate — accentuate
  axsept — accept
  axseptable — acceptable
  axseptance — acceptance
  axseptible — acceptable
  axsesary — accessary
  axsess — access
  axsessable — accessible
  axsessible — accessible
ay, ayes (yes)
ayatollah
aye (yes)
  aye — eye (see)
  aysure — azure
azalea
  azalia — azalea
  azbestos — asbestos
Aztec, Aztec, Aztecs
  azthma — asthma
azure
azury

Bb

abble, -led, -ling (chatter)

babble	bauble (trifle)
babble	bubble (globule)
babboon	baboon

abe

abel (confusion)

babey	baby
babie	baby

aboon

babtsim	baptism
babtize	baptize

aby, babies

aby-sitter

accarat

baccilus	bacillus
bach	batch
bacheler	bachelor

achelor

acillus, bacilli

ack, -ed, -ing

ackache

backake	backache
backammon	backgammon

ackbone

acker

ackfire, -fired, -firing

ackgammon

ackground

ackhand

acking

acklash

acklog, -logged, -logging

ackpack

ackroom

backround	background

ack-seat driver

ackstage

ackstitch, -ed, -ing

backstop, -stopped, -stopping

backstroke, -stroked, -stroking

back-to-back

backwards

backwash

backyard

bacon

bacteria

bad, worse, worst (not good)

bade (asked)

badge

badger

badly

badminton

baffle, -fled, -fling

bag, bagged, bagging

bagatelle

bagel

baggage

baggidge	baggage

baggy, baggier, baggiest

bagpipes

baige	beige

bail (court)

bail	bale (bundle)
bailif	bailiff

bailiff

bait (fishing)

bait	bate (hold)

baize, baized, baizing (fabric)

baize	bays (water)
baje	badge

bake, baked, baking

baker

bakery

balaclava

balad	ballad

balalaika

balance, -anced, -ancing

balanse	balance
balast	ballast
balay	ballet

balcony, -conies

bald (hairless)

bald	bawled (cried)

balderdash

balding

baldness
bale, baled, baling (bundle)
  bale — bail (court)
baleful, -ly
  balefull — baleful
  balerina — ballerina
  balero — bolero
  balet — ballet
  baliff — bailiff
ball (sphere, dance)
  ball — bawl (cry)
ballad (song)
ballad, ballet (dance)
ballad, ballot (vote)
ballast
ballerina
ballet (dance)
ballistics
balloon
balloonist
ballot, -ted, -ting (vote)
ballpoint
  ballsa — balsa
  ballsam — balsam
balm
balmy, balmier, balmiest (good)
  balonee — baloney
baloney
  baloon — balloon
  balot — ballot
balsa
balsam
balustrade
bamboo
bamboozle, -zled, -zling
ban, banned, banning
banal, -ly
banana
band, banded, banding (strip)
band (group)
  band — banned (forbidden)
bandage, -daged, -daging
bandanna
  bandey — bandy
bandicoot
  bandige — bandage

bandit
  bandoleer — bandolier
bandolier
bandsaw
bandwagon
bandy, -died, -dying
  baner — banner
  bangel — bangle
banger
bangle
banish, -ed, -ing
banishment
banister
banjo, banjos
bank, -ed, -ing
bankbook
banker
banknote
  bankrupcy — bankruptcy
bankrupt
bankruptcy
banksia
  bankwet — banquet
  bannana — banana
banned (forbidden)
  banned — band (strip, group)
banner
banns (notices)
banquet, -queted, -queting
bans (forbids)
  bans — banns (notices)
bantam
bantamweight
banter, -ed, -ing
  bantum — bantam
banyan
  baonet — bayonet
baptism
baptismal
Baptist
baptize, -tized, -tizing
bar, barred, barring
  baracks — barracks
  barage — barrage
barb
barbarian

arbaric	
arbarism	
arbarize, -ized, -izing	
arbarous, -ly	
barbarus	barbarous
arbecue, -cued, -cuing	
arbed wire	
arbell	
barbeque	barbecue
arber	
arbiturate	
ard (poet)	
bard	barred
	(stopped)
are, bared, baring (uncover)	
are, barer, barest (uncovered)	
bare	bear (animal)
areback	
arefaced	
arefoot	
areheaded	
barel	barrel
arely	
baren	baron (noble)
baren	barren (sterile)
bareskin	bearskin
argain, -ed, -ing	
argainer	
bargan	bargain
arge, barged, barging	
argee	
baricade	barricade
barier	barrier
aring (uncovering)	
baring	barring (stop)
baring	bearing (hold)
barister	barrister
aritone	
arium	
ark, -ed, -ing	
arkeep	
arley	
barlie	barley
barm	balm
barmade	barmaid
armaid	
arman, -men	

barmy	balmy (good)
barn	
barnacle	
barnacled	
barnicle	barnacle
barometer	
barometric	
baron (nobleman)	
baron	barren (sterile)
baroness, (noblewoman)	
baronet	
baronial	
baroque	
barow	barrow
barracade	barricade
barrack, -ed, -ing	
barracks	
barracuda	
barrage, -raged, -raging	
barrel, -ed, -ing	
barren (sterile)	
barren	baron (noble)
barrenness	
barricade, -caded, -cading	
barrier	
barring (stop)	
barring	baring
	(uncovering)
barrister	
barrol	barrel
barrow	
bartender	
barter, -ed, -ing	
basal, -ly	
basalt	
base, based, basing (support)	
base, baser, basest (dishonorable)	
base	bass (low tone)
baseball	
basement	
baset	basset
bash, -ed, -ing	
bashful, -ly, -ness	
basic	
basilica	
basillus	bacillus
basin	

basinette	bassinette
basis, bases	
basit	basset
bask, -ed, -ing	
basketball	
baskit	basket
basoon	bassoon
bas-relief	
bass (low tone)	
bass	base (support)
bass clef	
basset	
bassinette	
bassit	basset
bassoon	
bastard	
bastardizasion	bastardization
bastardization	
bastardry	
baste, basted, basting	
basterd	bastard
bastion	
bat, batted, batting	
batch	
bate, bated, bating (hold breath)	
bate	bait (fishing)
baten	baton (stick)
baten	batten (timber)
bater	batter
batery	battery
bath (noun)	
bathe, bathed, bathing (verb)	
bathing, suit	
bathroom	
batik	
batiste	
batle	battle
batler	battler
baton (stick)	
baton	batten (timber)
batt (insulating)	
batt	bat (baseball)
battalion	
battaliun	battalion
battel	battle
batten (timber)	
batter	

battering ram	
battery, -ries	
battle, battled, battling	
battleaxe	
battledress	
battler	
battleship	
batty, battier, battiest	
baty	batty
bauble (trifle)	
bauble	babble (chatter)
bauble	bubble (globule)
baught	bought
baulk, -ed, -ing	
bauxite	
bawble	bauble
bawdie	bawdy
bawdiness	
bawdy, -dier, -diest	
bawl, -ed, -ing (cry)	
bawl	ball (sphere, dance)
bawlsa	balsa
bay (water)	
bays	baize (fabric)
bayliff	bailiff
baynet	bayonet
bayonet	
bayou	
baythe	bathe
bazaar (fair)	
bazaar	bizarre (odd)
bazar	bazaar
bazooka	
be, been, being (exist)	
be	bee (insect)
beach, -ches (shore)	
beach	beech (tree)
beachcomber	
beachcomer	beachcomber
beacon	
bead, -ed, -ing	
beady, beadier, beadiest	
beaf	beef
beafeater	beefeater
beafy	beefy
beagel	beagle

beagle		beautisian	beautician
beak		beauty, beauties	
beaker		beauty shop	
beam, -ed, -ing		beaver	
bean (food)		becalmed	
bean	been (be)	became	
bean	bin (box)	because	
beanie		beck	
bear (animal)		beckon, -ed, -ing	
bear, borne, bearing (carry)		become, became, becoming	
bear	bare (uncover)	becon	beacon
bearback	bareback	becos	because
beard		bed, bedded, bedding	
bearer		bedeck, -ed, -ing	
bearfaced	barefaced	bedevel	bedevil
bearfoot	barefoot	bedevil, -ed, -ing	
bearheaded	bareheaded	bedlam	
bearing (hold)		bedlum	bedlam
bearing	baring	Bedouin	
	(uncovering)	bedowin	Bedouin
bearskin		bedpan	
beast		bedraggled	
beastliness		bedraguled	bedraggled
beastly, beastlier, beastliest		bedridden	
beat, beaten, beating (strike)		bedriden	bedridden
beat	beet (food)	bedrock	
beatel	beetle	bedroom	
beater		bedside	
beatific		bedspread	
beatify, -fied, -fying (happy)		bedspred	bedspread
beatify	beautify	bedstead	
	(adorn)	bedsted	bedstead
beatitude		bee (insect)	
beatle	beetle	bee	be (exist)
beatnik		beech (tree)	
beatroot	beetroot	beech	beach (shore)
beau, beaus, beaux (suitor)		beechcomber	beachcomber
beau	bough (branch)	beecon	beacon
beau	bow (bend)	beed	bead
beaut		beef	
beauteous, -ly		beefsteak	
beautician		beefy, beefier, beefiest	
beautie	beauty	beegle	beagle
beautiful, -ly		beehive	
beautify, -fied, -fying (adorn)		beeker	beaker
beautify	beatify (happy)	beeline	
beautious	beauteous	beem	beam

been (be)
- been
- been

bean (food)
bin (box)

beep, -ed, -ing
beeper
beer (ale)
- beer
- beerd
- beest
- beeswaks

bier (coffin)
beard
beast
beeswax

beeswax
beet (food)
- beet
- beetel

beat (strike)
beetle

beetle
- beever

beaver

befall, -fell, -fallen, -falling
befit, -fitted, -fitting
- befor

before

before
beforehand
befuddle, -dled, -dling
- befudle

befuddle

beg, begged, begging
began
- begar

beggar

beggar
beggarly
- beggin
- begginer
- begile

begin
beginner
beguile

begin, began, begun, beginning
beginner
begone
begonia
begrime, begrimed, begriming
begrudge, -grudged, -grudging
- begruge

begrudge

beguile, -guiled, -guiling
begun
behalf
behave, -haved, -having
behavior
behavioral
behead, -ed, -ing
- behed

behead

beheld

behest
behind
- behive

beehive

beige
- beije

beige

being
- bekos
- bekweath
- bekwest
- bel
- bel

because
bequeath
bequest
bell (ring)
belle (girl)

belabor, -ed, -ing
belated, -ly
belay, -layed, -laying
belch, -ed, -ing
- beleaf
- beleavable
- beleave
- beleif
- beleive
- belfrey

belief
believable
believe
belief
believe
belfry

belfry, -fries
Belgian
- beli
- belicose

belie
bellicose

belie, -lied, -lying
belief
believable, -bly
- believible

believable

believe, -lieved, -lieving
- beligerence
- beligerency
- beligerense
- beligerent
- beline
- belittel

belligerence
belligerency
belligerence
belligerent
beeline
belittle

belittle, -tled, -tling
bell (ring)
belle (girl)
bellicose, -ly
belligerence
belligerency
belligerent, -ly
bellow, -ed, -ing (roar)
- bellow

below (under)

bellows
belly, bellies

belly, bellied, bellying
bellyache
belong, -ed, -ing
belongings
　belose　　　　　　bellows
beloved
　belovid　　　　　　beloved
below (under)
　below　　　　　　bellow (roar)
　belows　　　　　　bellows
belt, -ed, -ing
　bely　　　　　　　belly
bemoan, -ed, -ing
bemused
bench, benches
benchmark
bend, bent, bending
bender
beneath
benediction
benefactor
benefactress
benefice
beneficence
beneficent, -ly
beneficial, -ly
beneficiary, -aries
　benefis　　　　　　benefice
　benefisense　　　　beneficence
　benefisent　　　　　beneficent
　benefishal　　　　　beneficial
　benefisharey　　　　beneficiary
benefit, -ed, -ing
benevolence
　benevolense　　　　benevolence
benevolent, -ly
　benifit　　　　　　benefit
benign, -ly
　benine　　　　　　benign
bent
　benum　　　　　　benumb
benumb
benzene (coal tar)
benzine (petroleum)
bequeath
　bequeeth　　　　　bequeath
bequest

berate, -rated, -rating
　beray　　　　　　beret
bereave, -reaved, -reaving
　bereeve　　　　　bereave
bereft
beret
　bereve　　　　　　bereave
　berglar　　　　　　burglar
　beri　　　　　　　berry (fruit)
　beri　　　　　　　bury (in earth)
　berial　　　　　　burial
beri-beri
　berie　　　　　　　berry (fruit)
　berp　　　　　　　burp
berry, berries (fruit)
　berry　　　　　　bury (cover)
berserk
berth (ship)
　berth　　　　　　birth (born)
　bery　　　　　　　berry (fruit)
　bery　　　　　　　bury (cover)
　beseach　　　　　beseech
beseech, -ed, -ing
　beseige　　　　　besiege
beset, -set, -setting
beside
besides
besiege, -sieged, -sieging
best
bestial, -ly
bestiality
bestir, -stirred, -stirring
bestow, -ed, -ing
bestowal
　bestro　　　　　　bistro
bet, bet, betting
beta
beta particle
betel nut
　betel　　　　　　beetle
betoken, -ed, -ing
betray, -ed, -ing
betrayal
betrayer
betrothal
better
betterment

between
betwixt
  beuty — beauty
bevel, -ed, -ing
beverage
  beveridge — beverage
  bevie — bevy
  bevrage — beverage
bevy, bevies
bewail
beware
  bewayl — bewail
  bewear — beware
  bewhere — beware
  bewhich — bewitch
bewilder, -ed, -ing
bewilderment
bewitch
  bewtician — beautician
  bewty — beauty
beyond
  bezerk — berserk
biannual, -ly (twice a year)
  biannual — biennial (every two years)
bias, biased, biasing
bias binding
  biass — bias
  biassed — biased
  Bibel — Bible
Bible
  bibliografy — bibliography
bibliographer
bibliography, -phies
  bicame — became
bicameral
bicarbonate
bicentenary
bicentennial
biceps
  bich — bitch
  bicicle — bicycle
bicker, -ed, -ing
bicuspid
bicycle
bid, bade, bidding
  biday — bidet

biddy, -dies
bide, bided, biding
bidet
  bidevil — bedevil
biennial, -ly (every two years)
  biennial — biannual (twice a year)
bier (coffin)
  bier — beer (ale)
  bifell — befell
bifocal
bifurcate, -cated, -cating
big, bigger, biggest
bigamist
bigamy
  bigan — began
  biggot — bigot
bight (bay)
  bight — bite (cut)
  bight — byte (computer)
  bigile — beguile
  bigin — begin
  biginer — beginner
  bigining — beginning
  bigone — bygone
bigot
bigoted, -ly
bigotry
  bigrudge — begrudge
  bigun — begun

> For bih- words, look under **beh-**.

  bikameral — bicameral
bike
bikini
  bikweath — bequeath
  bikwest — bequest
  bil — bill
  bilabor — belabor
  bilated — belated
bilateral, -ly
  bilaw — by-law
  bilay — belay
  bild — build
  bilding — building
bile

bileave	believe		biodegradable	
bileif	belief		bioethics	
bilet	billet		biografer	biographer
bilge			biografical	biographical
biliards	billiards		biografy	biography
bilief	belief		biographer	
bilievable	believable		biographical, -ly	
bilingual, -ly			biography, -phies	
bilingwal	bilingual		biokemist	biochemist
bilion	billion		biologey	biology
bilious, -ly, -ness			biological, -ly	
bilittle	belittle		biologist	
bilius	bilious		biology	
bilk, -ed, -ing			biopsey	biopsy
bill, -ed, -ing			biopsy	
billet, -ed, -ing			biorhythm	
billfold			biosphere	
billiards			bipartisan	
billion			bipartite	
billit	billet		bipartizan	bipartisan
billow (wave)			bipass	bypass
billygoat			biped	
bilong	belong		biplane	
bilow	below (under)		biproduct	byproduct
bilow	billow (wave)		birate	berate
bilyards	billiards		birch	
bilyon	billion		bird	
bilyus	billious		birdie	
bimoan	bemoan		bird's-eye	
bimuse	bemuse		bireave	bereave
bin (box)			bireft	bereft
bin	bean (food)		biro	
bin	been (be)		**birth (born)**	
binary			birth	berth (ship)
bind, bound, binding			**birthday**	
binder			**birthrate**	
bineath	beneath		bisalt	basalt
binevolent	benevolent		**biscuit**	
binge			biscut	biscuit
bingo			bisecktion	bisection
binine	benign		**bisect, -ed, -ing**	
binoculars			**bisection**	
binomial, -ly			**bisector**	
binominal, -ly			biseech	beseech
binumb	benumb		biseege	besiege
biochemist			biseige	besiege
biochemistry			biseksual	bisexual

bisen	bison	bitwixt	betwixt
bisentenary	bicentenary	biuld	build
bisentennial	bicentennial	bivalve	
biseps	biceps	bivouac, -acked, -acking	
biset	beset	bivuac	bivouac
bisexual, -ly		biwail	bewail
bisexuality		biway	byway
bishop		biwear	beware
bishopric		biwich	bewitch
bisicle	bicycle	biwilder	bewilder
biside	beside	biwitch	bewitch
bisier	busier	biword	byword
bisily	busily	bizar	bazaar (fair)
biskit	biscuit	bizar	bizarre (odd)
bismuth		bizarre, -ly (odd)	
bisness	business	bizare	bazaar (fair)
bison, -son		bizier	busier
bisotted	besotted	bizily	busily
bistander	bystander	bizmuth	bismuth
bistir	bestir	bizness	business
bistow	bestow	bizy	busy
bistowal	bestowal	blab, blabbed, blabbing	
bistro		blabber, blabbered, blabbering	
bisun	bison	blabbermouth	
bisy	busy	blaber	blabber
bit		black	
bitch, -ches		blackball	
bitchiness		blackberry, -ries	
bitchumen	bitumen	blackbird	
bitchy		blackboard	
bite, bitten, bit, biting (cut)		blackbord	blackboard
bite	bight (bay)	blacken, -ed, -ing	
bite	byte (computer)	blackguard	
biter	bitter	blackhead	
bitoken	betoken	blackjack	
bitray	betray	blacklist	
bitrayal	betrayal	blackmail	
bitrothal	betrothal	blackmale	blackmail
bitten (bite)		blackout	
bitten	bittern (bird)	blacksmith	
bitter, -ly		bladder	
bittern (bird)		blade	
bitterness		blader	bladder
bitters		blaggard	blackguard
bitumen		blaid	blade
bituminous		blaim	blame
bitween	between	blaimless	blameless

blair blare
blaise blaze
blaiser blazer
blame, blamed, blaming
blameless
blameworthy
blamonge blancmange
blanch, -ed, -ing
blancmange
bland, -ly, -ness
blandish
blandishment
blank
blanket
blare, blared, blaring
blasay blasé
blasé
blasfeem blaspheme
blasfemus blasphemous
blasfemy blasphemy
blaspheme, -phemed, -pheming
blasphemous, -ly
blasphemy, -mies
blast, -ed, -ing
blast-off
blatancy
blatant, -ly
blather
blaze, blazed, blazing
blazer
blazon
bleach, -ed, -ing
bleachers
blead bleed
bleak, -ly, -ness
blear, -ed, -ing
blearily
bleary, blearier, blearist
bleat, -ed, -ing
bleech bleach
bleed, bled, bleeding
bleeder
bleek bleak
bleep
bleer blear
bleet bleat
blemish, -ed, -ing

blench, -ed, -ing
blend, -ed, -ing
blender
blert blurt
bless, -ed, -ing
blew (to blow)
blew blue (color)

> For other blew- words, look
> under **blue-**.

blight, -ed, -ing
blighter
blimp
blind, -ed, -ing
blind, -ly, -ness
blindfold
blindman's buff
blink, -ed, -ing
blinker
blip
bliss
blissful, -ly
blister, -ed, -ing
blistery
blite blight
bliter blighter
blithe, -ly
blithering
blits blitz
blitz, -ed, -ing
blizard blizzard
blizzard
blo blow
bloat, -ed, -ing
blob
bloc (group)
block, -ed, -ing (stop)
blockade, -kaded, -kading
blockage
blockaid blockade
blockbuster
blockidge blockage
blond, blonde
blone blown
blood
bloodbath
bloodcurdling

blooded
bloodless
blood poisoning
blood pressure
bloodshed
bloodshot
bloodstream
bloodthirsty
bloody, bloodied, bloodying
bloody, bloodier, bloodiest
bloom, -ed, -ing
blooper
blosom   blossom
blossom
blot, blotted, blotting
blot   bloat
blotch, -ed, -ing
blotchy
blouse
blow, blew, blown, blowing
blower
blowfly
blowhole
blowout
blowpipe
blowse   blouse
blowtorch
blowup
blu   blue (color)
blu   blew (to blow)
blubber
blubbery
bluber   blubber
bludgeon

> For all other **blud-** words, look
> under **blood-**.

blue (color)
blue   blew (to blow)
blue, bluer, bluest
bluebird
bluebottle
bluecollar
blueprint
blues
bluf   bluff
bluff, -ed, -ing

bluish
blunder, -ed, -ing
blunt, -ed, -ing
blur, blurred, blurring
blurb
blurr   blur
blurt, -ed, -ing
blush, -ed, -ing
bluster, -ed, -ing
blustery
blustry   blustery
boa
boa constrictor
boar (pig)
boar   boor (rude)
boar   bore (drill)
board, -ed, -ing
board (wood)
board   bored (drill)
boarder (lodger)
boarder   border (edge)
boast, -ed, -ing
boastful, -ly
boat
boater
boathouse
boating
boatswain
bob, bobbed, bobbing
bobbel   bobble
bobbin
bobble
bobby, -bies
bobby pin, bobby pins
bobcat
bobin   bobbin
boble   bobble
bobslay   bobsleigh
bobsled
bobsleigh
bobtail
boch   botch
bochulism   botulism
boddy   body
bodess   bodice
bodice
bodie   body

bodigard	bodyguard	bomberdeer	bombardier
bodiley	bodily	bombshell	
bodily		bomer	bomber
bodis	bodice	bona fide	
body, bodies		bonanza	
body, bodied, bodying		bonbon	
bodyguard		bond, -ed, -ing	
body language		bondage	
bodywork		bone, boned, boning	
bog, bogged, bogging		bonet	bonnet
bogey, bogies		bonfire	
boggel	boggle	bonit	bonnet
boggle, -gled, -gling		bonsai	
bogus		bonus	
bogy	bogey	bony, bonier, boniest	
bohemian		boo, booed, booing	
boi	boy (male)	boob	
boi	buoy (afloat)	boobie	booby
boiancy	buoyancy	boo-boo	
boiant	buoyant	booby, -bies	
boicot	boycott	boodle	
boil, -ed, -ing		boodwar	boudoir
boiler		boofant	bouffant
boilermaker		book, -ed, -ing	
boisterous, -ly		bookay	bouquet
boisterus	boisterous	bookcase	
bokay	bouquet	bookeeping	bookkeeping
boks	box	bookie	
bolaro	bolero	bookish, -ly	
bold, -ly (brave)		bookkeeping	
bold	bowled (ball)	bookmaker	
bolder (braver)		bookmark	
bolder	boulder (rock)	bookworm	
bole (trunk)		boolevard	boulevard
bole	bowl (ball, dish)	boom, -ed, -ing	
bolero		boomerang	
boll (pod)		boon	
Bolshevik		boondoggle	
Bolshevism		boor (rude)	
bolster, -ed, -ing		boor	boar (pig)
bolt		boor	bore (drill)
bom	bomb	boorgeois	bourgeois
bomb, -ed, -ing		boorjgeoisie	bourgeoisie
bombardier		boost, -ed, -ing	
bombardment		booster	
bombastic		boot	
bomber		bootee (shoe)	

bootee	booty (plunder)		bort	bought
booteek	boutique		bos	boss
booth			bosie	bossy
bootie	bootee (shoe)		bosily	bossily
bootie	booty (plunder)		bosom	
bootik	boutique		boss, -ed, -ing	
bootleg, -legged, -legging			bossom	bosom
bootlegger			bossy, bossier, bossiest	
bootstrap			bosy	bossy
booty, -ties (plunder)			bot	boat
booty	bootee (shoe)		botaney	botany
booze, boozed, boozing			botanical, -ly	
boozer			botanist	
bora (ceremony)			botany	
bora	borer (driller)		botch, -ed, -ing	
boracic			boter	boater
boraks	borax		both	
borasic	boracic		bother	
borax			bothersome	
borbon	bourbon		bothersum	bothersome
bord	board (plank)		botom	bottom
bord	bored (tired)		bottel	bottle
border (edge)			bottle, -tled, -tling	
border	boarder (lodger)		bottlebrush	
border, -ed, -ing			bottleneck	
borderline			bottom -ed, -ing	
bording	boarding		bottomless	
bordom	boredom		botul	bottle
bordy	bawdy		botulism	
bore, bored, boring (drill)			boudoir	
bore	boar (pig)		bouffant	
bore	boor (rude)		bougainvillea	
boredom			bough (branch)	
borer (driller)			bough	bean (suitor)
borer	bora (ceremony)		bough	bow (bend)
born (birth)			bought	
born	borne (carry)		bouillon (soup)	
borne (carry)			bouillon	bullion (metal)
borne	born (birth)		boukay	bouquet
boronia			boulder (rock)	
borough (town)			boulder	bolder (braver)
borough	burrow (hole)		boulevard	
borow	borrow		bounce, bounced, bouncing	
borrow, -ed, -ing			bouncer	
borrower			bound, -ed, -ing	
borsch			boundary, -ries	
			boundry	boundary

bounteous, -ly
bountiful, -ly
  bountious — bounteous
bounty, -ties
bouquet
bourbon
bourgeois
bourgeoisie
  bourgwah — bourgeois
  bourgwahzey — bourgeoisie
bout
  bouteek — boutique
boutique
bovine
bow, -ed, -ing (bend)
  bow — bough (branch)
  bow — beau (suitor)
bowel (intestine)
bower
bowie knife
bowl (ball, dish)
  bowl — bole (trunk)
  bowl — boll (pod)
bowleg
bowler
bowline
  bownce — bounce
  bownd — bound
  bowndary — boundary
  bownse — bounce
  bownser — bouncer
  bownteous — bounteous
  bowntiful — bountiful
  bowt — bout
box, -ed, -ing
boxcar
boxer
boy (child)
  boy — buoy (float)
  boyansy — buoyancy
  boyant — buoyant
  boycot — boycott
boycott, -ed, -ing
  boykot — boycott
  boyle — boil
  boysterus — boisterous
bra, bras (brassiere)

brace, braced, bracing (clamp)
bracelet
bracken
bracket, -ed, -ing
brackish
  brackit — bracket
  braclete — bracelet
  brade — braid
brag, bragged, bragging
  bragart — braggart
braggart
bragger
Brahma
Brahman, -mans
braid
  brail — braille
braille
brain
brainstorm
brainwash, -ed, -ing
brainy, brainier, brainiest
braise, braised, braising (cook)
  braise — braze (solder)
  braisen — brazen
  brakable — breakable
  brakage — breakage
  brakaway — breakaway
  brakdown — breakdown
brake, braked, braking (stop)
  brake — break (divide)
  brakeneck — breakneck
  braker — breaker
  brakewater — breakwater
  brakidge — breakage
  braking — breaking
  brakish — brackish
  brale — braille
  brambel — bramble
bramble
  bramin — Brahman
bran
branch, -ches
branch, -ed, -ing
brand, -ed, -ing
brandish, -ed, -ing
brandy, -dies
  brane — brain

braney · brainy
bras (brassieres)
  bras · brass (metal)
  brase · brace (clamp)
brash
  brasier · brassiere (bra)
  brasier · brazier (burner)
  braslet · bracelet
brass
brassiere (bra)
brassy, brassier, brassiest
  brasy · brassy
brat
bravado, -does, -dos
brave, braver, bravest
bravely
bravery, -ries
  bravly · bravely
bravo, -voes, -vos
  bravrey · bravery
  brawd · broad
brawl, -ed, -ing
brawn
brawny, brawnier, brawniest
bray, -ed, -ing
  brayd · braid
  braylle · braille
  brayn · brain
braze, brazed, brazing (solder)
  braze · braise (cook)
brazen, -ly, -ness
brazier (burner)
  brazier · brassiere (bra)
brazil nut
breach, -ed, -ing (break)
  breach · breech (gun)
bread (food)
  bread · bred (produced)
breadth (width)
  breadth · breath (air)
breadwinner
break, broke, broken, breaking
  (divide)
  break · brake (stop)
breakable
breakage
breakaway

breakdance
breakdown
breaker
breakfast
  breakible · breakable
break-in
breakthrough
breakup
breakwater
bream (fish)
breast
breastbone
breastfeed, -fed, -feeding
breastplate
breast stroke
breastwork
breath (air)
  breath · breadth (width)
breathe, breathed, breathing (verb)
breather
breathless, -ly
breathtaking
bred (produced)
  bred · bread (food)
  bredth · breadth
  bree · brie
breech, -ches (gun)
  breech · breach (break)
breed, bred, breeding
breeder
breeding
  breef · brief
breeze, breezed, breezing
breezily
breezy, breezier, breeziest
  breif · brief
  brest · breast
  brest stroke · breast stroke
  breth · breath (air)
  breth · breadth (width)
  brethless · breathless
brethren
  brethtaking · breathtaking
breve
breviary, breviaries
brevity, -ties
brew, -ed, -ing (beer)

brewed   brood (worry)
brewer
brewery, -ries
brews   bruise (hurt)
breze   breeze
brezy   breezy
briar
bribe, bribed, bribing
bribery, -ries
bric-a-brac
brick, -ed, -ing
brickette   briquette
bricklayer
brickyard
bridal (marry)
bridal   bridle (horse)
bride
bridegroom
bridel   bridal (marry)
bridel   bridle (horse)
bridesmade   bridesmaid
bridesmaid
bridge, -dged, -dging
bridle, -dled, -dling (horse)
bridle   bridal (marry)
brie
brief, -ly
briefcase
brier
brig
brigade, -gaded, -gading
brigadeer   brigadier
brigadier
brigand
brige   bridge
bright, -ly, -ness
brighten, -ed, -ing
brilliance
brilliant, -ly
brilliantine
brilyanse   brilliance
brilyansy   brilliancy
brilyant   brilliant
brim, brimmed, brimming (edge)
brim   bream (fish)
brimful
brimstone

brindled
brine
briney   briny
bring, brought, bringing
brink
brinkmanship
briny, brinier, briniest
briquette
brisel   bristle
brisk, -ly
brisket
brisle   bristle
bristle, -tled, -tling
bristly
Britain
brite   bright
briten   brighten
British
britle   brittle
brittle, brittler, brittlest
brittleness
broach, -ed, -ing (mention)
broach   brooch (pin)
broad, -ly
broadcast, -cast, -casting
broadcaster
broaden, -ed, -ing
broad-minded
brocade, -caded
broccoli
broch   broach
                      (mention)
broch   brooch (pin)
brochure
brocoli   broccoli
brog   brogue
brogue
broil, -ed, -ing
broken, -ly
brokenhearted
broker
brokerage
brokeridge   brokerage
brolly, -lies
bromide
bromine
bronchial

bronchitis
bronco, -cos
  bronkial — bronchial
  bronkitis — bronchitis
bronze, bronzed, bronzing
brooch, -ches (pin)
brood (worry)
  brood — brewed (beer)
broody, broodier, broodiest
brook, -ed, -ing
broom
  broonette — brunette
  broose — bruise
  broot — brute
  brootal — brutal
  brootality — brutality
  brootish — brutish
  brorn — brawn
  brort — brought
  broshure — brochure
  brosure — brochure
broth
brothel
brother
brotherhood
brother-in-law, brothers-in-law
brotherliness
brotherly
brow, brows (forehead)
browbeat, -beat, -beaten, -beating
brown
  brownee — brownie
brownie
browse, browsed, browsing
browser
  browze — browse (read)
bruise, bruised, bruising (hurt)
  bruise — brews (beer)
bruiser
bruit (rumor)
  bruit — brute (beast)
brunch
brunet
brunette
brunt
  bruse — brews (beer)
  bruse — bruise (hurt)

brush, -ed, -ing
brushwood
brushwork
  brusk — brusque
brusque, -ly, -ness
brutal, -ly
brutality, -ties
brute (beast)
  brute — bruit (rumor)
brutish
bubble, -bled, -bling (globule)
  bubble — babble (chatter)
  bubble — bauble (triple)
bubbly, -lier, -liest
bubonic plague
  bucaneer — buccaneer
buccaneer
buccaneering
  bucher — butcher
buck, -ed, -ing
  buckaneer — buccaneer
  buckel — buckle
bucket, -ed, -ing
bucketful, bucketfuls
buckle, -led, -ling
buckshot
buckskin
bucktooth, -teeth
bucolic
bud, budded, budding
Buddhism
Buddhist
buddy, -dies
budge, budged, budging
budgerigar
budget, -eted, -eting
budgetary
budgie
  budgrigar — budgerigar
  Budhism — Buddhism
  Budhist — Buddhist
  buf — buff
  bufalo — buffalo
  bufay — buffet
  bufer — buffer
buff
buffalo, -loes, -los

buffay	buffet
buffer	
buffet (food)	
buffet, -ed, -ing (hit)	
buffoon	
buffoonery, -eries	
bufit	buffet
bufoon	buffoon
bufoonery	buffoonery
bug, bugged, bugging	
bugbare	bugbear
bugbear	
bugel	bugle
buget	budget
buggy, -gies	
bugle, -gled, -gling	
bugler	
bugy	buggy
build, built, building (construct)	
build	billed (account)
builder	
build-up	
buiscut	biscuit
buisness	business

For **buk-** words, look under **buc-**.

bul	bull
bulb	
bulbous	
buldog	bulldog
buldoze	bulldoze
bulet	bullet
buletin	bulletin
bulevard	boulevard
bulfight	bullfight
bulfrog	bullfrog
bulheaded	bull-headed
bulion	bullion
bulk	
bulkhead	
bulky, bulkier, bulkiest	
bulldog	
bulldoze, -dozed, -dozing	
bulldozer	
bullet	
bulletin	

bullfight	
bullfrog	
bullheaded	
bullhorn	
bullion (metal)	
bullion	bouillon (soup)
bullock	
bullring	
bull's-eye	
bull terrier	
bullwark	bulwark
bully, -lies	
bully, -lied, -lying	
bulock	bullock
bulring	bullring
bulrush	
bulseye	bull's-eye
bulwalk	bulwark
bulwark	
buly	bully
bulyon	bullion
bum, bummed, bumming (loaf)	
bumbel	bumble
bumble, bumbled, bumbling	
bump, -ed, -ing (strike)	
bumper	
bumpey	bumpy
bumpiness	
bumpkin	
bumptious, -ly, -ness	
bumpy, bumpier, bumpiest	
bumtious	bumptious
bunch, -ches	
bunch, -ed, -ing	
bunchberry, -berries	
buncum	bunkum
bundel	bundle
bundle, -dled, -dling	
buney	bunny
bung, -ed, -ing	
bungaloe	bungalow
bungalow	
bungel	bungle
bungelow	bungalow
bungkum	bunkum
bungle, -gled, -gling	
bungler	

bunie   bunny
bunion
bunk
bunker, -ed, -ing
bunkhouse
bunkum
bunny, -nies
Bunsen burner
bunt
bunting
     buny   bunny
     bunyon   bunion
buoy, -ed, -ing (float)
     buoy   boy (child)
buoyancy
     buoyansy   buoyancy
buoyant, -ly
     burbel   burble
burble, -bled, -bling
     burbon   bourbon
     burch   birch
     burd   bird
burden, -ed, -ing
burdensome
     burdensum   burdensome
     burdie   birdie
     burdseye   bird's-eye
bureau, -eaus, -eaux
bureaucracy, -cies
     bureaucrasy   bureaucracy
bureaucrat
bureaucratic
buret
burette
     burgandy   burgundy
     burgel   burgle
burgeon, -ed, -ing
     burger   burgher
burgess
burgher
burglar
burglarize, -ized, -izing
burglary, -ries
burgle, -gled, -gling
     burgler   burglar
burgundy
burial

burl, -ed, -ing
burlap
     burlesk   burlesque
burlesque, -lesqued, -lesquing
     burlie   burly
burly, -lier, -liest
burn, burned, burning
burnable
burner
burnish, -ed, -ing
     buro   bureau
     buro   burro
     burocrasy   bureaucracy
     burocrat   bureaucrat
     burow   bureau
     burow   burrow (hole)
burp, -ed, -ing
burr, burred, burring
     burra   borough (town)
burro, -ros (donkey)
     burro   bureau
     burrocracy   bureaucracy
     burrocrat   bureaucrat
burrow, -ed, -ing (hole)
     burrow   borough (town)
     burrow   burro (donkey)
     burry   bury (cover)
bursar
bursary, -ries
     burser   bursar
     bursery   bursary
burst, burst, bursting
     burth   berth (ship)
     burth   birth (born)
bury, buried, burying (cover)
     bury   berry (fruit)
bus, busses, buses
bus, bussed, bussing or bused, busing
busby, -bies
     busel   bustle
bush, -ed, -ing
bushel
bushfire
     bushie   bushy
bush league
bushman, -men
bushwhack, -ed, -ing

bushwhacker
bushy, bushier, bushiest
busier
busily
business
businesslike

busom	bosom
bussle	bustle

bust, -ed, -ing

bustel	bustle

buster
bustle, -tled, -tling
bust-up

busul	bustle

busy, busied, busying
busy, busier, busiest
busybody, -bodies
but (contrary)

but	butt (end)

butane
butcher, -ed, -ing

buteek	boutique
buten	button
buter	butter
buterfly	butterfly
butey	beauty
butician	beautician
butify	beautify
butique	boutique
butishun	beautician
butlar	butler

butler

butock	buttock
buton	button
butress	buttress

butt, -ed, -ing (end)

butt	but (contrary)

butter, -ed, -ing
buttercup
butterfingers
butterfly, -flies
butterscotch
buttock
button
buttonhole, -holed, -holing
buttress, buttresses
buxom, -ly

buy, bought, buying (purchase)

buy	by (near to)
buy	bye (sport)

buyer

buz	buzz
buzard	buzzard
buzer	buzzer
buz-saw	buzz saw

buzz, -ed, -ing
buzz, -es
buzzard
buzzer
buzz saw
by (near to)

by	bye (sport)
by	buy (purchase)

bye (sport)

bye	by (near to)
bye	buy (purchase)

bye-bye, bye-byes
by-election

byennial	biennial
byer	buyer
byfocal	bifocal

bygone

bying	buying
byke	bike

bylaw

byle	bile
bymetallic	bimetallic
bymonthly	bimonthly
byopsey	biopsy
bypartisan	bipartisan
bypartite	bipartite

bypass

byped	biped
byplane	biplane

byproduct

bysect	bisect
bysection	bisection
bysexual	bisexual

bystander
byte (computer)

byte	bite (chew)

byway
byword
Byzantine

Cc

cab
cabage — cabbage
cabal
cabana
cabaray — cabaret
cabaret
cabbage
cabboose — caboose
cabby, cabbies
cabel — cable
cabin
cabinet
cable, -bled, -bling
caboodle
caboose
cabul — cable
cacao, -caos (tree)
cacao — cocoa (drink)
caccus — caucus
cach — cache
cach — catch
cachay — cachet
cache, cached, caching (hide)
cache — cash (money)
cachet
cachou — cashew
cachword — catchword
cackel — cackle
cackle, -led, -ling
cacktus — cactus
cacky — khaki
cacofony — cacophony
cacophony, -nies
cactus, -ti, -tuses
cad
cadaver
cadaverous, -ly
caddie, -died, -dying (golf)

caddie — caddy (box)
caddy, -ies (box)
caddy — caddie (golf)
cadence
cadense — cadence
cadenza
cadet
cadge, cadged, cadging
cadjole — cajole
cadmium
Caesar
Caesarean section
cafay — cafe
cafe
cafeteria
caffee — coffee
caffeine
caffeteria — cafeteria
cafiene — caffeine
cafiteria — cafeteria
caftan
cage, caged, caging
cagey, cagier, cagiest
cahoots
cain — cane
caisson
cajole, -joled, -joling
cake, caked, caking
calabash
calaboose
calamari
calamine
calamitous, -ly
calamity, -ties
calarie — calorie
calcareous
calcarious — calcareous
calcification
calcify, -fied, -fying
calcium
calculable
calculate, -lated, -lating
calculater — calculator
calculation
calculative
calculator
calculus, -luses, -li

caldron
Caledonian
calendar (time)
calender (machine)
calendula
calf, calves
   calf   calve (give birth)
calfskin
caliber
calibrate, -brated, -brating
calibration
calibrator
   calicks   calyx
calico, -coes, -cos
   calif   caliph
   caligraphy   calligraphy
   caling   calling
caliper
caliph
   calipso   calypso
calisthenics
   calix   calyx
calk (fill horse shoe)
   calk   caulk (fill)
   calk   cork (stopper)
call, -ed, -ing (cry out)
   call   caul (membrane)
   callamity   calamity
   calldron   cauldron
caller
calligrapher
calligraphy
calliper
callisthenics
callosity, -ties
callous, -ly, -ness (cruel)
   callous   callus (skin)
callow
callus, calluses (skin)
   callus   callous (cruel)
calm, -ly, -ness
calorie
calorific
calorimeter
   calory   calorie

   calow   callow
   calsify   calcify
   calsium   calcium
calumniate, -ated, -ating
calumniation
calumnious, -ly
   calumnius   calumnious
calumny, -nies
   calus   callous (cruel)
   calus   callus (skin)
Calvary (crucifixion)
   Calvary   cavalry (troops)
calve, calved, calving (give birth)
   calve   calf (animal)
Calvinism
Calvinist
calypso, -sos
calyx, calyces, calyxes
cam
   camaflage   camouflage
camaraderie
camber
cambric
came
camel
camelhair
camellia
   camember   Camembert
Camembert
cameo, -os
camera
cameraman
   cameradery   camaraderie
   camfer   camphor
   camio   cameo
camisole
   camle   camel
camouflage, -flaged, -flaging
camp, -ed, -ing
campaign
   campain   campaign
campanology
   campas   campus
camper
camp fire
campground
   campher   camphor

camphor
  campsight   campsite
campsite
campus, -es
camshaft
  camul   camel
can, could (able to)
can, canned, canning (tinned)
  canabis   cannabis
Canadian
canal
canape
canary, -ries
canasta
cancan
cancel, -ed, -ing
  cancelation   cancellation
cancellation
cancer
cancerous
  cancerus   cancerous
  candel   candle
candelabrum
  candellight   candlelight
  candelstick   candlestick
  cander   candor
  candey   candy
candid (open)
  candid   candied (sugar)
candidate
candied (sugar)
  candied   candid (open)
candle
candlelight
candlestick
candor
candy, -dies
candy, candied, candying (sugar)
cane, caned, caning (hit)
canebrake
  caned   canned (tinned)
  canee   canny
  canery   cannery
cane sugar
  canibal   cannibal
  canibalism   cannibalism
  canie   canny

canine
canister
cannabis
  cannary   canary
canned (tinned)
  canned   caned (hit)
cannelloni
cannery, -ries
cannibal
cannibalism
canniness
cannon (gun)
  cannon   canon (law)
cannot
canny, -nier, -niest

> For other cann- words,
> look under **can-**.

canoe, -es
canoe, -noed, -noeing
canoeist
canon (law)
  canon   cannon (gun)
canonical
canonization
canonize, -nized, -nizing
  canoo   canoe
  canooist   canoeist
canopy, -pies
  cansel   cancel
  canselasion   cancelation
  canser   cancer
  canserous   cancerous
cant (insincere)
can't (cannot)
cantaloupe
cantankerous, -ly
  cantankerus   cantankerous
cantata
canteen
canter, -ed, -ing
cantilever
canto, -tos
canton
cantor
  canue   canoe
canvas, -es (tent)

canvas	canvass (gather)	capsule	
		captain, -ed, -ing	
canvass, -ed, -ing (gather)		captaincy	
canvass	canvas (tent)	capter	captor
cany	canny	captin	captain
canyon		caption	
cap, capped, capping		captious, -ly, -ness	
capability, -ties		captius	captious
capable, -bly		captivate, -vated, -vating	
capacious, -ly		captivation	
capaciter	capacitor	captive	
capacitor		captivity, -ties	
capacity, -ties		captor	
capasitor	capacitor	capture, -tured, -turing	
capasity	capacity	capuccino	cappuccino
capchure	capture	caracter	character
cape		caracteristic	characteristic
caper, -ed, -ing		carafe	
capible	capable	caraffe	carafe
capilary	capillary	caramel	
capillary, -laries		carat (weight)	
capital (head)		carat	caret (mark)
capitalizasion	capitalization	carat	carrot (food)
capitalism		carate	karate
capitalist		caravan, -vanned, -vanning	
capitalistic		caraway	
capitalization		carbine	
capitalize, -lized, -lizing		carbohydrate	
capitol (building)		carbon	
capitulate, -lated, -lating		carbonate, -nated, -nating	
capitulation		carbon dioxide	
capon		carbonize, -nized, -nizing	
cappuccino		carbon monoxide	
		carboy	
		carbuncle	

For all other **capp-** words,
look under **cap-**.

caprice		carburetor	
capricious, -ly, -ness		carcanoma	carcinoma
Capricorn		carcass	
caprise	caprice	carcinogen	
caprisious	capricious	carcinogenic	
capshin	caption	carcinoma, -mata, -mas	
capshis	captious	carcus	carcass
capsicum		card, -ed, -ing	
capsion	caption	cardagan	cardigan
capsize, -sized, -sizing		cardboard	
capstan		cardbord	cardboard
		cardiac	

cardigan
cardinal, -ly
  cardiograf — cardiograph
cardiologist
cardiology
cardiovascular
  cardnal — cardinal
cardshark
care, cared, caring
  carean — careen
careen
career, -ed, -ing
carefree
careful, -ly
careless, -ly, -ness
caress, -ed, -ing
caressingly
caret (mark)
  caret — carat (weight)
  caret — carrot (food)
caretaker
cargo, -goes, -gos
Caribbean
caribou, -bou
caricature, -tured, -turing
caricaturist
  caricter — character
  caricteristic — characteristic
  caridge — carriage
  carie — carry (bear)
  carier — carrier
caries (decay)
  caries — carries (bear)
  carillion — carillon
carillon
  carillyon — carillon
  carion — carrion
  carisma — charisma
carmine
carnage
carnal, -ly
carnality
  carnasion — carnation
carnation
  carneje — carnage
carnival
carnivore

carnivorous, -ly (flesh-eating)
  carniverous — coniferous (tree)
carol, -ed, -ing (sing)
  carol — carrel (desk)
  carol — corral (yard)
caroler
  carot — carat (weight)
  carot — carrot (food)
carouse, -roused, -rousing
carousel (merry-go-round)
carp, -ed, -ing
carpenter
carpentry
carpet, -ed, -ing
carrel (study)
  carrel — carol (song)
  carrel — corral (yard)
carriage
carrier
carries (bears)
  carries — caries (decay)
carrion
carrot (food)
  carrot — carat (weight)
  carrot — caret (mark)
carry, -ried, -rying
  carryon — carrion
  carsinoma — carcinoma
cart, -ed, -ing
carte blanche
cartel
cartilage
  cartilege — cartilage
  cartilidge — cartilage
  cartografy — cartography
cartographer
cartographic
cartography
carton
cartoon, -ed, -ing
cartoonist
cartridge
  cartrige — cartridge
  cartune — cartoon
cartwheel
carve, carved, carving (cut)

cary / carry
casava / cassava
cascade, -caded, -cading
case, cased, casing
caseen / casein
casein
casement
caserole / casserole
casette / cassette
cash, -ed, -ing (money)
cash / cache (hide)
cashay / cachet
casheer / cashier
cashew
cashier
cashmear / cashmere
cashmere
cashoo / cashew
casia / cassia
casing
casino, -nos
cask (barrel)
caskade / cascade
casket
caskit / casket
casock / cassock
casque (helmet)
cassava
cassel / castle
casserole
casset / cassette
cassette
cassia
cassock (dress)
cassock / Cossack (horseman)
cassowary, -ries
cast, cast, casting (fling)
cast / caste (class)
castanet
castaway
caste (class)
caster, castor (sugar)
caster / castor (oil)
castigate, -gated, -gating
castigation
cast-iron

castle, -tled, -tling
castor (oil)
castrait / castrate
castrate, -trated, -trating
castration
casual, -ly (offhand)
casual / causal (cause of)
casuality / casualty
casualty, -ties
casuarina
casuistic
casuistry, -tries
casulty / casualty
catachism / catechism
cataclysm (upheaval)
cataclysm / catechism (book)
cataclysmic
catacomb
catalist / catalyst
catalitic / catalytic
catalize / catalyze
catalog, -ed, -ing
cataloger
catalyst
catalytic
catalyze, -lyzed, -lyzing
catamaran
catapiler / caterpillar
catapult
catar / catarrh
cataract
catarh / catarrh
catarrh
catarrhal
catastrofic / catastrophic
catastrofy / catastrophe
catastrophe
catastrophic, -ally
catcall, -ed, -ing
catch, caught, catching
catcher
catchew / cashew
catchment
catchword
catchy, catchier, catchiest

catechism (book)
  catechism   cataclysm
                      (upheaval)
catechist
catechize, -chized, -chizing
categorical, -ly
categorist
categorize, -rized, -rizing
category, -ries
  catel   cattle
cater, -ed, -ing
caterer
caterpillar
  caterpiller   caterpillar
  caterwall   caterwaul
caterwaul
catfish
catgut
catharsis
cathartic
cathedral
catheter
cathode
catholic (universal)
Catholic (religion)
Catholicism
Catholicity
  caticize   catechize
  catigoric   categoric
  catigorize   categorize
  catigory   category
  catikism   catechism
  catish   cattish
catkin
catlike
catnap, -ed, -ing
cat-o'-nine-tails
  cattegory   category
  cattel   cattle
  catterpillar   caterpillar
cattle
cattish, -ly
catty, -tier, -tiest
catwalk
Caucasian
caucus, -ed, -ing
caught (did catch)

caught
  cauk   caulk
caul (membrane)
  caul   call (cry)
cauldron
  cauliflour   cauliflower
cauliflower
caulk, -ed, -ing (fill)
causal, -ly (cause of)
  causal   casual
                   (offhand)
causality, -ties
  causasion   causation
causation
causative, -ly
cause, caused, causing
causeway
caustic, -ally
cauterize, -rized, -rizing
  causion   caution
  causious   cautious
caution, -ed, -ing
cautionary
cautious, -ly
cavalcade, -caded, -cading
  cavaleer   cavalier
cavalier
cavalry, -ries (troops)
  cavalry   Calvary
                   (crucifixion)
cavalryman, -men
cave, caved, caving
caveman, -men
cavern
cavernous
caviar
cavil, -ed, -ing
cavity, -ties
  caw   core (heart)
  caw   corps (group)
  Cawcasian   Caucasian
  cawcus   caucus
cay
cayenne
  cayote   coyote
cease, ceased, ceasing (stop)
  cease   seize (grab)

court (law)
caulk

cease   seas (oceans)
cease   sees (looks)
cease-fire
ceaseless, -ly, ness
cedar
cede, ceded, ceding (yield)
  cede   seed (plant)
  ceder   cedar
  ceeling   ceiling (roof)
  ceese   cease
  cefalic   cephalic
ceiling (roof)
  ceiling   sealing (close)
celebrant (person)
celebrate, -brated, -brating
                  (festivity)
celebration
celebrity, -ties
celerity
celery (food)
  celery   salary (wage)
celestial, -ly
celibacy, -cies
  celibasy   celibacy
celibate (chaste)
  celibrant   celebrant
  celibrate   celebrate
cell (prison)
  cell   sell (goods)
cellar (room)
  cellar   seller (goods)
  celler   seller (goods)
cellist
cello, -los
  cellofane   cellophane
cellophane
cellular
  celluler   cellular
celluloid
cellulose
  celofane   cellophane
Celsius
cement, -ed, -ing
  cematary   cemetery
cemetery, -teries (graveyard)
  cemetery   symmetry
                  (even)

  cemical   chemical
  cemist   chemist
  cemistry   chemistry
  cenotaf   cenotaph
censer (incense)
  censer   censor (books)
  censor   censure
                (condemn)
  censor   sensor (device)
  censer   censure
                (condemn)
  censership   censorship
  censhure   censure
censor (books)
  censor   censer (incense)
censorious, -ly
censorship
censurable
censure, -sured, -suring (condemn)
  censurible   censurable
  censure   censer (incense)
  censure   censor (remove)
  censure   sensor (device)
census (count)
  census   senses
                (feelings)
cent (coin)
  cent   scent (perfume)
  cent   sent (away)
  centapede   centipede
centaur
centavo
centenarian
centenary, -ries
  centenery   centenary
centennial, -ly
center, -ed, -ing
centerboard
centerfold
centerpiece
Centigrade
centigram
centimeter
centipede
  centor   centaur
central, -ly
  centralizasion   centralization

centralism
centralist
centrality
centralization
centralize, -lized, -lizing
centrifugal, -ly
centrifuge
centripetal, -ly
centrist
centuple, -pled, -pling
centurion
century, -ries
cephalic
ceramic
ceramicist
ceramics
ceramist

> For any **cerc**- words,
> look under **circ**-.

cereal (grain)
  cereal   serial (part)
  cerebelum   cerebellum
cerebellum, -bella
cerebral
cerebrate, -brated, -brating
cerebration
cerebrum, -bra
ceremonial, -ly
ceremonious, -ly
  ceremonius   ceremonious
ceremony, -monies
  cerial   cereal (grain)
  cerial   serial (part)
  ceribellum   cerebellum
  ceribrum   cerebrum
cerise

> For any **cerk**- words,
> look under **circ**-.

certain, -ly (sure)
  certain   curtain (fabric)
certainty, -ties
  certan   certain
  certanty   certainty
  certenty   certainty
certifiable, -fiably

certificate, -cated, -cating
certification
certifier
certify, -fied, -fying
  certin   certain
  certinty   certainty
certitude
cervical
  cerviks   cervix
cervix, cervixes, cervices
  cesarean   Caesarean
  cesasion   cessation
  cesation   cessation
  ceshion   session (time)
  cesion   cession (yield)
  cespool   cesspool
cessation
cession(yield)
  cession   session (time)
cesspool
chablis
cha-cha
  chacoal   charcoal
chafe, chafed, chafing (rub)
  chafe   chaff (straw)
chaff (straw)
chaffinch, -es
chagrin, -ed, -ing
chain
chain reaction
chain saw
chain-smoke, -smoked, -smoking
chain smoker
chain stitch, -ed, -ing
chain store
chair, -ed, -ing
chair lift
chairman, -men
chairperson
chairwoman, -women
  chaise (chair)   chase (pursue)
chalet
chalice
  chalinge   challenge
  chalis   chalice
chalk, -ed, -ing
challenge, -lenged, -lenging

challenger	
chamba	chamber
chamber	
chamberlain	
chamberlin	chamberlain
chambermade	chambermaid
chambermaid	
chameleon	
chamee	chamois
chamfer, -ed, -ing	
chamie	chamois
chamois	
champ, -ed, -ing	
champagne	
champion, -ed, -ing	
championship	
champiun	champion
chance, chanced, chancing	
chancel	
chanceler	chancellor
chancelery	chancellery
chanceller	chancellor
chancellery, -ries	
chancellor	
chancellorship	
chancelor	chancellor
chancery, -ceries	
chancy, chancier, chanciest	
chandeleer	chandelier
chandelier	
chandler	
chane	chain
chanel	channel
chane reaction	chain reaction
chane saw	chain saw
changable	changeable
change, changed, changing	
changeable, -bly	
changeling	
changeover	
changible	changeable
channel, -ed, -ing	
chanse	chance
chansel	chancel
chansellery	chancellery
chansellor	chancellor
chansey	chancy

chant, -ed, -ing	
chaos	
chaotic, -ally	
chap, chapped, chapping	
chaparral	
chapel	
chaperon, chaperone	
chapile	chapel
chaple	chapel
chaplain	
chaplaincy	-
chaplet	
chaplin	chaplain
chapter	
char, charred, charring	
character	
characteristic, -ally	
characterize, -rized, -rizing	
charade	
charaid	charade
charcoal	
chare	chair
chareman	chairman
chareperson	chairperson
charewoman	chairwoman
charey	chary
charge, charged, charging	
charger	
chariot	
charioteer	
charisma	
charismatic	
charitable, -bly, -bleness	
charitible	charitable
charity, -ties	
charlady, -ladies	
charlatan	
charleston	
charm, -ed, -ing	
charmer	
chart, -ed, -ing	
charter, -ed, -ing	
chartreuse	
chartreuze	chartreuse
chary, charier, chariest	
chase (pursue)	chaise (chair)
chase, chased, chasing	

chased (follow)
  chased   chaste (pure)
  chasen   chasten
chaser
  chasis   chassis
chasm
  chassie   chassis
chassis, chassis
chaste (pure)
  chaste   chased (follow)
chasten, -ed, -ing
chastener
chastise, -tised, -tising
chastisement
chastiser
chastity
chat, chatted, chatting
chateau, -teaus, -teaux
  chatel   chattel
  chater   chatter
  chatily   chattily
  chatiness   chattiness
Chattanooga
chattel
chatter, -ed, -ing
chatterbox, -boxes
chattily
chattiness
chatty, -tier, -tiest
  chaty   chatty
  chauffer   chauffeur
chauffeur
chauvinism
chauvinist
chauvinistic, -ally
cheap (price)
  cheap   cheep (sound)
cheapen, -ed, -ing
cheapish, -ly
cheapskate
  chear   cheer
  chearful   cheerful
  chease   cheese
cheat, -ed, -ing
cheater
check (money)
check, -ed, -ing (stop)

  Check   Czech (person)
checkbook
checkers
checking account
checkmate, -mated, -mating
checkout
checkpoint
checkroom
checkup
  chedar   cheddar
cheddar
cheekily
cheekiness
cheeky, cheekier, cheekiest
cheep, -ed, -ing (sound)
  cheep   cheap (price)
cheer, cheered, cheering
  cheerey   cheery
cheerful, -ly, -ness
  cheerie   cheery
cheerily
cheeriness
cheery, -rier, -riest (happy)
  cheery   cherry (fruit)
cheese
cheeseburger
cheesecake
cheesecloth
cheesy, -sier, -siest
  cheet   cheat
  cheeta   cheetah
cheetah
  cheeter   cheetah
chef
chef-d'oeuvre, chefs-d'oeuvre
  cheif   chief
  cheiftan   chieftain
  chelist   cellist
  chelo   cello
chemical, -ly
chemise
chemist
  chemistrey   chemistry
chemistry, -tries
  chemize   chemise
chemotherapist
chemotherapy

chenille
  cherie — cherry
cherish, -ed, -ing
Cherokee, -kee, -kees
cheroot
  cherp — chirp
cherry, -ries (fruit)
  cherry — cheery (happy)
cherub, cherubim, cherubs
cherubic, -ally
  chery — cheery (happy)
  chery — cherry (fruit)
  ches — chess
  chesbord — chessboard
chess
chessboard
  chessnut — chestnut
chest
chesterfield
chestnut
chevalier
chevron (stripe)
chew, -ed, -ing (eat)
chewing gum
  chews — choose (select)
chewy
chic (stylish)
  chic — sheik (ruler)
chicanery, -ries
Chicano
chick (young bird)
chicken feed
chicken pox
chickpea
chickweed
chicle
chicory, -ries
chide, chided, chiding
chidingly
chief, chiefs
chiefly
chieftain
chieftaincy
chiffon
chiffonier
  chifon — chiffon
chignon

Chihuahua
  chil — chill
chilblain
  chilblane — chilblain
child, children
  childbaring — childbearing
childbearing
  childberth — childbirth
childbirth
childhood
childish, -ly, -ness
childlike
childproof
Chile (country)
chili, -ies (spice)
  chili — chilly (cold)
chill, -ed, -ing
chilli, -ies (spice)
  chilli — chilly (cold)
chilliness
chilly, -lier, -liest (cold)
  chilly — chilli (spice)
chime, chimed, chiming
chimera, -ras
chimeric, -ally
  chimnee — chimney
chimney, -neys
chimpanzee
chin
china (dishes)
China (country)
chinchilla
Chinese
chink, -ed, -ing
chintz, chintzes
chintzy
chip, chipped, chipping
chipboard
  chipmonk — chipmunk
chipmunk
  chiropodey — chiropody
chiropodist
chiropody
  chiropracter — chiropractor
chiropractic
chiropractor
chirp, -ed, -ing

chirpy, -pier, -piest
chisel, -ed, -ing
chiseler
chit
chitchat
chivalrous, -ly
   chivalrus   chivalrous
chivalry
chive
chloride
chlorinate, -nated, -nating
chlorination
chlorine
   chlorofill   chlorophyll
chloroform, -ed, -ing
chlorophyll
   chocalate   chocolate
chock, -ed, -ing
chock-full
   choclat   chocolate
chocolate
choice, choicer, choicest
choir (singers)
   choir   quire (measure)
   choise   choice
choke, choked, choking
choker
choler (anger)
   choler   collar (neck)
   choler   color (hue)
cholera
choleric
cholesterol
chomp, -ed, -ing
   choo   chew
choose, chose, chosen, choosing
(select)
   choose   chews (eats)
choosy
chop, chopped, chopping
chopper
choppy, -pier, -piest
   chopsooey   chop suey
chopstick
   chopy   choppy
choral, -ly (sing)
   choral   coral (reef)

   charal   corral (yard)
chorale (tune)
chord (music)
   chord   cord (string)
chore
   choreograf   choreograph
choreograph, -ed, -ing
choreographer
choreographic
choreography
chorister
chortle, -tled, -tling
chorus, -ruses
chorus, -rused, -rusing
chose
chosen
chow
chowder
chow mein
   chrisalis   chrysalis
chrism
   Chrismas   Christmas
Christ
   Christain   Christian
christen, -ed, -ing
christendom
Christian
Christianity
Christmas
chromatic, -ally
chrome
chromium
chromosome
   chronalogical   chronological
chronic, -ally
   chronical   chronicle
chronicle, -cled, -cling
chronicler
chronologer
chronological, -ly
chronology, -gies
chronometer
chrysalis, chrysalises
chrysanthemum
chubbiness
chubby, -bier, -biest
chuck, -ed, -ing

chuckle, chuckled, chuckling
chuck wagon
chuff, -ed, -ing
chug, chugged, chugging
chum
chummy, -mier, -miest
chump
chunk
chunkiness
chunky, -kier, -kiest
church, -es
churl
churlish, -ly
churn, -ed, -ing

churp — chirp
chute (drop)

chute — shoot (gun)
chutney, -neys
chutzpah

cianide — cyanide
cibernetics — cybernetics
cicada, -dae, -das
cicatrix, cicatrices, cicatrixes

> For all other cic- words,
> look under cyc-.

cider

cifer — cipher
cigar

cigaret — cigarette
cigarette

cignet — cygnet (swan)
cignet — signet (ring)
cilestial — celestial
cilium, cilia

cilinder — cylinder
cilindrical — cylindrical
cimbal — cymbal(music)
cimbal — symbol (sign)
ciment — cement
cinamon — cinnamon
cinch, -ches
cincture
cinder
Cinderella
cinema
cinematic, -ally

cinematographic
cinimatography

cineraria

cinic — cynic
cinical — cynical
cinima — cinema
cinimon — cinnamon
cinnamon

cinosure — cynosure
cipher

cipress — cypress
circa

circalate — circulate
circit — circuit
circiut — circuit
circle, -cled, -cling
circlet
circuit, -ed, -ing
circuit breaker
circuitous, -ly
circuitry
circular, -ly
circularity
circularize, -rized, -rizing
circulate, -lated, -lating
circulation
circulator
circulatory
circumcise, -cised, -cising
circumcision
circumference

circumferense — circumference
circumnavigate, -gated, -gating
circumnavigation
circumnavigator
circumscribe, -ribed, -ribing
circumscription
circumspect
circumspection
circumstance

circumstanse — circumstance
circumstantial, -ly
circumvent, -ed, -ing
circumvention
circus, circuses
cirrhosis

cirriculum — curriculum

cirrosis   cirrhosis
cirrus
cist   cyst
cistern
cistitis   cystitis
citadel
citation
citazen   citizen
cite, cited, citing (quote)
   cite   sight (see)
   cite   site (place)
   citie   city
citizen
citric acid
   citris   citrus
citron
citronella
   citros   citrus
citrous
citrus
city, cities
civet
civic
   civies   civvies
   civik   civic
civil, -ly
civilian
civility, -ties
   civilizasion   civilization
civilization
civilize, -lized, -lizing
   civit   civet
civvies
clad
cladding
claim, -ed, -ing
claimable
   claimabile   claimable
claimant
claimer
clairvoyance
clairvoyant
clam, clammed, clamming
   clamable   claimable
clamber, -ed, -ing
   clame   claim
   clamer   clamor

   clamerus   clamorous
clamminess
clammy, -mier, -miest
clamor, -ed, -ing
clamorous, -ly
clamp, -ed, -ing
   clamy   clammy
clan
clandestine, -ly
clang, -ed, -ing
clangor
clangorous, -ly
clank, -ed, -ing
clannish, -ly
clap, clapped, clapping
clapboard
clapper
claptrap
claret
   clarical   clerical
clarify, -fied, -fying
   clarificasion   clarification
clarification
clarifier
clarinet
clarinetist
clarion
clarionet
clarity
   clark   clerk
   claryon   clarion
clash, -ed, -ing
   clasify   classify
clasp, -ed, -ing
   clasroom   classroom
class, classes
classable
   classible   classable
classic
classical, -ly
classicism
classicist
classifiable
   classificasion   classification
classification
classify, -fied, -fying
classless

classroom
classy, classier, classiest
clatter, -ed, -ing
clause (grammar)
   clause — claws (animal)
   claustrofobia — claustrophobia
claustrophobia
   clavicel — clavicle
clavichord
   clavicord — clavichord
clavier, klavier
claw, -ed, -ing
claws (animal)
   claws — clause (grammar)
clay
clayey
clean, -ed, -ing
cleanliness
cleanse, cleansed, cleansing
cleanser
clean-shaven
clear, -ed, -ing
clearance
clearly
clearness
cleat
cleavage
cleave, cleaved, cleaving
   cleavedge — cleavage
cleaver
   cleek — clique
   cleerance — clearance
   cleeshay — cliché
   cleet — cleat
   cleeve — cleave
   cleevage — cleavage
   cleever — cleaver
clef
cleft
clematis
clemency
   clemensy — clemency
clement
clench, -ed, -ing
   clenliness — cleanliness
   clense — cleanse

clergy, -gies
clergyman, -men
clergywoman, -women
cleric
clerical, -ly
clerk
clever, cleverer, cleverest
cleverly
cleverness
   clew — clue
   clichay — cliché
cliché, -chés
click, -ed, -ing (sound)
   click — clique (group)
clicker
   clidesdale — clydesdale
client
clientele
   clientell — clientele
cliff
cliffhanger
climacteric (crucial)
climactic (climax)
   climaks — climax
climate (weather)
climatic, -ally
climatologist
climatology
climax, -maxes
climb, -ed, -ing (upward)
clime (region)
clinch, -ed, -ing
clincher
cling, clung, clinging
clinic
clinical, -ly
clink, -ed, -ing
clinker, -ed, -ing
clip, clipped, clipping
clipper
clique (group)
   clique — click (sound)
clitoris
   clitris — clitoris
cloak
cloak-and-dagger
cloakroom

clobber, -ed, -ing
clock, -ed, -ing
clockwise
clockwork
clod
clodhopper
clog, clogged, clogging
cloister, -ed, -ing
cloistral
cloke   cloak
clone, cloned, cloning
cloride   chloride
clorinate   chlorinate
clorine   chlorine
clorofil   chlorophyll
cloroform   chloroform
clorophyll   chlorophyll
close, closed, closing (shut)
close, closer, closest (near)
closed-circuit
closeness
closet, -ed, -ing
closure
clot, clotted, clotting
cloth, cloths (fabric)
clothe, clothed, clad, clothing (attire)
clothes (garments)
clothier
cloud, -ed, -ing
cloudburst
cloudless, -ly
cloudy, cloudier, cloudiest
clout, -ed, -ing
clove
cloven
cloven-hoofed
clover
cloverleaf, -leaves
clowd   cloud
clowdless   cloudless
clowdy   cloudy
clown, -ed, -ing
clownish, -ly
clowt   clout
cloy, -ed, -ing
cloyster   cloister

club, clubbed, clubbing
clubhouse
cluch   clutch
cluck, -ed, -ing
clue, clued, cluing
clump, -ed, -ing
clumpy
clumsily
clumsiness
clumsy, -sier, -siest
clung
clurgy   clergy
cluster, -ed, -ing
clutch, -ed, -ing
clutter, -ed, -ing
Clydesdale
coach, -ed, -ing
coachman, -men
coacksial   coaxial
coagulate, -lated, -lating
coagulation
coagulator
coaks   coax
coal
coalesce, -lesced, -lescing
coalescence
coalescent
coaless   coalesce
coalessence   coalescence
coalessent   coalescent
coalfield
coalision   coalition
coalition
coalitionist
coal mine
coal miner
coarse, coarser, coarsest (rough)
coarse   course (path)
coarsen, -ed, -ing
coast, -ed, -ing
coastal
coaster
coastgard   coastguard
coastguard
coastline
coat, -ed, -ing
coax, -ed, -ing

coaxial			cocktale	cocktail
coaxingly		cocky, cockier, cockiest	
coaxiul	coaxial	coco, -cos (palm tree)	
cobalt		cocoa (drink)	
cobble, -bled, -bling		cocoa	cacao (tree)
cobbler		coconut	
cobblestone		cocoon	
coble	cobble	coddle, -dled, -dling	
cobler	cobbler	code, coded, coding	
coblestone	cobblestone	codecks	codex
COBOL		codeen	codeine
cobolt	cobalt	codefy	codify
cobra		codeine	
cobweb		codex, codices	
cocaine		codger	
cocane	cocaine	codicil	
cocanut	coconut	codiene	codeine
cocatoo	cockatoo	codification	
coccix	coccyx	codifier	
coccyx, coccyges		codify, -fied, -fying	
coch	coach	codisil	codicil
cochineal		codle	coddle
cochineel	cochineal	coed	
cock, -ed, -ing		coeducation	
cockade		coeducational	
cockatoo		coefficient	
cockatrice		coefishent	coefficient
cockatriss	cockatrice	coegsist	coexist
cockcrow		coequal, -ly	
cockelshell	cockleshell	coequality	
cockerel		coercable	coercible
cocker spaniel		coerce, -erced, -ercing	
cocket	coquette	coercible	
cocketry	coquetry	coercion	
cockeyed		coercive, -ly	
cockfight		coerse	coerce
cockily		coersible	coercible
cockiness		coersion	coercion
cockle		coersive	coercive
Cockney, -neys		coeval, -ly	
cockpit		coevil	coeval
cockroach, -es		coexist, -ed, -ing	
cockroch	cockroach	coexistence	
cockscomb		coexistense	coexistence
cockshure	cocksure	coexistent	
cocksure		cofee	coffee
cocktail		cofer	coffer

coffey — coffee
coff — cough
coffee
coffer
coffin
cofin — coffin
cog
cogatate — cogitate
cogency
cogenital — congenital
cogent, -ly
coger — codger
cogitate, -tated, -tating
cogitation
cogitative
cognac
cognate
cognision — cognition
cognition
cognitive
cognizance
cognizanse — cognizance
cognizant
cohabit, -ed, -ing
cohabitation
cohearent — coherent
cohere, -hered, -hering
coherence
coherense — coherence
coherent, -ly
cohesion
cohesive, -ly
coheshon — cohesion
cohort
coiffure (hairdresser)
coiffeur — coiffure (hairstyle)
coiffure (hairstyle)
coiffure — coiffeur (hairdresser)
coil, -ed, -ing
coin, -ed, -ing
coinage
coincide, -cided, -ciding
coincidence
coincident, -ly
coinidge — coinage

coinsidence — coincidence
coinsident — coincident
coitus
coke
coket — coquette
cokoon — cocoon
cola
colander
colapse — collapse
cold, -er, -est
cold blooded
cold hearted
cole — coal
colender — colander
coler — choler (anger)
colera — cholera
coleric — choleric
colesterol — cholesterol
coleus
colic
colicky
colition — coalition
colitis
collaborate, -rated, -rating
collaboration
collaborater — collaborator
collaborator
collage (collection)
collage — college (school)
collapse, -lapsed, -lapsing
collapsible
collar, -ed, -ing (neck)
collar — choler (anger)
collar — color (hue)
collarbone
collate, -lated, -lating
collerater — collactor
collateral
collation
collator
colleague
collect, -ed, -ing
collectable
collectible
collection
collective, -ly
collectivism

collector
college (school)
  college   collage (collection)
collegian
collegiate
  coller   choler (anger)
  coller   collar (neck)
collide, -lided, -liding
collie
collier
collinear, -ly
collision (crash)
collocate, -cated, -cating
collocation
  collonial   colonial
colloquial, -ally
colloquialism
colloquy, -quies
collusion (fraud)
collusive, -ly
cologne
colon
  colonade   colonnade

> For other col- words,
> look under **coll-**.

colonel (army)
  colonel   kernel (core)
colonial, -ly
colonization
colonize, -nized, -nizing
colonizer
colonnade
colony, -nies
color, -ed, -ing (hue)
  color   choler (anger)
  color   collar (neck)
coloratura
colorblind
colorful, -fully
colossal, -ly
colossus, -lossuses
colt
coltish, -ly
  colum   column
columbine

column

> For other col- words,
> look under **coll-**.

columnist
coma (sleep)
  coma   comma (mark)
  comand   command
comatose
comb, -ed, -ing
combat, -ed, -ing
combatant
combative, -ly
comber
  combinasion   combination
combination
combine, -bined, -bining
  combustable   combustible
combustible
combustibility
combustion
come, came, come, coming
comeback
comedian
comedienne
comedy, -dies
comeliness
comely, -lier, -liest
  comence   commence
  comend   commend
comestibles
comet
comeuppance
  comfert   comfort
  comfertable   comfortable
  comferter   comforter
comfort, -ed, -ing
comfortable, -bly
comforter
  comfortible   comfortable
comfortless, -ly
comfy, -ier, -iest
comic
comical, -ly

> Look under **comm-** if the
> word is not under **com-**.

comma (mark)
  comma   coma (sleep)
command, -ed, -ing (order)
commandant
commander
commandment
commando, -dos, -does
  commerasion   commeration
commemorate, -rated, -rating
commemoration
commemorative, -ly
commence, -menced, -mencing
commencement
commend, -ed, -ing (praise)
commendable, -bly
  commendasion   commendation
commendation (praise)
  commendation   condemnation
                           (censure)
commendatory
  commendible   commendable
  commense   commence
commensurable, -bly
commensurate
  commensurible   commensurable
comment, -ed, -ing
commentary, -aries
  commentater   commentator
commentator
  commentry   commentary
  commer   comma
commerce
commercial, -ly
commercialism
commercialization
commercialize, -lized, -lizing
  commersial   commercial
  commersialize   commercialize
  commisar   commissar
  commisariat   commissariat
  commisary   commissary
commiserate, -rated, -rating
commiseration
  commision   commission
  commisioner   commissioner
commissar (Soviet bureaucrat)
commissariat (Soviet govt. dept.)

commission
commissioner (bureaucrat)
commit, -mitted, -mitting
  commital   committal
  commitee   committee
commitment
committal
committee
  commizerate   commiserate
  commodaty   commodity
commode
commodious, -ly
commodity, -ties
  commodoor   commodore
commodore
common, -ly, -ness
commonality, -ties
commoner
  commonist   communist
commonplace
commonsense
commonwealth
  commonwelth   commonwealth
  commosion   commotion
commotion
communal, -ly
commune, -muned, -muning
communicable
  communicabile   communicable
communicate, -cated, -cating
  communicater   communicator
communication
communicative
communicator
  communikay   communiqué
communion
communiqué
communism
communist
communistic
community, -ties
commutation
commute, -muted, -muting
commuter

> Look under **comm-** if the
> word is not under **com-**.

compact
   compair   compare (liken)
companion
companionable, -bly
companionship
company, -nies
   companyon   companion
comparable, -bly
comparative, -ly
compare, -pared, -paring
   comparible   comparable
comparison
compartment
compartmentalize, -ized, -izing
   compas   compass
   compasion   compassion
   compasionate compassionate
compass, -es
compass, -ed, -ing
compassion
compassionate, -nated, -nating
   compatable   compatible
compatibility
compatible, -bly
   compatition   competition
compatriot
compel, -pelled, -pelling
compendium, -diums, -dia
compensate, -sated, -sating
   compensater   compensator
compensation
compensator
compensatory
   compensatry   compensatory
   compeny   company
   compere   compare
   competant   competent
   competative   competitive
compete, -peted, -peting
competency
   competense   competence
competent, -ly
   competiter   competitor
competition
competitive, -ly
competitor
compilation

compile, -piled, -piling
compiler
   compinsation compensation
   complacation   complication
complacency, -cies
complacent, -ly (smug)
complain, -ed, -ing
complainant
complaint
complaisant (obliging)
   complanant   complainant
   complane   complain
   complant   complaint
   complasense   complacence
   complasent   complacent
   complection   complexion
complement, -ed, -ing (complete)
   complement   compliment
                    (praise)
complementary (completing)
   complementary complimentary
                    (free)
complete, -pleted, -pleting
completion
complex, -ly
complexion
complexity, -ties
compliable
compliance
compliant, -ly
complicate, -cated, -cating
complication
complicity
   complient   compliant
complier
compliment, -ed, -ing (praise)
   compliment   complement
                 (completely)
complimentary (free)
   complimentary complementary
   complisity   complicity
comply, -plied, -plying
component
comportment
compose, -posed, -posing
composedly
composer

composet	composite
composite, -ly	
compositer	compositor
composition	
compositor	
compost	
composure	
compot	compote
compote	
compound, -ed, -ing	
compoundable	
compoundible	compoundable
comprable	comparable
comprehend, -ed, -ing	
comprehendingly	
comprehensible, -bly	
comprehension	
comprehensive, -ly, -ness	
compress, -ed, -ing	
compressable	compressible
compresser	compressor
compressibility	
compressible	
compression	
compressor	
comprisal	
comprise, -prised, -prising	
comprize	comprise
compromise, -mised, -mising	
comptroller	
compulsery	compulsory
compulsion	
compulsive, -ly, -ness	
compulsorily	
compulsory	
compunction	
compuntion	compunction
computability	
computation	
compute, -puted, -puting	
computer	
computerization	
computer program	
computer terminal	
computibility	computability
comrad	comrade
comrade	

comradeship	
comtroller	comptroller

> Look under **comm-** if the
> word is not under **com-**.

con, conned, conning	
conbine	combine
concave, -ly	
concavity, -ties	
conceal, -ed, -ing	
concealable	
conceilible	concealable
concealment	
concede, -ceded, -ceding	
conceed	concede
conceit	
conceited, -ly	
conceivable	
conceivably	
conceive, -ceived, -ceiving	
conceivible	conceivable
concensus	consensus
concentrate, -trated, -trating	
concentration	
concentric	
concentricity	
concepsion	conception
concept	
conception	
conceptual, -ly	
conceptualize, -lized, -lizing	
concern, -ed, -ing	
concert, -ed, -ing (band)	
concert	consort (partner)
concertina	
concertmaster	
concerto, -tos, -ti	
concession	
conch, conchs, conches	
concherto	concerto
concideration	consideration
conciet	conceit
concieted	conceited
concievable	conceivable
concieve	conceive
conciliate, -ated, -ating	

concilliater	conciliator	condemnation (censure)	
conciliation		condemnation	commerdation
conciliator			(praise)
conciliatory		condemnatory	
concise, -ly, -ness		condence	condense

> Look under **cons-** if the
> word is not under **conc-**.

		condencer	condenser
conclave		condensasion	condensation
conclude, -cluded, -cluding		condensation	
conclushion	conclusion	condense, -densed, -densing	
conclusion		condenser	
conclusive, -ly, -ness		condensor	condenser
concocion	concoction	condescend, -ed, -ing	
concoct, -ed, -ing		condescension	
concoction		condiment	
concomitance		condisend	condescend
concomitancy		condisension	condescension
concomitant, -ly		condision	condition
concord		condit	conduit
concordance		condition, -ed, -ing	
concordanse	concordance	conditional, -ly	
concordant		condolance	condolence
concorse	concourse	condolatory	
concourse		condole, -doled, -doling	
concreet	concrete	condolence	
concrete, -creted, -creting		condolense	condolence
concretely, -creteness		condolingly	
concubine		condominium	
concupiscence		condonation	
concupiscent		condone, -doned, -doning	
concupissense	concupiscence	condor	
concupissent	concupiscent	conducive	
concur, -curred, -curring		conducktion	conduction
concurence	concurrence	conduct, -ed, -ing	
concurent	concurrent	conductable	conductible
concurrence		conducter	conductor
concurrent, -ly		conductible	
concus	concuss	conductibility	
concusion	concussion	conduction	
concuss, -ed, -ing		conductivity, -ties	
concussion		conductor	
condament	condiment	conductress	
condaminium	condominium	conduit	
condansation	condensation	condusive	conducive
condem	condemn	cone	
condemn, -ed, -ing		conect	connect
		conection	connection
		conective	connective

confection
confectionary, -aries (factory)
confectionery, -eries (candy)
confedence   confidence
confederacy, -cies
confederasy   confederacy
confederate, -rated, -rating
confederation
confer, -ferred, -ferring
conference
conferm   confirm
confess, -ed, -ing
confesser   confessor
confession
confessional
confessor
confetti
confidant (trusted man)
confidant   confident (sure)
confidante (trusted woman)
confide, -fided, -fiding
confidence
confident (sure)
confident   confidant
              (trusted man)
confidential   confidential
confidential, -ly
confidentiality
configerasion   configuration
configuration
confine, -fined, -fining
confinement
confirm, -ed, -ing
confirmable
confirmasion   confirmation
confirmation
confiscate, -cated, -cating
confiscation
conflagrasion   conflagration
conflagration
conflict, -ed, -ing
confluence
confluent
conform, -ed, -ing
conformable, -bly
conformible   conformable
conformist

conformity, -ties
confound, -ed, -ing
confownd   confound
confrence   conference
confront, -ed, -ing
confrontation
confurm   confirm
confuse, -fused, -fusing
confusion
confutation
confute, -futed, -futing
conga
congeal, -ed, -ing
congeel   congeal
congeneal   congenial
congenial, -ly
congeniality
congenital, -ly
conger
congest, -ed, -ing
congestion
congestive
conglomerate, -rated, -rating
conglomeration
congradulation   congratulation
congragation   congregation
congratulate, -lated, -lating
congratulation
congratulatory
congregate, -gated, -gating
congregation
congregational
congress
congressional
congrewent   congruent
congrewus   congruous
congruence
congruent
congruity, -ties
congruous, -ly
conic
conical, -ly
conifer
coniferous (tree)
coniferous   carniverous
              (flesh eating)
conjeckture   conjecture

conjecturable, -bly
conjecture, -tured, -turing
  conjenial   congenial
  conjestion   congestion
conjoin, -ed, -ing
conjoint, -ly
conjugal, -ly
conjugality
conjugate, -gated, -gating
conjugation
  conjugel   conjugal
  conjuice   conduce
  conjuncktion   conjunction
conjunct, -ly
conjunction
conjunctional, -ly
conjunctive, -ly
conjunctivitis
conjuncture
conjuration
conjure, -jured, -juring
conjurer, conjuror
conk, -ed, -ing
  conker   conquer
  conkwest   conquest
con man, -men
connect, -ed, -ing
connection
connective, -ly
connector
  connewbial   connubial
conning tower
connivance
  connivanse   connivance
connive, -nived, -niving
  connoiseur   connoisseur
connoisseur
connotation
connote, -noted, -noting
connubial, -ly
  conosseur   connoisseur
  conote   connote
conquer, -ed, -ing
conquerable
  conquerer   conqueror
  conquerible   conquerable
conqueror

conquest
conquistador
consanguine
consanguineous, -ly
consanguinity
  consaquence   consequence
  consceintious   conscientious
conscience (sense)
  conscience   conscious
                   (aware)
  consciensious   conscientious
conscientious, -ly
conscious, -ly, -ness
conscript, -ed, -ing
conscription
  conseal   conceal
  conseat   conceit
consecrate, -crated, -crating
consecration
consecutive
  consede   concede
  consekwence   consequence
consensus
consent, -ed, -ing
  consentrate   concentrate
consequence
consequent
consequential, -ly
  consern   concern
  conservasion   conservation
  conservatery   conservatory
conservation
conservational
conservationist
conservative, -ly
conservatism
conservatory, -tries
conserve, -served, -serving
  consession   concession
  consicrate   consecrate
consider, -ed, -ing
considerable, -ably
considerate, -ly
consideration
  considerible   considerable
consign, -ed, -ing
consignable

consignee
consigner
  consignible   consignable
consignment
consignor
  consiliate   conciliate
  consine   consign
  consinee   consignee
  consinement   consignment
  consinor   consignor
  consise   concise
consist, -ed, -ing
consistence
consistency, -cies
  consistense   consistence
  consistensy   consistency
consistent, -ly
consolable
  consoladasion   consolidation
consolation
console, -soled, -soling
consoler
  consolible   consolable
consolidate, -dated, -dating
consolidation
consolidator
consommé
consonance
  consonense   consonance
consonant, -ly
consort, -ed, -ing (partner)
  consort   concert (band)
consortium, -tia
conspicuous, -ly, -ness
conspiracy, -cies
  conspirasy   conspiracy
  conspirater   conspirator
conspirator
conspiratory
  conspiratry   conspiratory
conspire, -spired, -spiring
constable
constabulary, -ries
constancy
  constansy   constancy
constant, -ly
  constapation   constipation

constellation
  constent   constant
consternation
  constible   constable
constipate, -pated, -pating
constipation
constituency, -cies
  constituensy   constituency
constituent
constitute, -tuted, -tuting
constitution
constitutional, -ly
constrain, -ed, -ing
constraint
  constricksion   constriction
constrict, -ed, -ing
constriction
  construcksion   construction
construct, -ed, -ing
  constructer   constructor
construction
constructive, -ly
constructor
construe, -strued, -struing
consul (diplomat)
  consul   council (meeting)
  consul   counsel (advice)
consular
consulate
  consuler   consular
consult, -ed, -ing
consultant
consultation
consultative
  consultent   consultant
consulter
consumable
consume, -sumed, -suming
consumer
consumerism
consummate, -mated, -mating
consummation
consummative
  consummé   consommé
  consumpsion   consumption
consumption

consumptive, -ly
contack | contact
contact, -ed, -ing
contact lenses
contageous | contagious
contagion
contagious
contajus | contagious
contain, -ed, -ing
container
containerization
containment
contamanate | contaminate
contaminate, -nated, -nating
contamination
contane | contain
contanement | containment
contaner | container
contemparary | contemporary
contemplate, -plated, -plating
contemplation
contemplative, -ly
contemporaneous, -ly
contemporary, -raries
contempt
contemptable | contemptible
contemptible, -bly
contemptuous, -ly
contend, -ed, -ing
contender
contension | contention
contenental | continental
content
contented, -ly, -ness
contention
contentious, -ly
contentment
conterdiction | contradiction
contest, -ed, -ing
contestant
contestent | contestant
context
contextual, -ly
contiguity
contiguous, -ly
continence
continense | continence

continent
continental
contingency, -cies
contingensy | contingency
contingent, -ly
continnuasion | continuation
continous | continuous
continual, -ly
continuance
continuanse | continuance
continuation
continue, -ued, -uing
continuity, -ties
continuous, -ly
continuum, -tinuums, -tinua
contoar | contour
contort, -ed, -ing
contortion
contortionist
contour
contraband
contrabution | contribution
contraception
contraceptive, -ly
contracktion | contraction
contract, -ed, -ing
contracter | contractor
contraction
contractor
contractual
contradicktion | contradiction
contradict, -ed, -ing
contradiction
contradictory, -ries
contralto, -ti
contrapsion | contraption
contraption
contrarily
contrariness
contrariwise
contrary, -ries
contrasepsion | contraception
contraseptive | contraceptive
contrast, -ed, -ing
contravene, -vened, -vening
contravension | contravention
contribute, -buted, -buting

contributer → contributor
contribution
contributor
contributory
contributry → contributory
contrisiun → contrition
contrite, -ly
contrition
contrivance
contrivanse → contrivance
contrive, -trived, -triving
control, -trolled, -trolling
controllability
controllable
controller
controllible → controllable
controversal → controversial
controversial, -ly
controversy, -sies
contumely, -lies
contuse, -tused, -tusing
contusion
contusive
contuson → contusion
conubial → connubial
conundrum
conurbation
convalesce, -lesced, -lescing
convalescence
convalescense → convalescent
convalescent
convaless → convalesce
convalessence → convalescence
convect, -ed, -ing
convecter → convector
convection
convective, -ly
convector
convene, -vened, -vening
convener → convenor
convenience
conveniense → convenience
convenient, -ly
convenor
convension → convention
convent
convention

conventional, -ly
conventionalism
converge, -verged, -verging
conversant, -ly
conversasion → conversation
conversation
conversational, -ly
conversationalist
converse, -versed, -versing
conversely
conversent → conversant
conversion
convert, -ed, -ing
convertable → convertible
converter
convertible, -ly
convex, -ly
convexity, -ties
convey, -ed, -ing
conveyance
conveyancer
conveyancing
conveyanse → conveyance
conveyor
convicktion → conviction
convict, -ed, -ing
conviction
convienence → convenience
convincable → convincible
convince, -vinced, -vincing
convincible
convincingly
convivial, -ly
convivialty
convocation
convoke, -voked, -voking
convolusion → convolution
convolute, -luted, -luting
convolution
convolve, -volved, -volving
convoy, -ed, -ing
convulsant
convulse, -vulsed, -vulsing
convulsion
convulsive, -ly
conyac → cognac
coo, cooed, cooing

cooger	cougar		copyrite	copyright
cook, -ed, -ing			copywriter	
cookbook			coquet, -quetted, -quetting	
cookery			coquetry	
cookie, cookies			coquette	
cookoo	cuckoo		coquettish, -ly	
cool, -ed, -ing			corageous	courageous
coolant			coral (reef)	
cooler			coral	choral (sing)
coop, -ed, -ing			coral	chorale (tune)
co-op			coral	corral (yard)
cooper			corcus	caucus
cooperage			cord (rope)	
cooperate, -rated, -rating			cord	chord (music)
cooperation			cordage	
cooperative, -ly			corded	
coopon	coupon		cordial, -ly	
coopt, -ed, -ing			cordiality	
coordinate, -nated, -nating			cordige	cordage
coordination			cordon, -ed, -ing	
coordinator			cordon bleu	
coot			corduroy	
coparison	comparison		core, cored, coring (center)	
cope, coped, coping (put up with)			core	caw (cry)
copier			core	corps (group)
copilot			corect	correct
copious, -ly, -ness			corection	correction
cop-out			corective	corrective
copper			corelate	correlate
copperhead			corequisite	
copperplate			coreografy	choreography
coppy	copy		corespond	correspond
copra			corespondence	correspondence
cops	copse		corespondense	correspondence
copse			corespondent (divorce)	
copter			corespondent	correspondent
copula, -lae			corgi	
copulate, -lated, -lating			coriander	
copulation			coridoor	corridor
copulative, -ly			Corinthian	
copy, copies			coriografy	choreography
copy, copied, copying			corispond	correspond
copybook			corispondence	correspondence
copycat, -catted, -catting			corispondent	correspondent
copyer	copier		corister	chorister
copyist			cork, -ed, -ing (stopper)	
copyright, -ed, -ing (licence)			cork	calk (fill)

cork	caulk (fill)	corpulence	
corker		corpulense	corpulence
corkscrew, -ed, -ing		corpulent, -ly	
corm		corpus, -pora	
cormorant		corpuscle	
corn		corpuscular	
corncob		corpusle	corpuscle
cornea, -neas, -neae		corragation	corrigation
corneal		corral, -ralled, -ralling (yard)	
corned beef		corral	choral (sing)
corneel	corneal	corral	chorale (tune)
corner, -ed, -ing		corral	coral (reef)
cornerstone		correcktion	correction
cornet		correct, -ed, -ing	
cornflower		correction	
cornia	cornea	correctional	
cornice, -niced, -nicing		corrective, -ly	
cornstalk		correlate, -lated, -lating	
cornucopia		correlation	
corny, -nier, -niest		correlative, -ly	
coroborate	corroborate	correlativity	
coroborator	corroborator	correspond, -ed, -ing	
coroboree	corroboree	correspondence	
corode	corrode	correspondent	
corola	corolla	corresponding, -ly	
corolary	corollary	corridor	
corolla		corroborate, -rated, -rating	
corollary, -ries		corroborater	corroborator
corona, -nas, -nae		corroboration	
coronary		corroborative, -ly	
coronary thrombosis		corroborator	
coronasion	coronation	corrodable	corrodible
coronation		corrode, -roded, -roding	
coroner		corrodible	
coronet		corrollary	corollary
corosion	corrosion	corrosion	
corosive	corrosive	corrosive, -ly	
corparation	corporation	corrugate, -gated, -gating	
corperal	corporal	corrugated iron	
corporal, -ly		corrugation	
corporate, -ly		corrupt, -ed, -ing	
corporation		corruptable	corruptible
corporeal, -ly		corruptible, -bly	
corps (group)		corruptibility	
corps	corpse (body)	corruption	
corpse (body)		corsage	
corpse	corps (group)	corsair	

corsation	causation	costliness	
corse	coarse (rough)	costly, -lier, -liest	
corse	course (path)	costume, -tumed, -tuming (dress)	
corsen	coarsen	costume	custom (habit)
corset		cot	
corsit	corset	cotage	cottage
cort	caught (held)	cotchineal	cochineal
cort	court (law)	cote (shelter)	
cort marshal	court martial	cote	coat (garment)
cortage	cortege	coterie	
cortege		coton	cotton
corterize	cauterize	cottage	
cortex, -tices		cotter pin	
cortier	courtier	cotton	
cortion	caution	cottonwood	
cortious	cautious	cottony	
cortisan	courtesan	cou daytar	coup d'état
cortisone		couch	
cortizone	cortisone	cougar	
cortly	courtly	cough, -ed, -ing	
cortroom	courtroom	could	
cortship	courtship	couldn't (could not)	
cortyard	courtyard	couldnt	couldn't
corugate	corrugate	coulter	
corupt	corrupt	councel	council (meeting)
coruptible	corruptible	councel	counsel (advice)
coruption	corruption	council (meeting)	
corus	chorus	council	consul (diplomat)
corvet	corvette	council	counsel (advice)
corvette		counciler	councilor
cosign, -ed, -ing		councilor (member)	
cosmetic		councilor	counselor
cosmetically		counsel, -ed, -ing (advise)	
cosmic		counsel	consul (diplomat)
cosmografy	cosmography	counsel	council (meeting)
cosmography, -phies		counseler	counselor
cosmology		counselor (adviser)	
cosmonaut		counselor	councilor (member)
cosmonort	cosmonaut	count, -ed, -ing	
cosmopolitan		countdown	
cosmos		countenance, -nanced, -nancing	
Cossack		countenanse	countenance
cost, cost, costed, costing			
cost	coast		
co-star, -starred, -starring			
coster			
costguard	coastguard		

counter
counteract, -ed, -ing
counteraction
counteractive, -ly
counterattack, -ed, -ing
counterbalance, -anced, -ancing
counterculture
counterespionage
   counterfeet   counterfeit
counterfeit, -ed, -ing
counterfeiter
counterintelligence
countermand, -ed, -ing
counterpane
counterpart
counterpoint
counterproductive
counterrevolution
counterrevolutionary, -aries
countersign, -ed, -ing
countersignature
   countersine   countersign
   counterwait   counterweight
counterweight
countess
   countie   county
countless
country, -tries
countryman, -men
countryside
county, -ties
coup, coups
   coupay   coupé
coup de grace
coup d'état
coupé
couple, -led, -ling
couplet
coupon
courage
courageous, -ly
courier (messenger)
   courier   currier (leather)
course (path)
   course   coarse (rough)
court, -ed, -ing (law)
   court   caught (held)

   courtecy   courtesy
courtesan
courtesy, -sies (manners)
   courtesy   curtsy (bow)
courthouse
courtier
courtly, -lier, -liest
   court marshal   court martial
court martial
courtroom
courtyard
cousin
couture
couturier
covenant
cover, -ed, -ing
coverage
covert, -ly
cover-up
covet, -ed, -ing
covetous, -ly
covey, -eys
coward (scared)
   coward   cowered
            (cringed)
cowardice
   cowardiss   cowardice
cowardly
cowboy
cower, -ed, -ing (cringe)
   cowered   coward (scared)
cowl, -ed, -ing
cowlick
cowling

> For cown- words,
> look under coun-.

cowslip
cox
coxcomb
   coxe   coax
coxswain
coy, -ly
   coyn   coin
coyote
   cozmetic   cosmetic
   cozmic   cosmic

cozy
crab, crabbed, crabbing
crab apple
crabby, -bier, -biest
crack, -ed, -ing
crackdown
cracker
crackle, -led, -ling
crackpot
cradle, -dled, -dling
craft
craftily
craftiness
craftsman, -men
craftsmanship
crafty, -tier, -tiest
crag
craggy, -gier, -giest
   crain   crane
cram, crammed, cramming
cramp, -ed, -ing
cranberry, -ries
crane, craned, craning
cranial, -ly
cranium, -nia
crank, -ed, -ing
crankcase
crankiness
crankshaft
cranky, -kier, -kiest
cranny, -nies
craps
crapulous
crash, -ed, -ing
crass
crate, crated, crating
crater
cravat
crave, craved, craving
craven, -ly
crawfish
crawl, -ed, -ing
crawler
   crayen   crayon
crayfish
craze, crazed
crazily

craziness
crazy, -zier, -ziest
   creachure   creature
creak, -ed, -ing (squeak)
   creak   creek (stream)
creaky, -kier, -kiest
cream, -ed, -ing
creaminess
creamy, -mier, -miest
   creap   creep
crease, creased, creasing
create, -ated, -ating
   creater   creator
creation
creative, -ly, -ness
creativity
creator
creature
crèche
   credability   credibility
   credable   credible
credence
   credense   credence
   credensial   credential
credential
credibility
credible (believable)
credibly
credit, -ed, -ing
creditable, -bly (honor)
credit card
   crediter   creditor
   creditible   creditable
creditor
credo, -dos
credulity
credulous, -ly, -ness
creed
creek (stream)
   creek   creak (squeak)
creel
   creem   cream
creep, crept, creeping
creeper
creepiness
creeps
creepy, -pier, -piest

cremate, -mated, -mating
cremation
crematorium
creme
crenellate, -lated, -lating
Creole
creosote, -soted, -soting
crepe, creped, creping
crept
crepuscular
crescendo, -dos
crescent
    cresh   crèche
    creshendo   crescendo
cress
    cressent   crescent
crest, -ed, -ing
crestfallen, -ly
cretin
cretinism
cretinous
    creture   creature
    crevase   crevasse
    crevase   crevice
crevasse (deep crack)
crevice (narrow crack)
crew, -ed, -ing
crew-cut
crewel (yarn)
    crewel   cruel (harsh)
crews (sailors)
    crews   cruise (ship)
crib, cribbed, cribbing
    cribage   cribbage
cribbage
    cribbidge   cribbage
crick
cricket
cricketer
    crickit   cricket
crier
crime
criminal, -ly
criminality, -ties
criminalization
criminalize, -ized, -izing
    criminel   criminal

criminologist
criminology
crimp, -ed, -ing
crimpy, -pier, -piest
crimson
cringe, cringed, cringing
crinkle, -kled, -kling
crinkly
crinoline
cripple, -pled, -pling
    cript   crypt
    criptic   cryptic
    criptograf   cryptograph
    criptogram   cryptogram
    criptograph   cryptograph
    crisalis   chrysalis
    criscross   crisscross
crisis, -ses
crisp, -ed, -ing
crispness
crispy
crisscross
    Crist   Christ
    cristal   crystal
    cristaline   crystalline
    cristalize   crystallize
    cristen   christen
    Cristendom   Christendom
    Cristian   Christian
    Cristianity   Christianity
    criteek   critique
criterion, -teria
critic (judge)
critical, -ly
criticism
criticize, -cized, -cizing
critique (criticism)
    critisize   criticize
croak, -ed, -ing
crochet, -ed, -ing
crock
    crockadile   crocodile
crockery
crocodile
crocus, crocuses
croissant
    crokay   croquet

cromatic — chromatic
crome — chrome
cromosome — chromosome
crone
crony, -nies
crood — crude
crook
crooked, -ly, -ness
crookedness
croon, -ed, -ing
crooner
crop, cropped, cropping
crop-dust, -ed, -ing
crop-duster
cropper
croquet (sport)
croquette (food)
crosier
cross, -ed, -ing
crossbar
crossbones
crossbow
crossbreed, -bred, -breeding
cross-check
cross-country
crosscut, -cut, -cutting
cross-examination
cross-examine, -ined, -ining
cross-examiner
cross-eyed
crossfertilization
crossfertilize, -lized, -lizing
cross-pollinate, -nated, -nating
cross-purpose
cross-reference, -renced, -rencing
crossroads
cross section
cross stitch, -ed, -ing
crosswise
crossword puzzle
crotch
crotchet
crotchety
crouch, -ed, -ing
croup
croupier
crouton

crow, crowed, crowing
crowbar
crowd, -ed, -ing
crown, -ed, -ing
crow's foot, -feet
crow's nest
crucial, -ly
crucibel — crucible
crucible
crucifix
crucifixion
cruciform, -ly
crucify, -fied, -fying
crude, cruder, crudest
crudeness
crudely
crudity, -ties
crueler, cruelest (harsh)
cruel
cruel — crewel (yarn)
cruelty, -ties
cruet
cruise, cruised, cruising (ship)
cruise — crews (sailors)
cruiser
crulty — cruelty
crum — crumb
crumb, -ed, -ing
crumble, -bled, -bling
crummy, -mier, -miest
crumpet
crumple, -pled, -pling
crunch, -ed, -ing
crunchy, -chier, -chiest
crusade, -saded, -sading
crusader
crush, -ed, -ing
crushal — crucial
crusible — crucible
crusifix — crucifix
crust
crustacean
crustasean — crustacean
crustiness
crusty, crustier, crustiest
crutch, -ed, -ing
crux, cruxes, cruces

cruze — cruise
cry, cries
cry, cried, crying
crypt
cryptic, -ally
cryptogram
cryptograph
cryptographer
cryptographic
cryptography
crysalis — chrysalis
crystal
crystalline
crystallization
crystallize, -lized, -lizing
cub
cubbyhole
cube, cubed, cubing
cubic
cubical, -ly (cube-shaped)
cubicle (room)
cubism
cubist
cuboard — cupboard
cubyhole — cubbyhole
cuckold, -ed, -ing
cuckoldry
cuckoo
cucumber
cud
cuddle, -dled, -dling
cuddlesome
cuddly
cudgel, -ed, -ing
cudgerie
cudly — cuddly
cudos — kudos
cue, cued, cuing (billiards)
cuff, -ed, -ing
cuisine
culcher — culture
cul-de-sac
culer — color
culinary
cull, -ed, -ing
culminate, -nated, -nating
culmination

culots — culottes
culottes
culpability
culpable, -bly
culpible — culpable
culprit
cult
cultavate — cultivate
cultist
cultivate, -vated, -vating
cultivater — cultivator
cultivation
cultivator
cultural, -ly
culture, -tured, -turing
cultured pearl
culture shock
culvert
cumbersome, -ly
cumbersum — cumbersome
cumfurt — comfort
cumin
cummerbund
cumpass — compass
cumquat — kumquat
cumulative, -ly
cumulus
cuning — cunning
cunning, -ly
cuntry — country
cup, cupped, cupping
cupboard
cupbord — cupboard
cupful, cupfuls
Cupid
cupidity
cupola
cuppa
cur
curable, -bly
curacao
curacy, -cies
curage — courage
curant — currant (fruit)
curare
curate
curater — curator

curative, -ly
curator
curatorial
curb, -ed, -ing
curcuit   circuit
curd
curdle, -dled, -dling
cure, cured, curing
currency   currency
curent   current (flow)
curette, -retted, -retting
curfew
curiculum   curriculum
curio, curios
curiosity, -ties
curious, -ly
curius   curious
curl, -ed, -ing
curler
curlew
curling
curly, -lier, -liest
curmudgeon
curnel   colonel
currage   courage
curragus   courageous
currant (fruit)
currant   current (flow)
currency, -cies
currensy   currency
current (flow)
current   currant (fruit)
currently
curriculum, -lums, -la
curriculum vitae
currier (leather)
currier   courier
                (messenger)
curry, -ries
curry, -ried, -rying
curse, cursed, cursing
cursive, -ly
cursor
curt, -ly
curtail, -ed, -ing
curtailment
curtain, -ed, -ing (fabric)

curtain   certain (sure)
curtale   curtail
curteous   courteous
curtsy, -sies (bow)
curtsy, -sied, -sying (bow)
curtsy   courtesy
                (manners)
curvaceous
curvaseous   curvaceous
curvature
curve, curved, curving
curvilinear
cushion, -ed, -ing
cushon   cushion
cushy, cushier, cushiest
cusine   cuisine
cusp
cuspid
cuss
cussed, -ly
custamer   customer
custard
custodial
custodian
custom (habit)
custom   costume (dress)
customarily
customary, -aries
custom-built
customer
custom-made
cut, cut, cutting
cutback
cute, cuter, cutest
cuteness
cutical   cuticle
cuticle
cutlass
cutlery
cutlet
cutoff
cutter
cutthroat
cuttlefish
cuvenant   covenant
cuver   cover
cuvet   covet

cuvey	covey
cyanide	
cybernetics	
cyclamate	
cyclamen	
cycle, cycled, cycling	
cyclic	
cyclist	
cycloid	
cyclone	
cyclonic	
cygnet (swan)	
cygnet	signet (ring)
cylinder	
cymbal (instrument)	
cymbal	symbol (sign)
cymbalist	
cymbidium	
cynic	
cynical, -ly	
cynicism	
cynoshure	cynosure
cynosure	
cypher	
cypress	
cyst	
cystitis	
cytology	
czar	
czarina	
czarist	
Czech (person)	
Czech	check (stop)
Czech	check (money)
Czechoslovak	
Czechoslovakia	
Czechoslovakian	

Dd

dab, dabbed, dabbing
dabble, -bled, -bling
   dabris   debris
dachshund
   dacor   decor
   dacquiri   daiquiri
dad
daddy-long-legs
   daes   dais
daffodil
daffy, daffier, daffiest
   dafodil   daffodil
dagger
dahlia
   dail   dale
daily
   daim   dame
   daintie   dainty
daintily
dainty, -tier, -tiest
daiquiri, -ries
   dair   dare
   dairey   dairy (milk)
dairy, -ries (milk)
   dairy   diary (book)
dais
   daisie   daisy
daisy, daisies
   dalee   dally
   dalia   dahlia
   dalight   daylight
dally, -lied, -lying
Dalmatian
   daly   daily
dam, dammed, damming (water)
   dam   damn (swear)
damage, -aged, -aging
damageable

damask
dame
   damedge   damage
   damestic   domestic
damn, -ed, -ing (swear)
   damn   dam (water)
damnable, -bly
   damnasion   damnation
damnation
   damnible   damnable
damp
dampen, -ed, -ing
damper
damsel
dance, danced, dancing
dancer
dandelion
dander
   dandilion   dandelion
dandle, -dled, -dling
dandruff
dandy, dandier, dandiest
   dane   deign
   dangel   dangle
danger
dangerous, -ly
dangle, -gled, -gling
   danjer   danger
   danjerus   dangerous
   danse   dance
   dappel   dapple
dapper, -ly
dapple, -pled, -pling
   darby   derby
dare, dared, daring
daredevil
   darey   dairy (milk)
dark, -ly, -ness
darken, -ed, -ing
   darkin   darken
darkroom
   darlin   darling
darling
darn, -ed, -ing
dart, -ed, -ing
darter
dash, -ed, -ing

dashboard
   dashbord — dashboard
   dashound — dachshund
dastard, -ly
   dasy — daisy
data (plural noun)
database
date, dated, dating
   datente — détente
   dater — data
   datim — datum
datum (singular noun), data
daub
   daudle — dawdle
   daufin — dauphin
daughter
daunt, -ed, -ing
dauntless
dauphin
   dauter — daughter
davenport
   dawb — daub
dawdle, -dled, -dling
dawn, -ed, -ing
   dawnt — daunt
day
   daybrake — daybreak
daybreak
daydream
   daycor — decor
   dayify — deify
   dayis — dais
   dayity — deity
   daylia — dahlia
daylight
   daylite — daylight
   dayly — daily
   dayn — deign
daze, dazed, dazing (stun)
   daze — days (time)
   dazy — daisy
dazzle, -zled, -zling
dazzler
deacon
   deactavate — deactivate
deactivate, -ated, -ating
dead, -ly

deadbeat
dead center
deaden, -ed, -ing
deadline
deadlock
deadly, -lier, -liest
deadpan
dead reckoning
dead weight
deadwood
deaf
deafen, -ed, -ing
   deaft — deft
deal, dealt, dealing
dealer
   deam — deem
dean
dear, -ly (loved)
   dear — deer (animal)
dearth
death
death adder
deathly
death wish

> Look under **di-** if the
> word is not under **de-**.

debacle
   debanair — debonair
debar, -barred, -barring
debase, -based, -basing
debasement
debatable, -bly
debate, -bated, -bating
   debatible — debatable
debauch, -ed, -ing
debauchery, -ries
   debbit — debit
debenture
debilitate, -tated, -tating
debilitation
debility, -ties
debit, -ed, -ing
   debochery — dabauchery
debonair
   debrie — debris
debrief, -ed, -ing

debris
debt
  debter · debtor
debtor
  debue · debut
debug, -bugged, -bugging
debunk, -ed, -ing
debut
debutante
decade
decadence
  decadense · decadence
decadent, -ly
decamp, -ed, -ing
decant, -ed, -ing
decanter
decapitate, -tated, -tating
decapitation
  decathalon · decathlon
decathlon
decay, -ed, -ing
decease, -ceased, -ceasing
deceit
deceitful, -ly, -ness
deceive, deceived, deceiving
decelerate, -rated, -rating
December
decency, -cies
decent, -ly (fair)
  decent · descant (music)
  decent · descent (down)
  decent · dissent (differ)
decentralization
decentralize, -lized, -lizing
  decepsion · deception
deception
deceptive, -ly
decibel
  decibell · decibel
decide, -cided, -ciding
decidedly
deciduous
  deciet · deceit
  decieve · deceive
  decifer · decipher
decimal
decimate, -mated, -mating

decipher, -ed, -ing
decision
decisive, -ly, -ness
deck, -ed, -ing
  deckade · decade
  deckadence · decadence
deckchair
  deckchare · deckchair
  deckerate · decorate
deckhand
deckle
declaim, -ed, -ing
  declamasion · declamation
declamation
declarable
declaratory
  declaratry · declaratory
declare, -clared, -claring
  declarible · declarable
declassify, -fied, -fying
decline, -clined, -clining
  decmal · decimal
decode, -coded, -coding
decompose, -posed, -posing
decomposition
  decompresion · decompression
decompress, -ed, -ing
decompression
decongestant
decor
decorate, -rated, -rating
decoration
decorative, -ly
decorous, -ly
decorum
  decorus · decorous
decoy, -ed, -ing
decrease, -creased, -creasing
decree, -creed, -creeing (law)
  decree · degree (step)
  decreese · decrease
decrepit
decrepitude

> Look under **di-** if the word is not under **de-**.

decry, -cried, -crying

ded	dead
dedacate	dedicate
deden	deaden

dedicate, -cated, -cating
dedication

dedly	deadly

deduce, -duced, -ducing

deducksion	deduction

deduct, -ed, -ing

deductable	deductible

deductible
deduction
deed

deel	deal

deem, -ed, -ing

deen	dean

deep, -ly
deepen, -ed, -ing
deep-freeze, -frozen, -freezing
deer (animal)

deer	dear (loved)

deescalate, -lated, -lating

def	deaf

deface, -faced, -facing

defacit	deficit

de facto

defamasion	defamation

defamation
defamatory

defamatry	defamatory

defame, -famed, -faming (slander)

defame	deform (distort)

default, -ed, -ing
defaulter
defeat, -ed, -ing
defeatism
defeatist
defecate, -cated, -cating

defecktion	defection

defect, -ed, -ing

defecter	defector

defection
defective, -ly
defector

defeet	defeat
defen	deafen

defend, -ed, -ing

defendant

defendent	defendant
defensable	defensible

defense
defensible
defensive, -ly, -ness
defer, -ferred, -ferring (postpone)

defer	differ (disagree)
deferance	deference

deference

deferense	deference
deferensial	deferential

deferential, -ly

deferr	defer

> For **deff-** words,
> look under **def-**.

defiance

defianse	defiance

defiant, -ly
deficiency, -cies
deficit

defience	defiance

defile, -filed, -filing

definate	definite

define, -fined, -fining

definision	definition
definit	definite

definite, -ly
definition
definitive, -ly

defishency	deficiency
defishent	deficient
defisit	deficit

deflate, -flated, -flating
deflation
deflationary

deflecksion	deflection

deflect, -ed, -ing
deflection

definte	definite

defoliant
defoliate, -ated, -ating
defoliation
deform, -ed, -ing (distort)

deform	defame (slander)

deformity, -ies
defraud, -ed, -ing
defrauder
  defrawd   defraud
defray, -ed, -ing
defreeze, -frozen, -freezing
defrost, -ed, -ing
deft, -ly, -ness
defunct
defuse, -fused, -fusing
defy, -fied, -fying

> Look under **di-** if the word is
> not under **de-**.

degeneracy
  degenerasy   degeneracy
degenerate, -rated, -rating
degeneration
  degradasion   degradation
degradation
degrade, -graded, -grading
degree (step)
  degree   decree (law)
  degridasion   degradation
  dehidrate   dehydrate
dehumidify, -fied, -fying
dehydrate, -drated, -drating
dehydration
  deifie   deify
deify, -fied, -fying
deign
  dein   deign
  deisel   diesel
  deitee   deity
deity, -ties
  dejecksion   dejection
dejection
  dejenerate   degenerate
  dekay   decay
delay, -ed, -ing
  delecate   delicate
delectable, -bly
  delectible   delectable
delegate, -gated, -gating
delegation
  delerious   delirious
delete, -leted, -leting

deleterious, -ly
deletion
  delfinium   delphinium
deli
deliberate, -rated, -rating
deliberately
deliberation
deliberative, -ly
delicacy, -cies
delicate, -ly
delicatessen
delicious, -ly
  delicous   delicious
  deligate   delegate
delight, -ed, -ing
delightful, -ly
delimit, -ed, -ing
delineate, -ated, -ating
delineation
  deliniate   delineate
  delinkwency   delinquency
  delinkwent   delinquent
  delinquancy   delinquency
delinquency
delinquent
delirious, -ly
delirium
  delirius   delirious
  delisious   delicious
  delite   delight
  deliteful   delightful
deliver, -ed, -ing
deliverance
  deliverence   deliverance
delivery, -eries
dell

> For other **dell-** words, look
> under **del-**.

  delood   delude
delphinium
  delt   dealt
delta
delude, -luded, -luding
deluge, -uged, -uging
  deluks   deluxe
delusion

delusive, -ly
delusory
delve, delved, delving
demagog
demagogy
demand, -ed, -ing
demarcate, -cated, -cating
demarcation
demean, -ed, -ing
   demeaner   demeanor
demeanor
demented, -ly
dementia
demerit
demigod
demilitarized zone
   diminish   diminish
demise
   demize   demise
demo
demobilization
demobilize, -lized, -lizing
democracy, -cies
   democrasy   democracy
democrat
democratic, -ally
democratization
   demografy   demography
demographic, -ally
demography
demolish, -ed, -ing
   demolision   demolition
demolition
demolitionist
demon
demonic
demonology
demonstrable, -bly
demonstrate, -strated, -strating
   demonstrater   demonstrator
demonstration
demonstrator
   demonstrible   demonstrable
demoralize, -lized, -lizing
demote, -moted, -moting
demur, -murred, -murring (object)
   demur   demure (coy)

demure, -murer, -murest (coy)
   demure   demur (object)
den
   dence   dense
   dencher   denture
   dencity   density
   denem   denim
dengue
   deni   deny
denial
denigrate, -grated, -grating
denigration
denim
denizen

> For denn- words,
> look under den-.

denominate, -nated, -nating
   denominater   denominator
denomination
denominational, -ly
denominator
denotable
denote, -noted, -noting
   denotible   denotable
denounce, -nounced, -nouncing
denouncement
   denownse   denounce
dense, denser, densest
densely
   densitee   density
density
dent, -ed, -ing
dental
dentist
dentistry
denture
denude, -nuded, -nuding
denunciate, -ated, -ating
deny, denied, denying
   deoderant   deodorant
   deoderize   deodorize
deodorant
deodorize, -rized, -rizing
   deparcher   departure
depart, -ed, -ing
department

departmental, -ly

departure

depen   deepen

depend, -ed, -ing

dependable, -bly

dependance   dependence

dependant (noun)

dependence

dependency, -cies

dependent, -ly (adjective)

dependible   dependable

depick   depict

depicksion   depiction

depict, -ed, -ing

depiction

depilatory, -ries

depillatory   depilatory

depleet   deplete

deplesion   depletion

deplete, -pleted, -pleting

depletion

deploi   deploy

deplorable, -bly

deplore, -plored, -ploring

deplorible   deplorable

deploy, -ed, -ing

deployment

depo   depot

deport, -ed, -ing

deportation

deportee

deposatory   depository

depose, -posed, -posing

deposit, -ed, -ing

depositer   depositor

deposition (oath)

deposition   disposition (mood)

deposition   dispossession (deprivation)

depositor

depository, -ries

depot

For **depp-** words, look under **dep-**.

depraved (evil)

depraved   deprived (strip)

depravity, -ties

deprecate, -cated, -cating (disapprove)

deprecation

depreciate, -ated, -ating (reduce)

depreciation

depredasion   depredation

depredation

depresiate   depreciate

depresion   depression

depresive   depressive

depresor   depressor

depress, -ed, -ing

depressant

depressent   depressant

depresser   depressor

depression

depressive, -ly

depressor

depressurize, -ized, -izing

depresurize   depressurize

depricate   deprecate

deprive, -prived, -priving (strip)

deprived   depraved (evil)

depth

deputation

depute, -puted, -puting

deputey   deputy

deputize, -tized, -tizing

deputy, -ties

deragatory   derogatory

Look under **di-** if the word is not under **de-**.

derail, -ed, -ing

derailment

derale   derail

derange, -ranged, -ranging

derby, -bies

deregister, -ed, -ing

derelicksion   dereliction

derelict

dereliction

derick   derrick

deride, -rided, -riding

derigible   dirigible

derision
derisive, -ly
  derison — derision
  derivasion — derivation
derivation
derivative
derive, -rived, -riving
dermatitis
dermatologist
dermatology
derogatory
derrick

> For other **derr-** words, look
> under **der-**.

  dert — dirt
  derth — dearth
  derty — dirty
dervish
  desalate — desolate
  desalinasion — desalination
desalination
  desastrous — disastrous
descant (music)
descend, -ed, -ing
descendant (noun)
descendent (adjective)
descent (down)
  descent — decent (fair)
  descent — dissent (differ)
  desciple — disciple
describe, -scribed, -scribing
  descripsion — description
description
descriptive, -ly
descry, -cried, -crying
  desease — disease
  deseat — deceit
  deseave — deceive
desecrate, -crated, -crating
desecration
  desegragate — desegregate
desegregate, -gated, -gating
desegregation
  desel — diesel
  deselerate — decelerate
  Desember — December

  desency — decency
  desend — descend
desensitize, -tized, -tizing
  desent — decent
  desent — descent
  desentralize — decentralize
desert, deserts (land)
desert, -ed, -ing (leave)
  desert — dessert (food)
deserter
desertion
deserve, -served, -serving
de-sex, -ed, -ing
  desibel — decibel
  desicate — desiccate
  desicasion — desiccation
desiccate, -cated, -cating
desiccation
  deside — decide
  desiduous — deciduous
  desifer — decipher
design, -ed, -ing
designate, -nated, -nating
designation
  desimal — decimal
  desimate — decimate
  desimul — decimal
  desine — design
  desipher — decipher
desirability
desirable, -bly
desire, -sired, -siring
  desirible — desirable
desirous
  desirus — desirous
desist, -ed, -ing
  desizion — decision
desk
  deskant — descant

> Look under **di-** if the word is
> not under **de-**.

desolate, -lated, -lating
desolation
  despach — despatch
despair, -ed, -ing
  despare — despair

despatch, -ed, -ing
  despensable   dispensable
desperado, -does, -dos
desperate, -ly (rash)
  desperate   disparate
                    (unlike)
desperation
despicable, -bly
  despicible   despicable
despise, -spised, -spising
despite
despoil, -ed, -ing
  despolasion   despolation
despoliation
despondency
  despondensy   despondency
despondent, -ly
despot
despotic
despotism
  desprate   desperate
dessert (food)
  dessert   desert (land)
  dessert   desert (leave)
  desserter   deserter
  destatute   destitute
  destinasion   destination
destination
destine, -tined, -tining
destiny, -nies
  destitusion   destitution
destitute
destitution
destroy, -ed, -ing
destroyer
  destrucktion   destruction
destruct, -ed, -ing
  destructable   destructible
destructible
destruction
destructive, -ly
desultory
  det   debt
detach, -ed, -ing
detachable
  detachible   detachable
detail, -ed, -ing

detain, -ed, -ing
detainee
detainment
  detale   detail
  detane   detain
  detecksion   detection
detect, -ed, -ing
detectable
  detecter   dectector
  detectible   detectable
detection
detective
detector
  detektive   detective
  detension   detention
détente
detention
deter, -terred, -terring (prevent)
  deter   debtor (owes)
  deteranse   deterrence
  deterant   deterrant
  deterent   deterrent
detergent
  deterjent   detergent
deteriorate, -rated, -rating
deterioration
determinant
  determinasion   determination
determination
determine, -mined, -mining
determinism
deterrence
deterrent
detest, -ed, -ing
detestable, -bly
  detestasion   detestation
detestation
  detestible   detestable
  deth   death
detonate, -nated, -nating
  detonater   detonator
detonation
detonator
detour, -ed, -ing
  detracksion   detraction
detract, -ed, -ing (take)
  detract   distract (divert)

detracter	detractor
detraction	
detractor	
detramental	detrimental
detriment	
detrimental, -ly	
detterent	deterrent
dettonate	detonate
dettor	debtor
deuce	
deutschmark	
devaluation	
devalue, -valued, -valuing	
devestasion	devastation
devastate, -tated, -tating	
devastation	
devel	devil
develop, -ed, -ing	
develope	develop
developement	development
developer	
development	
developmental, -ly	
deviance	
deviancy	
devianse	deviance
deviansy	deviancy
deviant, -ly	
deviate, -ated, -ating	
deviation	
device (thing)	
device	devise (plan)
devide	divide
devient	deviant
devil	
devilish, -ly	
devilment	
devilry	
devil's advocate	
devine	divine
devious, -ly	
devise, -vised, -vising (plan)	
devise	device (thing)
devius	devious
devoid	
devolusion	devolution
devolution	

devolutionary	
devolve, -volved, -volving	
devote, -voted, -voting	
devotee	
devotion	
devour, -ed, -ing	
devout, -ly	
dew (water)	
dew	do (act)
dew	due (owing)
dewdrop	
dewey	dewy
dewy, dewier, dewiest	
dexterity	
dexterous, -ly	
dexterus	dexterous

> Look under **de-** if the word is not under **di-**.

diabeetes	diabetes
diabetes	
diabetic	
diabolic	
diabolical, -ly	
diadem	
diafanus	diaphanous
diafram	diaphragm
diagnose, -nosed, -nosing	
diagnosis, -ses	
diagnostic	
diagnostician	
diagnostisian	diagnostician
diagonal, -ly	
diagram (sketch)	
diagram	diaphragm (anatomy)
diagrammatic, -al, -ally	
dial, -ed, -ing	
dialect	
dialectic	
dialectician	
dialectision	dialectician
dialisis	dialysis
dialize	dialyze
dialog	
dialogue	
dialysis, -ses	

dialyze, -lyzed, -lyzing
diameter
diametrical, -ly
diamond
diaper (cloth)
   diaper   dipper (ladle)
diaphanous, -ly
   diaphanus   diaphanous
diaphragm (anatomy)
   diaphragm   diagram
                    (sketch)
   diarea   diarrhea
diarist
diarrhea
diary, -ries (book)
   diary   dairy (milk)
diatonic, -ally
diatribe
   dibase   debase
   dibate   debate
dibs
dice, diced, dicing
dicey
dichotomy, -mies
   diciple   disciple
dick
dickens
dickey
   dicotomy   dichotomy
   dicksion   diction
   dicksionary   dictionary
dictate, -tated, -tating
   dictater   dictator
dictation
dictator
dictatorial, -ly
diction
dictionary, -aries
dictum, -ta, -tums
did
didactic, -ally
diddle, -dled, -dling
   didgit   digit
   didgitalis   digitalis
didn't (did not)
   didnt   didn't
die (singular of dice)

die, dies (tool)
die, died, dying (death)
   die   dye (color)
die back
die-cast
   diefy   deify
diehard
   dieing   dying (death)
   dieing   dyeing (color)
   diel   dial
   dielect   dialect
dieresis, diereses
   diernal   diurnal
diesel
diet, -ed, -ing
dietary
dietician
   dietisian   dietician

> For dif- words, look under
> **diff-**.

differ, -ed, -ing (disagree)
   differ   defer
                    (postpone)
difference
   differense   difference
   differensial   differential
   differensiate   differentiate
   differensiasion differentiation
different, -ly
differential, -ly
differentiate, -ated, -ating
differentiation
difficult
difficulty, -ties
   diffidanse   diffidence
diffidence
diffident, -ly
diffuse, -fused, -fusing
   diffusion   diffusion
diffusion
   diflect   deflect
   diftheria   diphtheria
dig, dug, digging
   diger   digger
digest, -ed, -ing
   digestable   digestible

digestible
digestion
digger
digit
digital
digital computer
digitalis
dignify, -fied, -fying
dignitary, -taries
  dignitry — dignitary
dignity, -ties
  digresion — digression
digress, -ed, -ing
digression
dike or dyke
  diktionary — dictionary
  dil — dill
dilapidated
dilapidation
dilate, -lated, -lating
dilation
dilatory
  dilema — dilemma
dilemma
  diletante — dilettante
dilettante, -ti
  dilidali — dillydally
diligence
  diligense — diligence
diligent, -ly
dill
dilly
dillydally
dilution
diluvial
diluvian

> Look under **de-** if the word is
> not under **di-**.

dim, dimmed, dimming
dim, dimmer, dimmest
dime
dimension
dimensional, -ly
  dimer — dimmer
diminish, -ed, -ing
  diminusion — diminution

diminution
diminutive, -ly
  dimise — demise
dimity, -ties (thread)
dimmer
  dimond — diamond
  dimoralize — demoralize
  dimpile — dimple
dimple, -pled, -pling
dimwit
dimwitted, -ly
din, dinned, dinning
  dinamic — dynamic
  dinamite — dynamite
  dinamo — dynamo
  dinasaur — dinosaur
  dinasty — dynasty
dine, dined, dining
diner (eating)
  diner — dinner (food)
ding
ding-dong
dinghy, -ghies (boat)
dingo, -goes, -gos
dingy, -gier, -giest (dull)
dinky, dinkier, dinkiest
dinner (food)
  dinner — diner (eating)
dinosaur
  dinosoar — dinosaur
  dinosore — dinosaur
dint
diocese
diode
  diokside — dioxide
dioxide
dip, dipped, dipping
  diper — diaper
  diper — dipper
diphtheria
diphthong
diploma
diplomacy, -cies
  diplomasy — diplomacy
diplomat
diplomatic, -ally
dipper (ladle)

dipper	diaper (cloth)	disapproval	
dipsomania		disapprove, -proved, -proving (condemn)	
dipsomaniac			
diptych		disapprove	disprove (refute)
dire, direr, direst		disarmament	
direcksion	direction	disarray	
direct, -ed, -ing		disasociate	disassociate
direct current		disassociate, -ated, -ating	
directer	director	disassociation	
directery	directory	disaster	
direction		disasterous	disastrous
directional		disastrous, -ly	
directive		disatisfy	dissatisfy
directly		disavow, -ed, -ing	
director		disavowal	
directory, -ries		disband, -ed, -ing	
dirge		disbandment	
dirigable	dirigible	disbeleif	disbelief
dirigible		disbeleive	disbelieve
dirk		disbelief	
dirt		disbelieve, -lieved, -lieving	
dirtily		disburse, -bursed, -bursing (pay)	
dirty, dirtied, dirtying		disburse	disperse (scatter)
dirty, dirtier, dirtiest		disc	
disable, -bled, -bling		discard, -ed, -ing	
disabuse, -bused, -busing		disc brake	disk brake
disadvantage, -taged, -taging		discern, -ed, -ing	
disadvantageous, -ly		discernable	discernible
disadvantige	disadvantage	discernible, -bly	
disadvantij	disadvantage	discernment	
disaffecktion	disaffection	discharge, -charged, -charging	
disafect	disaffect	discipal	disciple
disaffect, -ed, -ing		disciple	
disaffection		disciplinarian	
disagree, -greed, -greeing		disciplinary	
disagreeable, -bly, -ableness		discipline, -plined, -plining	
disagreeible	disagreeable	disc jockey	
disagreement		disclaim, -ed, -ing	
disallow, -ed, -ing		disclaimer	
disalow	disallow	disclame	disclaim
disapear	disappear	disclaimor	disclaimer
disapoint	disappoint	disclose, -closed, -closing	
disappear, -ed, -ing		discloshure	disclosure
disappearance		disclosure	
disappearanse	disappearance	disclozure	disclosure
disappoint, -ed, -ing			
disappointment			

disco
discolor, -ed, -ing
discoloration
discomfert → discomfort
discombobulate, -lated, -lating
discomfit, -ed, -ing (thwart)
discomfit → discomfort
discomfort, -ed, -ing (pain)
discomforture

> Look under **de-** if the word is
> not under **di-**.

discompose, -posed, -posing
discomposhur → discomposure
discomposure
disconcert, -ed, -ing
disconnecktion → disconnection
disconnection
disconsert → disconcert
disconsolate, -ly
discontent
discontinue, -tinued, -tinuing
discontinuity
discontinuous, -ly
discord
discordance
discordanse → discordance
discordant, -ly
discotheque
discount, -ed, -ing
discourage, -raged, -raging
discouragement
discourse, -coursed, -coursing
discourteous, -ly
discourtesy
discourtious → discourteous
discover, -ed, -ing
discoverer
discoveror → discoverer
discovery, -eries
discovry → discovery
discownt → discount
discredit, -ed, -ing
discreditable, -bly
discreditible → discreditable
discreet (prudent)
discreet → discrete (apart)

discrepancy
discrepansy → discrepancy
discression → discretion
discrete (apart)
discretion
discretionary
discretionery → discretionary
discribe → describe
discriminate, -nated, -nating
discriminater → discriminator
discrimination
discriminator
discriminatory
discriminatry → discriminatory
discripsion → description
discriptive → descriptive
discuridge → discourage
discursive, -ly
discurtious → discourteous
discus (sport)
discusion → discussion
discuss, -ed, -ing (talk)
discussion
disdain, -ed, -ing
disdainful, -ly
disdaneful → disdainful
dise → dice
disease
diseased (sick)
diseased → deceased (dead)
diseave → deceive
diseecktion → dissection
disect → dissect
disembark, -ed, -ing
disembarksion → disembarkation
disembarkation
disemble → disembowel
disembodied
disembowel, -ed, -ing
diseminate → disseminate
disenchant, -ed, -ing
disenchantment
disension → dissension
disentangle, -gled, -gling
disentanglement
disentry → dysentery
disern → discern

disernible	discernible
disertasion	dissertation
diservise	disservice
disesed	diseased
disfaver	disfavor

disfavor, -ed, -ing

disfiger	disfigure

disfigure, -ured, -uring
disfranchise, -chised, -chising
disfranchisement

disgise	disguise

disgorge, -gorged, -gorging
disgrace, -graced, -gracing
disgraceful, -ly

disgracefull	disgraceful

disgruntled
disguise, -guised, -guising
disgust, -ed, -ing
disgustedly
dish, -ed, -ing

disharmoney	disharmony

disharmony

disharten	dishearten

dishcloth
dishearten, -ed, -ing
disheveled

dishevelled	disheveled
dishoner	dishonor

dishonest, -ly
dishonesty
dishonor, -ed, -ing
dishonorable, -bly

dishonorible	dishonorable
disidence	dissidence
disident	dissident
disign	design

disillusion, -ed, -ing
disillusionment

disilusion	disillusion
disimbark	disembark
disimilar	dissimilar
disimulate	dissimulate
disinclinasion	disinclination

disinclination
disincline, -clined, -clining
disinfect, -ed, -ing
disinfectant

disinfectent	disinfectant

disinherit, -ed, -ing
disinheritance

disinheritanse	disinheritance
disintagrate	disintegrate
disintegrasion	disintegration

disintegrate, -grated, -grating
disintegration
disinter, -terred, -terring
disinterment
disinterested, -ly

disintigrate	disintegrate
disipasion	dissipation
disipate	dissipate
disiple	disciple
disiplinary	disciplinary
disipline	discipline

disjoint, -ed, -ing
disk
disk brake

diskwalify	disqualify
diskwiet	disquiet
diskwolify	disqualify
dislexia	dyslexia

dislike, -liked, -liking
dislocate, -cated, -cating
dislocation
dislodge, -lodged, -lodging

disloge	dislodge

disloyal, -ly
disloyalty, -ties
dismal, -ly
dismantle, -tled, -tling
dismay, -ed, -ing
dismember, -ed, -ing
dismemberment

dismisal	dismissal

dismiss, -ed, -ing
dismissal
dismount, -ed, -ing

dismownt	dismount
disobay	disobey
disobediance	disobedience

disobedience

disobediense	disobedience

disobedient, -ly
disobey, -ed, -ing

disoblige, -bliged, -bliging

disoluble	dissoluble
disolusion	dissolution
disolute	dissolute
disolve	dissolve
disonance	dissonance
disonanse	dissonance
disonant	dissonant
disone	disown
disoner	dishonor
disonerable	dishonorable
disonest	dishonest

> Look under **de-** if the word is not under **di-**.

disorder

disorderley	disorderly

disorderliness
disorderly

disorganizasion	disorganization

disorganization
disorganize, -nized, -nizing
disorient
disorientate, -tated, -tating
disown, -ed, -ing

dispach	dispatch
dispair	despair

disparage, -raged, -raging
disparagement
disparagingly
disparate, -ly (unlike)

disparate	desperate (rash)
disparidge	disparage
disparige	disparage

disparity, -ties

dispasionate	dispassionate

dispassion
dispassionate, -ly
dispatch, -ed, -ing
dispel, -pelled, -pelling

dispencable	dispensable
dispencary	dispensary
dispence	dispense

dispensable

dispensible	dispensable

dispensary, -saries

dispensasion	dispensation

dispensation
dispensatory, -ries
dispense, dispensed, dispensing
dispenser

dispensible	dispensable
dispepsia	dyspepsia

dispersal
disperse, -persed, -persing (scatter)

disperse	disburse (pay)

dispersion

dispicable	despicable

dispirit, -ed, -ing

dispise	despise
dispite	despite

displace, -placed, -placing
displaceable
displacement

displacible	displaceable
displacment	displacement
displase	displace

display, -ed, -ing
displease, -pleased, -pleasing
displeasure

displese	displease
displeshur	displeasure
displesure	displeasure

disport, -ed, -ing
disposable
dispose, -posed, -posing

disposesion	dispossession
disposess	dispossess
disposible	disposable
disposision	disposition
disposision	deposition (oath)

disposition (mood)

disposition	dispossession (deprivation)

dispossess, -ed, -ing (deprive)
dispossession (deprivation)
disprin

disproporsion	disproportion

disproportion
disproportionate, -ly
disprove, -proved, -proving (refute)

disprove — disapprove (condemn)
dispursal — dispersal
dispurse — disperse
dispursion — dispersion
disputable, -bly
disputation
disputatious
dispute, -puted, -puting
disputible — disputable
disqualificasion — disqualification
disqualification
disqualify, -fied, -fying
disquiet, -ed, -ing
disquietude
disquite — disquiet
disregard, -ed, -ing
disreguard — disregard
disrepair
disrepare — disrepair
disreputable, -bly
disreputible — disreputable
disrespect
disrespectful, -ly
disrigard — disregard
disrispect — disrespect
disrobe, -robed, -robing
disrupsion — disruption
disrupt, -ed, -ing
disruption
disruptive, -ly
dissapate — dissipate
dissapear — disappear
dissapoint — disappoint
dissaprove — disapprove
disatisfacksion — dissatisfaction
dissatisfaction
dissatisfy, -fied, -fying
disscord — discord
dissect, -ed, -ing
dissemble, -bled, -bling
disseminasion — dissemination
disseminate, -nated, -nating
dissemination
dissension
dissent, -ed, -ing (differ)
dissent — decent (fair)

dissent — descant (music)
dissent — descent (down)
dissenter
dissertasion — dissertation
dissertation
disservice
disserviceable
disservicible — disserviceable
dissidence
dissidense — dissidence
dissident, -ly
dissimilar, -ly
dissimilarity
dissimulasion — dissimulation
dissimulate, -lated, -lating
dissimulation
dissipate, -pated, -pating
dissipation
dissociate, -ated, -ating
dissociation
disoloot — dissolute
dissolable — dissoluble
dissoluble
dissolusion — dissolution
dissolute, -ly
dissolution
dissolvable
dissolve, -solved, -solving
dissolvible — dissolvable
dissonance
dissonanse — dissonance
dissonant, -ly
disstil — distil
dissuade, -suaded, -suading
distaff
distance, distanced, distancing
distanse — distance
distant, -ly
distaste
distasteful, -ly
distastefull — distasteful
distemper, -ed, -ing
distend, -ed, -ing
distension — distention
distent — distant
distention
disterb — disturb

disterbance — disturbance
distil, -tilled, -tilling
distillasion — distillation
distillation
distillery, -eries
distillry — distillery
distincksion — distinction
distinct, -ly
distinction
distinctive, -ly
distinguish, -ed, -ing
distinguishable, -bly
distingwish — distinguish
distink — distinct
distort, -ed, -ing
distortion
distracksion — distraction
distract, -ed, -ing (divert)
distract — detract (take)
distraction
distraught, -ly
distrawt — distraught
distress, -ed, -ing
distressful, -ly
distressfull — distressful
distressingly
distributer — distributor
distribution
distributive, -ly
distributor
districk — district
district
distrust, -ed, -ing
disturb, -ed, -ing
disturbance
disturbanse — disturbance
disunion
disunite, -nited, -niting
disunity, -ties
disurn — discern
disurnible — discernible
disuse, -used, -using
diswade — dissuade
diswasion — dissuasion
diswasive — dissuasive
ditch, -ed, -ing
ditch, ditches

dither
dito — ditto
ditto
ditty, -ties
dity — ditty
divan
dive, dived or dove, diving
divebomb
diver
diverge, -verged, -verging
divergence
divergense — divergence
divergent, -ly
diverse, -ly
diversificasion — diversification
diversification
diversify, -fied, -fying

> Look under **de-** if the word is
> not under **di-**.

diversion
diversionary
diversity, -ties
divert, -ed, -ing
divest, -ed, -ing
divestable — divestible
divestible
divide, -vided, -viding
dividend
divider
divinasion — divination
divination
divinatory
divine, -vined, -vining
divinely
diviner
divinitey — divinity
divinity, -ties
divisable — divisible
diviser — divisor
divisible, -bly
division
divisional, -ly
divisive, -ly
divisor
divizion — division
divizive — divisive

divorce, -vorced, -vorcing
divorcée
  divorse — divorce
  divorsee — divorcée
divulge, -vulged, -vulging
divulgence
  divulgense — divulgence
divvy, -vied, -vying
Dixie
  dizier — dizzier
  diziest — dizziest
  dizmal — dismal
  dizolve — dissolve
  dizy — dizzy
dizzily
dizziness
dizzy, dizzier, dizziest
do, did, done, doing (act)
  do — dew (water)
  do — doe (animal)
  do — due (owing)
dobbin
  dochshund — dachshund
docile, -ly
docility
dock, -ed, -ing
docket
  dockit — docket
dockyard
  docter — doctor
doctor, -ed, -ing
doctoral
doctorate
  doctrate — doctorate
  doctrin — doctrine
  doctrinair — doctrinaire
doctrinaire
doctrinal, -ly
doctrine
  doctrinil — doctrinal
document, -ed, -ing
documentary, -ries
documentation
  documentery — documentary
dodder, -ed, -ing
doddery
doddle

  doder — dodder
dodge, dodged, dodging
dodger
  dodje — dodge
dodo, -does, -dos
doe (animal)
  doe — dough (bread)
doer
does (do)
  does — doze (sleep)
doesn't (does not)
  doesnt — doesn't
  dof — doff
doff, -ed, -ing
  doffin — dauphin
dog, dogged, dogging
  dogerel — doggerel
dogfight
dogfish
  dogfite — dogfight
doggerel
doghouse
dogie (calf)
dogleg
doglegged
dogma, -mas, -mata
dogmatic
dogmatical, -ly
dogmatism
dogmatist
dog paddle
  doilie — doily
doily, -lies
  dol — dole (pay)
  dol — doll (toy)
doldrums
dole, doled, doling (pay)
  dole — doll (toy)
  dolerus — dolorous
  dolfin — dolphin
doll, -ed, -ing (dress up)
  doll — dole (pay)
dollar (money)
  doller — dollar
dollop
dolly, dollies
dolomite

dolor (sorrow)
dolorous, -ly
  dolorus → dolorous
dolphin
dolt
doltish, -ly
domain
  domane → domain
dome
domed
domestic, -ally
domesticate, -cated, -cating
  domesticasion → domestication
domestication
domesticity
  domestisity → domesticity
domicile, -ciled, -ciling
domiciliary
dominance
  dominanse → dominance
dominant, -ly
  dominasion → domination
dominate, -nated, -nating
  dominater → dominator
domination
dominative
dominator
  dominear → domineer
domineer, -ed, -ing
  dominent → dominant
dominion
domino, -noes
domino effect
  dominyon → dominion
  domisile → domicile
  dommimate → dominate
don, donned, donning
donate, -nated, -nating
  donater → donator
donation
donator
done (finished)
  done → dun (color)
  done → dun (demand)
  doner → donor
dong, -ed, -ing
donkey, -keys

  donky → donkey
donnybrook
donor
don't (do not)
  dont → don't
donut
  dooch → douche
doodad
doodle, -dled, -dling
doom, -ed, -ing
doomsday
door (barrier)
  door → dour (stern)
doorbell
doorjamb
  doosh → douche
dope, doped, doping
dopey, dopier, dopiest
  dophin → dauphin
  dore → door
dormancy
  dormansy → dormancy
dormant
  dormatory → dormitory
dorsal
dory, -ries
dosage
dose, dosed, dosing
  dosege → dosage
  dosier → dossier
  dosige → dosage
  dosije → dosage
  dosile → docile
  dosility → docility
  dosn't → doesn't
dossier
dot, dotted, dotting
dotage
dote, doted, doting
  dotige → dotage
  dotije → dotage
dotterel
dottle
dotty, dottier, dottiest
  doubel → double
  doubile → double
double, -led, -ling

double agent
double-barreled
double bass
double-breasted
double-cross, -ed, -ing
double-date
double-dealing
double exposure
double header
double-jointed
double standard
doublet
double time
doubloon
doubt, -ed, -ing
doubtful, -ly
  doubtfull   doubtful
doubtingly
doubtless, -ly
douche, douched, douching
  douel   dowel
dough
doughboy
doughnut
doughty, -tier, -tiest
doughy, -hier, -hiest (soft)
  doughy   dowry (gift)
dour, -ly, -ness
douse, doused, dousing
  dout   doubt
  doutful   doubtful
  doutless   doubtless
  douty   doughty
dove
dovetail
  dovetale   dovetail
  dow   dhow (boat)
  dow   doe (animal)
  dow   dough (bread)
dowager
  dowdie   dowdy
dowdily
dowdiness
dowdy, -dier, -diest
  dowery   dowry
  dowey   doughy
down, -ed, -ing

down and out
downcast
  downey   downy
downfall
downfallen
downgrade, -graded, -grading
downhearted, -ly
downhill
down payment
  downpore   downpour
downpour
downright, -ly
  downrite   downright
downstairs
downstream
down-to-earth
downtown
downtrodden
down under
downward, -ly
  downwerd   downward
downwind
downy, downier, downiest
  dowrie   dowry
dowry, -ries (gift)
  dowry   doughy (soft)
dowse, dowsed, dowsing
  dowt   doubt
  dowtey   doughty
  dowtful   doubtful
  dowtless   doubtless
doxology, -gies
doyen
doze, dozed, dozing (sleep)
  doze   does (do)
dozen, dozens
drab, drabber, drabbest
  draconean   Draconian
Draconian
draft, -ed, -ing (plan)
  draft   draught (beer)
draft board
draftsman, -men
drafty, -tier, -tiest
drag, dragged, dragging
  dragatory   derogatory
dragnet

dragon
dragonfly, -flies
dragoon, -ed, -ing
drag race
drain, -ed, -ing
drainage
drainige → drainage
drainpipe
drake
dram
drama
dramatic, -ally
dramatics
dramatist
dramatizasion → dramatization
dramatization
dramatize, -tized, -tizing
drape, draped, draping
draper
drapery, -eries
drastic, -ally
draught (beer)
draught → draft (plan)
draw, drew, drawn, drawing
drawback
drawbridge
drawer
drawing board
drawl, -ed, -ing
drawn
dray
dread, -ed, -ing
dreadful, -ly
dreadnought
dream, dreamed, dreamt, dreaming
dreamer
dreamily
dreamless, -ly
dreamworld
drearily
dreariness
dreary, drearier, dreariest
dred → dread
dredful → dreadful
dredge, dredged, dredging
dredger

drednort → dreadnought
dreem → dream
drege → dredge
dregs
dremt → dreamt
drench, -ed, -ing
drery → dreary
dres → dress
dresie → dressy
dresige → dressage
dresmaker → dressmaker
dress, -ed, -ing
dressage
dress circle
dress down
dresser
dressing-down
dressmaker
dressmaking
dressy
drew
dri → dry
dribble, -bled, -bling
dribbler
dribs and drabs
dried
drier
driest
drift, -ed, -ing
drifter
driftwood
drill, -ed, -ing
drily
drink, drank, drunk, drinking
drinkable
drinkible → drinkable
drive-in
drivel, -ed, -ing
driver
driveway
drizzle, -zled, -zling
drizzly
droll
drollery, -eries
drolly
dromedary, -daries
drone, droned, droning

drool, -ed, -ing
droop, -ed, -ing
droopy, -pier, -piest
drop, dropped, dropping
dropkick
droplet
dropout
dropper
dropsy
dross
drought
  drousy   drowsy
  drout   drought
drove
drover
drown, -ed, -ing
drowse, drowsed, drowsing
drowsily
drowsy, drowsier, drowsiest
  drowt   drought
drub, drubbed, drubbing
drudge, drudged, drudging
drudgery, -eries
drug, drugged, drugging
  druge   drudge
  drugery   drudgery
drugstore
drum, drummed, drumming
drummer
drumstick
drunk
drunkard
drunken, -ly
drunkenness
dry, dried, drying
dry, drier, driest
dry cell
dry-clean
dryer
dryly
dryness
dual, -ly (two)
  dual   duel (fight)
dualism
duality
dub, dubbed, dubbing
  dubbel   double

  dubeous   dubious
dubious, -ly
  dubius   dubious
  duble   double
  dubly   doubly
ducal, -ly
  duce   deuce
duchess, -es, (noblewoman)
duchy, duchies (land)
duck, -ed, -ing
duckbill
duckling
  ducktile   ductile
duct
ductile
dud
dude
dudgeon
due (owing)
  due   dew (water)
  due   do (act)
  duece   deuce
  duedrop   dewdrop
duel, -ed, -ing (fight)
  duel   dual (two)
duelist
duet
duettist
duffer
duffle
dugout
duke
  dul   dull
dulcet
  dulie   duly
dull
dullard
dullish, -ly
dullness
dullsville
dully
  dulset   dulcet
duly
  dum   dumb
dumb, -ly
dumbbell
  dumbell   dumbbell

dumbfound, -ed, -ing
dumbness
   dumfound   dumbfound
dummy, -mies
dummy, -mied, -mying
   dumness   dumbness
dump, -ed, -ing
dumper
dumpling
   dumy   dummy
dun (color)
dun, dunned, dunning (demand)
   dun   done (finished)
dunce
dunderhead
dune
dung
dungaree
   dungen   dungeon
dungeon
dunk, -ed, -ing
   dunkey   donkey
   dunse   dunce
duodenal
duodenum
dupe, duped, duping
   duplacate   duplicate
   duplecks   duplex
duplex
duplicate, -cated, -cating
duplication
duplicity, -ties
   duplisity   duplicity
durable, -bly
durability
   durasion   duration
duration
duress
   durge   dirge
   durible   durable
during
   durt   dirt
   durtie   dirty
   durty   dirty
dusk
duskiness
dusky, duskier, duskiest

dust, -ed, -ing
duster
dustman, -men
dustpan
dusty, dustier, dustiest
   dutable   dutiable
Dutch courage
duteous, -ly
dutiable
dutiful, -ly
duty, -ties
   duv   dove
duvet
   duvtail   dovetail
   duvtale   dovetail
dux
   duzen   dozen
dwarf, dwarfs, dwarves
dwarf, -ed, -ing
dwarfish, -ly
dwell, dwelt or dwelled, dwelling
dwindle, -dled, -dling
   dworf   dwarf
dye, dyed, dyeing (color)
   dye   die (dead)
   dyed   died (dead)
   dyehard   diehard
   dyeing   dying (death)
dyer
dynamic, -ally
dynamics
dynamism
dynamite, -mited, -miting
dynamo, -mos
dynasty, -ties
dysentery
   dysentry   dysentery
dysfunction
dyslectic
dyslexia
dyslexic
dyspepsia
dyspeptic
dystrophy

Ee

each
eager
eagle
eaglehawk
eaglet
  eal   eel
ear
earache
eardrum
  earfone   earphone
  earie   eerie (weird)
  earie   eyrie (nest)
  earing   earring
earl
early, -lier, -liest
earmark, -ed, -ing
earmuff
earn, -ed, -ing (gain)
  earn   urn (jug)
earner
earnest, -ly, -ness
earnings
earphone
earring
earshot
earth
earthbound
earthen
earthenware
earthiness
earthling
earthly, -lier, -liest
earthquake
earthworm
earthy, earthier, earthiest
earwig
ease, eased, easing
easel

easement
easily
east
  easten   eastern
Easter
easterly
eastern
eastward, -ly
easiness
easy, easier, easiest
eat, ate, eaten, eating
eatable
eater
  eatible   eatable
eau de Cologne
  eavening   evening
eaves
eavesdrop, -dropped, -dropping
eavesdropper
ebb, -ed, -ing
  ebbony   ebony
ebony, -onies
  ebuliense   ebullience
  ebulient   ebullient
ebullience
ebullient, -ly
eccentric, -ally
eccentricity, -ties
ecclesiastic
ecclesiastical, -ly
  ecco   echo
  ecentric   eccentric
  ech   each
echelon
echidna
echo, echoes
echo, echoed, echoing
eclair
  eclare   eclair
eclectic, -ally
  eclesiastic   ecclesiastic
eclipse, eclipsed, eclipsing
ecliptical, -ly
  ecologey   ecology
ecological, -ly
ecologist
ecology

econamy — economy
economic
economical, -ly
economics
economist
economize, -mized, -mizing
economy, -mies
ecosphere
ecosystem
ecotoxicity
ecsema — eczema
ecsentric — eccentric
ecstasy, -sies
ecstatic, -ally
ecumenical, -ly
ecumenism
eczema
edable — edible
Edam
edem — Edam
eddy, eddies
eddy, eddied, eddying
edelweiss
edge, edged, edging
edgey — edgy
edginess
edgy, -gier, -giest
edible
edibility
edict
edie — eddy
edify, -fied, -fying
edit, -ed, -ing
editer — editor
edition (book)
edition — addition (add)
editor
editorial, -ly
educable
educate, -cated, -cating
education
educational, -ly
educationalist
educative
educator
educible — educable
Edwardian

edy — eddy
eeger — eager
eegle — eagle
eel
eenin — oenin
eer — ear
eerie, eerier, eeriest (weird)
eerie — eyrie (nest)
eerily
eeriness
eermark — earmark

For ef- words,
look under eff-.

efface, -faced, -facing
effecacious — efficacious
effect, -ed, -ing (result)
effect — affect (pretend)
effective, -ly, -ness
effectual, -ly
effeminacy
effeminasy — effeminacy
effeminate, -ly
effervesce, -vesced, -vescing
effervescence
effervescent, -ly
effervesent — effervescent
effervess — effervesce
effervessence — effervescence
efficacious, -ly
efficacy, -cies
efficasious — efficacious
efficiency, -cies
efficiensy — efficiency
efficient, -ly
effigy, -gies
effloresce, -resced, -rescing
efflorescence
efflorescent
effluent
effluvium, -via, -viums
effort
effortless, -ly
effrontery, -teries
effrontrey — effrontery
effusion
effusive, -ly

efigy	effigy
eg	egg
egalitarian	
egalitarianism	
egg, -ed, -ing	
egg cup	
egghead	
eggplant	
eggshell	
eggwhite	
eggwite	eggwhite
Egipt	Egypt
Egiptian	Egyptian
egis	aegis
ego, egos	
egocentric	
egocentricity	
egoism	
egoist	
egoistical, -ly	
egosentric	egocentric
egotism	
egotist	
egotistical, -ly	
egress	
egret	

For egs- or egz- words,
look under ex-.

Egypt	
Egyptian	
eiderdown	
eight (number)	
eight	ate (food)
eighteen	
eighth	
eightieth	
eighty, eighties	
eightyeth	eightieth
eisteddfod	
either (each)	
either	ether (drug)
ejaculate, -lated, -lating	
ejaculation	
ejecktion	ejection
eject, -ed, -ing	
ejection	

ejector	
eke, eked, eking	
eklipse	eclipse
eko	echo

For eks- words,
look under ex-.

ekumenical	ecumenical

For ekw- words,
look under eq-.

elaborate, -rated, -rating	
elaborately	
elaboration	
élan	
eland	
elapse, elapsed, elapsing	
elastic, -ally	
elasticity	
elastisity	elasticity
elate, elated, elating	
elbow, -ed, -ing	
elbowroom	
elder, -ly	
elderberry, -ries	
eldest	
elecktion	election
elecktric	electric
elect, -ed, -ing	
electer	elector
election	
electioneer, -ed, -ing	
elective	
elector	
electoral, -ly	
electorate	
electric	
electrical, -ly	
electrician	
electricity	
electrificasion	electrification
electrification	
electrify, -fied, -fying	
electrision	electrician
electrisity	electricity
electrocardiogram	
electrocardiograph	

electrocute, -cuted, -cuting
electrode
electrolysis
electromagnet
electromagnetic
electromotive
electron
electronic
electronics
electroplate, -plated, -plating
electrostatic
elegance
  eleganse — elegance
elegant, -ly
elegy, -gies (poem)
  elegy — eulogy (praise)
element
elemental, -ly
elementary
  elementery — elementary
  elementul — elemental
elephant
elephantine
  elevan — eleven
elevate, -vated, -vating
  elevater — elevator
elevation
elevator
eleven
eleventh
elf, elves
elfin
elfish
  elfs — elves
elicit, -ed, -ing (draw)
  elicit — illicit (unlawful)
  elifant — elephant
  eligable — eligible
  eliganse — elegance
  eligant — elegant
eligible, -bly
eligibility
  elikser — elixir
  eliment — element
  elimentry — elementary
eliminate, -nated, -nating
  eliminater — eliminator

eliminator
  elipse — ellipse
  elipsis — ellipsis
elision
elite
elitism
elitist
  elivate — elevate
elixir
Elizabethan
elk
ellipse
ellipsis, -ses
elliptical, -ly
  ellite — elite

> For ell- words,
> look under **el-**.

elm
  elocusion — elocution
elocution
elocutionist
  elokwence — eloquence
elongate, -gated, -gating
elongation
elope, eloped, eloping
elopement
  eloquant — eloquent
eloquence
  eloquense — eloquence
eloquent, -ly
else
  elsewere — elsewhere
elsewhere
  elswhere — elsewhere
elucidate, -dated, -dating
elucidation
elucidatory
elude, eluded, eluding (avoid)
  elude — allude (say)
  elusidate — elucidate
elusion (evade)
  elusion — allusion (reference)
  elusion — illusion (trick)
elusive, -ly (avoid)
  elusive — allusive (refer)

elusive	illusive (tricky)	embraceible	embracable
elves		embrase	embrace
emaciate, -ated, -ating		embrio	embryo
emaciation		embroider, -ed, -ing	
emanate, -nated, -nating		embroidery, -deries	
emanation		embroil, -ed, -ing	
emancipate, -pated, -pating		embryo, -os	
emancipater	emancipator	embryonic	
emancipation		emend, -ed, -ing (correct)	
emancipationist		emend	amend (change)
emancipator		emerald	
emanent	eminent	emerey	emery
emansipate	emancipate	emerge, emerged, emerging	
emasculate, -lated, -lating		emergence	
emasculation		emergency	
emasiate	emaciate	emergense	emergence
embalm, -ed, -ing		emergensy	emergency
embankment		emergent	
embarass	embarrass	emerie	emery
embargo, -goes		emeritus	
embargo, -goed, -going		emery	
embark, -ed, -ing		emetic	
embarkasion	embarkation	emfasema	emphysema
embarkation		emfasize	emphasize
embarrass, -ed, -ing		emfatic	emphatic
embarrassment		emigrant (person leaving)	
embassy, -sies		emigrant	immigrant (person entering)
embed, -bedded, -bedding			
embellish, -ed, -ing		emigrate, -grated, -grating (leave)	
embellishment		emigrate	immigrate (enter)
ember			
embezle	embezzle	eminence (high)	
embezzle, -zled, -zling		eminense	eminence
embezzlement		eminent, -ly (known)	
embitter, -ed, -ing		eminent	imminent (near)
emblazon, -ed, -ing		emisary	emissary
emblem		emision	emission
emblematic, -ally		emissary, -saries	
embodie	embody	emission	
embodiment		emit, emitted, emitting	
embody, -bodied, -bodying		emitter	
embolism		emollient	
embomb	embalm	emolument	
embos	emboss	emosion	emotion
emboss, -ed, -ing		emotion	
embrace, -braced, -bracing			
embraceable			

emotional, -ly
emotionless, -ly
emotive, -ly
empanel, -ed, -ing
empathy
  emperer   emperor
emperor
emphasis, -ses
emphasize, -sized, -sizing
emphatic, -ally
emphysema
empire (nations)
  empire   umpire
            (referee)
empirical, -ly (experiment)
  empirical   imperial (rule)
empiricism
empiricist
  empirisism   empiricism
employ, -ed, -ing
employable
employee
employer
  employible   employable
employment
emporium, -poriums, -poria
empower, -ed, -ing
empress
  emptie   empty
emptiness
empty, -tied, -tying
empty, -tier, -tiest
  emrald   emerald
emu
emulate, -lated, -lating
emulation
emulsion
  emulson   emulsion
  enabile   enable
enable, -bled, -bling
enact, -ed, -ing
enactment
enamel, -ed, -ing
  enamer   enamor
enamor, -ed, -ing
encapsulate, -lated, -lating
encephalitis

encephalogram
enchant, -ed, -ing
enchantment
enchilada
  enciclical   encyclical
  enciclopedia   encyclopedia
encircle, -cled, -cling
encirclement
enclave
enclose, -closed, -closing
  encloshur   enclosure
enclosure
encode, -coded, -coding
encompass, -ed, -ing
encore, -cored, -coring
encounter
  encownter   encounter
encourage, -raged, -raging
encouragement
encroach, -ed, -ing
encumber, -ed, -ing
encumbrance
  encumbranse   encumbrance
encyclical
encyclopedia
encyclopedic
end, -ed, -ing
endanger, -ed, -ing
endear, -ed, -ing
endearment
endeavor, -ed, -ing
  endeer   endear
endemic, -ally
  endever   endeavor
endive
endless, -ly
endorse, -dorsed, -dorsing
endorsement
endow, -ed, -ing
endowment
endurable, -bly
endurance
  enduranse   endurance
endure, -dured, -during
  endurible   endurable
endways, endwise
enema

enemy, -mies
energetic, -ally
energy, -gies
enervate, -vated, -vating
enervative
enfeeble, -bled, -bling
   enfeebile   enfeeble
enfold, -ed, -ing
enforce, -forced, -forcing
enforceable
enforcement
enforcer
   enforse   enforce
   enforseable   enforceable
enfranchise, -chised, -chising
engage, -gaged, -gaging
engagement
engender, -ed, -ing
   engenue   ingenue
engine
   enginear   engineer
engineer, -ed, -ing
English
engrave, -graved, -graving
engraver
engross, -ed, -ing
engulf, -ed, -ing
enhance, -hanced, -hancing
enhancement
   enhanse   enhance
enigma
enigmatic, -ally
   enima   enema
   enimy   enemy
   enithing   anything
   eniwhere   anywhere
   enjender   engender
   enjin   engine
   enjineer   engineer
   enjoi   enjoy
   enjoible   enjoyable
   enjoiment   enjoyment
enjoin, -ed, -ing
enjoy, -ed, -ing
enjoyable, -bly
   enjoyible   enjoyable
enjoyment

enlarge, -larged, -larging
enlargement
enlarger
enlighten, -ed, -ing
enlightenment
enlist, -ed, -ing
enlistment
   enliten   enlighten
enliven, -ed, -ing
en masse
enmity, -ties (hostility)
   enmity   amity
                  (friendship)
ennoble, -bled, -bling
enoblement
ennui
   enoble   ennoble
enormity, -ties
enormous, -ly
   enormus   enormous
enough
enquire, -quired, -quiring
enquirer
   enquiror   enquirer
enquiry, -ries
enrage, -raged, -raging
   enrap   enwrap
enrich, -ed, -ing
enrichment
enroll, -ed, -ing
enrollment
en route
ensconce, -sconced, -sconcing
   ensconse   ensconce
ensemble
   ensephalitis   encephalitis
   ensew   ensue
ensign
   ensine   ensign
   ensircle   encircle
ensue, -sued, -suing
en suite
ensure, -sured, -suring
   ensweet   en suite
entail, -ed, -ing
   entale   entail
entangle, -gled, -gling

entanglement		enunciation	
entente		enunsiate	enunciate
enter, -ed, -ing		enuresis	
enteritis		enurgy	energy
enterprise		envelop, -ed, -ing (wrap up)	
enterprising, -ly		envelope (stationary)	
entertain, -ed, -ing		enviabel	enviable
entertainer		enviable, -bly	
entertainment		envie	envy
entertane	entertain	envious, -ly	
entertainor	entertainer	envirament	environment
enthrall, -ed, -ing		environment	
enthuse, -thused, -thusing		environmental, -ly	
enthusiasm		environmentalism	
enthusiast		environmentalist	
enthusiastic, -ally		environs	
entice, -ticed, -ticing		envisage, -aged, -aging	
entire, -ly		envisidge	envisage
entirety		envius	envious
entise	entice	envoy	
entitel	entitle	envy, -vies	
entitey	entity	envy, envied, envying	
entitle, -tled, -tling		enwrap, enwrapped, enwrapping	
entitlement		enzime	enzyme
entity, -ties		enzyme	
entorage	entourage	epalepsy	epilepsy
entourage		epaulet	
entrails		epawlet	epaulet
entrance		ephemeral, -ly	
entranse	entrance	epic (poem)	
entrant		epic	epoch (age)
entre	entree, entrée	epical, -ly	
entreat, -ed, -ing		epicenter	
entreaty, -treaties		epicure	
entree, entrée		epicurean	
entreet	entreat	epidemic	
entreprener	entrepreneur	epidemical, -ly	
entrepreneur		epidermal	
entrepreneurial		epidermis	
entrust, -ed, -ing		epigraf	epigraph
entry, -tries		epigram	
enuff	enough	epigrammatic, -ally	
enumerable		epigraph (quotation)	
enumerate, -rated, -rating		epilepsy	
enumeration		epileptic	
enumerible	enumerable	epilogue, epilog	
enunciate, -ated, -ating		episcopacy, -cies	

episcopal
Episcopalian
episode
episodic, -ally
  epissel   epistle
  epitaf   epitaph
epitaph (inscription)
epithet (word)
epitome
epitomize, -mized, -mizing
epoch (age)
  epoch   epic (poem)
epochal
  epok   epoch
  eppigram   epigram
equable, -bly
equal, equaled, equaling
equality, -ties
equalize, -lized, -lizing
equanimity, -ties
equate, equated, equating
  equater   equator
equation
equator
equatorial
equestrian
  equety   equity
equidistant, -ly
equilateral
equilibrium
equine
  equinocks   equinox
equinoctial
equinox
equip, equipped, equipping
equipment
equitable, -bly
  equitible   equitable
equity, -ties
equivalence
  equivalense   equivalence
equivocal, -ly
equivocate, -cated, -cating
equivocation
era (age)
  era   error
           (mistake)

eradicable, -bly
eradicate, -cated, -cating
eradication
  erand   errand
  erant   errant
erase, erased, erasing
eraser
erasion
  erata   errata
  eratic   erratic
  erban   urban
  erbane   urbane
  erbanity   urbanity
  erbanize   urbanize
  erchin   urchin
  erecktion   erection
erect, -ed, -ing
erection
  erer   error
  erge   urge
  ergent   urgent
ergonomics
  erie   eerie (weird)
  erie   eyrie (nest)
  erk   irk
  erksome   irksome
  erl   earl
  erly   early
ermine
  ern   earn
           (money)
  ern   urn (vessel)
  ernest   earnest
erode, eroded, eroding
erogenous
  eroneous   erroneous
  eror   error
Eros
erosion
erosive
erotic, -ally (love)
erotica
eroticism
eroticize, -cized, -cizing
  erotisism   eroticism
err, -ed, -ing
errand (trip)

errant (deviate)
errant — arrant (notorious)
erratic, -ally (irregular)
erratum, -ta
erroneous, -ly
erronious — erroneous
error (mistake)
error — era (age)
errupt — erupt
ersatz
erstwhile
erth — earth
erthen — earthen
erthly — earthly
erudition
erupt, -ed, -ing
eruption (outburst)
eruption — irruption (break in)
erwig — earwig
esay — essay
escalate, -lated, -lating
escalater — escalator
escalation
escalator
escapade
escape, -caped, -caping
escapee
escaper
escapement
escapism
escapist
escapor — escaper
escarpment
eschew, -ed, -ing
eschue — eschew
escort, -ed, -ing
escutcheon
esel — easel
esence — essence
esential — essential
eshelon — echelon
Eskimo, -mos
eskwire — Esquire
esophagus, gi
esoteric, -ally (secret)

esoteric — exoteric (commonplace)
especial, -ly
espesial — especial
espionage
esplanade
esplanaid — esplanade
espousal
espouse, -poused, -pousing
espowse — espouse
espresso
esprit
espy, -pied, -pying
Esquire
essay, -ed, -ing (try)
essay — assay (analyze)
essayist
essence
essense — essence
essential, -ly
establish, -ed, -ing
establishment
estate
esteem, -ed, -ing
estemation — estimation
Ester — Easter
estern — eastern
estimabel — estimable
estimable, -bly
estimate, -mated, -mating
estimater — estimator
estimation
estimator
estrange, estranged, estranging
estrangement
estrogen
estuary, -aries
et cetera
etch, -ed, -ing (engrave)
etch — itch (scratch)
etcher
eternal, -ly
eternity, -ties
ether (drug)
ether — either (each)
ethereal, -ly
ethic

ethical, -ly
ethics
ethnic, -ally
ethnology
ethos
  etimology   etymology
etiologist
etiology
etiquette
etymology, -gies
eucalyptus, -tuses, -ti
euchre, -chred, -chring
Euclidean

> For euf- words, look under
> **euph-**.

eugenics
  Euklidean   Euclidean
eulogize, -gized, -gizing
eulogy, -gies (praise)
  eulogy   elegy (poem)
eunuch
euphemism
euphemistic, -ally
euphony, -nies
euphoria
euphoric
  Eurapean   European
Eurasian
eureka
eurhythmics
  eurithmics   eurhythmics
European
euthanasia
evacuate, -uated, -uating
evacuation
evacuee
evade, evaded, evading
evaluate, -ated, -ating
evaluation
evanesce, -nesced, -nescing
  evangalist   evangelist
evangelical, -ly
evangelism
evangelist
  evaperate   evaporate
evaporate, -rated, -rating

evaporation
evasion
evasive, -ly
eve
  evedence   evidence
even, -ed, -ing
evening
evenly
evenness
event
eventual, -ly
eventuality, -ties
eventuate, -ated, -ating
ever
evergreen
everlasting, -ly
every
everybody
everyday
everyone
everything
everywhere
  eves   eaves
  evicktion   eviction
evict, -ed, -ing
  evicter   evictor
eviction
evictor
evidence, -denced, -dencing
evident, -ly
evil, -ly
evince, evinced, evincing
  evinse   evince
eviscerate, -rated, -rating
evocative
evoke, evoked, evoking
evolution
evolve, evolved, evolving
evolvement
  evry   every
ewe (sheep)
  ewe   yew (tree)
  ewe   you (pronoun)
exacerbate, -bated, -bating
exacerbation
  exackly   exactly
exact, -ed, -ing

exactitude
exactly
exactness
exagerate   exaggerate
exaggerate, -rated, -rating
exaggeration
exalt, -ed, -ing (honor)
exalt   exult (rejoice)
exaltation
examination
examine, -ined, -ining
examiner
exampel   example
example
exaserbate   exacerbate
exasperate, -rated, -rating
exasperation
exatic   exotic
excavate, -vated, -vating
excavater   excavator
excavation
excavator
exceed, -ed, -ing (surpass)
exceed   accede (agree)
exceedingly
excel, -celled, -celling
excell   excel
excellence
excellency, -cies
excellense   excellence
excellent, -ly
except, -ed, -ing (omit)
except   accept (receive)
exception
exceptional, -ly
excerpt
excess (extra)
excess   access (approach)
excessive, -ly
exchange, -changed, -changing
exchangeable
exchequer
excise, -cised, -cising (tax, cut)
excise   exercise (exertion)
excise   exorcize (expel)

excision
excitable, -bly
excite, -cited, -citing
excitement
excitible   excitable
excize   excise
exclaim, -ed, -ing
exclamation
exclamatory
exclamatry   exclamatory
exclame   exclaim
exclude, -luded, -luding
exclusion
exclusive, -ly
excluson   exclusion
excommunicate, -cated, -cating
excommunication
excrement
excrescence
excresion   excretion
excressense   excrescence
excreta
excrete, -creted, -creting
excretion
excretory
excruciating, -ly
excursion
excusable, -bly
excuse, -cused, -cusing
execrable, -bly
execrate, -crated, -crating
execute, -cuted, -cuting
executer   executor
execution
executioner
executionor   executioner
executive
executor
exemplary
exemplify, -fied, -fying
exempt
exemptable   exemptible
exemptible
exemption
exemtion   exemption
exercise, -cised, -cising (exertion)
exercise   excise (tax, cut)

exercise   exorcize (expel)

exert, -ed, -ing

exertion

ex gratia

exhalation

exhale, -haled, -haling

exhaust, -ed, -ing

exhaustion

exhaustive, -ly

exhibit, -ed, -ing

exhibiter   exhibitor

exhibition

exhibitionism

exhibitionist

exhibitor

exhilarate, -rated, -rating

exhilaration

exhorbitant   exorbitant

exhort, -ed, -ing

exhortation

exhume, -humed, -huming

exhumation

exibit   exhibit

exibition   exhibition

exigency, -cies

exigensy   exigency

exile, -iled, -iling

exist, -ed, -ing

existence

existense   existence

existensial   existential

existent

existential, -ly

existentialism

existentialist

exit

exodus

exonerate, -rated, -rating

exorbitant, -ly

exorcism

exorcist

exorcize, -cized, -cizing (expel)

exorcize   excise (tax, cut)

exorcize   exercise (exertion)

exorsism   exorcism

exorst   exhaust

exort   exhort

exortation   exhortation

exoteric, -ally (commonplace)

exoteric   esoteric (secret)

exotic, -ally

expand, -ed, -ing

expanse

expansion

expansive, -ly, -ness

expatiate, -ated, -ating (digress)

expatriate, -ated, -ating (exile)

expatriation

expect, -ed, -ing

expectancy, -cies

expectant, -ly

expectation

expectorant

expectorate, -rated, -rating

expediency

expediensy   expediency

expedient, -ly

expedite, -dited, -diting

expedition

expeditionary

expeditious, -ly, -ness

expel, -pelled, -pelling

expend, -ed, -ing

expendable

expendature   expenditure

expenditure

expense

expensive, -ly

expergate   expurgate

experience, -enced, -encing

experiment, -ed, -ing

experimental, -ly

experimentation

expert, -ly

expertise

expiate, -ated, -ating (atone)

expiation

expiration

expire, -pired, -piring

expiry, -ries

explain, -ed, -ing

explanation

explanatory

explane	explain	exquisite, -ly, -ness	
explanetry	explanatory	exseed	exceed
expletive		exsel	excel
explicable, -bly		exselence	excellence
explicate, -cated, -cating		exserpt	excerpt
explicible	explicable	ex-serviceman, -men	
explicit, -ly		extant (exist)	
explisit	explicit	extant	extent (space)
explode, -ploded, -ploding		extasy	ecstasy
exploit, -ed, -ing		extatic	ecstatic
exploitation		extemporaneous, -ly	
exploration		extempore	
exploratory		extend, -ed, -ing	
explore, -plored, -ploring		extendable	extendible
explorer		extendible	
exploror	explorer	extension	
explosion		extensive, -ly	
explosive, -ly		extenson	extension
exponent		extent	
exponential, -ly		extent	extant (exist)
export, -ed, -ing		extenuate, -ated, -ating	
exporter		extenuation	
exportor	exporter	extercate	extricate
exposay	exposé	exterier	exterior
expose, -posed, -posing		exterior	
exposé		exterminate, -nated, -nating	
expostulate, -lated, -lating		exterminater	exterminator
exposure		extermination	
expound, -ed, -ing		exterminator	
expozier	exposure	external, -ly	
expresion	expression	extinct	
expresive	expressive	extinction	
express, -ly		extinguish, -ed, -ing	
express, -ed, -ing		extinguisher	
expression		extinktion	extinction
expressionism		extol, -tolled, -tolling	
expressionist		extort, -ed, -ing	
expressive, -ly		extortion	
expresso	espresso	extortionate, -ly	
expressway		extortioner	
expropriate, -ated, -ating		extortionist	
expropriation		extra	
expulsion		extracktion	extraction
expunction		extract, -ed, -ing	
expunge, -punged, -punging		extractable	
expurgate, -gated, -gating		extraction	
expurgation		extracurricular	

extradision — extradition
extradite, -dited, -diting
extradition
extramarital
extraneous, -ly
extraordinary
extrapolate, -ated, -ating
extrapolation
extrasensory
extraterrestrial
extravagance
extravagancy
extravagant, -ly
extravaganza
extravert — extrovert
extremast — extremist
extreme, -tremer, -tremest
extremely
extremism
extremist
extremity, -ties
extricate, -cated, -cating
extrication
extrovert
extrude, -truded, -truding
extrusion
exuberance
exuberanse — exuberance
exuberant, -ly
exude, -uded, -uding
exult, -ed, -ing (rejoice)
exult — exalt (honor)
exultant, -ly
exultation
exume — exhume
eye, eyed, eyeing (see)
eye — aye (yes)
eyeball
eyebrow
eyelash
eyelet
eyelid
eyesight
eyesore
eyetooth, -teeth
eyewash
eyewitness, -nesses

eyrie (nest)
  eyrie — eerie (weird)
  eze — ease
  ezel — easel
  ezy — easy

Ff

fable
fabric
fabricate, -cated -cating
fabrication
fabulous, -ly
fabulus — fabulous
facade
face, faced, facing
faceless
facelift
facesious — facetious
facet, -eted, -eting
facetious, -ly
facia (panel)
facial, -ly
facile, -ly
facilitate, -tated, -tating
facility, -ties (ease)
facility — felicity (happy)
facist — fascist
facsimile
fact
facter — factor
faction
factionalism
factor
factory, -ries
factotum
factual, -ly
faculty, -ties
fad
faddish, -ly
fade, faded, fading
fag, fagged, fagging
faggot
fagot — faggot
Fahrenheit
fail, -ed, -ing

faillure — failure
fail-safe
failure
  faim — fame
  faimus — famous
fain (gladly)
  fain — feign (pretend)
faint, -ed, -ing (weak)
  faint — feint (pretend)
fair, -ly, -ness (honest)
  fair — fare (price)
fairway
  fairwell — farewell
fairy, -ries
fairytale
  fait — fate
  faitful — fateful
fait accompli
faith
faithful, -ly
faithless, -ly
fake, faked, faking
faker (fraud)
fakir (holy)
  faksimile — facsimile
  falacious — fallacious
  falacy — fallacy
  falanx — phalanx
  falasy — fallacy
falcon
falconry
  fale — fail
  falesy — fallacy
  falible — fallible
  falic — phallic
fall, fell, fallen, falling
  fallable — fallible
fallacious, -ly
fallacy, -cies
fallible, -bly
fallout
fallow
  fallus — phallus
  falow — fallow
false, falser, falsest
falsehood
falsetto, -tos

falsification
falsify, -fied, -fying
  falt   fault
falter, -ed, -ing
falteringly
  falure   failure
  falus   phallus
fame
familial
familiar, -ly
familiarity, -ties
familiarization
familiarize, -rized, -rizing
  familier   familiar
family, -lies
famine
famished
famous, -ly
  famus   famous
fan, fanned, fanning
fanatic
fanatical, -ly
fanaticism
fancier
fanciful, -ly
fancy, -cies
fancy, -cied, -cying
fancy, -cier, -ciest
  fane   fain (glad)
  fane   feign (pretend)
  fanfair   fanfare
fanfare
fang
fanlight
  fansie   fancy
  fansiful   fanciful
  fansy   fancy
  fantam   phantom
  fantasey   fantasy
fantasia
fantasize, -sized, -sizing
fantastic, -ally
fantasy, -sies
  fantom   phantom
far, farther, farthest
far, further, furthest
  faranyx   pharynx

faraway
farce
fare, fared, faring (progress)
  fare   fair (honest)
  Farenhite   Fahrenheit
farewell
farfetched
farm, -ed, -ing
  farmacist   pharmacist
  farmacy   pharmacy
  farmasist   pharmacist
farmer
farmhouse
farmland
farrago, -goes
faroff
farrier
farrow, -ed, -ing
farsighted
farther (away)
  farther   father (parent)
farthing
  faryngitis   pharyngitis
  farytale   fairytale
fascinate, -nated, -nating
fascination
fascism
fascist
  fase   face
  fase   phase
  fasen   fasten
  faset   facet
  fasetious   facetious
  fashal   facial
fashion, -ed, -ing
fashionable, -bly
  fashism   fascism
  fashist   fascist
  fashon   fashion
  fashonable   fashionable
  fasilitate   facilitate
  fasility   facility
  fasinate   fascinate
  fasination   fascination
fast, -ed, -ing
fasten, -ed, -ing
fastener

fastidious, -ly, -ness
  fastidius   fastidious
fat
fat, fatter, fattest
fatal, -ly
fatalism
fatalist
fatalistic, -ally
fatality, -ties
fate (destiny)
  fate   fete (fair)
  fateague   fatigue
fated
fateful, -ly
  faten   fatten
father, -ed, -ing (parent)
  father   farther (away)
fatherhood
father-in-law, fathers-in-law
fatherland
fatherly
fathom, -ed, -ing
fathomable
fatigue, -tigued, -tiguing
fatten, -ed, -ing
fatty, -tier, -tiest
fatuous, -ly
faucet
fault, -ed, -ing
faultless, -ly
faulty, faultier, faultiest
faun (god)
  faun   fawn (deer)
fauna
faux pas
  faver   favor
  faverite   favorite
  faveritism   favoritism
favor, -ed, -ing
favorable, -bly
favorite
favoritism
fawn, -ed, -ing (deer)
  fawn   faun (god)
  fawna   fauna
  fayshal   facial
faze, fazed, fazing (daunt)

faze   phase (stage)
  feacher   feature
  feable   feeble
fealty, -ties
fear, -ed, -ing
fearful, -ly
  fearfull   fearful
fearless, -ly, -ness
fearsome, -ly
  feasable   feasible
feasible, -bly
feasibility
feast, -ed, -ing
feat (act)
  feat   feet (body)
feather, -ed, -ing
feather bed
featherweight
feathery
feature, -tured, -turing
febrile
February
  Febuary   February
feces
  fech   fetch
feckless, -ly, -ness
fecund
fecundity
  fedaration   federation
federal, -ly
federalism
federalist
federate, -rated, -rating
federation
fee
feeble, -bler, -blest
feebleness
feebly
feed, fed, feeding
feedback
feeder
feel, felt, feeling
  feeld   field
feeler
  feend   fiend
  feest   feast
feet (body)

feet feat (act)
feetus fetus
feign, -ed, -ing (pretend)
 feign fain (glad)
 feild field
 feind fiend
feint, -ed, -ing (pretend)
 feint faint (weak)
feisty, feistier, feistiest
 fekund fecund
 fekundity fecundity
felicitate, -tated, -tating
felicitation
felicitous, -ly
felicity, -ties (happy)
 felicity facility (ease)
feline, -ly
 felisitous felicitous
 felisity felicity
fell
fellow
fellowship
felon
felonious, -ly
felony, -nies
 felow fellow
felt
female
feminine, -ly
femininity
feminism
feminist
femme fatale
femur
fence, fenced, fencing
fend, -ed, -ing
fender
 fenix phoenix
fennel
 fenomenon phenomenon
 fenominal phenomenal
 fense fence
fer fir (tree)
fer fur (pelt)
feral
 feret ferret
 ferie ferry

 ferl furl
 ferlong furlong
ferment, -ed, -ing (yeast)
 ferment foment (incite)
fermentation
fern
fernery, -ries
ferny
 fernice furnace
 fernish furnish
 ferniture furniture
ferocious, -ly
ferocity
 ferosious ferocious
ferret, -ed, -ing
ferrous
ferrule, -ruled, -ruling (tip)
 ferrule ferule (rod)
ferry, -ries
ferry, -ried, -rying
ferryboat
 ferther further
 ferthest furthest
fertile, -ly
fertility
fertilization
fertilize, -lized, -lizing
fertilizer
ferule (rod)
 ferule ferrule (tip)
fervency
fervent, -ly
 ferver fervor
fervid, -ly
fervor
 fery ferry
 fesant pheasant
 fesible feasible
festal, -ly
fester, -ed, -ing
festival
festive, -ly
festivity, -ties
festoon, -ed, -ing
feta (cheese)
fetal
fetch, -ed, -ing

fete, feted, feting (fair)
  fete — fate (destiny)
  feter — fetter (chain)
  fether — feather
fetid, -ly
fetish
fetishism
fetlock
fetter, -ed, -ing (chain)
fettle
fetus
feud, -ed, -ing
feudal, -ly
feudalism
fever
fevered
feverish, -ly
few
  fewd — feud
  fewdal — feudal
fey, -ly
fez, fezzes
  fezant — pheasant
  fial — file (papers)
  fial — phial (tube)
fiancé (man)
fiancée (woman)
  fiansey — fiancée
fiasco, -cos
fib, fibbed, fibbing
fibber (liar)
fiber (strand)
fiberboard
fiberglass
fibroid
fibrosis
fibrositis
fibrous, -ly
  fibrus — fibrous
fibula
fickle, -kly, -ness
fickleness
  ficktion — fiction
fiction
fictional, -ly
fictitious, -ly
fiddle, -dled, -dling

fiddler
fiddlesticks
fidelity, -ties
fidget, -ed, -ing
fidgety
  fidle — fiddle
field, -ed, -ing
fielder
  fieldor — fielder
field day
field glasses
field goal
field hockey
field house
field trip
fiend (evil)
  fiend — friend (companion)
fiendish, -ly
fierce, fiercer, fiercest
fiercely
fierceness
  fierey — fiery
  fierse — fierce
fiery, fierier, fieriest
fiesta
fife
fifteen
fifteenth
fifth
fiftieth
fifty
  fiftyeth — fiftieth
fifty-fifty
fig
  figer — figure
  figerative — figurative
  figet — fidget
fight, fought, fighting
fighter
figment
figuration
figurative, -ly
figure, -ured, -uring
figurehead
  figuretive — figurative
figurine

Fiji
Fijian
  fiksation — fixation
  fiksative — fixative

> For fila- words,
> look under **phila-**.

filch, -ed, -ing
file, filed, filing (paper)
  file — phial (vial)
  filet — fillet
filial, -ly
filibuster
  filie — filly
filigree
  filip — fillip
Filipino
  Filippines — Philippines
  filistine — philistine
fill, -ed, -ing
filler
fillet
fillip
filly, -lies
film, -ed, -ing
filmy, filmier, filmiest

> For filo- words,
> look under **philo-**.

filter, -ed, -ing
filth
filthily
filthiness
filthy, filthier, filthiest
filtrate, -trated, -trating
filtration
  fily — filly
fin
final, -ly (end)
finale (last part)
finalist
finality, -ties (conclusiveness)
finalization
finalize, -lized, -lizing
finally (conclusively)
  finally — finely
       (elegantly)

finance, -nanced, -nancing
financial, -ly
financier
  finanse — finance
finch, -ches
find, found, finding (discover)
finder
fine, fined, fining (penalty)
fine, finer, finest (quality, sunny)
finely (elegantly)
  finely — finally
       (conclusively)
fineness (being fine)
finery, -ries
finesse, -nessed, -nessing (skill)
finger
fingernail
fingerprint
fingertip
finical, -ly
finicky
finis (conclusion)
finish, -ed, -ing
finite, -ly
fiord
fir (tree)
  fir — fur (pelt)
fire, fired, firing
fire alarm
firearm
firebreak
fire drill
fire escape
fire extinguisher
firefly, -flies
fireman, -men
fireplace
fireproof
fire screen
fireworks
firm, -ed, -ing
firmament
first, -ly
first aid
firsthand
fiscal, -ly (money)
  fiscal — physical (body)

fish, fishes, fish
fishbowl
fisherman, -men
fishery, -ries
fishhook
fishion → fission
fishnet
fishy, fishier, fishiest
fisile → fissile
fision → fission

> For other fisi- words,
> look under **physi-**.

fiskle → fiscal
fissile
fission
fissure, -sured, -suring
fist
fisticuff
fistula, -las, -lae
fit, fitted, fitting
fit, fitter, fittest
fite → fight
fitful, -ly
fitfull → fitful
fitness
fitter
five
fix, fixed, fixing
fixated
fixation
fixative
fixcher → fixture
fixity, -ties
fixture
fizz, -ed, -ing
fizzel → fizzle
fizzle, -zled, -zling
fizzy, -zier, -ziest
fjord
flabbergast, -ed, -ing
flabbily
flabbiness
flabby, -bier, -biest
flabergast → flabbergast
flaby → flabby
flaccid, -ly

flaccidity
flack
flag, flagged, flagging
flagellate, -lated, -lating
flagon
flagpole
flagrant, -ly (glaring)
flagrant → fragrant (odor)
flagrent → flagrant
flagship
flagstone
flail, -ed, -ing
flair (talent)
flair → flare (blaze)
flak
flake, flaked, flaking
flakey → flaky
flakily
flaky, flakier, flakiest
flamable → flammable
flamboyance
flamboyancy
flamboyant, -ly
flame, flamed, flaming
flamenco, -cos
flameproof
flamethrower
flamingo, -gos, -goes
flammable
flammible → flammable
flan
flanel → flannel
flange, flanged, flanging
flank, -ed, -ing
flannel, -ed, -ing
flannelette
flap, flapped, flapping
flapjack
flapper
flare, flared, flaring (blaze)
flare → flair (talent)
flash, -ed, -ing
flashback
flashbulb
flashcube
flash-gun
flashlight

flashy, flashier, flashiest
flask
flat, flatted, flatting
flat, flatter, flattest
flatbed
  flaten — flatten
  flater — flatter
flatfoot, -feet
flatfooted
Flathead
flatten, -ed, -ing
flatter, -ed, -ing
flatterer
flattery, -teries
flatulence
  flatulense — flatulence
flatulent, -ly
flaunt, -ed, -ing
flautist
  flaver — flavor
flavor, -ed, -ing
flaw, -ed, -ing (fault)
  flaw — floor (room)
flax
flaxen
flay, -ed, -ing
flea (insect)
  flea — flee (escape)
flea-bitten
  fleat — fleet
flecks (spots)
  flecks — flex (bend)
fledge, fledged, fledging
flee, fled, fleeing (escape)
  flee — flea (insect)
fleece, fleeced, fleecing
fleeciness
fleecy, fleecier, fleeciest
  fleese — fleece
fleet, -ly, -ness
fleeting, -ly
  flegling — fledgling
  flegmatic — phlegmatic
  fleks — flecks (spots)
  fleksible — flexible
  flem — phlegm
  flert — flirt

flesh
fleshy, fleshier, fleshiest
fleur-de-lis, fleurs-de-lis
flew (fly)
  flew — flu (ill)
  flew — flue (passage)
flex, -ed, -ing (bend)
  flex — flecks (spots)
flexible, -bly
flextime
  fli — fly
flibbertigibbet
flick, -ed, -ing
flicker, -ed, -ing
flier
flight
flightiness
flighty, -tier, -tiest
flimsily
flimsiness
flimsy, -sier, -siest
flinch, -ed, -ing
fling, flung, flinging
flint
flinty, flintier, flintiest
flip, flipped, flipping
  flipansy — flippancy
  flipant — flippant
  fliper — flipper
flip-flop
flippancy
flippant, -ly
flipper
flirt, -ed, -ing
flirtation
flirtatious, -ly
flit, flitted, flitting
  flite — flight
  flo — floe (ice)
  flo — flow (pour)
float, -ed, -ing
floatation
floater
flock, -ed, -ing
flocks (groups)
  flocks — phlox (plant)
floe (ice)

floe   flow (pour)
flog, flogged, flogging
flood, -ed, -ing
floodgate
floodlight, -lit, -lighting
floor, -ed, -ing (room)
    floor   flaw (fault)
floorboard
    flooride   fluoride
    floot   flute
flop, flopped, flopping
floppily
floppy, -pier, -piest
floppy disc
flora, floras, florae
floral, -ly
florescence (flowering)
    florescence   fluorescence
          (giving light)
florescent
    florescent   fluorescent
florid, -ly
    floridate   fluoridate
florin
    florish   flourish
florist
floss
flossy, flossier, flossiest
flotation
    flote   float
flotilla
flotsam and jetsam
flounce, flounced, flouncing
flounder, -ed, -ing
    flounse   flounce
flour (grain)
    flour   flower (plant)
flourish, -ed, -ing
flout, -ed, -ing
flow, -ed, -ing (pour)
    flow   floe (ice)
flower, -ed, -ing (plant)
    flower   flour (grain)
flowerbed
flowery, -rier, -riest
flown
    flownder   flounder

    flownse   flounce
    flowt   flout
    flox   phlox
flu (ill)
    flu   flew (fly)
    flu   flue (passage)
fluctuate, -ated, -ating
fluctuation
flue (passage)
    flue   flew (fly)
    flue   flu (ill)
fluency
    fluensy   fluency
fluent, -ly
fluff, -ed, -ing
fluffiness
fluffy, fluffier, fluffiest
fluid, -ly
fluidity
fluke, fluked, fluking
    fluks   flux
fluky, flukier, flukiest
flunk, -ed, -ing
fluoresce, -resced, -rescing
fluorescence (giving light)
fluoridate, -dated, -dating
fluoridation
    flurish   flourish
flurry, -ries
flurry, -ried, -rying
    flurt   flirt
    flurtation   flirtation
    flury   flurry
flush, -ed, -ing
fluster, -ed, -ing
flute, fluted, fluting
flutter, -ed, -ing
fluvial
flux
fly, flies (insect)
fly, flew, flown, flying (travel)
flyblown
flycatcher
flyleaf, -leaves
flyweight
flywheel
foal, -ed, -ing

foam, -ed, -ing
fob, fobbed, fobbing
  fobia   phobia
focaccia
focal, -ly
focalize, -lized, -lizing
focus, -ci, -cuses
focus, -cused, -cusing or -cussed, -cussing
fodder
foe
  foe pas   faux pas
fog, fogged, fogging
fogginess
foggy, -gier, -giest (misty)
foghorn
fogy, -gies (old-fashioned)
foible
  foier   foyer
foil, -ed, -ing
foist, -ed, -ing
  foks   fox
fold, -ed, -ing
folder
  fole   foal
foliage
foliated
foliation
  folicle   follicle
  folie   folly
folio, -lios
folk
folk dance
  folklaw   folklore
folklore
folk song
follicle
  follicul   follicle
follow, -ed, -ing
follower
folly, -lies
  folow   follow
  foly   folly
  fome   foam
foment, -ed, -ing (incite)
  foment   ferment (yeast)
fond, -ly

fondant
  fondel   fondle
fondle, -dled, -dling
fondness
fondue
  fone   phone
  fonetic   phonetic
  fonograf   phonograph
font
  fony   phony
food
foodstuff
fool, -ed, -ing
foolery, -eries
foolhardiness
foolhardy, -dier, -diest
foolish, -ly
foolishness
foolproof
foolscap
foot, feet
football
foothill
foothold
footing
footlights
footloose
footman, -men
footnote
footpath
footprint
footsore
footstep
footwork
fop
foppish, -ly
for (with the purpose of)
  for   fore (front)
  for   four (number)
forage, -raged, -raging
foray
  forbarance   forbearance
forbear, -bore, -borne, -bearing
forbearance
forbid, -bad, -bidden, -bidding
  forbode   forebode
  forcable   forcible

forcasle	forecastle	forethought	
forcast	forecast	forever	
forcastle	forecastle	forewarn, -ed, -ing	
force, forced, forcing		foreword (book)	
forceful, -ly, -ness		foreword	forward (ahead)
forceps, -ceps, -cipes		forfeit, -ed, -ing	
forcible, -bly		forfeiture	
forclose	foreclose	forfit	forfeit
ford, -ed, -ing		forfiture	forfeiture
fordable		forgary	forgery
fore (front)		forge, forged, forging	
fore	four (number)	forgery, -eries	
forearm		forget, -got, -gotten, -getting	
forebear		forgetful, -ly	
forebode, -boded, -boding		forget-me-not	
forecast, -ed, -ing		forgettable	
forecaster		forgive, -gave, -given, -giving	
forecastle		forgiveness	
forecastor	forecaster	forgo, -went, -gone, -going (give up)	
foreclose, -closed, -closing		forgo	forego (go before)
forefather			
forefinger			
forego, -gone, -going (go before)			
forego	forgo (give up)		

For for- words, also
look under **fore-**.

foreground		forige	forage
forehand		forin	foreign
forehead		fork, -ed, -ing	
foreign		forklift	
foreigner		forlorn, -ly	
foreignor	foreigner	form, -ed, -ing	
foreknow, -knew, -knowing		formal, -ly	
foreknowledge		formality, -ties	
foreman, -men		formalize, -lized, -lizing	
foren	foreign	format	
forener	foreigner	formation	
forerunner		formative, -ly	
foresee, -saw, -seeing		former, -ly	
foreshadow, -ed, -ing		Formica	
foreshore		formidable, -bly	
foresight		formidible	formidable
foreskin		formula, -las, -lae	
forest, -ed, -ing		formulate, -lated, -lating	
forestall, -ed, -ing		formulater	formulator
forester		formulation	
forestry		formulator	
foretaste, -tasted, -tasting		forn	faun (god)
foretell, -told, -telling		forn	fawn (deer)

fornicate, -cated, -cating
fornication
forsake, -sook, -saken, -saking
  forse — force
  forseps — forceps
  forsful — forceful
  forsible — forcible
  forsight — foresight
fort (building)
  fort — fought (fight)
forte (strength)
  forteen — fourteen
forth (away)
  forth — fourth (number)
forthcoming
forthright
forthwith
fortieth
fortification
fortify, -fied, -fying
fortitude
fortnight
fortnightly
  fortnite — fortnight
fortress
fortuitous, -ly
  fortuitus — fortuitous
fortunate, -ly
fortune
fortuneteller
forty, -ties
  fortyeth — fortieth
forum, forums, fora
forward (ahead)
  forward — foreword (book)
  fosfate — phosphate
  fosforesent — phosphorescent
  fosforus — phosphorus
  fosil — fossil
fossil
foster, -ed, -ing

For **foto-** words,
look under **photo-**.

foul, -ed, -ing (dirt)
  foul — fowl (bird)

found, -ed, -ing
foundation
founder, -ed, -ing
foundling (child)
  foundling — fondling (touching)
foundry, -dries
fount
fountain
four (number)
  four — fore (ahead)
four flusher
fourfold
  fourt — fort (soldiers)
  fourt — fought (fight)
fourteen
fourteenth
fourth, -ly (number)
  fourth — forth (away)
  fourty — forty
fowl (bird)
  fowl — foul (offensive)
  fownd — found
  fowndation — foundation
  fowndry — foundry
  fownt — fount
  fowntain — fountain
fox, foxes or fox
foxhole
fox trot
fox-trot, fox-trotted, fox-trotting
foxy, foxier, foxiest
  foyble — foible
foyer
fracas
  fracktion — fraction
  fracktious — fractious
fraction
fractional, -ly
fractious, -ly
fracture, -tured, -turing
fragile, -ly
fragility, -ties
fragment, -ed, -ing
fragmentary
fragmentation
fragmented

fragmentry	fragmentary	freehand	
fragrance		freehold	
fragranse	fragrance	free-lance, -lanced, -lancing	
fragrant, -ly (odor)		free lancer	
fragrant	flagrant (glaring)	freeload, -ed, -ing	
frail, -ly		freeloader	
frailty, -ties		freely	
frame, framed, framing		freeman, -men	
frame-up		Freemason	
framework		Freemasonry	
franc (money)		freesia	
franc	frank (mark)	freestanding	
franchise		freestyle	
frangipanni, -nies		freeway	
frank, -ed, -ing (mark)		freewheel, -ed, -ing	
frank	franc (money)	freeze, froze, frozen, freezing (cold)	
frankfurter		freeze	frieze (band)
frankincense		freezer	
frantic, -ally		freight, -ed, -ing	
frase	phrase	freighter	
frate	freight	freind	friend
fraternal, -ly		frekwency	frequency
fraternity, -ties		frekwent	frequent
fraternization		French	
fraternize, -nized, -nizing		frend	friend
fraud		frendly	friendly
fraudulance	fraudulence	frendship	friendship
fraudulence		frenetic, -ally	
fraudulense	fraudulence	frenzie	frenzy
fraudulent, -ly		frenzied	
fraught		frenzy, -zies	
fraut	fraught	frenzy, -zied, -zying	
frawd	fraud	frequency, -cies	
frawdulence	fraudulence	frequensy	frequency
frawdulent	fraudulent	frequent, -ly	
frawt	fraught	fresco, -coes	
fray, -ed, -ing		fresh, -er, -est	
frazzel	frazzle	fresh, -ly	
frazzle, -zled, -zling		freshen, -ed, -ing	
freak		freshener	
freakish, -ly		freshness	
freckle, -led, -ling		freshwater	
free, freed, freeing		fresko	fresco
free, freer, freest		fret, fretted, fretting	
freeborn		fretful, -ly	
freedom		fretwork	
		Freudian	

fri	fry	fro	
friabel	friable	frock	
friable		frog	
friar (monk)		frogman, -men	
friar	fryer (pan)	Froidian	Freudian
fricassee, -seed, -seeing		frolic, -icked, -icking	
fricktion	friction	frolicsome, -ly	
friction		frond	
frictional, -ly		front, -ed, -ing	
Friday		frontage	
fridge		frontal, -ly	
friend (companion)		fronteer	frontier
friend	fiend (evil)	frontier	
friendliness		frontige	frontage
friendly, -lier, -liest		froogal	frugal
friendship		frooition	fruition
Friesian		froot	fruit
frieze (band)		frootful	fruitful
frieze	freeze (cold)	frost, -ed, -ing	
frigate		frostbite, -bit, -bitten, -biting	
fright		frostily	
frighten, -ed, -ing		frosty, -tier, -tiest	
frightful, -ly		froth, -ed, -ing	
frightfull	frightful	frothiness	
frigid, -ly		frothy, frothier, frothiest	
frigidity, -ties		frown, -ed, -ing	
frigidness		frowzy, -zier, -ziest	
frigid zone		froze	
frill, -ed, -ing		frozen, -ly	
fringe, fringed, fringing		fructose	
frippery, -ries		frugal, -ly	
frisk, -ed, -ing		frugality, -ties	
friskily		fruision	fruition
frisky, friskier, friskiest		fruit, -ed, -ing	
frite	fright	fruiterer	
friteful	frightful	fruit fly	
friten	frighten	fruitful, -ly	
friter	fritter	fruition	
fritter, -ed, -ing		fruitless, -ly	
frivolity, -ties		fruity, -tier, -tiest	
frivolous, -ly		frump	
frivolus	frivolous	frumpish, -ly	
friz, frizz		frunt	front
frizz, frizzed, frizzing		fruntal	frontal
frizzel	frizzle	fruntier	frontier
frizzle, -zled, -zling		frusstration	frustration
frizzy, frizzier, frizziest		frustrate, -trated, -trating	

frustration

frut	fruit
fruterer	fruiterer
frutful	fruitful
frutie	fruity

fry, fried, frying

fry, fries

fryer (pan)

fryer	friar (monk)
fucher	future
fucheristic	futuristic

fuchsia

fudal	feudal
fudalism	feudalism
fuddel	fuddle

fuddle, -dled, -dling

fude	feud

fudge, fudged, fudging

fuel, -ed, -ing

fuel injection

fuel injector

fugitive

fugue

ful	full

fulcrum, -crums, -cra

fulfil, -filled, -filling

fulfill, -ed, -ing

fulfillment

full

fullback

full-blooded

fullfil	fulfil

fully

full-fledged

fulminate, -ated, -ating

fulscap	foolscap

fulsome, -ly

fulsomeness

fumbel	fumble

fumble, -bled, -bling

fumbler

fume, fumed, fuming

fumigant

fumigate, -gated, -gating

fumigater	fumigator

fumigation

fumigator

fun

funcktion	function

function

functional, -ly

functionalism

functionary, -ries

fund, -ed, -ing

fundamental, -ly

funel	funnel

funeral

funereal, -ly

fungicide

fungus, fungi

funicular

funily	funnily

funk

funky

funnel, -ed, -ing

funnies

funnily

funny, -nier, -niest

fur, furred, furring (pelt)

fur	fir (tree)

furbish, -ed, -ing

furie	furry (fur)
furie	fury (anger)
furier	furrier

furious, -ly

furius	furious

furl, -ed, -ing

furlong

furlough

furm	firm
furmament	firmament
furment	ferment
furmentation	fermentation
furn	fern

furnace

furnish, -ed, -ing

furnishings

furniture

furor

furrier

furrow, -ed, -ing

furry, -rier, -riest (fur)

furst	first

further

furtherance
furthest
furtive, -ly
fury, -ries (anger)
  fus   fuss
fuse, fused, fusing
fuselage
  fusha   fuchsia
  fusier   fussier
  fusiest   fussiest
  fusilade   fusillade
  fusilage   fuselage
fusilier
fusillade
fusion
fuss, -ed, -ing
fusspot
fussy, -sier, -siest
futile, -ly
futility, -ties
future
futurism
futuristic
fuzz
fuzzily
fuzziness
fuzzy, -zier, -ziest
  fyord   fiord
  fyord   fjord

> For fysi- words, look
> under **physi-**.

Gg

gab, gabbed, gabbing
gabardine
gabble, -bled, -bling (talk)

gabel	gabble (talk)
gabel	gable (roof)

gable (roof)
gadget
Gaelic

gaf	gaff (hook)
gaf	gaffe (mistake)

gaff (hook)
gaffe (mistake)
gag, gagged, gagging
gaga
gage (challenge)

gage	gauge (measure)
gaget	gadget

gaggle

gagit	gadget
gagle	gaggle

gaiety, -ties

gail	gale

gaily
gain, -ed, -ing
gainful, -ly
gainsay, -said, -saying
gait (walk)

gait	gate (opening)

gaiter

gaitey	gaiety

gal
gala (festival)

galaksy	galaxy
galant	gallant
galantry	gallantry
galawe	galore

galaxy, -axies

gale

galery	gallery
galey	galley
galivant	gallivant

gall, -ed, -ing
gallant, -ly
gallantry, -tries
galleon
gallery, -leries
galley, -leys
gallivant, -vanted, -vanting
gallon
gallop, galloped, galloping (pace)
gallows
gallstone
Gallup poll (survey)

galon	gallon
galop	gallop (pace)

galore
galoshes

galows	gallows
galup poll	Gallup poll

galvanize, -nized, -nizing

galy	galley

gambit
gamble, -bled, -bling (chance)
gambol, -ed, -ing (frolic)
game, gamed, gaming
gamesmanship
gamin (urchin)
gamma
gammon (bacon)
gamut
gamy, gamier, gamiest
gander
gang
gangling
ganglion, -glia
gangplank

gangreen	gangrene

gangrene
gangrenous

gangrenus	gangrenous

gangster
gangway
gannet
gantry, -tries

gap
gape, -ed, -ing
gar, garfish
garage, -raged, -raging
   garantee   guarantee
   garantee   guaranty
   garantor   guarantor
garb, -ed, -ing
garbage
   garbel   garble
   garbige   garbage
garble, -bled, -bling
   gard   guard
garden, -ed, -ing
gardener
gardenia
   gardian   guardian
   gargel   gargle
gargle, -gled, -gling
   gargoil   gargoyle
gargoyle
garish, -ly
   garison   garrison
garland, -ed, -ing
garlic
garment
garner, -ed, -ing
garnet
garnish, -ed, -ing
garnishee, -sheed, -sheeing
   garnit   garnet
   garrage   garage
garrison, -ed, -ing
   garrlic   garlic
   garrot   garrotte
garrote, -ed, -ing, garrotte, -rotted,
-rotting
garrulity
garrulous, -ly
garter
   garulous   garrulous
gas, gases
gas, gassed, gassing
gasbag, -bagged, -bagging
   gasebo   gazebo
   gaselene   gasoline
gaseous

gash, -ed, -ing
   gasious   gaseous
gasket
gasmask
gasoline
gasp, -ed, -ing
   gassey   gassy
gassy, -sier, -siest
   gastley   ghastly
gastric
gastritis
gastroenteritis
gastronome
gastronomy
gate (opening)
   gate   gait (walk)
gateau, -teaux
gatecrash, -ed, -ing
   gater   gaiter
gateway
gather, -ed, -ing
gauche
   gaudie   gaudy
gauge, gauged, gauging (measure)
   gauge   gage (challenge)
gaunt, -ly, -ness
gauntlet
gauze
gave
gavel
   gavot   gavotte
gavotte
   gawdie   gaudy
gawk, -ed, -ing
gawky, -kier, -kiest
   gawl   gall
   gawnt   gaunt
   gawntlet   gauntlet
   gawse   gauze
gay, gayer, gayest
   Gaylic   Gaelic
   gayn   gain
   gaysha   geisha
gaze, gazed, gazing
gazebo, -bos, -boes
   gazel   gazelle
gazelle

gazette, -etted, -etting
gear, -ed, -ing
gearbox, -boxes
gearshift
gearwheel
gecko, -os, -oes
geek
   geershift   gearshift
   gees   geese
geese
geezer
Geiger counter
geisha, -shas
gel, gelled, gelling
   gelatin   gelatine
gelatine
gelatinous
   gelatinus   gelatinous
gelato
geld, gelded, gelding
gelignite
gem, gemmed, gemming
Gemini
gendarme, -darmes
gender
gene
genealogist
genealogy, -gies
   genee   genie
general, -ly
generality, -ties
generalize, -ized, -izing
generate, -ed, -ing
   generater   generator
generation
generation gap
generator
generic
generical, -ly
generosity, -ties
generous, -ly
   generus   generous
genesis, -ses (origin)
genetic
genetical, -ly
genetics
   geney   genie

genial, -ly
genie
   geniology   genealogy
genital
genius, geniuses (talent)
genocide
   genoside   genocide
genre
gent
genteel, -ly (proper)
   genteel   gentle
gentile, Gentile (Christian)
gentility, -ties
gentle, -tler, -tlest (mild)
gentleman, -men
gentlewoman, -women
   gentrey   gentry
   gentrificasion   gentrification
gentrification
gentry
   genufleck   genuflect
genuflect, -ed, -ing
   genuin   genuine
genuine, -ly
genuineness
genus, genera (Biol.)
   geny   genie
   geofysics   geophysics
   geografey   geography
geography, -phies
geologist
geology, -gies
   geometrey   geometry
geometric
geometrical, -ly
geometry, -tries
   geomettric   geometric
geophysicist
geophysics
georgette
   geraffe   giraffe
geranium
   gerd   gird
   gerder   girder
   gerdle   girdle
geriatric
   gerilla   gorilla

gerilla	guerrilla	gient	giant
gerkin	gherkin	giesha	geisha
gerl	girl	gift	
germ		gifted	
German		giftwrap, -wrapped, -wrapping	
germane		gig	
germinal		gigalo	gigolo
germinate, -nated, -nating		gigantic, -ally	
gerontology		giggle, -gled, -gling	
gerrymander, -ed, -ing		gigle	giggle
gerth	girth	gigolo, -los	
gerund		gil	gill
gescha	gesture	gild, -ed, -ing (gold)	
geser	geyser	gild	guild (union)
gess	guess	gile	guile
gest	guest	gill	
gestate, -tated, -tating		giloteen	guillotine
gestation		gilotine	guillotine
gesticulate, -lated, -lating		gilt (gold)	
gesture, -tured, -turing		gilt	guilt (offense)
get, got, getting		gilty	guilty
getaway		gim	gym
getto	ghetto	gimick	gimmick
geyser		gimkana	gymkhana
gezelle	gazelle	gimlet	
ghastly, -lier, -liest		gimlit	gimlet
gherkin		gimmick	
ghetto, ghettos, ghettoes		gimmicky	
ghool	ghoul	gimnasium	gymnasium
ghost, -ly		gimnastics	gymnastics
ghoul		gin, ginned, ginning	
ghoulish, -ly, -ness		ginea	guinea
giant		gineapig	guineapig
gibber		ginecology	gynecology
gibberish		gingam	gingham
gibbet, -ed, -ing		ginger	
gibe, gibed, gibing (mock)		gingerley	gingerly
gibe	jibe (sail)	gingerly	
giber	gibber	gingham	
giberish	gibberish	gingivitis	
gibbet	gibbet	ginjer	ginger
giblet		ginseng	
gidance	guidance	ginsing	ginseng
gidanse	guidance	gip	gyp
giddy, -dier, -diest		gipsie	gipsy
gide	guide	gipsum	gypsum
gidy	giddy	gipsy, -sies	

giraffe

gird, -ed, -ing

  girdel · girdle

girder

girdle, -dled, -dling

girl

  girm · germ

  girocompass · gyrocompass

  giroscope · gyroscope

girth

  gise · guise

gist

  gitar · guitar

give, gave, given, giving

  giy · guy

  gizard · gizzard

gizmo

gizzard

glacial, -ly

glacier (ice)

  glacier · glazier (person)

glad, gladder, gladdest

glade

  gladen · gladden

  gladiater · gladiator

gladiator

  glamer · glamor, glamour

glamor, glamour

glamorous, -ly

glance, -ed, -ing

gland

glandular

  glanduler · glandular

  glanse · glance

glare, glared, glaring

  glas · glass

  glasial · glacial

  glasier · glacier

glasnost

glass, glasses

glassware

glassy, -sier, -siest

glaucoma

  glawcoma · glaucoma

glaze, glazed, glazing

glazier (person)

  glazier · glacier (ice)

  glea · glee

gleam, -ed, -ing

glean, -ed, -ing

glee

  gleem · gleam

  gleen · glean

glib, glibber, glibbest

  glicerine · glycerine

glide, glided, gliding

glider

glimmer, -ered, -ering

glimpse, glimpsed, glimpsing

  glimse · glimpse

glint, -ed, -ing

  glisen · glisten

  gliserin · glycerine

glisten, -ed, -ing

glitch

glitter, -ed, -ing

  glo · glow

gloat, -ed, -ing

glob

global, -ly

globe

globule

  gloo · glue

  gloocose · glucose

gloom

gloomily

gloomy, -mier, -miest

  glooten · gluten

  glorie · glory

glorify, -fied, -fying

glorious, -ly

  glorius · glorious

glory, glories

glory, gloried, glorying

  glos · gloss

  glosary · glossary

gloss, glossed, glossing

glossary, -ries

  glossie · glossy

glossy, glossier, glossiest

  glote · gloat

glove

glow, -ed, -ing

glower, -ed, -ing

glucose
glue, glued, gluing
glum, -ly
glut, glutted, glutting
gluten (glue)
  glutten   glutton
glutton (eat)
  gluv   glove
glycerine
gnarled (knotty)
  gnarled   knurled
                (ridged)
gnash, -ed, -ing
gnat
gnaw, gnawed, gnawing (bite)
  gnaw   nor (conj.)
gnome
gnu, gnus
go, went, gone, going
goad, -ed, -ing
goal
goalkeeper
goat
goatee
gob
  gobbel   gobble
gobble, -bled, -bling
gobbledygook
gobbler
go-between
  goble   gobble
goblet
goblin
go-cart
  goche   gauche
God or god
godchild, -children
goddess
Godfearing
Godforsaken
godly, -lier, -liest
godparent
godsend, -sent, -sending
Godspeed
goes
gofer
  gofer   gopher (animal)

goggle, -gled, -gling
  gogle   goggle
goiter
gold
golden, -ly
goldfield
goldfish
goldmine
  gole   goal (aim)
golf (sport)
  golf   gulf (bay)
golly
  gon   gone
gondola
gondolier
gone
goner
gong
gonorrhea
goo
good, better, best
  gooda   Gouda
goodby, goodbys, goodbye, -byes
good night
goodwill
gooey, gooier, gooiest
goof, goofed, goofing
goofball
  gool   ghoul
  goolash   goulash
  goormand   gourmand
  goormay   gourmet
goose, geese
  gooseberie   gooseberry
gooseberry, -ries
goosestep, -stepped, -stepping
gopher (animal)
  gopher   gofer (worker)
gore, gored, goring
gorge, gorged, gorging
  gorgeos   gorgeous
gorgeous, -ly
gorilla (ape)
  gorilla   guerrilla
                (soldier)
gormandize, -dized, -dizing
gorse

gory, gorier, goriest		grafics	graphics
gosamer	gossamer	grafite	graphite
goshawk		grafiti	graffiti
gosip	gossip	graft, grafted, grafting	
gosling		grail	
gospel		grain (seed)	
gossamer		grainy	granny
gossip, -ed, -ing			(grandmother)
gost	ghost	graling	grayling
gote	goat	gram	
Gothic		gramar	grammar
Gouda		gramarian	grammarian
gouge, gouged, gouging		gramatical	grammatical
goul	ghoul	gramer	grammar
goulash		gramerfone	gramophone
gourd		grammar	
gourmand		grammarian	
gourmet		grammatical, -ly	
gout		gramophone	
goven	govern	grampus, grampuses	
goverment	government	granade	grenade
govern, -ed, -ing		granary, -ries	
governer	governor	grand	
governess		grandeur	
government		grandiloquent, -ly	
governmental, -ly		grandiose, -ly	
governor		grandiosity	
govner	governor	grandparent	
gowge	gouge	grandstand	
gowt	gout	grane	grain
goyter	goiter	grange	
grab, grabbed, grabbing		granit	granite
grace, graced, gracing		granite	
graceful, -ly, -ness		grannie	granny
gracious, -ly, -ness		granny, grannies (grandmother)	
gradasion	gradation	granny	grainy (gritty)
gradation		grant, -ed, -ing	
grade, graded, grading		granular	
grader		granulate, -lated, -lating	
gradient		granule	
gradual, -ly		grany	granny
graduate, -ated, -ating		grape	
graduation		grapefruit, grapefruit	
graf	graph	grapevine	
graffiti (plural noun)		graph, -ed, -ing	
graffito (singular noun)		graphic	
grafic	graphic	graphical, -ly	

graphics
graphite
  graple   grapple
grapnel
grapple, -pled, -pling
  gras   grass
  grase   grace
  grashoper   grasshopper
  grasious   gracious
grasp, -ed, -ing
grass
grasshopper
glassland
grassroots
grassy, -sier, -siest
grate (fireplace)
grate, grated, grating (shred)
  grate   great (large)
grateful, -ly
  gratificasion   gratification
gratification
gratify, -fied, -fying
gratingly
gratis
gratitude
  gratuitey   gratuity
gratuitous, -ly
gratuity
  gravatation   gravitation
grave
gravel, -ed, -ing
gravelly
  gravie   gravy
gravitate, -tated, -tating
gravitation
gravity, -ties
gravure
  gravvity   gravity
gravy, -vies
gray
  grayhownd   greyhound
  grayl   grail
grayling
  grayn   grain
graze, grazed, grazing
grazier
grease, greased, greasing (oil)

greasepaint
great (large)
  great   grate (shred)
  greatful   grateful
  grede   greed
Greece (country)
greed
greedily
greedy, greedier, greediest
  greef   grief
green
greenery, -eries
greenhorn
greenhouse
Greenpeace
  greese   grease
greet, -ed, -ing
gregarious, -ly
  gregarius   gregarious
  greif   grief
  greive   grieve
  greivus   grievous
gremlin
grenade
grenadier
grenadine
  grene   green
  grenery   greenery
  grenhorn   greenhorn
  grenhous   greenhouse
  grennade   grenade
  grese   grease
  grete   greet
  grevance   grievance
  grevanse   grievance
  greve   grieve
  grevous   grievous
grew
  grewsome   gruesome
greyhound
grid
  griddel   griddle
griddle, -dled, -dling
gridiron
gridlock
grief
grief-stricken

grievance
  grievanse → grievance (mythology)
grieve, -ed, -ing
grievous, -ly
griffin (mythology)
  griffin → griffon (dog)
griffon (dog)
  griffon → griffin (mythology)
grill, -ed, -ing (cook)
grille (screen)
  griller → guerrilla (soldier)
grim, grimmer, grimmest
grimace, -maced, -macing
  grimase → grimace
grime, grimed, griming (dirt)
grimy, grimier, grimiest
grin, grinned, grinning (smile)
grind, ground, grinding
grinder
grindstone
  grined → grind
grip, gripped, gripping (hold)
gripe, griped, griping (pain)
grippe (flu)
  grisel → gristle (fiber)
grisly, -lier, -liest
  grissle → gristle (fiber)
grist
gristle (fiber)
grit, gritted, gritting
  grizzle → gristle (fiber)
grizzly, -lier, -liest
  gro → grow
groan, groaned, groaning (moan)
  groan → grown (mature)
grocer
grocery, -ceries
grog
groggy, -gier, -giest
groin
  grone → groan
  grone → grown
  groo → grew
  grool → gruel

groom, -ed, -ing
  groop → group
groove, grooved, grooving
  groovey → groovy
groovy, -vier, -viest
  grooyere → gruyère
grope, groped, groping
  gros → gross
  groser → grocer
gross, grosses
  grotesk → grotesque
grotesque, -ly
  groto → grotto
grotto, -toes, -tos
grouch, -ed, -ing
  groun → grown
ground, -ed, -ing
groundhog
groundless, -ly
  groundsheat → groundsheet
groundsheet
groundskeeper
groundswell
groundwater
groundwork
group, -ed, -ing
grouse, groused, grousing
grout, -ed, -ing
grove
grovel, -ed, -ing
  grovle → grovel
grow, grew, grown, growing
grower
growl, -ed, -ing
grown (mature)
  grown → groan (moan)
  grownd → ground
  growse → grouse
growth
grub, grubbed, grubbing
grubby, -bier, -biest
grudge, -ed, -ing
gruel
grueling
gruesome, -ly, -ness
  gruesum → gruesome
  gruf → gruff

gruff, -ly, -ness		guitar	
gruge	grudge	gul	gull
grumbel	grumble	gulash	goulash
grumble,-led, -ling		gulch	
grumpie	grumpy	gulet	gullet
grumpy, -pier, -piest		guley	gully
grunt, -ed, -ing		gulf (bay)	
grusome	gruesome	gulf	golf (sport)
grusum	gruesome	gulible	gullible
gruvel	grovel	gulie	gully
gruvaire	gruyère	gull, -ed, -ing	
gruyère		gullet	
G-string		gullible, -bly	
guano, -nos		gullibility	
guarantee, -teed, -teeing		gully, gullies	
guaranter	guarantor	gulp, -ed, -ing	
guarantor		guly	gully
guaranty, -tied, -tying		gum, gummed, gumming	
guaranty, -ties		gumbo	
guard, -ed, -ing		gumboil	
guardian		gummy, -mier, -miest	
guava		gumnut	
gudgeon		gumption	
Guernsey, -seys		gumshoe	
guerrilla (soldier)		gun, gunned, gunning	
guerrilla	gorrilla (ape)	gung ho	
guess, -ed, -ing		gunk	
guest		gunman, -men	
guesthouse, -houses		gun metal	
gufaw	guffaw	gunnel	gunwale
guffaw, -awed, -awing		gunner	
guidance		gunnery, -eries	
guide, guided, guiding		gunny, -nies	
guideline		gunnysack	
guild (union)		gunpoint	
guild	gild (gold)	gunpowder	
guile		gunshot	
guileless, -ly		gun-shy	
guillotine, -tined, -tining		gunslinger	
guiloteen	guillotine	gunsmith	
guilotine	guillotine	gunwale	
guilt (offense)		guppy, -pies	
guiltily		gurdle	girdle
guilty, -tier, -tiest		gurgel	gurgle
guinea		gurgle, -gled, -gling	
guinea pig		gurnerd	gurnard
guise, guised, guising		gurth	girth

guru, gurus
gush, gushed, gushing
gusset

gussit	gusset
gussto	gusto

gust, -ed, -ing
gustatory
gusto
gut, gutted, gutting

guter	gutter
guteral	guttural
gutersnipe	guttersnipe

gutless, -ly

gutsie	gutsy

gutsy, -sier, -siest
gutter
guttersnipe
guttural, -ly

guvern	govern
guverness	governess
guvernment	government
guvner	governor

guy

guyser	geyser
guzle	guzzle

guzzle, guzzled, guzzling

gwano	guano
gwava	guava
gybe	gibe

gym

gymkana	gymkhana

gymkhana
gymnasium, -nasiums, -nasia
gymnastics
gynecological
gynecologist
gynecology
gyp, gypped, gypping
gypsum
gypsy, -sies
gyrate, -ed, -ing
gyrocompass
gyroscope

Hh

habanera
habeas corpus
haberdasher
haberdashery, -ries
habet	habit
habetation	habitation
habias corpus	habeas corpus
habit
habitable, -bly
habitat
habitation
habitible	habitable
habitual, -ly
habituate, -ated, -ating
hach	hatch
hachery	hatchery
hachet	hatchet
hacienda
hack, -ed, -ing
hackel	hackle
hacker
hackie
hackle, -led, -ling
hackman, -men
hackney, -neyed, -neying
hacksaw
hackwork
haddock, haddocks, haddock
Hades
hadn't (had not)
hadnt	hadn't
haf	have
haft
hag
hagard	haggard
haggard, -ly
haggis
haggle, -gled, -gling

hagiography, -phies
| hagis | haggis |
| hagle | haggle |
haiku, haiku
hail (ice)
| hail | hale (robust, bring) |
hailstone
hailstorm
hair (head)
| hair | hare (animal) |
| hair | heir (inherit) |
haircut
hairdo, -dos
hairdresser
hairline
hairpiece
hairpin
hair-raising
hair-raiser
hairspring
hairstyle
hairstylist
hair-trigger
hairy, -rier, -riest
hake, hake, hakes
| halcion | halcyon |
halcyon
hale (robust)
hale, haled, haling (bring)
hale	hail (ice)
haleluya	hallelujah
halestone	hailstone
halestorm	hailstorm
half
half-back
half-baked
half-breed
half brother
half-caste
half-cocked
half dollar
half-hearted, -ly, -ness
half hour
half-life
half-mast
half measures

half mesures	half measures	hand, handed, handing	
half moon		handbag	
half sister		handball	
half size		handbill	
half time		handbook	
half-truth		handclap, -clapped, -clapping	
halfway		handcuff, -ed, -ing	
halfway house		handel	handle
half-wit		handey	handy
halibut, -buts		handeywork	handiwork
halilooya	hallelujah	handful, handfuls, handsful	
halitosis		handicap, -capped, -capping	
hall (room)		handicraft	
hall	haul (carry)	handie	handy
hallelujah		handiwork	
halleluyah	hallelujah	handkerchief, -chiefs, -chieves	
hallmark		handle, -dled, -dling	
hallow, -ed, (holy)		handlebar	
Halloween		handler	
hallucinate, -nated, -nating		handmade (article)	
hallucination		handmaid (servant)	
hallucinogen		hand-me-down	
halmark	hallmark	hand-off	
halo, -loes, -los (light)		handout	
halo	hallow (holy)	handpick, -ed, -ing	
halo	hello (greet)	handrail	
halogen		handriting	handwriting
Haloween	Halloween	handsaw	
halsyon	halcyon	handset	
halt, -ed, -ing		handshake	
halter		handsome (attractive)	
halusinate	hallucinate	handspring	
halusinogen	hallucinogen	handstand	
halve, halved, halving		hand-to-mouth	
halyard		handwriting	
halyerd	halyard	handy, -dier, -diest	
ham, hammed, hamming		handyman	
hamburger		hang, hung or hanged, hanging	
hamer	hammer	hangar (shed)	
hamlet		hangar	hanger (clothes)
hammer, -ed, -ing		hangdog	
hammerhead		hanger (clothes)	
hammock		hanger	hangar (shed)
hamper, -ed, -ing		hanger-on, hangers-on	
hamster		hang-glider	
hamstring, -strung, -stringing		hangkerchief	handkerchief
hanbook	handbook		

hangman
hangnail
hangout
hangover
hang-up
hank
hanker, -ed, -ing
hankerchief	handkerchief
hankuff	handcuff

hanky, hankies
hanky-panky
hansom (cab)
hansom	handsome (attractive)
hansum	handsome
hapen	happen

haphazard, -ly
hapie	happy

hapless, -ly
happen, -ened, -ening
happily
happy, happier, happiest
happy-go-lucky
hapy	happy
harang	harangue

harangue, -rangued, -ranguing
haras	harass

harass, -ed, -ing
harassment
harber	harbor

harbinger
harbor, -ed, -ing
hard, -ly, -ness
hardback
hardball
hard-bitten
hardboard
hard core
hard court
harden, -ed, -ing
hardheaded
hardhearted, -ly
hardie	hardy

hardhat
hardihood
hardiness
hardlie	hardly

hard line
hard-nosed
hardship
hardtop
hardware
hardwear	hardware

hardwood
hardworking
hardy, hardier, hardiest
hare (animal)
hare	hair (head)
hare	heir (inherit)

harebrained
harelip
harem
hark, -ed, -ing
harlot
harm, -ed, -ing
harmonic
harmonica
harmonious, -ly
harmonium
harmonius	harmonious

harmonize, -nized, -nizing
harmony, -nies
harness, -ed, -ing
harow	harrow

harp, -ed, -ing
harpoon
harpsichord
harpsicord	harpsichord

harpy
harrier
harrow, -ed, -ing
harry, -ried, -rying
harsh, -ly, -ness
hart (deer)
hart	heart (body)

> For all other **hart-** words, look under **heart-**.

harum-scarum
harvest, -ed, -ing
harvester
harvist	harvest
hary	hairy

has-been

hasen	hasten	hawnt	haunt
hash, -ed, -ing		hawse (ship)	
hashish		hawse	horse (animal)
hasn't (has not)		hawser	
hasnt	hasn't	hawthorn	
hasock	hassock	hawthorne	hawthorn
hasp		hawticulture	horticulture
hassel	hassle	hawty	haughty
hassle, -led, -ling		haxsaw	hacksaw
hassock		hay (grass)	
haste, -tily, -tiness		hay	hey
hasten, -ed, -ing			(interjection)
hasty, hastier, hastiest		hay fever	
hatch, -ed, -ing		haystack	
hatchary	hatchery	haywire	
hatchback		hazard	
hatchery, -eries		hazardous, -ly	
hatchet		haze, hazed, hazing	
hatchway		hazel	
hate, -ed, -ing		hazerd	hazard
hateful, -ly, -ness		hazerdous	hazardous
hatred		head, -ed, -ing	
hatrid	hatred	headache	
hatter		headake	headache
haughtily, haughtiness		head count	
haughty, -tier, -tiest		headdress	
haul, -ed, -ing (carry)		headfirst	
haul	hall (room)	headfone	headphone
haulage		headhunting	
hauler		headland	
haulige	haulage	headlight	
haunch		headline, -lined, -lining	
haunt, -ed, -ing		headlite	headlight
haute cuisine		headlong	
hav	have	headman	
have, had, having		headmaster	
haven		headmistress	
haven't (have not)		head-on	
havent	haven't	headphone	
haversack		headquarters	
havoc, -ocked, -ocking		headset	
hawk, -ed, -ing		headstand	
hawker		head start	
hawl	haul	headstone	
hawlage	haulage	headstrong	
hawnch	haunch	headwaiter	
hawnet	hornet	headwaters	

headway
headword
headwork
heady, -dier, -diest
heal (health)
   heal   heel (shoe)
   heal   he'll (he will)
healer (doctor)
health
healthy, -thier, -thiest
heap, -ed, -ing
hear, heard, hearing (listen)
   hear   here (place)
heard (listen)
   heard   herd (animals)
hearer
hearing aid
hearsay
hearse
heart (body)
heartache
heart attack
heartbeat
heartbreak
heartbroken, -ly
heartburn
hearten, -ed, -ing
heartfelt
hearth
heartless, -ly, -ness
heartrending, -ly
heartstrings
heartthrob
heart-to-heart
heartwarming
hearty, -tily
heat, -ed, -ing
heater
heath
heathen, -then, -thens
heather
heat wave
heave, heaved, heaving
heaven, -ly
heavy, -vier, -viest
heavy-duty
heavy-handed, -ly

heavyhearted, -ly
heavyset
heavyweight
Hebrew
   Hebroo   Hebrew
heck
heckle, -led, -ling
hectare
hectic, -ally
hector, -ed, -ing
he'd (he would)
   hed   head (body)
   hed   he'd (he would)
hedge, hedged, hedging
hedgehog
hedonism
heed, -ed, -ing
heedless, -ly
heehaw
heel (shoe)
   heel   heal (health)
   heel   he'll (he will)
   heeler   healer (doctor)
   heematology   hematology
   heemoglobin   hemoglobin
   heemophilia   hemophilia
   heep   heap
   heer   hear (listen)
   heer   here (place)
   heet   heat
   heeth   heath
   hefer   heifer
   heftie   hefty
heft, -ed, -ing
hefty, -tier, -tiest
   hege   hedge
heifer
height
heighten, -ed, -ing
   heighth   height
heinous, -ly, -ness
   heinus   heinous
heir (inherit)
   heir   hair (head)
   heir   here (place)
heir apparent, heirs apparent
heiress

heirloom
heir presumptive, heirs presumptive
heist
heist, -ed, -ing
  heith — height
  hel — hell
held
helicopter
helipad
heliport
helium
hell
he'll (he will)
  hell — he'll
hellbent
hellcat
Hellenic
hellfire
hello, -los (greeting)
  hello — halo (light)
hello, -loed, -loing
helm
helmet
helmsman, -men
  helo — hello
helot
help, -ed, -ing
helpless, -ly, -ness
helpmate
helter-skelter
  helth — health
  helthy — healthy
hem, hemmed, hemming
hematology
  hemisfear — hemisphere
hemisphere
hemlock
hemoglobin
hemophilia
hemorrhage, -haged, -haging
hemorrhoid
hemp
hemstitch, -stitched, -stitching
hen
  hena — henna
hence (from this time)
  hence — hens (fowl)

henchman, -men
henna
  henous — heinous
henpeck, -pecked, -pecking
hens (fowl)
  hens — hence (from this time)
hepatic
hepatitis
heptagon
herald, -ed, -ing
heraldic, -ally
  heraldrey — heraldry
heraldry, -dries
herb
herbaceous
herbage
herbalist
  herbaseous — herbaceous
herbicide
  herbiside — herbicide
herbivore
herbivorous
  herbivorus — herbivorous
herculean
herd (animals)
  herd — heard (listen)
herdsman, -men
here (place)
  here — hear (listen)
hereafter
hereby
hereditary (adjective)
  hereditery — hereditary
  hereditey — heredity
heredity, -ties (noun)
Hereford
herein
hereof
  heresay — hearsay
  heresie — heresy
heresy, -sies
heretic
hereto
hereunder
hereupon
herewith

hering	herring
heritable, -ly	
heritage	
heritije	heritage
herl	hurl
hermafrodite	hermaphrodite
hermaphrodite	
hermaphroditism	
hermatage	hermitage
hermetic	
hermetical, -ly	
hermit	
hermitage	
hermitige	hermitage
hernia, -nias	
hero, -roes	
heroic	
heroical, -ly	
heroicle	heroical
heroin (drug)	
heroine (female hero)	
heroism	
heron	
hero worship, -shipped, -shipping	
herpeas	herpes
herpes	
herrediraty	hereditary
herring, -rings, -ring	
herringbone	
hers (pronoun)	
herse	hearse (vehicle)
herself	
hert	hurt
hertle	hurtle
hertz	
he's (he is, has)	
hes	he's
hesian	hessian
hesitancy	
hesitansy	hesitancy
hesitant, -ly	
hesitate, -tated, -tating	
hesitation	
hessian	
heterogeneity, -ties	
heterogeneous, -ly (unlike)	
heterogenius	heterogeneous

heterogenous, -ly (foreign origin)	
heterosexual	
hethen	heathen
hether	heather
heuristic, -ally	
heve	heave
heven	heaven
hevenly	heavenly
hevily	heavily
hevy	heavy
hevywait	heavyweight
hew, hewed, hewn, hewing (cut)	
hew	hue (color)
hex	
hexagon	
hexagonal, -ly	
hexameter	
hey (interjection)	
hey	hay (grass)
heyday	

> For other **hi**- words, look under **hy**-.

hi (interjection)	
hi	high (up)
hiasinth	hyacinth
hiatus, -tuses	
hibernate, -nated, -nating	
hibiscus	
hibrid	hybrid
hiccup, -ed, -ing	
hich	hitch
hichhike	hitchhike
hick	
hickey	
hickory, -ries	
hicup	hiccup
hidden	
hide, hid, hiding	
hide-and-seek	
hideaway	
hidebound	
hideous, -ly, -ness	
hideout	
hidious	hideous
hier	hire
hierarchy, -chies	

hierarkey   hierarchy
hieroglific   hieroglyphic
hieroglyphic
hi-fi
high, -ly, -ness
high beam
highborn
highbrow
highchair
high-class
higher (up)
higher-up
    higher   hire (employ)
highfalutin
high fidelity
high-grade
high-handed, -ly, -ness
highland
highlight
high-minded, -ly, -ness
high-pitched
high-powered
high-pressure, -ed, -ing
high-rise
high-speed
high-spirited
high-strung
    hight   height
high-tension
high-test
highway
highwayman, -men
hijack, -ed, -ing
hike, -ed, -ing
    hil   hill
    hiland   highland
hilarious, -ly
    hilarius   hilarious
    hilight   highlight
    hilite   highlight
hill
hillbilly, -lies
hillock
hilly, hillier, hilliest
hilt
him (pronoun)
    him   hymn (song)

himself
hind
hinder, -ed, -ing
    hinderance   hindrance
hindquarter
hindrance
    hindranse   hindrance
hindsight
    hindsite   hindsight
Hindu
Hinduism
    hiness   highness
hinge, -ed, -ing
hint, -ed, -ing
hinterland
hip
    hipie   hippie
    hipopotamus   hippopotamus
    hippacritical   hypocritical
                              (deceitful)
hippie, -ies
Hippocratic (of Hippocrates)
hippopotamus, -muses, -mi
hipster
hire, hired, hiring (employ)
    hire   higher (up)
hireling
    hiroglific   hieroglyphic
hiss, -ed, -ing
    histerectomy   hysterectomy
    histeria   hysteria
    histery   history
histogram
historian
historic
historiography
history, -ries
    histrey   history
histrionic, -ally
hit, hit, hitting
hig-and-run
hitch, -ed, -ing
hitchhike, -hiked, -hiking
    hite   height
hither
hitherto
hive, -ed, -ing

hiway — highway

For other hi- words,
look under **hy-**.

ho — hoe
hoaks — hoax
hoard, -ed, -ing (gather)
hoard — horde (mob)
hoarding
hoare — whore
hoarse, hoarser, hoarsest (voice)
hoarse — hawse (ship)
hoarse — horse (animal)
hoary, hoarier, hoariest (old)
hoax, -ed, -ing
hob
hobbel — hobble
hobble, -bled, -bling
hobby, -bies
hobbyhorse
hobie — hobby
hobnail
hobnob, -nobbed, -nobbing
hobo, -bos, -boes
hock, -ed, -ing
hockey
hockie — hockey
hocus-pocus
hod
hoe, hoed, hoeing (tool)
hoes — hose (water)
hog, hogged, hogging
hogshead
hogshed — hogshead
hogwash
hoi polloi
hoist, -ed, -ing
hokem — hokum
hokum
hold, held, holding
holdup
hole, holed, holing (opening)
hole — whole (all)
holey (holes)
holey — wholly (all)
holiday
holie — holly (plant)

holie — holy (religion)
holie — wholly (all)
holihock — hollyhock
holiness
Holland
holler, -ed, -ing (shout)
hollow, -ly, -ness (hole)
holly, -lies (plant)
holly — wholly (all)
hollyhock
holocaust
holocost — holocaust
holow — hollow
holster
holy, -lier, -liest (religion)
holy — holly (plant)
holy — wholly (all)
homage
homburg
home, -ed, -ing
homebody
homebred
homecoming
home-grown
homeland
homeless
homely, -lier, -liest
homemade
homemaker
homeopathy
homeostasis
homeroom
home run
homesick
homespun
homestead
homestretch
homeward
homework
homicide
homige — homage
homiley — homily
homily, -lies
homiopathy — homeopathy
homiside — homicide
homogeneous, -ly (alike)
homogenius — homogeneous

homogenize, -nized, -nizing
  homonim   homonym
homogenous (corresponding)
homogeny
homonym
homophone
Homo sapiens
  homoseksual   homosexual
  homoseksuality homosexuality
homosexual
homosexuality
hone, honed, honing
honest, -ly
honesty
honey, honeys
honeybee
honeycomb
honeydew
honeymoon
honeysuckle
  honie   honey
honk, -ed, -ing
honky-tonk
Honolulu
honor, -ed, -ing
honorable, -bly
honorarium, -rariums, -raria
honorary
honorific, -ally
  hony   honey
hood, -ed, -ing
hoodlum
hoodwink, -ed, -ing
hoof, hoofs, hooves
hook, -ed, -ing
hookah (pipe)
hooker (prostitute)
  hookie   hooky
hookup
hookworm
hooky
  hoola-hoola hula-hula
hooligan
hoop (ring)
  hoop   whoop (cry)
  hooping coff whooping
                cough

hoopla
hooray
hoot, -ed, -ing
hootenanny, -nies
hooter
hop, hopped, hopping
hope, hoped, hoping
hope chest
hopeful, -ly, -ness
  hopefull   hopeful
hopeless, -ly, -ness
hopper
hopsacking
hopscotch
horde (group)
  horde   hoard (gather)
  hore   whore
  horendous horrendous
  horer   horror
  horible   horrible
  horid   horrid
  horific   horrific
  horify   horrify
horizon
horizontal, -ly
hormone
horn, -ed, -ing
hornbill
hornpipe
horn-rimmed
horny, -nier, -niest
horology
  horor   horror
horoscope
  horrable   horrible
horrendous, -ly
horrible, -bly
horrid, -ly
horrific
horrify, -fied, -fying
horror
hors d'oeuvre
horse, horses (animal)
horse, horsed, horsing (play around)
  horse   hawse (ship)
  horse   hoarse (voice)
horseback

horseflesh
horsefly
horsemanship
horseplay
horsepower
horse race
horseradish
horseshoe, -shoed, -shoeing
horsy, -sier, -siest
  hortaculture   horticulture
hortative, -ly
hortatory
  horthorn   hawthorn
horticulture
  hortie   haughty
hose, hosed, hosing (water)
  hose   hoes (tools)
hosiery
  hospetal   hospital
hospice
  hospiece   hospice
hospitable, -bly
hospital
hospitality, -ties
  hospitible   hospitable
host, -ed, -ing
hostage
  hostege   hostage
hostel
hostess
hostile, -ly
hostility, -ties
hot
hot, hotter, hottest
hot-blooded
hotel
hotelier
hotfoot
hothead
hotheaded, -ly, -ness
  hothed   hothead
  hotheded   hotheaded
hothouse
hot line
hotplate
hot potatoe
hot rod

hot seat
hotshot
hot tempered
hot-water bottle
hound, -ed, -ing
hound's-tooth
hour (time)
  hour   our (pronoun)
hourglass
houri, -ris
hourly
house, houses
house, housed, housing
houseboat
housebreaker
housebroken
housecoat
housefly, -flies
houseguest
household
housekeeper
housemaid
House of Representatives
house-to-house
housetrain
housewares
housewarming
housewife, -wives
housework
housing
hovel, -ed, -ing
hover, -ed, -ing
Hovercraft
how
howdy
however
howl, -ed, -ing
howler
  hownd   hound
  howse   house
how-to
hoyden
  hu   hew (cut)
  hu   hue (color)
hub
hubbub
hubby

huch | hutch
huckleberry, -berries
huckster
huddle, -dled, -dling
hue (color)
  hue | hew (cut)
  huf | huff
huff, -ed, -ing
hug, hugged, hugging
huge, huger, hugest
  hul | hull
hula-hula
  hulabaloo | hullabaloo
hulk
hull, -ed, -ing
hullabaloo
hum, hummed, humming
human (person)
humane, -ly (kind)
humanism
humanist
humanitarian
humanity, -ties
humankind
humanly
humble, -bled, -bling
humble, -bler, -blest
humbug, -bugged, -bugging
humdinger
humdrum
  humer | humor
  humerist | humorist
humerus, -meri (bone)
  humerus | humorous (funny)
humid, -ly
humidifier
humidify, -fied, -fying
humidity
humiliate, -ated, -ating
humiliation
humility, -ties
hummingbird
hummock
  humock | hummock
humor, -ed, -ing
humorist

humorous, -ly (funny)
  humorous | humerus (bone)
hump, -ed, -ing
humpback
humpy, -pier, -piest
humus
hunch, -ed, -ing
hunchback
hundred, -dreds
hundredfold
hundredth
  huney | honey
hunger
  hungrie | hungry
hungry, -grier, -griest
  hunie | honey
hunk
hunky-dory
  hunny | honey
hunt, -ed, -ing
  huntch | hunch
hunter
huntress
huntsman, -men
  huray | hurray
  hurd | heard (listen)
  hurd | herd (animals)
  hurdel | hurdle
  hurdiegurdie | hurdy-gurdy
hurdle, -dled, -dling
hurdy-gurdy, -dies
  huricane | hurricane
  hurie | hurry
hurl, -ed, -ing
  hurlie-burlie | hurly-burly
hurly-burly, -burlies
  hurmit | hermit
  hurnia | hernia
hurray (interjection)
  hurray | hurry (haste)
hurricane
hurry, -ried, -rying (haste)
  hurry | hurray (interjection)
  hurse | hearse
hurt, hurt, hurting
  hurtel | hurtle

hurtful, -fully
hurtle, -tled, -tling
  hurtz   hertz
  hury   hurry
husband
husbandry
hush, -ed, -ing
husk
  huskie   husky
husky, -kier, -kiest (hoarse)
husky, -kies (dog)
Hussars
  hussel   hustle
  hussey   hussy
hussy, -sies
hustings
hustle, -tled, -tling
hustler
hut
hutch
hyacinth
hybrid
hydra, -dras, -drae
hydrangea
hydrant
hydrate, -drated, -drating
hydration
hydraulic, -ally
hydrocarbon
hydrochloric acid
hydroelectric
  hydrofobia   hydrophobia
hydrofoil
hydrogen
hydrologist
hydrology
  hydrolic   hydraulic
hydrolysis, -ses
hydrometer
hydroplane, -planed, -planing
hydroponics
hydrosphere
hydrous
hydroxide
hyena
  hygene   hygiene
hygiene

hygienic, -ally
  hym   hymn
hymen
hymn (song)
  hymn   him (pronoun)
hymnal
hype, hyped, hyping
hyperactive
hyperbola, -las (curve)
hyperbole (overstatement)
hypercritical, -ally (overcritical)
  hypercritical   hypocritical
                      (pretending)
hypersensitive
hypertension
hyphen
hyphenate, -nated, -nating
hypnosis, -ses
hypnotherapy
hypnotism
hypnotize, -tized, -tizing
hypo
hypochondria
hypocrisy, -sies
hypocrite
hypocritical, -ally (pretending)
  hypocritical   hypercritical
                      (overcritical)
hypodermic
hypotenuse
hypothecate, -cated, -cating
hypothesis, -ses (supposition)
hypothesize, -sized, -sizing (frame a
hypothesis)
hypothetical, -ly
hysterectomy, -mies
hysteria
hysteric
hysterical, -ly
hysterectomy, -mies

Ii

ibis
ice, iced, icing
iceberg
icebound
icebox
icebreaker
ice-cold
ice cream
ice-cream cone
ice cube
ice pack
ice pick
ice-skate, -ed, -ing
iceskater

ich	itch

icicle
icing

iclesiastic	ecclesiastic
iclipse	eclipse

icon, icons
iconoclast

iconomist	economist
iconomy	economy

icy, icier, iciest
icily, -ness
idea
ideal, -ly (perfect)

ideal	idle (not busy)
ideal	idol (image)
ideal	idyll (writing)

idealism
idealize, -ized, -izing
idem
identical, -ly

identificasion	identification

identification
identify, -fied, -fying
identity, -ties

ideology, -gies

iderdown	eiderdown

ides

idia	idea
idill	idyll
idillic	idyllic

idiocy, -cies

idiology	ideology

idiom
idiomatic, -ally

idiosincrasy	idiosyncrasy

idiosyncrasy, -sies
idiot

idium	idiom

idle, idled, idling (inactive)

idle	idol (image)

idler
idly, -ness
idol (image)

idol	ideal (perfect)
idol	idle (not busy)
idol	idyll (writing)

idolatry, -tries
idolize, -lized, -lizing

idyl	idyll

idyll (writing)

idyll	ideal (perfect)
idyll	idle (not busy)
idyll	idol (image)

idyllic, -ally

ifface	efface
iffect	effect
Iffel	Eiffel
iffeminate	effeminate
ifficiency	efficiency
igalitarian	egalitarian

igloo, -loos

iglue	igloo

igneous

ignight	ignite

ignite, -nited, -niting
ignition

ignius	igneous

ignoble, -bly
ignominy, -minies

ignor	ignore

ignoramus, -muses

ignorance		ill	isle (island)
ignoranse	ignorance	ill-advised, -ly	
ignorant, -ly		ill-bred	
ignore, -nored, -noring		illegable	illegible
iguana		illegal, -ly	
igwana	iguana	illegible, -bly (unreadable)	
ijaculation	ejaculation	illegible	ineligible (not
ijection	ejection		qualified)
ikon, ikons		illegitimate, -ly	
ikuip	equip	ill-fated	
ikwivocal	equivocal	ill-favored	
ikwivocate	equivocate	ill-gotten	
il	I'll (I will)	illicit, -ly (unlawful)	
il	ill (sick)	illicit	elicit (evoke)
ilaberate	elaborate	Illinois	
iland	island	illiteracy	
ilapse	elapse	illiterate	
ilation	elation	ill-mannered, -ly	
ilastic	elastic	ill-natured, -ly	
ilate	elate	illness	
ile	aisle (path)	illogical, -ly	
Ile	I'll (I will)	ill-suited	
ile	isle (island)	ill-tempered	
ilect	elect	ill-timed	
ilection	election	ill-treat, -ed, -ing	
ilectorate	electorate	ill-treatment	
ilectrocute	electrocute	illuminate, -nated, -nating	
ilectronic	electronic	illumination	
ilegable	illegible	illumine, -mined, -mining	
ilegal	illegal	ill-usage	
ilegitimate	illegitimate	ill-use, -used, -using	
ileven	eleven	illusion (trick)	
ilicit	elicit	illusion	allusion
ilicit	illicit		(reference)
iliminate	eliminate	illusion	elusion
ilimination	elimination		(evasion)
ilipse	ellipse	illusive (tricky)	
iliptic	elliptic	illusive	allusive (refer)
ilisit	elicit	illusive	elusive (evade)
ilisit	illicit	illusory	
iliteracy	illiteracy	illustrate, -strated, -strating	
iliterate	illiterate	illustrater	illustrator
ilixir	elixir	illustration	
ilk		illustrative, -ly	
I'll (I will)		illustrator	
ill, worse, worst (sick)		illustrious, -ly, -ness	
ill	aisle (path)	ill will	

ilogical	illogical	imige	image
ilope	elope	imission	emission
ilucidate	elucidate	imit	emit
ilude	elude		

For other im- words, look under imm-.

iluminate	illuminate		
ilumination	illumination	imitate, -tated, -tating	
ilusidate	elucidate	imitation	
ilusion	allusion	immaculate, -ly	
ilusion	elusion	immanent (inherent)	
ilusion	illusion	immanent	eminent (known)
ilusive	allusive	immanent	imminent (near)
ilusive	elusive		
ilusive	illusive	immaterial, -ly	
ilustrate	illustrate	immature, -ly	
ilustration	illustration	immaturity	
ilustrator	illustrator	immeasurable, -bly	
ilustrious	illustrious	immediate, -ly	
I'm (I am)		immemorial, -ly	
Im	I'm	immense, -ly	
imaciate	emaciate	immerse, -mersed, -mersing	
imaculate	immaculate	immersion	
image, -aged, -aging		immesurable	immeasurable
imagery, -ries		immigrant (person entering)	
imagin	imagine	immigrant	emigrant (person leaving)
imaginary			
imagination		immigrate, -grated, -grating (enter)	
imaginative		immigrate	emigrate (leave)
imagine, -ined, -ining		imminent (near)	
imancipate	emancipate	imminent	eminent (known)
imancipation	emancipation		
imasiate	emaciate	imminent	immanent (inherent)
imaterial	immaterial		
imature	immature	immobile	
imaturity	immaturity	immobility	
imbalance		immoderate, -ly	
imbalanse	imbalance	immodest, -ly	
imbarrass	embarrass	immolate, -lated, -lating	
imbecile, -cilic		immoral, -ly	
imbeseal	imbecile	immortal, -ly	
imbibe, -bibed, -bibing		immortality, -ties	
imbroglio, -os		immortalize, -lized, -lizing	
imbue, -bued, -buing		immortel	immortal
imerge	emerge	immovable, -bly	
imergence	emergence	immovible	immovable
imergency	emergency	immune, -ly	
imergent	emergent		
imetic	emetic		

immunity
immunize, -nized, -nizing
immunology
immure, -mured, -muring
immutable, -bly
imolient	emollient
imolument	emolument
imotion	emotion
imotional	emotional
imotive	emotive

imp
impact, -ed, -ing
impair, -ed, -ing
impale, -paled, -paling
impalpable, -bly
impanel, -ed, -ing
| impare | impair |

impart, -ed, -ing
| impartal | impartial |

impartial, -ly
impasable	impassable
impasioned	impassioned
impasive	impassive

impassable, -bly
impasse
| impassible | impassable |

impassioned, -ly
impassive, -ly
| impatiant | impatient |

impatient, -ly
impeach, -ed, -ing
impeccable, -bly
| impecunios | impecunious |

impecunious, -ly
impede, -peded, -peding
impediment
| impeech | impeach |

impel, -pelled, -pelling
impenetrable, -bly
| impenge | impinge |

imperative, -ly
imperceptible, -bly
imperfect, -ly
imperial, -ly (rule)
| imperial | empirical |
| | (experiment) |

imperialism

imperil, -ed, -ing (endanger)
imperious, -ly
| imperius | imperious |

impermeable, -bly
| impermiable | impermeable |
| imperseptible | imperceptible |

impersonal, -ly
impersonate, -nated, -nating
impertinence
| impertinense | impertinence |

imperturbable, -bly
impervious, -ly
| impervius | impervious |

impetuous, -ly
impetus, -tuses
impiety, -ties
impinge, -pinged, -pinging
impious, -ly
impish, -ly
| impius | impious |

implacable, -bly
| implacible | implacable |

implant, -ed, -ing
implausible, -bly
| implament | implement |

implement, -ed, -ing
implicate, -cated, -cating
implication
implicit, -ly
| implie | imply |

implied
| implisit | implicit |

implode, -ploded, -ploding
implore, -plored, -ploring
| imployee | employee |

imply, -plied, -plying
impolite, -ly
impolitic, -ly
import, -ed, -ing
importance
| importanse | importance |

important, -ly
importunate, -ly
importune, -tuned, -tuning
impose, -posed, -posing
| imposible | impossible |
| imposision | imposition |

imposition
impossible, -bly
  imposter   impostor
impostor
imposture
  impotance   impotence
  impotant   impotent
impotence
impotent, -ly
impound, -ed, -ing
impoverish, -ed, -ing
impracticability
impracticable, -bly
impractical, -ly
  impracticible   impracticable
imprecate, -cated, -cating
imprecise, -ly, -ness
impregnable, -bly
  impregnible   impregnable
impregnate, -nated, -nating
  impres   impress
impresario, -os
  impresion   impression
  impreshunable impressionable
  impresionism   impressionism
  impresise   imprecise
  impresive   impressive
impress, -ed, -ing
impression
impressionable, -bly
impressionism
impressive, -ly, -ness
imprimatur
imprint, -ed, -ing
imprison, -ed, -ing
improbable, -bly
impromptu
  impromtu   impromptu
improper, -ly
  impropriaty   impropriety
impropriety, -ties
improve, -proved, -proving
improvement
improvident, -ly
improvise, -vised, -vising
imprudent, -ly
  impruve   improve

impudent, -ly
impugn, -ed, -ing
impulse
  impune   impugn
impunity
impure, -ly
impute, -puted, -puting
  imulsion   emulsion
  imune   immune
  imunology   immunology
  imurge   emerge
in (preposition)
  in   inn (hotel)
inability
  in absenshia   in absentia
in absentia
  inaccessable   inaccessible
inaccessible, -bly
inaccuracy, -cies
inactive, -ly
  inacuracy   inaccuracy
  inadekwat   inadequate
inadequate, -ly
inadvertent, -ly
inalienable, -bly
  inalienible   inalienable
inane, -ly (pointless)
  inane   insane (mad)
inanimate, -ly
  inappreciabel inappreciable
inappreciable, -bly
inappropriate, -ly
  inapropriate   inappropriate
inapt, -ly
inaptitude
inarticulate, -ly
inasmuch as
  inate   innate
  inatentive   inattentive
inattentive
  inaugral   inaugural
inaugural
inaugurate, -rated, -rating
inauspicious, -ly, -ness
  inbibe   imbibe
inborn
inbred

inbreed, -bred, -breeding
incalculable, -bly
incandescence
incandescent, -ly
  incandesence   incandescence
incantation
incapable, -bly
incapacitate, -tated, -tating
incapacity, -ties
  incapasitate   incapacitate
  incapasity   incapacity
  incapible   incapable
incarcerate, -rated, -rating
incarnate, -nated, -nating
  incarserate   incarcerate
incendiary, -aries
incense (perfume)
incense, -censed, -censing (angry)
incentive
inception
incessant, -ly
  incessent   incessant
incest
incestuous, -ly
inch, -ed, -ing
incidence (range of occurrence)
  incidence   instance
                  (example)
incident (occurrence)
  incident   instant (space
                  of time)
incidental, -ly
incinerate, -rated, -rating
  incinerater   incincerator
incinerator
incipient, -ly
incise, -cised, -cising
  inciser   incisor
incision
incisive, -ly
incisor
incite, -cited, -citing (urge)
  incite   insight (see)
incivility, -ties
inclement
inclination
incline, -clined, -clining

  inclose   enclose
include, -cluded, -cluding
inclusion
inclusive, -ly
incoherent, -ly
incognito
income
incommensurable, -bly
incommensurate, -ly
incommode, -moded, -moding
incommodity, -ties
incommunicability
incommunicable, -bly
incommunicado
incommunicative, -ly
incomparable, -bly
  incompatable   incompatible
incompatible, -bly
incompetence
incompetent, -ly
incomplete, -ly
incomprehensible, -bly
incomprehension
  incomunicado   incommunicado
inconceivable, -bly
  inconcievable   inconceivable
inconclusive, -ly
  incongrous   incongruous
incongruous, -ly
  inconseavable   inconceivable
inconsequent, -ly
inconsequential, -ly
inconsiderate, -ly
  inconsistant   inconsistent
inconsistent, -ly
inconsolable, -bly
  inconsolible   inconsolable
inconspicuous, -ly
inconstant, -ly
incontestable, -bly
  incontestible   incontestable
incontinence
incontinent
incontrovertible, -bly
inconvenience, -ienced, -iencing
inconvenient, -ly
  incorect   incorrect

incorigible — incorrigible
incorporate, -rated, -rating
incorporation
incorrect, -ly
incorrigible, -bly
incorrupt, -ly
incorruptible, -bly
increase, -creased, -creasing
incredable — incredible
incredible, -bly
incredulity
incredulous, -ly
incredulus — incredulous
increment
incremental
increse — increase
incriminate, -nated, -nating
incubate, -bated, -bating
incubater — incubator
incubator
inculcate, -cated, -cating
incum — income
incumbent, -ly
incumbrance
incur, -curred, -curring
incurable, -bly
incurible — incurable
incursion
incurson — incursion
indebted
indecent, -ly
indecipherable
indecision
indecisive, -ly
indecison — indecision
indeclinable
indeclinible — indeclinable
indecorous, -ly
indecorus — indecorous
indeed
indefatigable, -bly
indefatigible — indefatigable
indefeasible, -bly
indefeasible — indefeasible
indefensable — indefensible
indefensible, -bly
indefinable, -bly

indefinible — indefinable
indefinite, -ly
indeks — index
indelable — indelible
indelible, -bly
indelicate, -ly
indemnifie — indemnify
indemnify, -fied, -fying
indemnity, -ties
indent, -ed, -ing
indenture, -tured, -turing
independence
independent, -ly
in-depth
indescribable, -bly
indescribible — indescribable
indesent — indecent
indesiferable — indecipherable
indespensable — indispensable
indestructable — indestructible
indestructible, -bly
indeted — indebted
indeterminate, -ly
index, -dexes, -dices
indexation
Indian
India rubber
indicate, -cated, -cating
indicater — indicator
indicative, -ly
indicator
indices
indict, -ed, -ing
indictment
indiferent — indifferent
indifferent, -ly
indigenous, -ly
indigent, -ly
indigestable — indigestible
indigestible, -bly
indigestion
indignant, -ly
indignation
indignity, -ties
indigo, -gos, -goes
indipendent — independent
indirect, -ly

indiscreet, -ly
  indiscresion   indiscretion
  indiscrete   indiscreet
indiscretion
indiscriminate, -ly
  indisishun   indecision
  indisisive   indecisive
  indisoluble   indissoluble
indispensable, -bly
  indispensible   indispensable
indisposed
  indisposision   indisposition
indisposition
indisputable, -bly
  indisputible   indisputable
indissoluble, -bly
indistinct, -ly
indistinguishable, -bly
indite, -dited, -diting (write)
  indite   indict (accuse)
  inditment   indictment
individual, -ly
individualism
individualist
individuality, -ties
  indivisable   indivisible
indivisible, -bly
indoctrinate, -nated, -nating
indolent, -ly
indomitable, -bly
  indomitible   indomitable
indoor
indubitable, -bly
  indubitible   indubitable
induce, -duced, -ducing
  inducktion   induction
induct, -ed, -ing
  inducter   inductor
induction
inductive, -ly
inductor
indulge, -dulged, -dulging
indulgence
  indulgense   indulgence
indulgent, -ly
  industrey   industry
industrial, -ly

industrialism
industrialist
industrialize, -lized, -lizing
industrious, -ly
  industrius   industrious
industry, -tries
inebriate, -ated, -ating
inebriation
  inedable   inedible
inedible
  inefable   ineffable
  inefective   ineffective
  inefectual   ineffectual
ineffable
ineffective, -ly
ineffectual, -ly
inefficient, -ly

> For **ineks-** words, look
> under **inex-**.

inelegant, -ly
  ineligable   ineligible
ineligible, -bly
inept, -ly
inequality, -ties
inequitable, -bly
  inequitible   inequitable
inequity, -ties (unfairness)
  inequity   iniquity
              (wickedness)
ineradicable, -bly
  ineradicible   ineradicable
  inersha   inertia
inert, -ly
inertia
inescapable, -bly
  inescapible   inescapable
  inesential   inessential
inessential, -ly
inestimable, -bly
  inestimible   inestimable
inevitable, -bly
  inevitible   inevitable
inexact, -ly
inexcusable, -bly
inexhaustible, -bly
inexorable, -bly

inexorible / inexorable
inexpedient, -ly
inexpensive, -ly
inexperienced
inexperiense / inexperience
inexpert, -ly
inexplicable, -bly
inexplicit, -ly
inexpressible, -bly
in extremis
inextricable, -bly
infalible / infallible
infallible, -bly
infaltrate / infiltrate
infamey / infamy
infamous, -ly
infamus / infamous
infamy, -mies
infancy, -cies
infansy / infancy
infant
infanticide
infantiside / infanticide
infantile
infantrey / infantry
infantry
infatuate, -ated, -ating
infatuation
infecktion / infection
infect, -ed, -ing
infection
infectious, -ly
infelicity, -ties
infer, -ferred, -ferring
inference
inferense / inference
inferier / inferior
inferior
inferiority complex
inferm / infirm
infermarey / infirmary
infernal, -ly
inferno, -nos
infertile
infest, -ed, -ing
infidel
infidelity, -ties

infighting
infiltrate, -trated, -trating
infinite, -ly
infinitesimal, -ly
infinitey / infinity
infinitive, -ly
infinity, -ties
infirior / inferior
infirm, -ly
infirmary, -ries
inflamable / inflammable
inflamatry / inflammatory
inflame, -flamed, -flaming
inflammable, -bly
inflammation
inflammatory
inflatable
inflate, -flated, -flating
inflatible / inflatable
inflation
inflect, -ed, -ing
inflection
inflexible, -bly
inflict, -ed, -ing
infliction
inflow
influence, -enced, -encing
influense / influence
influensial / influential
influential, -ly
influenza
influks / influx
inform, -ed, -ing
informal, -ly
informant
information
informent / informant
informer
infrcaktion / infraction
infraction
infrared
infrastructure
infrekwency / infrequency
infrekwent / infrequent
infrequency
infrequent, -ly
infringe, -fringed, -fringing

infuriate, -ated, -ating
  infurnal   infernal
infuse, -fused, -fusing
infusion
  infuson   infusion
ingenious, -ly (clever)
  ingenius   ingenious
ingenue
ingenuity, -ties
  ingenuos   ingenuous
ingenuous, -ly (innocent)
ingest, -ed, -ing
ingestion
  Inglish   English
ingot
ingrain, -ed, -ing
  ingrasiate   ingratiate
ingrate
ingratiate, -ated, -ating
ingratitude
  ingrave   engrave
ingredient
ingress
ingrown
inhabit, -ed, -ing
inhalant
inhalation
inhale, -haled, -haling
  inhear   inhere
inhere, -hered, -hering
inherent, -ly
inherit, -ed, -ing
inheritance
  inheritanse   inheritance
  inhibision   inhibition
inhibit, -ed, -ing
inhospitable, -bly
inhospitality
  inhospitible   inhospitable
in-house
inhuman, -ly
inhumane, -ly
inhumanity, -ties
  inikwality   inequality
  inikwity   iniquity
  inikwitus   iniquitous
inimical, -ly

inimitable, -bly
inimitability
  inimitible   inimitable
  inings   innings
  iniquitey   iniquity
iniquitous, -ly
  iniquitus   iniquitous
iniquity, -ties (wickedness)
  iniquity   inequity
                 (unfairness)
  inital   initial
  initate   initiate
initial, -ed, -ing
initiate, -ated, -ating
initiation
initiative
  inititive   initiative
inject, -ed, -ing
injection
  injenue   ingenue
  injere   injure
injudicious, -ly
  injudisious   injudicious
injunction
  injunktion   injunction
injure, -jured, -juring
  injurey   injury
  injurius   injurious
injury, -ries
injustice
  injustise   injustice
ink
  inkeeper   innkeeper
inkling
  inkwest   inquest
  inkwire   enquire
  inkwisitive   inquisitive
  inkwisitor   inquisitor

> For other ink- words,
> look under inc-.

  inlade   inlaid
inland
in-law
inlay, -laid, -laying
inlet
inmate

in memoriam
inmost
inn (hotel)
   inn — in (prep.)
innards
innate, -ly
inner
   innerject — interject
innermost
innings
innkeeper
innocence
innocent, -ly
innocuous, -ly
innovate, -vated, -vating
innovation
innovative, -ly
innovatory
innuendo, -dos
innumerable, -bly
innumerate
   inocent — innocent
inoculate, -lated, -lating
inoculation
   inocuos — innocuous
   inofensive — inoffensive
inoffensive, -ly
inoperable, -bly
inoperative, -ly
   inoportune — inopportune
inopportune, -ly
   inordable — inaudible
   inordible — inaudible
inordinate, -ly
inorganic, -ally
   inorgural — inaugural
   inorgurate — inaugurate
   inormity — enormity
   inormous — enormous
   inorspisious — inauspicious
   inosence — innocence
   inosent — innocent
   inough — enough
   inovate — innovate
inpatient
   inpayshent — inpatient
input

inquest
inquietude
inquire, -quired, -quiring
inquiry, -ries
inquisitive, -ly, -ness
   inrage — enrage
inroad
   inrode — inroad
   insalation — insulation
insalubrious, -ly
   insalubrius — insalubrious
   insaine — insane
   insamnia — insomnia
insane, -ly (mad)
   insane — inane (pointless)
   insanitey — insanity
insanity, -ties (mental disorder)
   insatable — insatiable
insatiable, -bly
inscribe, -scribed, -scribing
inscription
inscrutable, -bly
inscrutability
insect
insecticide
   insectiside — insecticide
insecure, -ly
insecurity, -ties
inseminate, -nated, -nating
insemination
   insendiary — incendiary
   insensable — insensible
insensate, -ly
   insense — incense
insensible, -bly
insensibility, -ties
insensitive, -ly
insensitivity
   insentive — incentive
inseparable, -bly
   inseperible — inseparable
   insepsion — inception
insert, -ed, -ing
insertion
   insertitude — incertitude
   insesent — incessant

insest	incest	inspecktion	inspection
insestuous	incestuous	inspect, -ed, -ing	
inset, -set, -setting		inspecter	inspector
inshore	ensure (certain)	inspection	
inshore	insure (protect)	inspector	
inshorense	insurance	inspiration	
inside		inspire, -spired, -spiring	
insidense	incidence	instability	
insident	incident	instagate	instigate
insidental	incidental	install, -ed, -ing	
insidious, -ly		installation (to place)	
insidius	insidious	installment	
insight, (see)		instalment	
insight	incite (urge)	instance, -stanced, -stancing	
insignia		(example)	
insignificance		instance	incidence
insignificant, -ly			(range of
insincere, -ly			occurrence)
insincerity, -ties		instant, -ly (space of time)	
insinerate	incinerate	instant	incident
insinerater	incinerator		(occurrence)
insinsere	insincere	instantaneous, -ly	
insinserity	insincerity	instantanius	instantaneous
insinuate, -ated, -ating		instatution	institution
insipid, -ly		instead	
insipient	incipient	insted	instead
insiser	inciser	instep	
insision	incision	instigate, -gated, -gating	
insisive	incisive	instigater	instigator
insist, -ed, -ing		instigation	
insistance	insistence	instigator	
insistence		instilation	instillation
insistent, -ly		instill, -ed, -ing	
insite	incite (urge)	installation (to infuse)	
insite	insight (see)	instinct	
insivility	incivility	instinctive, -ly	
insobriety		instink	instinct
insofar		institute, -tuted, -tuting	
insolence		institution	
insolense	insolence	institutional, -ly	
insolent, -ly		institutionalize, -lized, -lizing	
insolubility		instrament	instrument
insoluble, -bly		instruct, -ed, -ing	
insolvency		instruction	
insolvensy	insolvency	instructive, -ly	
insolvent		instrument	
insomnia		instrumental, -ly	

instrumentalist		inteligense	intelligence
instrumentation		inteligensia	intelligentsia
instrument panel		inteligent	intelligent
insubordinate, -ly		inteligible	intelligible
insubordination		intellect	
insubstantial, -ly		intellectual, -ly	
insue	ensue	intelligence	
insufferable, -bly		intelligent, -ly	
insufficiency		intelligentsia	
insufficient, -ly		intemperance	
insufiency	insufficiency	intemperanse	intemperance
insufrable	insufferable	intemperate, -ly	
insular, -ly		intend, -ed, -ing	
insularity		intense, -ly	
insulate, -lated, -lating		intensify, -fied, -fying	
insulation		intension	intention
insulin		intensive, -ly	
insult, -ed, -ing		intent, -ly	
insuperable, -bly		intention	
insuperible	insuperable	intentional, -ly	
insurance (protection)		inter, -terred, -terring	
insurance	assurance	interact, -ed, -ing	
	(certainty)	interaction	
insure, -sured, -suring (guarantee)		inter alia	
insure	assure (certain)	intercede, -ceded, -ceding	
insurgence		intercept, -ed, -ing	
insurgency		intercepter	interceptor
insurgense	insurgence	interception	
insurgent		interceptor	
insurmountable, -bly		intercesser	intercessor
insurrection		intercession	
insurt	insert	intercessor	
insurtion	insertion	interchange, -changed, -changing	
intact		interchangeable, -bly	
intaglio, intaglios		intercom	
intail	entail	intercontinental	
intake		intercorse	intercourse
intangable	intangible	intercourse	
intangible, -bly		interdepartmental	
integer		interdependence	
integral, -ly		interdependency	
integrate, -grated, -grating		interdependent, -ly	
integrated circuit		interdict	
integration		interdisciplinary	
integrity		interelate	interrelate
intelect	intellect	interest, -ed, -ing	
intelectual	intellectual	interface, -faced, -facing	

interfear — interfere
interfere, -fered, -fering
interference
interfuse, -fused, -fusing
intergalactic
interier — interior
interim
interior
interject, -ed, -ing
interjecter — interjector
interjection
interjector
interlace, -laced, -lacing
interline, -lined, -lining
interlock, -ed, -ing
interloap — interlope
interlood — interlude
interlope, -loped, -loping
interloper
interlude
interlopor — interloper
intermarie — intermarry
intermarry, -ried, -rying
intermediary, -aries
intermediate, -ly
interment
intermesh, -ed, -ing
intermezzo, -zos, -zi
interminable, -bly
interminible — interminable
intermision — intermission
intermission
intermittent, -ly
intern
internal, -ly
internalization
internalize, -lized, -lizing
international, -ly
internationalism
internecine
internee
internisine — internecine
interogate — interrogate
interpersonal, -ly
interplay, -ed, -ing
interpolate, -lated, -lating
interpose, -posed, -posing

interpret, -ed, -ing
interpretation
interpreter
interpretor — interpreter
interracial, -ly
interregnum, -nums
interrelate, -lated, -lating
interrogate, -gated, -gating
interrogater — interrogator
interrogation
interrogative, -ly
interrogator
interrupt, -ed, -ing
interruption
intersect, -ed, -ing
intersection
intersede — intercede
intersepsion — interception
intersept — intercept
intersesion — intercession
intersperse, -spersed, -spersing
interspurse — intersperse
interstate (between states)
interstate — intestate (no will)
interstate — intrastate (within state)
interstice, -tices
intertwine, -twined, -twining
interuption — interruption
interurban
interval
interveiw — interview
intervene, -vened, -vening
intervener
intervenor — intervener
intervension — intervention
intervention
interview, -ed, -ing
interviewer
interviewor — interviewer
intervue — interview
interweave, -woven, -weaving
intestate (no will)
intestate — interstate (between states)

intestate	intrastate	intricacy, -cies	
	(within a state)	intricasy	intricacy
intestine		intricate, -ly	
intice	entice	intrigue, -trigued, -triguing	
intiger	integer	intrinsic, -ally	
intigral	integral	introduce, -duced, -ducing	
intigrate	integrate	introducksion	introduction
intimacy, -cies		introduction	
intimasy	intimacy	introductory	
intimate, -ly		introduse	introduce
intimate, -mated, -mating		introode	intrude
intimation		introosive	intrusive
intimidate, -dated, -dating		introspection	
intimidater	intimidator	introvert, -ly	
intimidation		intrude, -truded, -truding	
intimidator		intruder	
intirety	entirety	intrusion	
intoksicate	intoxicate	intrusive, -ly	
intolerable, -bly		intruson	intrusion
intolerance		intrust	entrust
intoleranse	intolerance	intuision	intuition
intolerant, -ly		intuition	
intonation		intuitive, -ly	
intone, -toned, -toning		inturn	intern
in toto		inturnal	internal
intoxicant		inuendo	innuendo
intoxicate, -cated, -cating		inumerable	innumerable
intoxication		inumerate	enumerate
intractable, -bly		inumeration	enumeration
intractible	intractable	inunciate	enunciate
intransigence		inundate, -dated, -dating	
intransigency		inundation	
intransigense	intransigence	inunsiate	enunciate
intransigensy	intransigency	inure, inured, inuring	
intransigent, -ly		inurt	inert
intransitive, -ly		inurtia	inertia
intrastate (within a state)		invacation	invocation
intrastate	interstate	invade, -vaded, -vading	
	(between	invagle	inveigle
	states)	invalid, -ly	
intrastate	intestate (no	invalidate, -dated, -dating	
	will)	invalidation	
intrauterine device		invaluable, -bly	
intravenous, -ly		invaluble	invaluable
intravenus	intravenous	invariability	
intreege	intrigue	invariable, -bly	
intrepid, -ly		invasion	

invatation	invitation	invoke, -voked, -voking	
invay	inveigh	involuntary, -tarily	
invazion	invasion	involuntery	involuntary
invective, -ly		involusion	involution
inveigh, -ed, -ing		involution	
inveigle, -gled, -gling		involve, -volved, -volving	
inveigel	inveigle	involvement	
invension	invention	invulnerable, -bly	
invent, -ed, -ing		invulnerible	invulnerable
inventer	inventor	invurce	inverse
invention		invurt	invert
inventive, -ly		inward, -ly	
inventor		inwardness	
inventory, -tories		inwood	inward
inverse, -ly		inyure	inure
inversion		iodene	iodine
inverson	inversion	iodine	
invert, -ed, -ing		ion (atom)	
invertebrate		ion	iron (metal)
invest, -ed, -ing		ionesfear	ionosphere
investagation	investigation	ionize, -nized, -nizing	
investigate, -gated, -gating		ionosphere	
investigater	investigator	iony	irony
investigation		iota	
investigator		iphemeral	ephemeral
investiture		iradiate	irradiate
investment		iradicate	eradicate
inveterate		irascable	irascible
invidios	invidious	irascibility	
invidious, -ly		irascible, -bly	
inviegh	inveigh	irase	erase
inviegle	inveigle	irate, -ly	
invigorate, -rated, -rating		irational	irrational
invincible, -bly (unbeatable)		ire	
invinsibul	invincible	ireny	irony
inviolable, -bly		ires	iris
inviolate, -ly			

<table>
For other ir- words,
look under irr-.
</table>

inviolible	inviolable	iridesense	iridescence
invisable	invisible	iridesent	iridescent
invisibility		iridescence	
invisible, -bly (unseen)		iris, irises	
invitation		Irish	
invite, -vited, -viting		irk	
in vitro		irksome, -ly	
invocation		irksum	irksome
invoice, -voiced, -voicing			
invoise	invoice		

irode	erode	irrespective, -ly	
iron, -ed, -ing (metal)		irresponsable	irresponsible
iron	ion (atom)	irresponsibility	
ironeus	erroneous	irresponsible, -bly	
ironic, -ally		irretraceable, -bly	
ironware		irretraseable	irretraceable
ironwork		irretrievable, -bly	
ironworker		irretrievible	irretrievable
irony, -nies		irrevelent	irrelevant
irosion	erosion	irreverence	
irotic	erotic	irreverent, -ly (disrespectful)	
irradiate, -ated, -ating		irreverent	irrelevant (not
irradiation			pertinent)
irrational, -ly		irreversable	irreversible
irreconcilable, -bly		irreversibility	
irrecoverable, -bly		irreversible, -bly	
irrecoverible	irrecoverable	irrevocable, -bly	
irredeemable, -bly		irrevocible	irrevocable
irredeemible	irredeemable	irridescent	iridescent
irreducable	irreducible	irrigate, -gated, -gating	
irreducibility		irrigation	
irreducible, -bly		irrisistible	irresistible
irrefutable, -bly		irritability	
irrefutible	irrefutable	irritable, -bly	
irregular, -ly		irritancy	
irregularity, -ties		irritansy	irritancy
irrelavent	irrelevant	irritant	
irrelevance		irritate, -tated, -tating	
irrelevancy		irritation	
irrelevansy	irrelevancy	irritible	irritable
irrelevant, -ly (not pertinent)		irrupsion	irruption
irrelevant	irreverent	irrupt, -ed, -ing	
	(disrespectful)	irruption (break in)	
irreligious, -ly		irruption	eruption
irreligous	irreligious		(outburst)
irrepairable	irreparable	irruptive, -ly	
irreparable, -bly		isalate	isolate
irreparible	irreparable	isatope	isotope
irreplacable	irreplaceable	ise	ice
irreplaceable, -bly		isicle	icicle
irrepresable	irrepressible	isight	eyesight
irrepressible, -bly		Islam	
irreproachable, -bly		Islamic	
irreproachible	irreproachable	island	
irresistable	irresistible	islander	
irresistible, -bly		isle (island)	
irresolute, -ly		isle	aisle (path)

isn't (is not)
   isnt   isn't
isobar
isolate, -lated, -lating
isolation
isolationism
isolationist
isosceles
   isoseles   isosceles
isotope
Israeli
   Isralie   Israeli
issue, issued, issuing
isthmus, -muses
   istmus   isthmus
   isue   issue
italic
itch, -ed, -ing (scratch)
   itch   etch (engrave)
item
itemize, -mized, -mizing
iterate, -rated, -rating
iteration
   iternal   eternal
   iternally   eternally
   iternity   eternity
itinerant, -ly
itinerary, -ries
it'll (it will)
   itll   it'll
it's (it is)
its (possessive)
   its   it's (it is)
itself
   ivacuate   evacuate
   ivacuation   evacuation
   ivade   evade
   ivaluate   evaluate
   ivaluation   evaluation
   ivaporate   evaporate
   ivaporation   evaporation
   ivasion   evasion
   ivasive   evasive
I've (I have)
   Ive   I've
   ivent   event
   iventual   eventual

   ivery   ivory
   ivey   ivy
   ivict   evict
   iviction   eviction
   ivoke   evoke
   ivolve   evolve
ivory, -ries
ivory tower
   ivry   ivory
ivy, ivies
Ivy League

Jj

jab, jabbed, jabbing
jabber
jacaranda
jack
jackal
jackass
jackdaw
   jackdoor   jackdaw
jacket
jackhammer
jack-in-the-box
jackknife, -knives
jack-of-all-trades
jack-o'-lantern
jackpot
jackrabbit
Jacobean
jade, jaded, jading
jag
jagged
jaguar
jail
jailbird
jailbreak
jailer, jailor
jalopy, -lopies
jam, jammed, jamming
jam (food)
   jam   jamb (door)
jamb (door)
   jamb   jam (food)
jamboree
   jamborie   jamboree
   jangel   jangle
jangle, -gled, -gling
   janiter   janitor
janitor
January

   Janurey   January
Japanese, -nese
jape, japed, japing
japonica
jar, jarred, jarring
jargon
   jasmin   jasmine
jasper
jaundice
jaundiced
   jaundise   jaundice
jaunt
   jauntie   jaunty
jaunty, -tier, -tiest
javelin
   javlin   javelin
jaw
jawbone
jawbreaker
   jawnt   jaunt
jay
jaywalk, -ed, -ing
jaywalker
   jaz   jazz
jazz
jazzy, -zier, -ziest
jealous, -ly
jealousy, -ousies
   jealus   jealous
jeans (trousers)
   jeans   genes (Biol.)
   jeapardy   jeopardy
   jear   jeer
   jeens   jeans
jeep
jeer, -ed, -ing
Jehovah
Jehovah's Witness, -es
jejune
   jelie   jelly
   jell   gel
jelly, -lies
jelly, -lied, -lying
jellyfish, -fish, -fishes
   jelous   jealous
   jely   jelly
jeopardize, -dized, -dizing

jeopardy		jingle, -gled, -gling	
jepardize	jeopardize	jingoism	
jepardy	jeopardy	jinks	jinx
jeranium	geranium	jinx, -es	
jerboa		jipsum	gypsum
jeribilt	jerry-built	jiration	gyration
jerk, -ed, -ing		jiro	gyro
jerkin		jiroscope	gyroscope
jerkwater		jist	gist
jerky, -kily		jiter	jitter
jersey		jitney	
jersie	jersey	jitter, -ed, -ing	
jest, -ed, -ing		jittery	
jester		jive, jived, jiving	
jesticulate	gesticulate	job, jobbed, jobbing (work)	
jestor	jester	Job (bible char.)	
Jesuit		jobber	
Jesus		jobholder	
jet, jetted, jetting		jockey, -eys	
jetison	jettison	jockey, -eyed, -eying	
jet lag		jockstrap	
jettison, -ed, -ing		jocky	jockey
jetty, -ties		jocose, -ly	
jety	jetty	jocosity, -ties	
jeuse	juice	jocular, -ly	
Jew		jocularity, -ties	
jewel, -ed, -ing (cut gem)		jocund, -ly	
jewel	joule (unit)	jocundity, -ties	
jeweler		jodhpurs	
Jewish		jodpurs	jodhpurs
Jewry (Jewish people)		jog, jogged, jogging	
jewry	jury (court)	jogger	
jib, jibbed, jibbing (refuse)		joggor	jogger
jibe, jibed, jibing (sail)		jogtrot	
jibe	gibe (scoff)	johnnycake	
jiffy, -fies		johnquil	jonquil
jify	jiffy	joi	joy
jig, jigged, jigging		join, joined, joining	
jigger		joiner	
jiggle, -gled, -gling		joint, -ly	
jigle	jiggle	joist	
jigsaw		joke, joked, joking	
jilt, -ed, -ing		joker	
jim	gym	jollitey	jollity
jimkana	gymkhana	jollity, -ties	
jin	gin	jolly, -lier, -liest	
jingel	jingle	jolt, -ed, -ing	

joly	jolly	judiciary, -aries	
jonquil		judicious, -ly	
Joo	Jew	judisial	judicial
Jooish	Jewish	judisiary	judiciary
jool	joule (unit)	judisious	judicious
Joone	June	judo	
joopiter	Jupiter	juel	jewel (gem)
joose	juice (liquid)	juel	joule (unit)
joote	jute	jug, jugged, jugging	
josle	jostle	juge	judge
jostle, -tled, -tling		juggement	judgement
jot, jotted, jotting		juggernaut	
joule (unit)		juggle, -gled, -gling	
joule	jewel (gem)	juggler (performer)	
journal		jugitsu	jujitsu
journalese		jugle	juggle
journalism		jugular (vein)	
journalist		juice (liquid)	
journel	journal	juiciness	
journey, -neys		juicy, -cier, -ciest	
journey, -neyed, -neying		juiniper	juniper
joust, -ed, -ing		Juish	Jewish
Jove		jujitsu	
jovial, -ly		jukebox	
joviality		jukstapose	juxtapose
jowl		julep	
joy		Juli	July
joyful, -ly		julip	julep
joyous, -ly		July	
joyride, -rode, -riding		jumble, -bled, -bling	
joystick		jumbo, -bos	
joyus	joyous	jumbuck	
jubalee	jubilee	jump, -ed, -ing	
jube		jumper	
jubilant, -ly		jump start	
jubilate, -lated, -lating		jump suit	
jubilation		jumpy, jumpier, jumpiest	
jubilee		junco, juncos, juncoes	
juce	juice (liquid)	junction	
judacature	judicature	juncture	
Judaism		June	
Judas		jungel	jungle
judge, judged, judging		jungle	
judgement		junier	junior
judgment		junior	
judicature		junipar	juniper
judicial, -ly		juniper	

junk
junket
junkie
  junkit — junket
  junktion — junction
  junkture — juncture
junta
Jupiter (planet)
  jurasdiction — jurisdiction
  jurer — juror
  juri — jury
juridical, -ly
  jurisdicktion — jurisdiction
jurisdiction
jurisprudence
  jurisprudense — jurisprudence
jurist
  jurk — jerk
  jurnal — journal
  jurney — journey
juror
  jursey — jersey
jury, -ries
  juse — juice
  jusie — juicy
just, -ly
  justafiable — justifiable
justice
justice of the peace
justifiable, -bly
justification
justify, -fied, -fying
  justise — justice
jut, jutted, jutting
jute
juvenile, -ly
  juwel — jewel (gem)
  juwel — joule (unit)
  juxapose — juxtapose
  juxaposition — juxtaposition
juxtapose, -posed, -posing
juxtaposition
  jym — gym
  jyroscope — gyroscope

Kk

Look under c if
the word is not under **k**.

kaleidoscope
kalidascope — kaleidoscope
kamikaze
kampong
kangaroo
kanine — canine
kaolin
kaos — chaos
kapok
kaput
karafe — carafe
karate
karma
karri — carry (bring)
kayak
kazoo
kean — keen
kebab
keel, -ed, -ing
keen, -ly, -ness
keep, kept, keeping
keeper
keepsake
keg
kelp
ken, kenned, kenning
kenel — kennel
kennel, -ed, -ing
keno
keosk — kiosk
kept
keratin
kerchief
kernel (core)
kernel — colonel (army)

keroseen — kerosene
kerosene
ketch
ketchup
kettel — kettle
kettle
kettledrum
kew — cue
kewi — kiwi
key, keys (lock)
key, keyed, keying (lock)
key — quay (wharf)
keyboard
keyhole
keypunch
key ring
keystone
keyword
khaki, -kis
kibble, -bled, -bling
kiak — kayak
kibbutz
kiche — quiche
kichen — kitchen
kick, -ed, -ing
kickback
kickoff
kickstand
kid, kidded, kidding
kidnap, -ed, -ing, -napped, -napping
kidney, -neys
kill, -ed, -ing (murder)
killer
killjoy
kiln (oven)
kilo
kilogram
kilojoule
kiloliter
kilometer
kilowatt
kilowatt-hour
kilt
kilter
kimono, -nos
kin
kind, -ly

kinderd   kindred
kindel   kindle
kindness
kindergarten
kindle, -dled, -dling
kindly, -lier, -liest
kindred
kinetics
king, -ly
kingdom
kingfisher
kingpin
kingsize, -d
kink, kinked, kinking
kinkey   kinky
kinkiness
kinky, -kier, -kiest
kinsfolk
kinship
kinsman, -men
kiosk
kipper
kirk
kiropody   chiropody
kismet
kiss, kissed, kissing
kissable
kit
kitchen
kite
kiten   kitten
kith
kitie   kitty
kitsch
kitten
kittenish, -ly
kitty, -ties
kity   kitty
kiwi
kiyak   kayak
kleptomania
knack
knapsack
knave (rogue)
knave   nave (church)
knead, -ed, -ing, (dough)
knead   need (want)

knee, kneed, kneeing
kneecap
kneel, knelt, kneeling
knell, -ed, -ing
knew (did know)
knew   gnu (animal)
knew   new (not old)
knickerbockers
knickknack
knife, knives
knife, knifed, knifing
knight (lord)
knight   night (time)
knighthood
knit, knitted, knitting (stitch)
knit   nit (insect)
knitwear
knob
knobbly
knobby, -bier, -biest
knock, -ed, -ing
knock down
knocker
knock knees
knockout
knoll
knot, knotted, knotting (tie)
knot   not (denial)
knothole
knotty, -tier, -tiest
know, knew, known, knowing
knowhow
know-it-all
knowledge
knowledgeable, -bly
knuckle, -led, -ling
knucklebone
knuckleduster
knurled
knurled   gnarned (knotted)
koala
kola   koala
kook
kookaburra
kooky, -kier, -kiest
Koran

kosher
koto
kowtow, -ed, -ing
kraal
kremlin
Krishna
kudos
Ku Klux Klan
kumquat
kung fu
   kurchief   kerchief

> For kw- words, look under
> **qu-**.

Ll

label, -ed, -ing
laber — labor
labial
labirinth — labyrinth
labium, -bia
lable — label
labor, -ed, -ing
laboratory, -ries
laborer
laborious, -ly
laborius — laborious
laboror — laborer
Labrador
labratory — laboratory
labrinth — labyrinth
laburnem — laburnum
laburnum
labyrinth
labyrinthine
lace, laced, lacing
lacerate, -rated, -rating
laceration
lach — latch
lack, -ed, -ing
lackadaisical, -ly
lacker — lacquer
lackey, -eys
lackey, -eyed, -eying
lacksative — laxative
lacky — lackey
lackluster
laconic, -ally
lacquer, -ed, -ing
lacross — lacrosse
lacrosse
lactate, -tated, -tating
lactation
lacteal, -ly

lactic
lactose
lad
ladder
lade — laid (placed)
ladel — ladle
laden
lader — ladder
ladie — lady
lading
ladle, -dled, -dling
ladul — ladle
lady, -dies
ladybird
ladybug
ladyfinger
lady-in-waiting
ladylike
lag, lagged, lagging
lagard — laggard
lager
laggard, -ly, -ness
laghable — laughable
lagoon
laid (placed)
laim — lame
lain (did lie)
lain — lane (passage)
lair (den)
lair — layer (thickness)
laissay fair — laissez faire
laissez faire
laitie — laity
laity
lake
lakross — lacrosse
laks — lax
laksative — laxative
lam, lammed, lamming (thrash)
lam — lamb (sheep)
lama
lamb (sheep)
lamb — lam (thrash)
lambaste, -basted, -basting
lambskin
lambswool

lame, lamed, laming
lame, lamer, lamest
lame duck
lament, -ed, -ing
lamentable, -bly
lamentation
laminate, -nated, -nating
lamp
lampoon, -ed, -ing
lamppost
lampray   lamprey
lamprey, -reys
lance, lanced, lancing
lancet
land, -ed, -ing
landfall
landfill
landform
landlady, -dies
landlocked
landlord
landlubber
landmark
landmass
landmine
landscape, -scaped, -scaping
landslide
landsman, -men
landward
lane (passage)
lane   lain (did lie)
lanelin   lanolin
langauge   language
language
languid, -ly
languish, -ed, -ing
languor
languorous, -ly
langwid   languid
langwidge   language
langwish   languish
lank, -ly
lankey   lanky
lanky, -kier, -kiest
lankey   lanky
lanlady   landlady
lanlord   landlord

lanolin
lanse   lance
lanser   lancer
lanset   lancet
lantana
lantern
lanyard
lap, lapped, lapping
lapel
lapidary, -ries
lapis lazuli
lapse, lapsed, lapsing
larceny, -nies
larcenous
larconic   laconic
lard
larder
large, -ly, -ness
large-hearted
large-scale
largess
lariat
laringitis   laryngitis
larinx   larynx
lark
larseny   larceny
larva, -vae (insect)
larva   lava (rock)
laryngitis
larynx, larynxes
lascivious, -ly, -ness
lase   lace
laser
laserate   lacerate
lash, -ed, -ing
lasitude   lassitude
lasivious   lascivious
lasoo   lasso
lasor   laser
lass
lassitude
lasso, -sos, -soes
lasso, -soed, -soing
last, lasted, lasting
last ditch
lastly
last-minute

latch, -ed, -ing
latchkey
late, later or latter, latest
late, later, latest (adjective), or last (adv.)
latecomer
lately
latency
  latensey — latency
latent, -ly
lateral, -ly
latex, latexes
lath (strip)
lathe (machine)
lather, -ed, -ing
Latin
  latise — lattice
latitude
  latreen — latrine
latrine
latter
lattice
laud, -ed, -ing (praise)
  laud — lord (ruler)
laudable, -bly
laudanum
laudatory
laugh, -ed, -ing
laughable
laughter
  laun — lawn
launch, launched, launching
launder, -ed, -ing
  laundrey — laundry
laundromat
laundry, -dries
laureate
laurel, -ed, -ing
  lauyer — lawyer
lava (rock)
  lava — larva (insect)
lavatory, -ries
lave, laved, laving
lavender
lavish, lavished, lavishing
  lavitory — lavatory
law (rule)

  law — lore (learn)
  lawd — laud (praise)
  lawd — lord (ruler)
  lawdable — laudable
lawful, -ly
lawless, -ly
lawn
  lawnch — launch
  lawnder — launder
  lawndrey — laundry
  lawndromat — laundromat
  lawndry — laundry
lawsuit
  lawsute — lawsuit
  lawwer — lawyer
lawyer
lax, -ly
  lax — lacks
  laxadasical — lackadaisical
laxative
laxity
lay, laid, laying (rest)
  lay — lei (flowers)
layaway
layer (thickness)
  layer — lair (den)
layette
layman, -men
layout
layover
laze, lazed, lazing
lazily
lazy, -zier, -ziest
lea (meadow)
  lea — lee (shelter)
leach, -ed, -ing (filter)
  leach — leech (worm)
lead, led, leading (show)
lead (metal)
  lead — led (shown)
leaden
leader
leaderless
leadership
leading lady
leading man
  leador — leader

leaf, leaves (tree)		leed	lead
leaf	lief (gladly)	leef	leaf
leaflet		leeflet	leaflet
league		leege	liege
leak (hole)		leegue	league
leak	leek (food)	leek (food)	
leakage		leek	leak (hole)
lean (thin)		leen	lean
lean, -ed, -ing (bend)		leep	leap
lean	lien (legal)	leer, -ed, -ing	
Leant	Lent (season)	lees	
leant	lent (did lend)	leese	lease
lean-to		leesh	leash
leap, leaped or leapt, leaping		leesion	lesion
leapfrog, -frogged, -frogging		leeve	leave
learn, -ed, -ing		leeward (sheltered)	
learner		leeward	lewd (lusty)
lease, leased, leasing		leeward	lured
leasehold			(attracted)
leash, -ed, -ing		leeward	lurid (shining)
leason	liaison	leeway	
least (smallest)		leewood	leeward
lest	lest (unless)	left	
leasure	leisure	leftenant	lieutenant
leasurely	leisurely	left-handed	
leather		leftist	
leatherneck		leftward	
leave, left, leaving		left-wing	
leaven, -ed, -ing		left-winger	
leaver	lever	leg, legged, legging	
lecherous, -ly		legacy, -cies	
lecherus	lecherous	legal, -ly	
lechery		legalism	
lectern		legality, -ties	
lecter	lector	legalization	
lector		legalize, -lized, -lizing (authorize)	
lecture, -tured, -turing (talk)		legand	legend
lecturer		legasion	legation
led (shown)		legasy	legacy
led	lead (metal)	legate	
ledge		legation	
ledger (book)		legel	legal
lee (shelter)		legend	
lee	lea (meadow)	legendary, -ries	
leeason	liaison	legendrey	legendary
leech (worm)		leger	ledger (book)
leech	leach (filter)	legeslation	legislation

leghorn
legibel — legible
legibility
legible, -bly
legion
legionary, -ries
legionnaire
legislate, -lated, -lating
legislater — legislator
legislation
legislative, -ly
legislator
legislature
legitimacy
legitimasy — legitimacy
legitimate, -mated, -mating
legume
lei, leis (flowers)
lei — lay (rest)
leisier — leisure
leisure, -ly
lejion — legion
lejionary — legionary
leksicografer — lexicographer
leksicografey — lexicography
leksicographer — lexicographer
leksicon — lexicon
leming — lemming
lemming
lemon
lemonade
lemur
lend, -t, -ing (assist)
lender
lendor — lender
length
lengthen, -ed, -ing
lengthily
lengthwise
lengthy, -thier, -thiest
lenience
leniency
leniense — lenience
leniensy — leniency
lenient, -ly
lenity, -ties
lens, lenses

lense — lens
Lent (season)
lenth — length
lentil (pea)
lentil — lintel (beam)
Leo
leopard
leotard
lepard — leopard
leper
leperd — leopard
leprechaun
leprechorn — leprechaun
leprosy
lept — leapt
lerch — lurch
lerk — lurk
lern — learn
lerynx — larynx
lese — lease
lesen — lessen (reduce)
lesen — lesson (study)
lesbian
lesbianism
lesion (injury)
leson — lessen (reduce)
leson — lesson (study)
less
lessee (tenant)
lessen (reduce)
lesser (smaller)
lesson (study)
lessor (landlord)
lest (unless)
lest — least (smallest)
lesure — leisure
let, let, letting
letdown
leter — letter
leter — liter
lethal, -ly
lethargey — lethargy
lethargic, -ally
lethargy, -gies
lethel — lethal
lether — leather
letter

letter carrier		liar (tell lies)	
letterhead		liar	lyre (music)
letter-perfect		liason	liaison
letterpress		libarian	librarian
lettuce		libary	library
letup		libel, -ed, -ing (slander)	
letuce	lettuce	libel	liable (obliged)
letuse	lettuce	libelus	libelous
leukemia		libelous, -ly	
leve	leave	liberal, -ly	
levee (bank)		liberalism	
levee	levy (tax)	liberate, -rated, -rating	
level, -ed, -ing		liberater	librator
leveler		liberation	
levelheaded		liberator	
levelheded	levelheaded	libertarian	
leven	leaven	libertey	liberty
lever, -ed, -ing		libertine	
leverage		liberty, -ties	
leviathan		libery	library
levie	levee (bank)	libidinal	
levie	levy (tax)	libido	
levitate, -tated, -tating		libility	liability
levitation		Libra	
levity, -ties		libralism	liberalism
levrage	leverage	librarian	
levy, levies (tax)		library, -ries	
levy, levied, levying (tax)		libretto, -tos, -ti	
levy	levee (bank)	librian	librarian
lewd, -ly (lusty)		lice (plural of louse)	
lewd	leeward (sheltered)	licence, -cenced, -cencing	
		licencious	licentious
lewd	lured (attracted)	license, -censed, -censing	
		licensee	
lewd	lurid (shining)	licensiate	licentiate
lexicografer	lexicographer	licensious	licentious
lexicografey	lexicography	licentiate	
lexicographer		licentious, -ly	
lexicographor	lexicographer	lichee	
lexicography		lichen	
lexicon		lick, -ed, -ing	
lezbian	lesbian	licker	liqueur (sweet drink)
li	lie		
liability, -ties		licker	liquor (drink)
liable (obliged)		licorice	
liable	libel (slander)	licorish	licorice
liaison		licoriss	licorice

lid
lie, lied, lying (untruth)
lie, lay, lain, lying (recline)
   lie   lye (solution)
lief (gladly)
   lief   leaf (tree)
liege
lien (law)
   lien   lean (bend, thin)
   liesure   leisure
lieu
lieutenant
life, lives
life belt
lifeboat
   lifeboy   lifebuoy
life buoy
lifeguard
lifeless, -ly
lifelike
lifeline
lifelong
lifesaver
lifestyle
lifetime
lift, -ed, -ing
liftoff
ligament
ligature
light, lighted or lit, lighting
lighten, -ed, -ing
lighter
lightfingered
lightheaded
lighthearted, -ly
lighthouse
lightly
lightning
lightweight
ligneous
lignite
likable
like, liked, liking
likelihood
likely, -lier, -liest
   likelyhood   likelihood

likeness
likewise
   likley   likely
   likorish   licorice
   likoriss   licorice

> For likw- words, look
> under **liqu-**.

lilac
   lilak   lilac
   lile   lisle
   lilie   lily
   lillac   lilac
lilliputian
lilt, -ed, -ing
lily, lilies
lily-livered
lily-white
limb (body)
   limb   limp (walk)
limber
limbo, -bos
lime, limed, liming
limelight
   limelite   limelight
limerick
   limersene   limousine
limestone
   limf   lymph
   limfatic   lymphatic
limit, -ed, -ing
limitation
limousine
limp, -ed, -ing (walk)
   limp   limb (body)
limpet
   limph   lymph
   limphatic   lymphatic
limpid
linage (number of lines)
linchpin
   linch   lynch
line, lined, lining (mark)
   line   lion (animal)
lineage (ancestry, number of lines)
lineal, -ly
lineament (detail)

linear, -ly
  lineige — lineage
linen
liner
linesman, -men
lineup
ling, lings
linger, -ed, -ing
lingerie
lingo, -goes
lingual, -ly
linguist
linguistic, -ally
  lingwal — lingual
  lingwist — linguist
  linier — linear
liniment (oil)
  liniment — lineament (detail)
link, linked, linking
linkage
links (joins)
  links — lynx (wildcat)
linnet
linoleum
  linolium — linoleum
Linotype, -typed, -typing
linseed
lint
lintel (beam)
  lintel — lentil (pea)
  linx — lynx
lion (animal)
  lion — line (mark)
lioness
lionhearted, -ly
lionize, -nized, -nizing
  liotard — leotard
lip, lipped, lipping
lip read, -read, -reading
lipstick
lip sync
liquefier
liquefy, -fied, -fying
liqueur (sweet drink)
  liqueur — liquor (drink)
liquid

liquidambar
liquidate, -dated, -dating
liquidation
liquidator
liquidity
liquor (drink)
  liquor — liqueur (sweet drink)
liquorice
  liquorise — liquorice
  lire — lyre
  liric — lyric
  lirical — lyrical
  lise — lice
  lisen — listen
  lisence — licence
  lisence — license
  lisen — listen
  lisensee — licensee
  lisentiate — licentiate
lisle
lisp, -ed, -ing
lissome
  lissum — lissome
list, -ed, -ing
listen, -ed, -ing
listless, -ly, -ness
lit
  litagation — litigation
litany, -nies
  litarel — literal
  litargy — liturgy
  lite — light
  litel — little
liter (unit)
  liter — litter (trash)
  literachure — literature
literacy
literal, -ly
literary, -ily
  literasy — literacy
  literat — literate
literate
literati
literature
  litergy — liturgy
  litewait — lightweight

lithe, -ly
lithesome
lithium
  lithograf — lithograph
lithograph
lithographic
lithography
litigant
litigate, -ed, -ing
  litigater — litigator
litigation
litigator
  litle — little
litmus
  litening — lightning
  litle — little
  litrature — literature
litter, -ed, -ing (trash)
  litter — liter (unit)
litterbug
little, less, least
  liturgey — liturgy
liturgical, -ly
liturgy, -gies
  liutenant — lieutenant
  liv — live
  livary — livery
live, lived, living
lived-in
livelihood
livelong
lively, -lier, -liest
  livelyhood — livelihood
liven, -ed, -ing
liver
liverish
liverwurst
livery, -ries
livestock
live wire
livid, -ly
  livlie — lively
  livrey — livery
  liying — lying
lizard
  lizerd — lizard
llama

  lo — low
load, -ed, -ing (burden)
  load — lode (ore)
loaf, loaves
loam, -ed, -ing
loan (lend)
  loan — lone (alone)
loath (unwilling)
loathe, loathed, loathing (hate)
loathsome, -ly
lob, lobbed, lobbing
lobby, -bies
lobby, -bied, -bying
lobe
lobotomy
lobster
  loby — lobby
local, -ly
locale
locality, -ties
localize, -lized, -lizing
locate, -cated, -cating
location
loch (lake)
lock (door)
locker
locket
lockjaw
locksmith
lockup
  locomoshun — locomotion
locomotion
locomotive
locus, loci
locust
locution
lode (ore)
  lode — load (burden)
lodestar
lodestone
lodge, lodged, lodging
lodger
  lofe — loaf
loft, lofted, lofting
loftily
lofty, -tier, -tiest
log, logged, logging

loganberrie	loganberry	long winded, -ly	
loganberry, -berries		loo	lieu
logarithm		loobricant	lubricant
logbook		loobricate	lubricate
loge	lodge	loocid	lucid
loger	logger	loocrative	lucrative
logerithm	logarithm	loodicrous	ludicrous
loggerhead		loofah	
logic		look, -ed, -ing	
logical, -ly		lookemia	leukemia
logicality		looker	lucre
logistics		look out	
loier	lawyer	lookwarm	lukewarm
loin		loom, -ed, -ing	
loincloth		loominus	luminous
loiter, -ed, -ing		loon	
loiterer		loonatic	lunatic
lol	loll	loony	
lolipop	lollipop	loop, -ed, -ing	
loll, -ed, -ing		loophole	
lollipop		loose, looser, loosest	
lome	loam	loose	lose (fail)
lone (alone)		loosen	
lone	loan (lend)	loosing	losing
loneliness		loot (booty)	
lonely, -lier, -liest		loot	lute (music)
loner		lop, lopped, lopping (cut)	
lonesome, -ly		lope, loped, loping (run)	
lonesum	lonesome	lopsided, -ly	
long, -ed, -ing		loquacious, -ly	
long-distance		loquacity	
longevity		loquasious	loquacious
longhair		lord (ruler)	
longhand		lord	laud (praise)
longing, -ly		lordly, -lier, -liest	
longitude		lore (traditions)	
longitudinal, -ly		lore	law (rule)
long-legged		lorel	laurel
long-lived		lorgnette	
long-playing		loriat	laureate
long-range		lornch	launch
longshoreman, -men		lornyet	lorgnette
longstanding		los	loss
longsuffering		lose, lost, losing (fail)	
long-term		lose	loose (not tight)
long time			
long ways		losenge	lozenge

loser
loss
lot
  lotery — lottery
  lothe — loathe
  lothsum — loathsome
  lotien — lotion
lotion
  lotis — lotus
lots
lottery, -teries
lotto
lotus
loud, -ly, -ness
loudmouth
loudspeaker
lounge, lounged, lounging
louse, lice or louses
louse, loused, lousing
  lousey — lousy
lousy, lousier, lousiest
lout
louver
love, loved, loving
loveliness
lovelorn
lovely, -lier, -liest
lover
  loves — loaves
low, lower, lowest
low beam
lowboy
lowbrow
low-cal
low-class
  lowd — loud
lowdown
lower, -ed, -ing
lower case
lower-class
low frequency
low gear
low-key
lowland
lowly, -lier, -liest
  lownge — lounge
low-pitchd

low-pressure
low-rise
  lowse — louse
  lowt — lout
low-tension
low tide
low voltage
loyal, -ly
loyalty, -ties
  loyle — loyal
lozenge
  lozinge — lozenge
  lu — lieu (instead)
luau
lubber, -ly
  luber — lubber
lubricant
lubricate, -cated, -cating
lubrication
  lucer — lucre
lucerne
lucid, -ly
Lucifer
luck, -ily
lucky, -kier, -kiest
lucrative, -ly
lucre
  lucsious — luscious
  lude — lewd
  ludecrous — ludicrous
ludicrous, -ly
luff, -ed, -ing
lug, lugged, lugging
  lugage — luggage
luggage
lugubrious, -ly, -ness
  lukemia — leukemia
  lukerative — lucrative
lukewarm
  luksuriant — luxuriant
  luksuriate — luxuriate
  luksurius — luxurious
  luksury — luxury
  lul — lull
  lulaby — lullaby
lull, -ed, -ing
lullaby, -bies

lumbago
lumbar (back)
lumber (timber)
lumberjack
luminance
luminary, -naries
luminescence
luminescent
  luminessence — luminescence
  luminessent — luminescent
luminosity, -ties
luminous, -ly
  luminus — luminous
lump, -ed, -ing
lunacy, -cies
lunar
  lunasy — lunacy
lunatic
lunch, -ed, -ing
luncheon
lung
lunge, lunged, lunging
lungfish
lupin
lupus
lurch, lurched, lurching
lure, lured, luring (attract)
  lured — leeward (sheltered)
  lured — lewd (lusty)
lurid, -ly (shining)
  lurid — leeward (sheltered)
  lurid — lewd (lusty)
lurk, lurked, lurking
  lurn — learn
luscious, -ly
lush, -ly
  lusid — lucid
  lusious — luscious
lust, lusted, lusting
luster, -less, lustrous
lustful, -ly
  lustfull — lustful
  lustie — lusty
lusty, -tier, -tiest
lute

lute — loot (booty)
Lutheran
  luv — love
  luvely — lovely
  luver — lover
  luvlier — lovelier
lux
  luxerious — luxurious
  luxery — luxury
luxuriance
luxuriant, -ly
luxuriate, -ated, -ating
  luxurient — luxuriant
luxurious, -ly
luxury, -ries
lyceum
lye (solution)
  lye — lie (untruth)
  lye — lie (recline)
lymph
lymphatic
lynch, -ed, -ing
lynx (animal)
  lynx — links (joins)
lyre (musical instrument)
  lyre — liar (tells lies)
lyric
lyrical, -ly
lyricist

Mm

ma'am
macabre
macadam
macadamia nut
macaroni
macaw
mace
Mach (speed)
  mach → match (equal)
machete
machination
machine, -chined, -chining
machinery, -ries
mackerel
macramé
macro economics
mad, madder, maddest
madam
madcap
madden, -ing, -ly
made (create)
  made → maid (girl)
Madeira
mademoiselle
  madera → Madeira
made-to-order
made-up
madhouse
madman
madness
Madonna
madrigal
maelstrom
maestro
Mafia
magazine
  maggit → maggot
maggot

magic
magical, -ly
magician
  magisian → magician
magisterial, -ly
magistrate
  magizine → magazine
magnanimity
magnanimous, -ly
magnate (wealth)
magnesium
magnet (attract)
magnetic, -ally
magnetism
magnetite
magnetization
magnetize, -tized, -tizing
magneto, -tos
  magnezium → magnesium
  magnificasion → magnification
magnification
magnificence
magnificent, -ly
magnifier
  magnifisense → magnificence
  magnifisent → magnificent
magnify, -fied, -fying
  magnifyer → magnifier
magnitude
magnolia
  magnolya → magnolia
magnum, -nums
  magot → maggot
magpie
  magpye → magpie
  mahem → mayhem
mahjong
mahogany
maid (girl)
  maid → made (create)
maiden
mail (letters)
  mail → male (man)
mailbag
mailbox, mailboxes
mailman, -men
maim, -ed, -ing

main (chief)
   main   mane (hair)
mainland
mainline, -lined, -lining
mainliner
mainstay
mainstream
maintain, -ed, -ing
maintenance
   maintenanse   maintenance
maize (corn)
   maize   maze (puzzle)
   majer   major
   majestey   majesty
majestic, -ally
majesty, -ties
   majong   mahjong
major
   majoraty   majority
majority, -ties
   makaber   macabre
   makadam   macadam
make, made, making
make-believe
makeshift
makeup
mako (shark)
maladapted
maladjusted
maladjustment
maladminister, -ed, -ing
malady, -dies (disease)
   malady   melody (music)
malaise
malapropism
   malard   mallard
malaria
   malase   malaise
male (man)
   male   mail (letters)
   maleable   malleable
   malefacktion   malefaction
   malefacter   malefactor
malefaction
malefactor
   malet   mallet
malevolence

   malevolense   malevolence
malevolent, -ly
malformation
malformed
   malfuncktion   malfunction
malfunction, -ed, -ing
   maliable   malleable
malice
malicious, -ly
malign, -ed, -ing
malignance
malignancy
malignant, -ly
   maline   malign
malinger, -ed, -ing
malingerer
   malingeror   malingerer
   malise   malice
   malisious   malicious
mall
mallard, -lard, -lards
malleability
malleable
mallet
   mallow   mellow
   malnutrision   malnutrition
malnutrition
malpractice
   malpractise   malpractice
   malstrom   maelstrom
malt (liquor)
   malt   molt (shed)
Malthusian
maltreat, -ed, -ing
maltreatment
   maltreet   maltreat
   mamal   mammal
   mamarey   mammary
   mame   maim
mammal
mammary
mammon
mammoth
   mamon   mammon
   mamoth   mammoth
man, men
man, manned, manning

manacle, -cled, -cling
  manacure   manicure
manage, -aged, -aging
manageability
manageable, -bly
management
manager
managerial, -ly
mañana
mandarin
mandate, -dated, -dating
mandatory, -ries
mandolin
mane (hair)
man-eater
  mane   main (chief)
  maner   manner (way)
  maner   manor (house)
maneuver, -ed, -ing
maneuverability
maneuverable
  maneuverible   maneuverable
mange
  mangel   mangle
manger
mangle, -gled, -gling
mango, -goes, -gos
mangrove
mangy, -gier, -giest
manhandle, -dled, -dling
manhole
manhood
manhunt
mania
maniacal, -ly
manic
manic-depression
manicdepressive
manicure, -cured, -curing
manifest, -ed, -ing
manifestation
manifesto, -tos
manifold
  manige   manage
manikin, mannikin (dwarf)
  manikin   mannequin (model)

Manila
  manipulasion   manipulation
manipulate, -lated, -lating
  manipulater   manipulator
manipulation
manipulative
manipulator
manipulatory
  manje   mange
  manjer   manger
  manjy   mangy
mankind
manlike
manly, -lier, -liest
manmade
manna (food)
  manna   manner (way)
  manna   manor (house)
  manndate   mandate
mannequin
manner (way)
  manner   manna (food)
  manner   manor (house)
mannered
mannerism
mannerly
  manneuver   maneuver
  mannipulate   manipulate
mannish
  manocle   monocle
man-of-war
  manogamy   monogamy
  manologue   monologue
manor (house)
  manor   manna (food)
  manor   manner (way)
manpower
manse
mansion
manslaughter
  manslorter   manslaughter
  manson   mansion
mantel (shelf)
  mantel   mantle (cloak)
mantelpiece
mantilla
mantis, -tises

mantissa
mantle (cloak)
   mantle   mantel (shelf)
manual, -ly
   manuever   maneuver
   manufackture   manufacture
manufacture, -tured, -turing
manure, -nured, -nuring
manuscript
many, more, most
   maonaise   mayonnaise
Maori, -ris
map, mapped, mapping
   mapel   maple
maple
mar, marred, marring
   maratal   marital
marathon
maraud, -ed, -ing
   marawed   maraud
marble, -bled, -bling
marcasite
March
march, -ed, -ing
marcher
marchioness
mare (horse)
   mare   mayor (chief)
   mareene   marine
margarine
margin
marginal, -ly
   mariage   marriage
   marie   marry
marijuana
marina
marinade, -naded, -nading
marinate, -nated, -nating
marine
mariner
   marionet   marionette
marionette
marital, -ly (wed)
   marital   marshal
                    (officer)
   marital   martial (brave)
maritime

   mariuana   marijuana
marjoram
mark, marked, marking
marker
market, -ed, -ing
markdown
marketable
marketplace
marksman, -men
marksmanship
   markuis   marquis
markup
marlin
marmalade
   marone   maroon
maroon, -ed, -ing
   marow   marrow
marquee (tent)
marquess, -es (nobleman)
marquis (nobleman)
marquise (noblewoman)
marquisette (fabric)
   marrage   marriage
marriage (wedding)
   marriage   mirage
                 (illusion)
marrow
marry, -ried, -rying (unite)
Mars (planet)
Marsala
marsh
marshal, -ed, -ing (officer)
   marshal   marital (wed)
   marshal   martial (brave)
marshland
marshmallow
marshy, -shier, -shiest
marsupial
mart
   marteni   martini
   marter   martyr
martial (brave)
   martial   marshal
                 (officer)
   martial   marital (wed)
martini
martyr

martyrdom
marvel, -ed, -ing
marvelous, -ly
Marxism
Marxist

mary	marry

marzipan

mas	mass
masacre	massacre
masage	massage

mascara
mascot
masculine, -ly
masculinity

mase	mace

mash, -ed, -ing

mashine	machine
mashinry	machinery
masive	massive

mask, -ed, -ing

maskerade	masquerade

masochism
masochist

masocism	masochism

mason
Masonic
masonite
masonry, -ries
masquerade, -raded, -rading
mass
massacre, -cred, -cring
massage, -saged, -saging (rub)

massage	message
	(errand)

masseur
massif (mountain)
massive, -ly (large)
mass media
mass-produce, -duced, -ducing

massur	masseur

mast
mastectomy, -mies
master, -ed, -ing

masterbate	masturbate

masterful, -ly
mastermind
masterpiece

masthead
masticate, masticated, masticating
mastiff
masturbate, -bated, -bating
masturbation
mat, matted, matting (rug)

mat	matt (dull)

matador
match, -ed, -ing (equal)

match	Mach (speed)

matchmaker
mate, mated, mating

mater	matter

material, -ly
materialism
materialist
materialization
materialize, -lized, -lizing
maternal, -ly
maternity
mathematical, -ly
mathematician
mathematics

mathematisian	mathematician
matinay	matinee

matinee

mating	matting
matress	mattress

matriarch
matriarchal
matriarchy, -chies
matricide
matriculate, -lated, -lating
matriculation
matrimony, -nies

matriside	matricide

matrix, matrices
matron, -ly
matt (dull)
matter
matting

mattle	mottle

mattock
mattress
maturation
mature, -tured, -turing
maturity

maudlin, -ly
  maukish   mawkish
maul, -ed, -ing
mausoleum, -leums, -lea
mauve
maverick
  mawgage   mortgage
mawkish, -ly, -ness
  mawl   maul
  mawsoleum   mausoleum
  maxamize   maximize
maxi
maxim
maximization
maximize, -mized, -mizing
maximum, -ma, -mums
maybe (perhaps)
may be (may happen)
May
mayhem
mayonnaise
mayor (chief)
  mayor   mare (horse)
mayoralty, -ties
mayoress
Maypole
maze (puzzle)
  maze   maize (corn)
mazurka
mead
meadow
meager, -ly
  meak   meek
meal
mean, meant, meaning (intend)
  mean   mien (show)
meander, -ed, -ing
meantime
meanwhile
  measels   measles
measles
measure, -ured, -uring
measurement
meat (flesh)
  meat   meet (contact)
  meat   mete (measure)
  mecanic   mechanic

  mecanism   mechanism
  mecanize   mechanize
mechanic
mechanical, -ly
mechanism
mechanization
mechanize, -nized, -nizing
medal, -ed, -ing (award)
medallion
  medcine   medicine
meddle, -dled, -dling (interfere)
meddler
  medeval   medieval
media
median
  mediasion   mediation
mediate, -ated, -ating
  mediater   mediator
mediation
meditator
medic
Medicaid
medical, -ly
Medicare
medicate, -cated, -cating
medication
medicinal, -ly
medicine
medicine chest
medicine man
medieval
medievalist
  mediocer   mediocre
mediocre
mediocrity, -ties
  medisinal   medicinal
  medisine   medicine
meditate, -tated, -tating
  meditater   meditator
meditation
meditator
medium, -dia, -diums
  medle   meddle
                  (interfere)
  medler   meddler
medley, -leys
  meddile   middle

meddlor	meddler	melodrama	
medow	meadow	melodramatic, -ally	
medsine	medicine	melody, -dies (music)	
meed	mead	melody	malady
meek, -ly, -ness			(disease)
meel	meal	melon	
meen	mean (intend)	melow	mellow
meen	mien (show)	melt, melted, melting	
meening	meaning	member	
meerschaum		membership	
meesels	measles	membrain	membrane
meet, met, meeting (contact)		memento, -tos	
meet	meat (flesh)	memo, memos	
meet	mete (measure)	memoir	
meeting house		memorabilia	
meeting place		memorable,-bly	
megafone	megaphone	memorandum, -dums, -da	
megahertz		memorey	memory
megalith		memorial	
megalomania		memorible	memorable
megalomaniac		memorize, -rized, -rizing	
megalopolis		memory, -ries	
megaphone		memrable	memórable
megaton		memwar	memoir
meger	meager	menace, -aced, -acing	
mekanic	mechanic	menajery	menagerie
mekanical	mechanical	menase	menace
mekanism	mechanism	mend, -ed, -ing	
mekanize	mechanize	mendacious, -ly	
melancholia		mendacity, -ties (lying)	
melancholic, -ally		mendasious	mendacious
melancholy, -cholies		mendasity	mendacity
melancolly	melancholy	mendicant	
Melanesian		mendicity (begging)	
meld, -ed, -ing		menial, -ly	
melee		meningitis	
meliflous	mellifluous	meninjitis	meningitis
meliorate, -rated, -rating		meniscus, -nisci	
meliorater	meliorator	menopause	
melioration		menopaws	menopause
meliorator		mension	mention
mellifluous, -ly, -ness		menstruate, -ated, -ating	
mellow, -ly, -ness		menstruation	
melodey	melody	mensuration	
melodic, -ally		menswear	
melodious, -ly, -ness		ment	meant
melodius	melodious		

mental, -ly
mental hospital
mentality, -ties
mentally retarded
menter — mentor
menthol
mentholated
mention, -ed, -ing
mentor
menu
merang — meringue
mercantile
mercenary, -naries
mercenrey — mercenary
mercer
mercerize
mercery
merchandise, -dised, -dising
merchant
merchantman, -men
merciful, -ly
merciless, -ly
mercurial, -ly
Mercury (planet)
mercury, -ries (element)
mercy, -cies
mercyful — merciful
merder — murder
mere, -ly
meretricious, -ly, -ness
meretrisious — meretricious
merge, merged, merging
merger
meridian
merie — merry
meringue
merino, -nos
merit, -ed, -ing
meritorious, -ly, -ness
meritorius — meritorious
mermade — mermaid
mermaid
merriment
merry, -rier, -riest
merry-go-round
merrymaking
merrymaker

mersenry — mercenary
mersy — mercy
mery — merry
mesa
mescaline
mesenger — messenger
mesh, -ed, -ing
mesige — message
mesmerism
mesmerize, -rized, -rizing
mess, -ed, -ing
message (communication)
message — massage (rub)
messenger
Messiah
Messianic
messmate
Messrs
messy, messier, messiest
mesure — measure
metabolic
metabolism
metabolize, -lized, -lizing
metafisical — metaphysical
metafisics — metaphysics
metafore — metaphor
metaforic — metaphoric
metaforical — metaphorical
metal, -ed, -ing (element)
metal — mettle (energy)
metalic — metallic
metallic
metallurgic
metallurgical, -ly
metallurgist
metallurgy
metamorfic — metamorphic
metamorfosis — metamorphosis
metamorphic
metamorphosis, -ses
metaphor
metaphoric
metamorphical, -ly
metaphysical, -ly
metaphysics
metastasize, -sized, -sizing
mete, meted, meting (measure)

mete	meat (flesh)	mica		
mete	meet (contact)	mice		
metearology	meteorology	micrawave	microwave	
meteor (streak)		microbe		
meteor	métier (trade)	microbial		
meteoric, -ally		microbic		
meteorite		microbiological		
meteorological, -ly		microbiologist		
meteoroid		microbiology		
meteorology		microchip		
meter		microcircuit		
methadical	methodical	microcosm		
methadone		microdot		
methane		micro economics		
methed	method	microelectronics		
meth		microencapsulate, -lated, -lating		
method		microfiche		
methodical, -ly		microfilm		
Methodist		microfish	microfiche	
methodology, -gies		microfone	microphone	
meticulous, -ly, -ness		microgram		
meticulus	meticulous	micrograph		
métier (trade)		micrometer		
métier	meteor (streak)	micron		
metiorology	meteorology	microorganism		
metranome	metronome	microphone		
metrapolitan	metropolitan	microprocessor		
metric		microprosessor	microprocessor	
metricate, -cated, -cating		microscope		
metrication		microscopic, -ally		
metric system		microsecond		
metronome		microsurgery		
metropolis, -lises		microwave		
metropolitan		midair		
mettaphor	metaphor	midday		
mettle (energy)		middel	middle	
mettle	metal (element)	middle		
mew, -ed, -ing		middle-aged		
mews (stables)		middle class		
mews	muse (think)	middleman, -men		
mezanine	mezzanine	middle-of-the-road		
mezzanine		middlewait	middleweight	
mi	my	middleweight		
miander	meander	middling		
miaow, -ed, -ing		middy, -dies		
miasma, -mata, -mas		midel	middle	
miasmic		midge		

midget		mililiter	milliliter
midil	middle	milimeter	millimeter
midling	middling	miliner	milliner
midnight		miling	milling
midnite	midnight	milinry	millinery
midriff		milion	million
midruff	midriff	milionair	millionaire
midshipman, -men		milipeed	millipede
midst		milisha	militia
midterm		militancy	
midwife, -wives		militansy	militancy
mien (show)		militant, -ly	
mien	mean (intend)	militarism	
miff		militarist	
mige	midge	militaristic	
might (power)		military	
might	mite (small)	militia	
mighty, -tier, -tiest		milk, -ed, -ing	
migit	midget	milkmaid, -maiden	
migraine		milkman, -men	
migrane	migraine	milksop	
migrant (noun)		milk-white	
migrate, -grated, -grating (verb)		milky, -kier, -kiest	
migration		Milky Way	
migratory		mill, milled, milling (grind)	
migreat	migrate (verb)	mill	mil
migrent	migrant (noun)		(measurement)
mika	mica	millennial, -ly	
mikado, -dos		millennium, -niums, -nia	
mikrofiche	microfiche	miller	
mikrofilm	microfilm	millet	
miksamotosis	myxomatosis	millibar	
mikschure	mixture	milligram	
mikser	mixer	milliliter	
mil (measurement)		millimeter	
mil	mill (grind)	milliner	
milatary	military	millinery	
mild, -ly, -ness		million	
mildew, -ed, -ing		millionaire	
mildue	mildew	millipede	
mile		millpond	
mileage		millrace	
milestone		millstone	
milenium	millennium	Milwaukee	
milet	millet	milyou	milieu
milibar	millibar	mime, mimed, miming	
milieu, -lieus, -lieux		mimeograph	

mimic, -icked, -icking
mimicry, -ries
mimosa
minaret
mince, minced, mincing
mincemeat
mincer
mind, minded, minding
mind-bending
mind-blowing
mind-expanding
mindful, -ly, -ness
mindless, -ly, -ness
mine, mined, mining
minefield
miner (worker)

miner	minor (less)
miner	myna (bird)

mineral
mineralogical, -ly
mineralogist
mineralogy

minerel	mineral

minestrone
minesweeper
mineworker

mingel	mingle

mingle, -led, -ling
mini
miniature
minibike
minibus
minim
minimal, -ly
minimize, -mized, -mizing
minimizer
minimum, -mums, -ma
minion

miniscule	minuscule

miniseries
miniskirt
minister
ministerial
ministrant
ministration
ministrative, -ly

ministrone	minestrone

ministry, -tries

minit	minute

mink, minks (animal)

minks	minx (girl)

Minnesota
minnow, -nows
minor (lesser)

minor	miner (worker)
minor	myna (bird)

minority, -ties

minow	minnow
minse	mince

minstrel
mint, -ed, -ing
minuet
minus
minuscule
minute, -ly, -ness
minute hand
Minuteman, -men
minx (girl)

minx	minks (animals)
minyouet	minuet
miopia	myopia
miow	miaow

miracle
miraculous, -ly

miraculus	miraculous

mirage (illusion)

mirage	marriage (wedding)

mire, mired, miring

mirer	mirror
miriad	myriad
miricle	miracle
mirrh	myrrh

mirror, -ed, -ing
mirth
mirthful, -ly, -ness

mis	miss
misadvenchure	misadventure

misadventure

misal	missal

misanthrope
misanthropic, -ally
misanthropist

misanthropy
misapprehension
  misapprehention   misapprehension
misappropriate, -ated, -ating
misappropriation
  misapropriate   misappropriate
misbehave, -haved, -having
miscarriage
miscarry, -ried, -rying
miscast, -cast, -casting
miscellaneous, -ly
miscellany, -nies
mischance
  mischanse   mischance
mischief
  mischievious   mischievous
mischievous, -ly, -ness
  mischif   mischief
  mischivus   mischievous
misconceive, -ceived, -ceiving
misconceiver
  misconcepsion   misconception
misconception
  misconcieve   misconceive
  misconcievor   misconceiver
misconduct
  misconseption   misconception
  misconstrew   misconstrue
misconstrue, -strued, -struing
miscount, -ed, -ing
miscreant
misdeed
  misdemeaner   misdemeanor
misdemeanor
  misdemener   misdemeanor
misdo, -did, -done, -doing
  mise   mice
  miselanius   miscellaneous
  miselany   miscellany
  miself   myself
  miseltoe   mistletoe
miser, -ly, -ness
miserable, -ly, -ness
  miserible   miserable
misery, -ries
misfit, -fitted, -fitting
misfortune

misgiving
mishap
  mishapen   misshapen
  mishion   mission
mishmash
  misile   missile
  misiltoe   mistletoe
  misis   misses
  misive   missive
mislay, -laid, -laying
  misle   missal (book)
  misle   missile
       (weapon)
mislead, -led, -leading
  misleed   mislead
  misnoma   misnomer
misnomer
misogynist
misogynous
misogyny
  misojonist   misogynist
  misojonous   misogynous
  misojony   misogyny
  misor   miser
  mispell   misspell
misplace, -placed, -placing
misplacement
  misplase   misplace
misprint, -ed, -ing
mispronounce, -nounced, -nouncing
  misrable   miserable
  misrible   miserable
misrepresent, -ed, -ing
  misrey   misery
miss (unmarried woman)
miss, missed, missing (fail)
missal (book)
  missal   missile
       (weapon)
  misselanius   miscellaneous
  misselany   miscellany
misshape, -shaped, -shaping
missile (weapon)
  missile   missal (book)
mission
missionary, -ries
Mississippi

missive
Missouri
misspell, -led, -ing
  missplace — misplace
  misstake — mistake
  misstress — mistress
mist (cloud)
  mist — missed (fail)
mistake, -took, -taking
mistaken
  misteltoe — mistletoe
mister
  misterey — mystery
  misterius — mysterious
  mistery — mystery
  mistic — mystic
  mistic — mystique
  mistify — mystify
mistletoe
mistreat, -ed, -ing
mistress
mistrial
  mistro — maestro
mistrust, -ed, -ing
misty, -tier, -tiest
misunderstand, -stood, -standing
misuse, -used, -using
mite (small)
  mite — might (power)
  miten — mitten
miter, -ed, -ing
  mith — myth
  mithical — mythical
  mithology — mythology
  mitie — mighty
mitigate, -gated, -gating
mitt
mitten
mix, mixed, mixing
  mixamotosis — myxomatosis
  mixchure — mixture
mixer
mixture
mixup
mizzenmast
mnemonics
  mo — mow

moan, moaned, moaning
moaner
moat (ditch)
  moat — mote (dust)
mob, mobbed, mobbing
mobile, -ly
  mobiliety — mobility
mobility
mobilization
mobilize, -lized, -lizing
  moble — mobile
moccasin
mock, -ed, -ing
mockery, -ries
mockingbird
  mockry — mockery
mockup
  modal — model
  modarate — moderate
  moddo — motto
mode
  modecum — modicum
model, -ed, -ing
  moden — modern
moderate, -rated, -rating
  moderater — moderator
moderation
moderator
modern, -ly
modernize, -nized, -nizing
modest, -ly
modesty, -ties
modicum
  modifi — modify
modification
modifier
modify, -fied, -fying
  modjule — module
  modlin — maudlin
modular
modulate, -lated, -lating
  modulater — modulator
modulation
modulator
module
  moduler — modular
mogul

mohair
Mohammedan
  mohare — mohair
moiety, -ties
  moischure — moisture
  moisen — moisten
moist, -ly, -ness
moisten, -ed, -ing
moisture
  mokasin — moccasin
molar
  molases — molasses
molasses
mold, -ed, -ing
molder, -ed, -ing
moldy, -dier, -diest
moldy, moldiness
mole
molecular, -ly
molecule
molehill
moleskin
molest, -ed, -ing
molestation
moll
  mollecule — molecule
mollify, -fied, -fying
mollusk, mollusc
Molotov cocktail
molt, -ed, -ing (shed)
  molt — malt (liquor)
molten
  molusk — mollusck
molybdenum
mom
moment
momentarily
momentary
momentous, -ly, -ness
momentum, -ta
  momint — moment
  monakey — monarchy
monarch
monarchal
monarchic, -al
monarchist

monarchy, -chies
monastery, -teries
monastic, -ally
monasticism
  monastry — monastery
Monday
  mone — moan
monetarism
monetary, -rily
money, moneys or monies
money-back
moneybags
moneychanger
moneyed
money-grubber
moneylender
moneymaker
money market
money order
  monga — monger
monger
Mongol
Mongolian
Mongolism
Mongoloid
mongoose, -gooses
mongrel
  mongrul — mongrel
  moniter — monitor
monitor, -ed, -ing
monk
monkey, -keys
monkey, -keyed, -keying
monkey wrench
  monnotny — monotony
  monocel — monocle
mono
monochromatic, -ally
monochrome
monochromic
monocle
monocled
monogamist
monogamous
  monogamus — monogamous
monogamy
  monograf — monograph

monogram, monogrammed,
monogramming
monograph
   monokrome   monochrome
   monokside   monoxide
monolith
monolithic
monologue, monolog
mononucleosis
monophonic, -ally
   monoplain   monoplane
monoplane
   monopolizasion monopolization
monopolization
monopolize, -lized, -lizing
monopoly, -lies
monorail
   monosilabic   monosyllabic
   monosilable   monosyllable
monosyllabic, -ally
monosyllable
   monosyllible   monosyllable
monotone
monotonous, -ly
   monotonus   monotonous
monotony
monoxide
monsoon
monster
monstrosity, -ties
monstrous, -ly, -ness
   monstrus   monstrous
montage
month
monument
monumental, -ly
moo, -ed, -ing
mooch, -ed, -ing
moocher
mood
moody, -dier, -diest
moon
moonbeam
moonless
moonlight
moonlighter
moonlit

moonrise
moonscape
moonshine
moonshot
moonstone
moonstruck
moonwalk
moony, -nier, -niest
moor, -ed, -ing (secure)
   moor   more (further)
Moor (Muslim)
moose, moose (animal)
   moose   mouse (rodent)
   moose   mousse (food)
moot
   moovable   movable
   moove   move
mop, mopped, mopping
mope, moped, moping
moped
moral, -ly (rules)
morale (zeal)
moralist
moralistic
morality, -ties
moralize, -lized, -lizing
morass
moratorium, -toria, -toriums
moray, -rays (eel)
   morays   mores (custom)
morbid, -ly, -ness
morbidity
mordant, -ly
   mordern   modern
more, most (further)
   more   moor (secure)
moreover
mores (custom)
   morfine   morphine
   morg   morgue
   morgage   mortgage
morganatic
morgue
moribund, -ly
Mormon
Mormonism
morn (morning)

morn	mourn (sorrow)	mother-in-law, mothers-in-law	
mornful	mournful	motherland	
morning (day)		motherless	
morning	mourning (sorrow)	motherly	
		mother-of-pearl	
moron		motif (figure)	
moronic		motif	motive (reason)
morose, -ly, -ness		motion, -ed, -ing	
morover	moreover	motivate, -vated, -vating	
morow	morrow	motivation	
morphine		motivational	
morrow		motive (reason)	
Morse code		motive	motif (figure)
morsel		motle	mottle
mortafy	mortify	motley	
mortal, -ly		moto	motto
mortality, -ties		motor, -ed, -ing	
mortar		motorbike	
mortarboard		motorboat	
mortgage, -gaged, -gaging		motorcade	
mortgagee		motorcycle	
mortgagor, mortgager		motorcyclist	
mortification		motorist	
mortify, -fied, -fying		motorize, -rized, -rizing	
mortise, -tised, -tising		mottle, -tled, -tling	
mortuary, -ries		motto, -toes, -tos	
mos	moss	mouce	mouse
mosaic		mouldy, -dier, -diest	
moselle		mound	
mosion	motion	mount, mounted, mounting	
mosk	mosque	mountain	
moskito	mosquito	mountaineer	
Moslem		mountainous	
mosque		mountainside	
mosquito, -toes		mountaintop	
moss		mounten	mountain
most, -ly		mountenous	mountainous
mot		mourn, -ed, -ing (sorrow)	
mote (dust)		mourn	morn (morning)
mote	moat (ditch)	mourner	
motel		mournful, -ly	
moter	motor	mourning (sorrow)	
motervate	motivate	mourning	morning (day)
moth, moths		mournor	mourner
mothballs		mouse, mice (rodent)	
moth-eaten		mouse, moused, mousing	
mother		mouse	moose (animal)

mouse	mousse (food)	muddy, -died, -dying	
moussaka		muddy, -dier, -diest	
mousse (food)		mudey	moody
mousse	moose (animal)	mudguard	
mousse	mouse (rodent)	mudle	muddle
moustache		mudslinger	
mousy, -sier, -siest		Muenster	
mouth, mouths		muezzin	
mouthful, -fuls		muff, -ed, -ing	
mouthpeace	mouthpiece	muffin	
mouthpiece		muffle, -fled, -fling	
mouthwash		muffler	
mouthwatering		mufflor	muffler
mouth-to-mouth		mufin	muffin
movable		mufti	
move, moved, moving		mug, mugged, mugging	
moveable, -ly		mugger	
moveible	movable	muggy, -gier, -giest	
movement		mug shot	
movie		mugwump	
mow, -ed, -ing		mukus	mucous (of
mower			mucus)
mownd	mound	mukus	mucus
mownt	mount	mulatto, -toes	
mowntain	mountain	mulberie	mulberry
mowntenous	mountainous	mulberry, -ries	
mowse	mouse	mulch, -ed, -ing	
mowth	mouth	mule	
mozaic	mosaic	muleteer	
mozzarella		mulish, -ly	
Mr., Messrs.		mull, -ed, -ing	
Mrs.		mullet, -lets, -let	
Ms.		mulligatawny	
much, more, most		mullion	
muchual	mutual	multaple	multiple
mucilage		multch	mulch
mucilaginous		multicultural	
muck, mucked, mucking		multifaceted	
muckraking		multifamily	
muck up		multifarious, -ly	
mucky, -kier, -kiest		multifarius	multifarious
mucous (of mucus)		multifaseted	multifaceted
mucus		multiform	
mud		multilateral, -ly	
muddie	muddy	multilevel	
muddle, -dled, -dling		multilingual	
muddler		multimedia	

multimillionaire
multinashional — multinational
multinational
multiple
multiple sclerosis
multiplex
multipli — multiply
multiplicand
multiplication
multiplicative, -ly
multiplicity, -ties
multiplier
multiplisity — multiplicity
multiply, -plied, -plying
multipurpose
multiracial
multisense
multistage
multistory
multitude
multitudinous
multitudinus — multitudinous
multiversity
multivitamin
mulyon — mullion
mum
mumble, -bled, -bling
mumbo jumbo
mumie — mummy
mumifi — mummify
mummer
mummificasion — mummification
mummification
mummify, -fied, -fying
mummy, -mies
mumps
mumy — mummy
munch, -ed, -ing
munchies
mundain — mundane
mundane, -ly
Munday — Monday
munetry — monetary
mungrel — mongrel
municipal, -ly
municipality, -ties
munie — money

munishun — munition
munisipality — municipality
munk — monk
munkey — monkey
munth — month
muny — money
mur — myrrh
mural
murder, -ed, -ing
murderer
murderess
murderor — murderer
murderous, -ly
murk, -ily, -iness
murky, -kier, -kiest
murmer — murmur
murmur, -ed, -ing
murrain
murth — mirth
murtle — myrtle
mus — mews (stables)
mus — muse (think)
muscat
muscatel
muscle, -cled, -cling (body)
muscle — mussel (mollusk)
musclebound
muscular, -ly
muscularity
Muse (mythology)
muse, mused, musing (think)
muse — mews (stables)
muse — Muse (mythology)
Muse — muse
musel — muscle (body)
musel — mussel (mollusk)
museum
mush, -ed, -ing
mushroom, -ed, -ing
mushy, mushier, mushiest
music
musical, -ly (of music)
musicale
musicale — musical

musician
musisian — musician
musk
muskatel — muscatel
musket
musketeer
musketry
muskmelon
musk ox
muskrat, -rats
musk rose
Muslim (religion)
muslin (fabric)
mussel (mollusk)
mussel — muscle (body)
must
mustache
mustash — mustache
mustang
mustard (spice)
muster, -ed, -ing (assemble)
musterd — mustard
mustie — musty
mutable
mutant, -ly
mutate, -tated, -tating
mutation
mute, muted, muting
mutent — mutant
muter — mutter
mutilate, -lated, -lating
mutilater — mutilator
mutilation
mutilator
mutinear — mutineer
mutineer
mutinous, -ly
mutinus — mutinous
mutiny, -nies
mutiny, -nied, -nying
muton — mutton
mutt
mutter, -ed, -ing
mutton
muttonchops
mutual, -ly
mutuality

muumuu
Muzak
muzzle, -zled, -zling
myna (bird)
myna — miner (worker)
myna — minor (less)
myopia
myopic
myriad
myrrh
myrtle
myself
mysterious, -ly, -ness
mysterius — mysterious
mystery, -ries
mystic (symbol)
mystical, -ly
mysticism
mystificasion — mystification
mystification
mystify, -fied, -fying
mystique (secret)
mystisism — mysticism
mystry — mystery
myth
mythical, -ly
mythology, -gies
myxomatosis

Nn

nab, nabbed, nabbing
  nabor · neighbor
nachos
  nachural · natural
  nachure · nature
  nack · knack
  nacker · nacre
nacre (shellfish)
nadir
nag, nagged, nagging
nagger
  naghty · naughty
nail, -ed, -ing
naive, naïve, -ly
naiveté, naïveté
naked, -ly, -ness
  nakid · naked
  nale · nail
namby-pamby, -bies
name, named, naming
nameable
name-dropper
nameless, -ly
namely
nameplate
namesake
  nanie · nanny
nankeen
nanny, -ies
nanny goat
nanometer
nanosecond
nap, napped, napping
  naparm · napalm
nape
napery
naphtha

naphthalene
  napie · nappy
napkin
nappy
  napsack · knapsack
  naptha · naphtha
  narate · narrate
  narative · narrative
narcissism
narcissistic
narcissus, -cissuses, -cissi
narcosis
narcotic
nark
  narl · gnarled
  narow · narrow
narrate, -rated, -rating
  narrater · narrator
narration
narrative, -ly
narrator
narrow, -ly
  narsissism · narcissism
  narsissistic · narcissistic
  narsisus · narcissus
nasal, -ly
nasalization
nasalize, -lized, -lizing
nascence
nascent
  nasel · nasal
  nash · gnash
  nashon · nation
  nashonal · national
  nastie · nasty
nasty, -tier, -tiest
  nat · gnat
natal
  natel · natal
  nateral · natural
  natile · natal
  naty · natty
nation
national, -ly
National Guard
nationalism
nationalist

nationalistic
nationality, -ties
nationalize, -lized, -lizing
nationalization
native
nativity

| Natsi | Nazi |
| natur | nature |

natural, -ly, -ness
naturalism
naturalist
naturalistic
naturalization
naturalize, -lized, -lizing
nature

| naty | natty |

naught, nought
naughty, -tier, -tiest
nausea
nauseate, -ated, -ating
nauseation
nauseous, -ly
nautical, -ly
nautilus, -luses, -li
naval (ship)

| naval (ship) | navel (body) |

nave (church)

| nave | knave (rogue) |
| navegator | navigator |

navel (body)
navel orange

| navie | navy |
| navigater | navigator |

navigable, -bly
navigate, -gated, -gating
navigation
navigator

navigible	navigable
navul	naval (ship)
navul	navel (body)

navy

| naw | gnaw |

nay (no)

nay	neigh (horse)
naybor	neighbor
nayl	nail

Nazi, -zis

Nazism

nead	knead (dough)
nead	need (want)
neadle	needle
neadless	needless
nealism	nihilism
nean	neon

neap
near, -ed, -ing
nearby
nearly, -ness
nearsighted, -ly, -ness
neat, -ly
nebula, -las, -lae
nebulous, -ly

nebulus	nebulous
neccesary	necessary
necesarey	necessary
necesitate	necessitate
necesitey	necessity

necessarily
necessary, -saries
necessitate, -tated, -tating
necessity, -ties
neck
neckerchief

| neckliss | necklace |

necklace
neckline

| necksus | nexus |

necktie
neckwear
necromancer
necromancy

necromanser	necromancer
necromansey	necromancy
necrofilia	necrophilia
necrofiliac	necrophiliac
necrofilism	necrophilism

necrophilia
necrophiliac
necrophilism
necropolis, -lises
nectar
nectarine
nee, née (name)

| nee | knee (limb) |

need, -ed, -ing (want)		nek	neck
need	knead (dough)	neklace	necklace
need	kneed (use	nekrofilia	necrophilia
	knee)	nekropolis	necropolis
needful		nektar	nectar
needle, -dled, -dling		nell	knell
needlecraft		nemesis, -ses	
needlepoint		nemisis	nemesis
needless, -ly, -ness		nemonics	mnemonics
needlework		neofite	neophyte
neel	kneel	Neolithic	
neer	near	neologism	
ne'er-do-well		neology	
neet	neat	neon	
nefarious, -ly, -ness		neophyte	
nefarius	nefarious	nephew	
nefew	nephew	nephrite	
negate, -gated, -gating		nephritic	
negation		nephritis	
negative, -tived, -tiving		nepotism	
negativity		Neptune (planet)	
neggotiate	negotiate	nerd	
neghbor	neighbor	nerture	nurture
neglect, -ed, -ing		nervana	nirvana
neglectful, -ly		nerve, nerved, nerving	
negligable	negligible	nerve center	
negligee		nerveless, -ly, -ness	
negligence		nerve-racking	
negligense	negligence	nerveous	nervous
negligent, -ly		nervous, -ly, -ness	
negligible		nervus	nervous
neglijay	negligee	nervy, -vier, -viest	
negoshiable	negotiable	nessessary	necessary
negoshiate	negotiate	nesessitate	necessitate
negotiable		nesessity	necessity
negotiate, -ated, -ating		nesle	nestle
negotiation		nest, -ed, -ing	
Negro, Negroes		nestle, -tled, -tling	
neice	niece	net, netted, netting	
neigh (horse)		netha	neither (nor)
neigh	nay (no)	netha	nether (below)
neighbor		nether (below)	
neighborhood		nether	neither (nor)
neighboring		netile	nettle
neighborly, -liness		nettle, -tled, -tling	
neither (nor)		nettlesome	
neither	nether (below)	nettul	nettle

network
  neumatic — pneumatic
neural
neuralgia
neuralgic
neuritic
neuritis
neurological, -ly
neurologist
neurology
neuron
neurone
neuroscience
neurosis, -ses
neurosurgeon
neurosurgery
neurotic, -ally
neuter, -ed, -ing
neutral, -ly
neutralism
neutrality
neutralization
neutralize, -lized, -lizing
  neutril — neutral
neutron
  neva — never
nevermore
nevertheless
new (not old)
  new — gnu (animal)
  new — knew (did know)
newborn
  newclear — nuclear
  newcleus — nucleus
newcomer
newfangled
newfound
Newfoundland
newly
newlywed
  newmatic — pneumatic
  newmonia — pneumonia
  newral — neural
  newrologist — neurologist
  newrone — neurone
  newrosis — neurosis

  newrotic — neurotic
news
news agency
news agent
newsboy
newscast, -cast, -casting
newscaster
  newscastor — newscaster
newsletter
newsmagazine
newsman, -men
newspaper
newspaperman, -men
newspeak
newsprint
newsreel
newsstand
newsworthy
newt
  newter — neuter
  newtralize — neutralize
  newtron — neutron
next
next-door
next of kin
nexus, nexuses, -us
  ni — nigh
  nialism — nihilism
nib
  nibbel — nibble
nibble, -bled, -bling
nibbler
nice, nicer, nicest
nicety, -ties
niche
nick, -ed, -ing
nickel
  nickerbockers — knickerbockers
  nickers — knickers
  nickle — nickel
  nicknack — knickknack
nickname, -named, -naming
  nicks — nix
nicotine
niece
  niether — neither
  nifarius — nefarious

nife	knife		ninie	ninny
niftie	nifty		ninny, -nies	
nifty, -tier, -tiest			ninteen	nineteen
nigel	niggle		ninth, -ly	
nigerd	niggard		nion	neon
niggard, -ly, -liness			nipie	nippy
niggle, -gled, -gling			niple	nipple
nigh			nipper	
night, -ly (time)			nipple	
night	knight (lord)		nippy, -pier, -piest	
nightcap			nirvana	
nightclothes			nise	nice
nightclub			nisety	nicety
nightdress			nit (insect)	
nightfall			nit	knit (stitch)
nightgown			nitch	niche
nighthawk			nite	knight (lord)
nightingale			nite	night (time)
nightjar			niter	
nightlife			nither	neither
nightlong			nitpick, -ed, -ing	
nightmare			nitpicker	
nightmarish			nitrate, -trated, -trating	
nightshade			nitration	
nightshirt			nitric	
nightsoil			nitrifi	nitrify
nightstick			nitrificasion	nitirification
nighttime			nitrification	
night watchman			nitrify, -fied, -fying	
nigle	niggle		nitrite	
niglect	neglect		nitrogen	
nihilism			nitrogenous	
nikotine	nicotine		nitrogliserine	nitroglycerin
nil			nitroglycerin, nitroglycerine	
nilon	nylon		nitrojen	nitrogen
nimbel	nimble		nitrous	
nimble, -bler, -blest			nitting	knitting
nimbus, -bi, -buses			nitty-gritty	
nimf	nymph		nitwit	
nimph	nymph		nives	knives
nine			nix	
ninepins			no (denial)	
nineteen			no	know (understand)
nineteenth			nobel	noble
ninetieth			nobie	knobby
ninety, -ties				
ninetyeth	ninetieth			

nobility, -ties
noble, nobler, noblest
noble, -ly, -ness
nobleman, -men
noblewoman, -men
nobody, -bodies
nock — knock
nocker — knocker
nocturnal, -ly
nocturne
nocuous
nod, nodded, nodding
noddy, -dies
node
nodular
nodule
Noel
noes (denials)
noes — knows (understand)
noes — nose (facial)
noggin (cup, head)
no-good
no-hitter
no-how
noise, noised, noising
noiseless
noisily
noisiness
noisemaker
noisome
noisy, noisier, noisiest
noisily, noisiness
noledge — knowledge
noll — knoll
nomad
nomadic
nomanee — nominee
no-man's-land
nom de plume
nome — gnome
nomenclature
nominal, -ly
nominate, -nated, -nating
nominater — nominator
nomination
nominative

nominator
nominee
nommad — nomad
non — none
nonabrasive
nonabsolute
nonabsorbent
nonacademic
nonacceptance
nonacid
nonactive
nonaddictive
nonadhesive
nonadjacent
nonadjustable
nonaggression
nonaggressiun — nonaggression
nonapplicable
nonassertive, -ly
nonathletic
nonbeliever
noncancerous
noncarbonated
non-Catholic
non-Caucasian
noncellular
nonchalance
non-Christian
noncoagulating
noncohesive
noncollectible
noncombatant
noncombustible
noncommercial
noncommercially
noncommissioned
noncommittal, -ly
noncommunicable
noncommunicative
noncommunist
noncompetitive
noncompliance
noncomplying
non compos mentis
non compus mentis — non compos mentis
nonconciliatory

nonconclusive, -ly -ness
nonconcurrence
nonconducting
nonconductive
nonconductor
nonconflicting
nonconformist
nonconformity
nonconstructive, -ly
nonconsumption
noncontagious
noncontributory
noncontroversial, -ly
nonconventional
nonconvertible
noncooperation
noncorrosive
noncredit
noncritical
nondairy
nondeductible
nondenominational
nondependence
nondescript
nondestructive
nondetachable
nondiscriminatory
nondistinctive, -ly, -ness
nondivisible
nondrinker
none (no one)
  none   nun (religion)
noneducable
noneducational
noneffective
noneffervescent
nonelastic
nonelectric
noneligible
nonemotional
nonenforcable
nonenforcement
nonentity, -ties
nonessential
nonetheless
nonexchangable
nonexistent

nonexpendable
nonexplosive
nonfactual
nonfat
nonfiction
nonfictional
nonfilterable
nonflammable
nonflexible
nonflowering
nonfulfillment
nonfunctional
nongaseous
nongovernmental
nonhabitual
nonhazardous
nonhereditary
nonhuman
nonimmunity
noninconclusive
nonincriminating
nonindependent
noninductive
nonindustrial
noninfectious
noninformative
noninhabitable
noninheritable
noninstitutional
noninterchangable
nonintersecting
nonintervention
nonintoxicant
nonintoxicating
nonirritant
nonirritating
nonjudicial
nonkosher
nonlethal
nonlinear
nonliterary
nonmalignant
nonmarketable
nonmaterial
nonmember
nonmetal
nonmigratory

nonmilitary
nonnegotiable
nonnutritious
nonobjective, -ly
nonobjectivity
nonobservance
nonoily
nonoperable
nonorganic
nonparallel
nonpareil
nonparticipation
nonpartisan
nonpaying
nonpayment
nonperformance
nonperishable
nonpermanent
nonperson
nonphysical
nonplussed
nonpoisonous
nonpolitical
nonporous
nonpossessive, -ly, -ness
nonprecious
nonpredictable
nonprescription
nonprescriptive
nonproducer
nonproductive
nonprofessional
nonprofit
nonproliferation
nonproprietary
nonpunishable
nonracial
nonradioactive
nonrealistic
nonreciprocal
nonrecognition
nonrecoverable
nonrecurrent
nonreader
nonredeemable
nonrefillable
nonreligious

nonremovable
nonrepresentational
nonrepresentative
nonresident
nonresistance
nonresistant
nonrestrictive
nonreturnable
nonrigid
nonsalaried
nonscheduled
nonscientific
nonseasonal
nonsectarian
nonsegregated
nonselective
nonsectarian
nonsence   nonsense
nonsense
nonsensical, -ly
non sequitur
nonshrinkable
nonskid
nonskilled
nonslip
nonsmoker
nonsmoking
nonsocial
nonspecialized
nonstaining
nonstarter
nonstick
nonstimulating
nonstop
nonstrategic
nonstriking
nonsurgical
nonsupport
nonsustaining
nontaxable
nontechnical
nontenured
nonthinking
nontoxic
nontransferable
non troppo
nonunion

nonuser		nosebag	
nonvascular		noseband	
nonvenomous		nosebleed	
nonverbal		nose-dive, -dived, -diving	
nonviable		nosegay	
nonviolence		nosepiece	
nonviolent, -ly		nosh, -ed, -ing	
nonvirulent		no-show	
nonvocal		nosily	
nonvocational		nosiness	
nonvoter		nostalgia	
nonwhite		nostalgic, -ally	
noodle			
noogar	nougat	nostrem	nostrum
nook		nostril	
noon		nostrim	nostrum
noonday		nostrum	
noontime		nosy, nosey, -sier, -siest	
noose		not (denial)	
nope		not	knot (tie)
nor (conjunction)		nota bene	
nor	gnaw (bite)	notability	
Nordic		notable, -bly	
norm		notarial, -ly	
normal, -ly		notary public, notaries public	
normalcy		notation	
normality		notch, -ed, -ing	
normalization		note, noted, noting	
normalize, -lized, -lizing		notebook	
Norman		notefy	notify
normative, -ly, -ness		notepaper	
norsia	nausea	notery public	notary public
norsiate	nauseate	noteworthy	
nort	naught, nought	nothing	
nortey	naughty	nothingness	
north		noticable	noticeable
northerly		notice, -ticed, -ticing	
northern		noticeable, -bly	
northerner		noticeible	noticeable
northernmost		notifiable	
northward, -ly		notificasion	notification
nortickel	nautical	notification	
nortie	naughty	notifier	
nose, nosed, nosing (detect)		notify, -fied, -fying	
nose	knows (understand)	notion	
		notional, -ly	
nose	noes (denial)	notoriety	
		notorios	notorious

notorious, -ly
   notorius — notorious
notwithstanding
   nougar — nougat
nougat
noun
nourish, -ed, -ing
nourishingly
nourishment
nouveau riche, nouveaux riches
nova
novel
novelette
novelist
novelization
novelize, -lized, -lizing
novella, novellas, novellae
novelty, -ties
November
novena
novice
novitiate
now
nowadays
no way
nowhere
   nowing — knowing
   nowledge — knowledge
noxious, -ly
   noxius — noxious
   nozzel — nozzle
nozzle
   nu — gnu (animal)
   nu — knew (did know)
   nu — new (not old)
nuance
   nuanse — nuance
nub
nubile
   nuckle — knuckle
nuclear
nuclear bomb
nuclear energy
nuclear family
   nuclear fishun — nuclear fission
nuclear fission

nuclear fusion
nuclear power
nuclear reaction
nuclear reactor
nucleus, -clei, -cleuses
nude
nudge, nudged, nudging
nudism
nudist
nudity
   nuge — nudge
nugget
nuisance
   nulifi — nullify
null
   nullificasion — nullification
nullification
nullify, -fied, -fying
   num — numb
   numatic — pneumatic
numb, numbed, numbing
numb, -ly, -ness
number, -ed, -ing
numberless
numerable
numeral
   numeracle — numerical
numerate, -rated, -rating
   numerater — numerator
numeration
numerator
numerical, -ly
   numericle — numerical
numerological
numerology
numerous, -ly, -ness
   numerus — numerous
numismatics
numismatist
   numskull — numbskull
   numonia — pneumonia
nun (religion)
   nun — none (no one)
nunnery, -neries
   nupshial — nuptial
nuptial
   nural — neural

nuralgia	neuralgia
nurchere	nurture
nuritis	neuritis
nurled	knurled
nurologist	neurologist
nurone	neurone
nurosis	neurosis
nurotic	neurotic

nurse, nursed, nursing
nursery, -eries
nursing home

nursrey	nursery

nurture, -tured, -turing

nurve	nerve
nusance	nuisance
nuse	news
nuspaper	newspaper

nut

nuter	neuter

nutcracker
nutmeg

nutral	neutral

nutrient
nutriment

nutrision	nutrition
nutrisious	nutritious

nutrition
nutritional, -ly
nutritionist
nutritious, -ly, -ness

nutron	neutron

nuts
nutshell
nutty, -tier, -tiest

nuty	nutty
nuzzel	nuzzle

nuzzle, -zled, -zling
nylon

nymf	nymph

nymph
nymphomania
nymphomaniac

Oo

oaf
oak
oar (boat)

oar	awe (dread)
oar	or (conj.)
oar	ore (rock)

oasis, oases
oat
oath, oaths
oatmeal

obalisk	obelisk
obay	obey
obbese	obese

obduracy

obdurasy	obduracy

obdurate
obedience

obediense	obedience

obedient, -ly

obeisanse	obeisance

obelisk
obese
obesity
obey, -ed, -ing
obituary, -aries

objecktion	objection
objay dart	objet d'art

object, -ed, -ing

objecter	objector

objection
objectionable, -bly

objectionible	objectionable

objective, -ly, -ness
objectivity
objector
objet d'art, objets d'art
oblation

obleek	oblique

obligate, -gated, -gating
obligation
obligatory
oblige, obliged, obliging

oblik	oblique

oblique, -ly, -ness
obliterate, -rated, -rating
obliteration
oblivion
oblivious, -ly, -ness

oblivius	oblivious

oblong
obloquy, -quies

obnoksious	obnoxious

obnoxious, -ly, -ness

obo	oboe

oboe
oboist

obsalete	obsolete

obscene, -ly
obscenity, -ties
obscurantism
obscurantist
obscure, -scured, -scuring
obscure, -scurer, -scurest
obscurity, -ties
obsecrate, -crated, -crating

obseen	obscene
obsekwies	obsequious

obsequious, -ly, -ness
observance
observant, -ly
observation
observatory, -tories

observatery	observatory

observe, -served, -serving

obsesion	obsession

obsess, -ed, -ing
obsession
obsessive, -ly
obsolescence
obsolescent

obsolesense	obsolescence
obsolesent	obsolescent

obsolete, -ly

obsolve	absolve

obstacel — obstacle
obstacle
  obstain — abstain
  obstatrician — obstetrician
obstetric, -al
obstetrician
obstetrics
  obstetrisian — obstetrician
obstinacy, -cies
  obstinasy — obstinacy
obstinate, -ly
obstreperous, -ly, -ness
  obstreperus — obstreperous
  obstrucktion — obstruction
obstruct, -ed, -ing
  obstructer — obstructor
obstruction
obstructive, -ly, -ness
obstructor
obtain, -ed, -ing
  obtane — obtain
  obtroode — obtrude
  obtroosive — obtrusive
obtrude, -truded, -truding
obtrusive, -ly, -ness
obtuse, -ly, -ness
obverse, -ly
obviate, -ated, -ating
obviation
obvious, -ly, -ness
  obvius — obvious
  obzervance — observance
  obzervation — observation
  ocasion — occasion
occasion, -ed, -ing
occasional, -ly
Occident
occidental
occlude, -cluded, -cluding
occlusion
  occluson — occlusion
  occular — ocular
occult
occultism
occupancy
occupant
  occupasion — occupation

occupation
occupational, -ly
  occupent — occupant
  occupi — occupy
occupy, -pied, -pying
occupier
occur, -curred, -curring
  occuranse — occurrence
occurrence
ocean
oceanarium, -iums, -ia
oceanfront
oceangoing
oceanic
  oceanografey — oceanography
oceanographer
oceanography
ocelot
ochre, ocher
  Ocktober — October
o'clock
  oclood — occlude
  ocloosion — occlusion
  Ocsident — Occident
octagon
octagonal, -ly
octahedron, -drons, -dra
octane
octave
octavo
octet
October
octogenarian
octopus, -puses, -pi
octosyllabic
ocular
  ocult — occult
  ocupancy — occupancy
  ocupant — occupant
  ocupi — occupy
  ocur — occur
  ocurence — occurrence
  od — odd
odd, -ly, -ness
  oddaty — oddity
oddball
oddity, -ties

oddment		officer	
odds		office worker	
odds-on		official, -ly	
odeclone	eau de Cologne	officialdom	
oderus	odorous	officiant	
odiferus	odoriferous	officiate, -ated, -ating	
odious, -ly, -ness		officious, -ly, -ness	
odissey	odyssey	offing	
odium		offise	office
odius	odious	offish	
odometer		offisial	official
odor, -less		offisious	officious
odoriferous, -ly		off-key	
odorous		off-limits	
odyssey		off-line	
Oedipus complex		off-load, -ed, -ing	
of (preposition)		off-peak	
of	off (away)	offprint	
ofal	offal	off-putting	
ofe	oaf	off-season	
ofence	offense	offset, -set, -setting	
ofend	offend	offshoot	
ofen	often	offshore	
ofense	offense	offside	
ofensive	offensive	offspring	
ofer	offer	offstage	
off (away)		off-the-record	
offace	office	off-the-shelf	
offal		offtrack	
off-beat		off-white	
off Broadway		oficial	official
off chance		oficiate	officiate
off color		oficious	officious
offence		ofis	office
offend, -ed, -ing		ofiser	officer
offender		ofishal	official
offendor	offender	ofishiate	officiate
offense		ofishus	officious
offensive, -ly, -ness		ofset	offset
offer, -ed, -ing		ofshoot	offshoot
offering		ofside	offside
offertory, -ries		ofspring	offspring
offhand		oft	
offhanded, -ly		often	
office		oftentimes	
officeholder		ogel	ogle
office hours		oger	ogre

ogle, ogled, ogling		Olimpic	Olympic
ogre		oliv	olive
ogress		olive	
oh (interjection)		omelet, omelette	
oh	owe (debt)	omen	
ohm		ominous, -ly, -ness	
ohmeter		ominus	ominous
oil, oiled, oiling		omision	omission
oilcan		omission	
oilcloth		omit, omitted, omitting	
oil field		omnibus, -buses	
oilly	oily	omnipotanse	omnipotence
oil paint		omnipotence	
oil rig		omnipotent, -ly	
oilskin		omnipresence	
oil well		omnipresent	
oily, oilier, oiliest		omnisense	omniscience
ointment		omnisent	omniscient
oister	oyster	omniscience	
ok	oak	omniscient, -ly	
ok	okay	omnivorous, -ly, -ness	
okay		omnivorus	omnivorous
oks	ox	on	
oksalic acid	oxalic acid	on (prep.)	own (possess)
oksidate	oxidate	once	
okside	oxide	once-over	
Oksident	Occident	oncoming	
oksidize	oxidize	oncore	encore
oksyacetylene	oxyacetylene	oncourse	
oksygen	oxygen	one (number)	
oksymoron	oxymoron	one	won (win)
old, older, oldest		one-armed bandit	
olden		one-liner	
old-fashioned		one-man	
oldie		oner	owner
oldish		onerous, -ly, -ness	
old-maid		onership	ownership
old-timer		onerus	onerous
oleaginous		oneself	
oleaginus	oleaginous	one-sided	
oleander		onest	honest
olfactory		onesty	honesty
olfactry	olfactory	onetime	
oligarch		one-to-one	
oligarchic		one-track mind	
oligarchy, -chies		one-upmanship	
oligarkey	oligarchy	one-way street	

one-way ticket
ongoing
  onian — onion
  oniks — onyx
onion, -y
onionskin
  onor — honor
  onley — only
on-line
onlooker
only
onomatopeia
onomatopeic, -ally
onomatopoetic, -ally
  onorary — honorary
  onorarium — honorarium
  onrable — honorable
  on route — en route
onrush
  onse — once
onset
onshore
onslaught
  onslawt — onslaught
onto
ontogeny
ontological
ontology
  ontray — entree
  ontreprener — entrepreneur
onus
onward
onyx
oomph
ooze, oozed, oozing
opacity
  opake — opaque
opal
opaline
opaque, -ly, -ness
  opasity — opacity
  opeate — opiate
open, -ed, -ing
open-air
open-and-shut
open-ended
opener

open-handed, -ly, -ness
open-heart surgery
openly
open-minded
openwork
opera
operability
operable, -bly
operate, -rated, -rating
  operater — operator
operatic, -ally
operation
operational
operative, -ly
operator
operetta
  operible — operable
  opeum — opium
ophthalmic
ophthalmologist
ophthalmology
opiate
opine, opined, opining
  opinian — opinion
opinion
opinionated
opium
  oponent — opponent
  oportune — opportune
  oportunity — opportunity
  opose — oppose
  oposite — opposite
  oposition — opposition
opossum
  oposum — opossum
opponent
opportune, -ly
opportunism
opportunist
opportunity, -ties
opposable
oppose, -posed, -posing
opposite, -ly, -ness (contrary)
  opposite — apposite (appropriate)
opposition
oppress, -ed, -ing

oppresser	oppressor	orangutan, orangoutan	
oppression		orater	orator
oppressive, -ly, -ness		oration	
oppressor		orator	
opprobrious, -ly		oratorical, -ly	
opprobrium		oratorio, -rios	
oprable	operable	oratory	
oprate	operate	oratrey	oratory
opresion	oppression	orb	
opress	oppress	orbit, -ed, -ing	
opressive	oppressive	orbital	
opsion	option	orbiter	
opshioul	optional	orbitor	orbiter
opt, -ed, -ing		orcestra	orchestra
optacal	optical	orcestral	orchestral
optative		orcestrate	orchestrate
opthalmic	ophthalmic	orchard	
opthalmology	ophthalmology	orchardist	
optic		orchestra	
optical, -ly		orchestral, -ly	
optician		orchestrate, -trated, -trating	
optics		orchestration	
optimal, -ly		orchid	
optimism		orcid	orchid
optimist		ordain, -ed, -ing	
optimistic, -ally		ordanal	ordinal
optimum, -ma, -mums		ordane	ordain
option		ordeal	
optional, -ly		order, -ed, -ing	
optisian	optician	orderly, -lies	
optometrist		orderliness	
optometry		ordinal	
opulence		ordinance (law)	
opulense	opulence	ordinarily	
opulent, -ly		ordinariness	
opus, opuses, opera		ordinary, -ries	
or (conjuction)		ordination	
or	awe (dread)	ordinry	ordinary
or	oar (boat)	orditer	auditor
or	ore (rock)	orditrey	auditory
ora	aura	ordnance (weapons)	
oracel	oracle	ordnance	ordinance (law)
oracle		ordnary	ordinary
oracular		ordure	
oral, -ly (spoken)		ore (rock)	
oral	aural (hear)	ore	oar (boat)
orange		ore	or (conj.)

ore	awe (dread)	orkid	orchid
oregano		ornament	
orfan	orphan	ornamental, -ly	
orfanage	orphanage	ornamentation	
orful	awful	ornate, -ly, -ness	
organ		ornery	
organdy, organdie, -ies		ornimant	ornament
organic, -ally		orning	awning
organick	organic	ornithologist	
organism		ornithology	
organismal		orotund, -ity	
organist		orphan	
organization		orphanage	
organize, -nized, -nizing		orris	
organza		orspisious	auspicious
orgasm		orstruck	awestruck
orgasmic		orsum	awesome
orgenism	organism	ort	aught
orger	auger (tool)	ort	ought
orger	augur (foretell)	orthapedic	orthopedic
orgey	orgy	orthedoks	orthodox
orgiastic		orthodontic	
orgy, -gies		orthodontics	
orical	auricle (ear)	orthodontist	
orical	oracle (seer)	orthodox	
oriel		orthodoxy	
Orient		orthografey	orthography
oriental		orthography, -phies	
orientate, -tated, -tating		orthopedic	
orientation		orthopedics	
orienteering		orthopedist	
orifice		orthority	authority
orifise	orifice	oscilation	oscillation
origami, -mis		oscillate, -lated, -lating (move)	
origin		oscillate	osculate (kiss)
original, -ly		oscillater	oscillator
originality		oscillation	
originate, -nated, -nating		oscillator	
originater	originator	oscillatory	
originator		oscilloscope	
oringe	orange	oscilloscopic, -ally	
oriole		osculate, -lated, -lating (kiss)	
orjy	orgy	osculate	oscillate (move)
orkestra	orchestra	osean	ocean
orkestral	orchestral	oseanic	oceanic
orkestrate	orchestrate	oselot	ocelot
orkestration	orchestration	osier	

osifi	ossify	ouster	
osmosis		oustor	ouster
ospray	osprey	out, -ed, -ing	
osprey, -preys		outage	
ossification		out-and-out	
ossifi	ossify	outback	
ossify, -fied, -fying		outbalance, -anced, -ancing	
ossilate	oscillate	outbid	
ossilation	oscillation	outbilding	outbuilding
ossiloscope	oscilloscope	outboard	
osteapath	osteopath	outbound	
ostensable	ostensible	outbrake	outbreak
ostensible, -bly		outbreak	
ostentation		outbuilding	
ostentatious, -ly		outburst	
osteopath		outcast	
osteopathic		outclass	
osteopathy		outcome	
ostracism		outcri	outcry
ostrasism	ostracism	outcrop	
ostracize, -cized, -cizing		outcry, -cries	
ostrasize	ostracize	outdated	
ostrich		outdistance, -ed, -ing	
ote	oat	outdo, outdid, -done, -doing	
oter	otter	outdoor	
oth	oath	outdoors	
other		outdoorsman, -men	
otherwise		outer	
otherworldly, -liness		outermost	
otiose		outer space	
otoman	ottoman	outfield	
otter		outfit, -fitted, -fitting	
ottoman, -mans		outfitter	
ouch		outflank, -ed, -ing	
ought (should)		outflow	
ought	aught (any part)	outfox, -ed, -ing	
		outgoing	
Ouija		outgrow, -grew, -grown, -growing	
oul	owl	outgrowth	
ounce		outguess	
ounse	ounce	outhouse	
our (pronoun)		outhowse	outhouse
our	hour (time)	outing	
ourly	hourly	outlandish, -ly	
ours		outlast, -ed, -ing	
ourself, -selves		outlaw	
oust, ousted, ousting		outlawry	

outlay
outlet
outline, -lined, -lining
outlive, -lived, -living
outlook
outlying
outmaneuver, -ed, -ing
outmoded
outmost
outnumber
out-of-date
out-of-towner
outpace, -ed, -ing
outpatient
  outpayshent   outpatient
outperform, -ed, -ing
outplay, -ed, -ing
outpoint, -ed, -ing
  outpooring   outpouring
outpost
outpouring
output, output, outputting
outrage, -raged, -raging
outrageous, -ly, -ness
  outragious   outrageous
outrank
outreach
outrider
outrigger
outright, -ness
  outrite   outright
outrun, -ran, -run, -running
outsell, outsold, outselling
outset
outshine, -shone, -shining
outside
outsider
outsize, outsized
outskirts
outsmart
outspoken, -ly, -ness
outspread
outstanding, -ly
outstretch, outstretched
outstrip, -stripped, -stripping
outvote, -ted, -ting
outward, -ly

outwear, -wore, -worn, -wearing
outweigh
outwit, -witted, -witting
outwork
outworn
  ouze   ooze
  ov   of
oval
  ovarey   ovary
ovary, -ries
ovate
ovation
oven
ovenproof
ovenware
  ovenwear   ovenware
over, -ly
overabundance
overact
overactive
overage
overaggressive
overall
overalls
overanxious
overarm
overawe, -awed, -awing
  overawl   overall
overbalance, -anced, -ancing
  overbalanse   overbalance
  overbare   overbear
overbear, -bore, -borne, -bearing
overbearing
overbid, -bid, -bidding
overblown
overboard
  overbord   overboard
overburden, -ed, -ing
overcareful
overcast, -cast, -casting
overcautious
overcharge, -charged, -charging
  overchure   overture
overcloud
overcoat
overcome, -came, -come, -coming
overcommit, -mitted, -mitting

overcompensate, -sated, -sating
overconfidence
overconfident
overconscientious
overcooked
overcritical
  overdew   overdue
overdo, -did, -done, -doing
overdose
overdraft
overdraw, -drew, -drawn, -drawing
overdress, -ed, -ing
overdressed
overdrive
overdue
overeager
overeat, -ate, -eaten, -eating
overeducated
overemphasis
overemphasize, -sized, -sizing
overestimate, -mated, -mating
overexcite, -cited, -citing
overexert, -ed
overexpose, -posed, -posing
overexposure
overextend, -ed, -ing
overfeed, -fed, -feeding
overfill, -ed, -ing
overflow, -ed, -ing
overfly, -flew, -flown, -ing
overfull
overgenerous
overglaze, -glazed, -glazing
overgrown
overhand
overhang, -hung, -hanging
overhasty
overhaul, -ed, -ing
  overhawl   overhaul
overhead
overhear, -heard, -hearing
overhearer
overheat
  overhed   overhead
  overherd   overheard
  overhere   overhear
overindulge, -dulged, -dulging

overindulgence
overindulgent
overjoyed
overkill
overland
overlap, -lapped, -lapping
overlay, -laid, -laying
overleaf
  overleef   overleaf
overlie, -lay, -lain, -lying (lie over)
  overlie   overly
overload
overlong
overlook
overlord
overly (excessively)
overmodest
overnight
  overnite   overnight
  overore   overawe
  overought   overwrought
overoptimism
overoptimistic
overpass
overpay, -paid, -paying
overplay
overpopulated
overpower, -ed, -ing
overpowering
overpraise, -praised, -praising
overprice, -priced, -pricing
overprint, -ed, -ing
overproduce, -duced, -ducing
overprotection
overprotective
overproud
overqualified
overrate, -rated, -rating
  overeach   overreach
  overeech   overreach
  overiding   overriding
overreach, -ed, -ing
overreacher
overreact, -ed, -ing
override, -rode, -ridden, -riding
  overrought   overwrought
overripe

overrule, -ruled, -ruling
overrun, -ran, -run, -running
  overule   overrule
  overun   overrun
overseas (abroad)
oversee, -saw, -seen, -seeing
overseer
oversell, -sold, -selling
oversensitive
oversew, ed, -sown, -ing
oversexed
overshadow, -ed, -ing
overshoe
overshoot, -shot, -shooting
oversight
  oversite   oversight
oversimplify, -fied, -fying
oversize
oversized
oversleep, overslept, -ing
overspecialize, -lized, -lizing
overspecialization
overspend, -spent, -spending
overspread
overstaffed
overstate, -stated, -stating
overstatement
overstay, -ed, -ing
overstep, -stepped, -stepping
overstimulate, -lated, -lating
overstock, -ed, -ing
overstrict
overstuffed
oversubscribed
oversupply, -plies
overt, -ly
overtake, overtook, -taken, -taking
  overtaks   overtax
overtax, -ed, -ing
over-the-counter
overthrow, -threw, -thrown, -throwing
overtime
overtired
overtone
overture
overturn, -ed, -ing

overuse, -used, -using
overvalue, -lued, -luing
overview
  overwait   overweight
overweening
overweight
  overwelm   overwhelm
  overwerk   overwork
overwhelm, -ed, -ing
overwind, -wound, -winding
overwork, -ed, -ing
overwrought
  overy   ovary
overzealous
  oveture   overture
oviduct
  ovin   oven
oviparous, -ly
ovoid (egg)
  ovoid   avoid (evade)
ovulate, -lated, -lating
ovulation
ovule
ovum, ova
  owa   hour (time)
  owa   our (pron.)
owe, owed, owing (debt)
  owe   oh (interjection)
owl
own, -ed, -ing
  ownce   ounce
owner
ownership
  ownly   only
  owst   oust
  owt   out
ox, oxen
oxblood
oxbow
oxeye
oxford
oxidate, -dated, -dating
oxidation
oxide
oxidizable
oxidization

oxidize, -dized, -dizing
oxidizer
  oxidizible   oxidizable
  oxidizor   oxidizer
  oxigenate   oxygenate
oxyacetylene
oxygen
oxygenate, -nated, -nating
oxygenation
oxymoron, -mora
oyster
oz, oz.
ozone
ozonosphere

Pp

pace, paced, pacing
 pacefist   pacifist
pacemaker
pacer
pacesetter
 pach   patch
 pachwork   patchwork
pacific, -ally
pacification
pacifier
pacifism
pacifist
pacify, -fied, -fying
pack, -ed, -ing (load)
package
 packedge   package
packet
packhorse
packinghouse
packsaddle
pact (agreement)
pad, padded, padding
 paddel   paddle
paddle, -dled, -dling
paddock
paddy, -dies (rice)
 paddy   patty (cake)
paddy wagon
padlock, -ed, -ing
 padock   paddock
padre
 pady   paddy
pagan
paganism
page, paged, paging
pageant
pageantry, -ries
 pagentry   pageantry

pageboy
paginate, -nated, -nating
pagination
pagoda
pail (bucket)
 pail   pale (colorless)
pain (ache)
 pain   pane (glass)
painful, -ly, -ness
painkiller
painless, -ly, -ness
painstaking, -ly
paint, -ed, -ing
paintbox
paintbrush
painter
painting
pair, -ed, -ing (two)
 pair   pare (trim)
 pair   pear (fruit)
pajamas
pal, palled, palling (friend)
palace
 palase   palace
palatable (taste)
palate (mouth)
 palate   palette (board)
 palate   pellet (ball)
 palate   pallet (bed)
palatial (palace)
pale, paled, paling (colorless)
 pale   pail (bucket)
paleographer
paleography
paleolithic
paleontologist
paleontology
Paleozoic
palette (board)
 palette   pallet (bed)
 paliate   palliate
 palid   pallid
palindrome
paling
palisade, -saded, -sading
pall, palled, palling (satiate)

pallbearer
pallet (bed)
   pallet   palette (board)
   pallet   pellet (ball)
palliate, -ated, -ating
palliation
palliative
pallid
pallor
palm, -ed, -ing
palmer
palmist
palmistry
palmy, -mier, -miest
palomino, -nos
   palor   pallor
palpable, -bly
   palpible   palpable
palpitate, -tated, -tating
palpitation
   palsie   palsy
palsied
palsy, -sies
   paltrie   paltry
paltry, -trier, -triest (petty)
   paltry   poultry (birds)
   pamplet   pamphlet
pampas
pamper, -ed, -ing
pamphlet
pan, panned, panning
panacea
panache
Panama hat, panama
   panash   panache
pancake
panchromatic
pancreas
pancreatic
panda (animal)
pandemonium
pander, -ed, -ing (indulge)
pane (glass)
   pane   pain (ache)
   paneful   painful
panegyric, -ally
panel, -ed, -ing

paneling
panelist
   panestaking   painstaking
panful
pang
panhandle, -ed, -ing
panhandler
panic, -icked, -icking
panicky
panic-stricken
   panigiric   panegyric
   panik   panic
pannier
panorama
panoramic
   pansie   pansy
pansy, -sies
pant, -ed, -ing
pantaloon
pantheism
pantheist
pantheistic
pantheon
panther
   panthion   pantheon
panties
pantomime, -mimed, -miming
   pantomine   pantomime
   pantray   pantry
pantry, -ries
pants
pantsuit
pantyhose
   panza   panzer
panzer
pap
papa
papacy, -cies
papal
   papasy   papacy
papaya
paper
paperback
paperboard
paperboy
paper clip
paperhanger

paperhanging
  paper-mache — papier-mâché
  paperwait — paperweight
paperweight
paperwork
papier-mâché
  papirus — papyrus
papist
papoose
  papouse — papoose
  pappa — papa
  pappoose — papoose
  papprika — paprika
  pappyrus — papyrus
  paprica — paprika
paprika
  papul — papal
papyrus, ruses, -ri
par
  parabel — parable
parable
parabola
parachute, -ed, -ing
  paracide — parricide
  paracleet — paraclete
parade, -raded, -rading
  paradice — paradise
paradigm
  paradime — paradigm
paradise
  paradoks — paradox
paradox
paradoxical, -ly
  parady — parody
  parafernalia — paraphernalia
paraffin
  parafin — paraffin
  parafrase — paraphrase
paragon
  paragraf — paragraph
paragraph
parakeet
  parakete — parakeet
  paralax — parallax
  paralel — parallel
  paralelagram — parallelogram
  paralisis — paralysis

  paralitic — paralytic
  paralize — paralyze
parallax
parallel, -leled, -leling
parallelogram
paralysis
paralytic
paralyze, -lyzed, -lyzing
paramedic
paramedical
parameter
  paramiter — parameter
  paramoor — paramour
paramount
paramour
  paramownt — paramount
paranoia
paranoiac
paranoid
parapet
paraphernalia
paraphrase, -phrased, -phrasing
paraplegic
  parashoot — parachute
  parashute — parachute
paraprofessional
parapsychology
parasite
parasitic
parasitism
paracitize, -tized, -tizing
paracitology
parasol
  parasoll — parasol
parasympathetic
paratrooper
parboil, -ed, -ing
  parboyle — parboil
parcel, -ed, -ing
parch, -ed, -ing
parchment
pardon, -ed, -ing
pardonable
pardoner
  pardonible — pardonable
  pardonor — pardoner
pare, pared, paring (trim)

pare — pair (two)
pare — pear (fruit)
paredigm — paradigm
parent
parentage
parental
parenthesis, -ses
parenthetic, -al, -ally
parenthood
parentige — parentage
par excellence
parfait
parfay — parfait
pariah
parie — parry
parish, parishes
parishioner
parishonor — parishioner
pariside — parricide
parity
park, -ed, -ing
parka
parket — parquet
parking meter
Parkinson's disease
parkway
parlance
parlanse — parlance
parlay, -ed, -ing (bet)
parlay — parley (talk)
parler — parlor
parley, -leyed, -leying (talk)
parley — parlay (bet)
parliament
parliamentarian
parliamentary
parliment — parliament
parlimentary — parliamentary
parlor
parm — palm
parmagiana
parmist — palmist
parochial
parochialism
parody, -dies
parody, -died, -dying
parokial — parochial

paroksism — paroxysm
parole, -roled, -roling
paroll — parole
parot — parrot
paroxysm
parquet
parrable — parable
parrade — parade
parralel — parallel
parranoia — paranoia
parricide
parrot
parry, parried, parrying
parse, parsed, parsing
parsel — parcel
parshal — partial
parshiality — partiality
parsimonious, -ly
parsimonius — parsimonious
parsimony
parsley
parsly — parsley
parsnip
parson
parsonage
part, -ed, -ing
partake, -took, -taken, -taking
partecle — particle
partesan — partisan
partial, -ly
partiality, -ties
participal — participle (noun)
participant
participate, -pated, -pating
participial (adjective)
participle (noun)
particel — particle
particle
particular, -ly
particularity
partie — party
partime — part-time
partisan
partision — partition
partisipant — participant
partisipate — participate

partisipeal	participial	passkey	
partisiple	participle	Passover	
partition, -ed, -ing		passport	
partly		password	
partner		past	
partridge		pasta (dough)	
partrige	partridge	pasta	pastor
part-time (adjective)			(minister)
part-timer		paste, pasted, pasting	
partway		pasteboard	
party, -ties		pastel	
party, -ied, -ying		pasterize	pasteurize
paruse	peruse	pastern	
pary	parry	pasteurize, -rized, -rizing	
pasable	passable	pasteurization	
pasage	passage	pastiche	
pascal	paschal	pastie	pasty
paschal		pastime	
paschure	pasture	pastor (minister)	
pase	pace	pastoral	
pasemaker	pacemaker	pastrami	
paserby	passerby	pastry, -tries	
pasible	passable	pasture, -ured, -uring	
pasific	pacific	pasty, -tier, -tiest	
pasify	pacify	pasword	password
pasinger	passenger	pat, patted, patting	
pasion	passion	patay	pâté
pasive	passive	patch, -ed, -ing	
pasivity	passivity	patchwork	
Pasover	Passover	patchy, patchier, patchiest	
pasport	passport	patchy, -ily, -iness	
pass, passed, passing		pâté	
passable, -bly		patella, -tellas, -tellae	
passage		paten (dish)	
passageway		paten	pattern (design)
passbook		patent, -ed, -ing	
passé		paternal, -ly	
passenger		paternalism	
passerby, passersby		paternity	
passible	passable	path	
passige	passage	pathetic, -ally (inadequate)	
passion, -less		pathetic	prophetic
passionate, -ly			(predictive)
passionflower		pathfinder	
passionfruit		pathogen	
passive, -ly, -ness		pathological, -ly	
passivity		pathology	

pathos		paverty	poverty
patie	patty	pavilion	
pathway		paw (foot)	
patience (calm)		paw	poor (needy)
patient (calm), patients (ill people)		paw	pore (skin)
patient, -ly		paw	pour (flow)
patina		pawcelain	porcelain
patio, patios		pawch	porch
patois, patois		pawk	pork
patriarch		pawkupine	porcupine
patriarchal		pawl	pall
patriarchy, -archies		pawlbarer	pallbearer
patriark	patriarch	pawlsied	palsied
patrician		pawlsy	palsy
patricide		pawltrey	paltry
patrimony, -al		pawn, -ed, -ing	
patriot		pawnbroker	
patriotic, -ally		pawnch	paunch
patriotism		pawnografey	pornography
patrisian	patrician	pawper	pauper
patriside	patricide	pawpus	porpoise
patrol, patrolled, patrolling		pawse	pause (stop)
patrolman, -men		pawselin	porcelain
patrol wagon		pawsion	portion
patron		pawsitey	paucity
patronage		pay, paid, paying	
patroness		payable	
patronige	patronage	payible	payable
patronize, -nized, -nizing		paycheck	
patronizing, -ly		payload	
patter, -ed, -ing		payment	
pattern, -ed, -ing (design)		paynt	paint
pattern	paten (dish)	payoff	
patty, -ties (cake)		payola	
patty	paddy (rice)	payroll	
paturnal	paternal	paysience	patience
paturnity	paternity	paysient	patient
patwa	patois	paytent	patent
paucity		pea	
paun	pawn	peacable	peaceable
paunch		peace (calm)	
paunchy		peace	piece (part)
pauper		peaceable, -bly	
pause, paused, pausing (stop)		peaceful, -ly, -ness	
pause	paws (feet)	peacekeeper	
pave, paved, paving		peacekeeping	
pavement		peacemaker	

peacetime
peach, peaches
peacock
peahen
pea jacket
peak, -ed, -ing (top)
   peak   peek (look)
   peak   pique (anger)
peal, -ed, -ing (ring)
   peal   peel (remove)
peanut
peanut butter
   peap   peep
pear (fruit)
   pear   pair (two)
   pear   pare (trim)
   pearage   peerage
   pearce   pierce
pearl (gem)
   pearl   purl (knit)
pearly, -ier, -iest
peasant
peasantry
peashooter
   peashuter   peashooter
peat
pebble
pecan
peccadillo, -loes, -los
peck, -ed, -ing
   pecock   peacock
pectin
pectoral
peculiar, -ly
peculiarity, -ties
pecuniary
   pedagog   pedagogue
pedagogic, -al
pedagogue
pedagogy
pedal, -ed, -ing (bike)
pedalboat
pedant
pedantic, -ally
peddle, -dled, -dling (sell)
   peddle   pedal (bike)
peddler

   peddlor   peddler
pederast
pederasty
pedestal, -ed, -ing
pedestrian
pediatrician
pediatrics
pedicure
pedigree
pedlar
pedometer
pedophile
pedophilia
peek, -ed, -ing (look)
   peek   peak (top)
   peek   pique (anger)
peel, -ed, -ing (remove)
   peel   peal (ring)
peep, -ed, -ing
peephole
peer, -ed, -ing (look)
   peer   pier (wharf)
peerage
peeress
peer group
peerless
peeve, peeved, -ving
peevish, -ly, -ness
peewee
peg, pegged, pegging
pegboard
   peice   piece
peignoir
pejorative, -ly
   pek   peck
   pekant   piquant
Pekingese
pelican
pellet (ball)
   pellet   palate (mouth)
   pellet   palette (board)
   pellet   pallet (bed)
pellmell (haste)
pellucid
pelt, -ed, -ing
   pelusid   pellucid
pelvic

pelvis
pen, penned, penning
penal
penalization
penalize, -lized, -lizing
penalty, -ties
penance
  penanse — penance
  penant — pennant
pence
penchant
pencil, -ed, -ing
pencil box
pendant
pendent
pending
pendulous
pendulum
  pendulus — pendulous
penetrable
penetrability
penetrate, -trated, -trating
penetration
  penetrible — penetrable
penguin
  pengwin — penguin
penicillin
  peniless — penniless
peninsula (noun)
peninsular (adjective)
penis, -nes, -nises
  penisilin — penicillin
penitence
  penitensial — penitential
  penitensiary — penitentiary
penitent, -ly
penitential
penitentiary, -ries
penknife, -knives
penmanship
pen name
pennant
penniless
pennon
penny, pennies
penny-pinching
penological

penologist
penology
pen pal
  pensave — pensive
  pense — pence
  pensil — pencil
pension
pensioner
  pensionible — pensionable
  pensionor — pensioner
pensive, -ly
pentagon, -al
  pentathalon — pentathlon
pentagram
pentameter
pentathlon
penthouse
  penthowse — penthouse
  pention — pension
pent-up
penultimate
penumbra, -brae, -bras
penurious
penury
  penut — peanut
peon
peony, -nies
people, -pled, -pling
pep, pepped, pepping
  peper — pepper
  pepermint — peppermint
  pepery — peppery
pepper
pepper-and-salt
peppercorn
peppermint
peppery
pep pill
pep talk
peptic
per
perambulate, -lated, -lating
perambulation
perambulator
per annum
per capita
perceive, -ceived, -ceiving

percent		performanse	performance
percentage		perfume, -fumed, -fuming	
percentige	percentage	perfumery, -ries	
percentile		perfunctory, -torily, -toriness	
perceptable	perceptible	perfunctry	perfunctory
perceptible, -bly		pergarey	perjury
perception		pergative	purgative
perceptive, -ly, -ness		pergatory	purgatory
perceptual, -ly		perge	purge
percession	procession	pergola	
perch, perches		perhaps	
perch, -ed, -ing		perhibit	prohibit
perchase	purchase	periferal	peripheral
percipience		perifery	periphery
percipient		peril, -ed, -ing	
percolate, -lated, -lating		perilous, -ly	
percolater	percolator	perilus	perilous
percolation		perimeter	
percolator		period	
percushun	percussion	periodic	
percussion		periodical, -ly	
percussionist		peripatetic	
per diem		peripheral, -ly	
perdision	perdition	periphery, -ries	
perdition		periscope	
peregrination		perish, -ed, -ing	
peregrine falcon		perishable	
peremptory, -torily		perishible	perishable
perennial, -ly		peritonitis	
perestroika		periwinkle	
perfecktion	perfection	perjector	projector
perfect, -ed, -ing		perjure, -jured, -juring	
perfectable	perfectible	perjurer	
perfectible		perjuror	perjurer
perfection		perjury, -ries	
perfectionism		perk, -ed, -ing	
perfectionist		perkusion	percussion
perfess	profess	perky, -kier, -kiest	
perficient	proficient	perky, -ily, -iness	
perfidious, -ly		perl	pearl (gem)
perfidius	perfidious	perl	purl (knit)
perfidy, -dies		perloin	purloin
perforate, -rated, -rating		permafrost	
perforation		permananse	permanence
perforce		permanence	
perform, -ed, -ing		permanency	
performance		permanent, -ly	

permeability
permeable
permeate, -ated, -ating
permeation
  permiate   permeate
  permisible   permissible
  permision   permission
permissible, -bly
permission
permissive, -ly
permit, -mitted, -mitting
permutation
permute, -muted, -muting
pernicious, -ly
  pernisious   pernicious
  perokside   peroxide
peroration
peroxide
  perpellant   propellant
  perpellent   propellent
perpendicular, -ly
perpendicularity
perpetrate, -trated, -trating
  perpetrater   perpetrator
perpetration
perpetrator
perpetual, -ly
perpetuate, -ated, -ating
perpetuation
perpetuity, -ties
  perport   purport
  perpose   purpose
perplex, -ed, -ing
perplexity
perquisite (profit)
  perquisite   prerequisite
                      (necessary)
  per say   per se
per se
  perse   purse
persecute, -cuted, -cuting (harass)
  persecute   prosecute (law)
  persecuter   persecutor
persecution
persecutor
  perseptible   perceptible
  persepsion   perception

  perseve   persevere
perseverance
  perseverence   perseverance
persevere, -vered, -vering
Persian
persimmon
persist, -ed, -ing
persistent, -ly
persistence, -cy
persnickety
person
personable
personage
personal, -ly (private)
  personal   personnel
                      (employees)
personality, -ties
personalize, -lized, -lizing
persona non grata, gratae
personate, -ated, -ating
  personible   personable
  personificasion   personification
personification
personify, -fied, -fying
personnel (employees)
  personnel   personal
                      (private)
perspective, -ly (view)
  perspective   prospective
                      (future)
  perspektive   perspective
perspicacious, -ly
perspicacity
perspicuous
  perspirasion   perspiration
perspiration
perspire, -spired, -spiring
persuadable
persuade, -suaded, -suading
  persuadible   persuadable
persuasion
persuasive, -ly, -ness
  persuede   persuade
  persuit   pursuit
  perswade   persuade
  perswasion   persuasion
pert, -ly, -ness

pertain, -ed, -ing
  pertane — pertain
pertinacious, -ly
pertinacity
pertinence
pertinent, -ly
perturb, -ed, -ing
perturbable
  perturbabile — perturbable
peruse, -rused, -rusing
pervade, -vaded, -vading
pervasion
pervasive, -ly, -ness
perverse, -ly, -ness
perversion
perversity, -ties
pervert, -ed, -ing
  pervertion — perversion
  pervurse — perverse
  pervursion — perversion
  pervurt — pervert
  pesant — peasant
  pesary — pessary
  pese — peace
  peseable — peaceable
  pesimism — pessimism
  pesimist — pessimist
peso
pessary, -ries
pessimism
pessimist
pest
pester, -ed, -ing
pesticide
pestilence
  pestilense — pestilence
pestilent
  pestiside — pesticide
pestle
  pesul — pestle
pet, petted, petting
peta
petal (flower)
  petal — pedal (bike)
  petal — peddle (sell)
petard
  peteet — petite

peter, -ed, -ing
  peticoat — petticoat
  petie — petty
  petishun — petition
petite
petition, -ed, -ing
petrel
petrify, -fied, -fying
petroleum
petticoat
petty, -tier, -tiest
petty, -ily, -iness
petulance
petulant, -ly
petunia
  peuter — pewter
  pevish — peevish
pew
pewter
phalanx, -anxes, -anges
  phalus — phallus
phallic
phallus, phalli, phalluses
phantasm
phantasmagoria
phantom
Pharaoh
pharisaic, -al, -ally
Pharisee
pharmaceutical
pharmacist
pharmacologist
pharmacology, -gic, -gical
pharmacy, -cies
pharyngitis
pharynx, pharynges, pharynxes
phase, phased, phasing (stage)
  phase — faze (daunt)
pheasant
phenacetin
  phenix — phoenix
phenomenal, -ly
phenomenon, -mena
phenotype
phenomone
  phesant — pheasant
phial (vial)

phial   file (paper)
philander, -ed, -ing
philanderer
   philanderor   philanderer
philanthropic, -ally
philanthropist
philanthropy
   philarmonic   philharmonic
philatelist
philharmonic
Philippines
   philosofer   philosopher
   philosofical   philosophical
   philosofy   philosophy
philosophic, -al, -ly
philosophize, -phized, -phizing
philosopher
   philosophor   philosopher
philosophy, -phies
philter

> For phis- words, look
> under **phys-**.

phlegm
phlegmatic, -ally
   phlem   phlegm
phlox
phobia
phobic
phoenix
phone
phonetic, -ally
   phonograf   phonograph
phonograph, -ic, -ically
phony, phonier, phoniest
   phosfate   phosphate
   phosforus   phosphorus
phosphate
phosphor
phosphoresce
phosphorescence
phosphorescent, -ly
phosphoric
phosphorus
photo, photos
photocopier
photocopy, -pies

photocopy, -copied, -copying
photoelectric
photoengrave, -graved, -graving
photoflash
photogenic
   photograf   photograph
photograph, -graph, -graphing
photographer
   photographor   photographer
photographic, -ally
photography
photogravure
photojournalist
photolithography
photometer, -tric
photomicrograph
photomural
photon
photoplay
photosensitive
photosphere
photostat, -stated, -stating
photosynthesis
photosynthesize, -ed, -ing
photosynthetic
phrase, phrased, phrasing
phraseology
phylactery, -teries
physic (medicine)
physical, -ly (body)
   physical   fiscal (money)
physician
physicist
physics
physiognomy, -mies
physiography, -ic
physiological, -ly
physiologist
physiology
physiotherapist
physiotherapy
physique (body)
pi (Greek letter)
   pi   pie (food)
pianist
piano, pianos
pianoforte

piatsa	piazza	piggyback	
piazza		pigheaded	
pibald	piebald	pigiback	piggyback
pica		pigin	pidgin (talk)
picador		pigin	pigeon (bird)
picancy	piquancy	piglet	
picayune		pigment	
piccolo, -los		pigmentation	
pich	pitch	pigmy, -mies	
picinic	picnic	pigpen	
pick, -ed, -ing		pigskin	
pickax, -ed, -ing		pigsty, -sties	
picket, -ed, -ing		pigtail	
picket line		pigtale	pigtail
pickle, -led, -ling		pijamas	pajamas
picklock		pike, piked, piking	
pickpocket		piker	
pick-me-up		pilchard	
pickup		pile, piled, piling	
picnic, -nicked, -nicking		pileup	
picnicker		pilfer, -ed, -ing	
pictorial, -ly		pilferage	
picture, -tured, -turing (image)		pilferer	
picture	pitcher (jug, thrower)	pilferige	pilferage
		pilgrim	
picturesque, -ly, -ness		pilgrimage	
pidgin (talk)		pilgrimige	pilgrimage
pidgin	pigeon (bird)	pilige	pillage
pie (food)		pilion	pillion
pie	pi (Greek letter)	pill	
piebald		pillage, -laged, -laging	
piece, pieced, piecing (part)		pillager	
piece	peace (calm)	pillar (column)	
pièce de résistance		pillbox, -boxes	
piecemeal		pillege	pillage
piecework		piller	pillar
pier (wharf)		pillion	
pier	peer (look)	pillory, -ries	
pierce, pierced, piercing		pillory, -ried, -rying	
pierse	pierce	pillow, pillows (cushion)	
piety, -ties		pillowcase	
pig		pilon	pylon
pigeon (bird)		pilory	pillory
pigeon	pidgin (talk)	pilot, -ed, -ing	
pigeonhole, -holed, -holing		pilotage	
pigeon-toed		pilotfish	
		pilothouse	

pilotless
  pilow — pillow
pimp, -ed, -ing
  pimpel — pimple
pimple
pimply
pin, pinned, pinning
  pinacle — pinnacle
pinafore
pinball
pince-nez
pincers
pinch, -ed, -ing
pincher
pinch-hit, -hit, -hitting
pinch-hitter
pincushion
pine, pined, pining
pineapple
pinfeather
ping, -ed, -ing
Ping-Pong
pinhole
pinion, -ed, -ing
pink, -ness
pinkeye
pinkie
pinkish
pinnacle
pinochle
pinpoint, -ed, -ing
pinprick
  pinsers — pincers
pinstripe, -d
pint
pinup
pinwheel
pinworm
  pionear — pioneer
pioneer, -ed, -ing
pious, -ly, -ness
pip
pipe, piped, piping
pipe dream
pipeline
piper
pipi

pipit
pippin
pipsqueak
piquancy
piquant, -ly
pique, piqued, piquing
piracy
  piramid — pyramid
piranha
  pirasy — piracy
pirate, -rated, -rating
piratical
  pire — pyre
  pirooet — pirouette
pirouette, -etted, -etting
piscatorial
Pisces
pistachio, -chios
pistil (flower)
pistol (gun)
piston
pit, pitted, pitting
  pitanse — pittance
pit-a-pat
pitch, -ed, -ing
pitch black
pitchblende
pitcher (jug, thrower)
  pitcher — picture (image)
pitchfork, -ed, -ing
piteous, -ly
  piter-pater — pitter-patter
pitfall
pith
  pithetic — pathetic
  pithon — python
pithy, pithier, pithiest
pitiable, -ly
pitiful, -fully
pitiless, -ly
pittance
  pittanse — pittance
pitter-patter
pituitary, -taries
pity, pities
pity, pitied, pitying
  pius — pious

pivot, -ed, -ing
pivotal
pixie, pixies
pixy, pixies
pizazz
pizza
pizzeria
pizzicato
placard, -ed, -ing
placate, -cated, -cating
placatory
place, placed, placing (position)
  place   plaice (fish)
placebo, -bos, -boes
placekick, -ed, -ing
placekicker
placement
placenta, -tas, -tae
placental
  placibo   placebo
placid, -ly
placidity
placket
  placque   plaque
  plagarism   plagiarism
  plage   plague
plagiarism
plagiarist
plagiarize, -rized, -rizing
plague, plagued, plaguing
plaice (fish)
plaid (cloth)
plain, -ly, -ness (clear)
  plain   plane (flat)
plainclothes
plainclothesman, -men
plainspoken
plaint
plaintiff (sue)
plaintive, -ly (sad)
plait, -ed, -ing (braid)
  plait   plate (dish)
  plaket   placket
plan, planned, planning
plane, planed, planing (flat)
  plane   plain (clear)
planet

planetarium
planetary
plank
plankton
planner
plant, -ed, -ing
  plantasion   plantation
plantation
planter
  plantif   plaintiff (sue)
  plantive   plaintive (sad)
plaque
  plase   place (position)
  plase   plaice (fish)
  plasebo   placebo
  plasenta   placenta
  plasid   placid
plasma
  plastec   plastic
plaster, -ed, -ing
plasterboard
plasterer
plastic
plasticity
plate, plated, plating (dish)
  plate   plait (braid)
plateau, -eaus, -eaux
platelet
  plater   platter
platform
  platichude platitude
platinum
  platipus   platypus
platitude
platitudinous
  plato   plateau
platonic
platoon
  platteau   plateau
platter
platypus, -puses, -pi
plaudits
  plausable   plausible
plausible, -bly
play, -ed, -ing
playable
playacting

playback
playbill
playbook
playboy
play-by-play
player
playful, -ly, -ness
playgoer
playground
playhouse
playlet
playmate
playoff
  playrite — playwright
playpen
playsuit
plaything
playtime
playwright
plaza
plea, pleas (request)
plead, -ed, -ing
  pleas — please (satisfy)
pleasant, -ly, -ness
pleasantry, -tries
please, pleased, pleasing (satisfy)
pleasurable, -bly
pleasure
  pleasurible — pleasurable
pleat, -ed, -ing
  plebean — plebeian
plebeian
plebiscite
  plebisite — plebiscite
plectrum, -tra, -trums
pledge, pledged, pledging
  plee — plea
  pleed — plead
  pleet — pleat
  plege — pledge
plenary
plenipotentiary, -ries
plenitude
plenteous
plentiful, -ly
  plentius — plenteous
plenty

  plesant — pleasant
  plese — pleas (requests)
  plese — please (satisfy)
  plesurable — pleasurable
  plesure — pleasure
plethora
pleurisy
  pli — ply
  plabel — pliable
pliable, -bly
pliancy
pliant, -ly
pliers
plight, -ed, -ing
plinth
  plite — plight
  pliwood — plywood
plod, plodded, plodding
plodder
ploddingly
  ploi — ploy
  ploomage — plumage
  plootocrasy — plutocracy
  ploovial — pluvial
plop, plopped, plopping
plot, plotted, plotting
plover
plow, -ed, -ing
ploy
pluck, -ed, -ing
plucky, -kier, -kiest
  pluerisy — pleurisy
plug, plugged, plugging
plum (fruit)
  plum — plumb (test)
plumage
plumb, -ed, -ing (test)
plumber
plume, plumed, pluming (preen)
  plumige — plumage
  plummer — plumber
plummet, -ed, -ing
plump, -ed, -ing
plunder, -ed, -ing
plunge, plunged, plunging
plural
pluralism

plurality, -ties
  plurasy   pleurisy
plus
plush
Pluto (planet)
plutocracy, -cies
plutocrat, -ic
plutonium
pluvial
ply, plies
  plyers   pliers
ply, plied, plying
plywood
pneumatic, -ally
pneumatics
pneumonia
poach, -ed, -ing
poacher
  poch   poach
pock
pocket, -ed, -ing
pocketbook
pocketful
pocketknife, -knives
pocket money
pocket watch
pockmarked
pod, podded, podding
podiatrist
podiatry
podium, -dia
poem
poet
poetess
poetic
poetical, -ly
poetry
pogrom
poignancy
poignant, -ly
  poinancy   poignancy
  poinant   poignant
poinsettia
point, -ed, -ing
pointblank
pointed, -ly
pointer

pointillism
pointillist
pointless, -ly
poise, poised, poising
poison, -ed, -ing
poisonous
poke, poked, poking
poker
pokey (jail)
poky, -kier, -kiest (small)
polar (region)
  polar   poler (horse)
polarity
polarization
polarize, -rized, -rizing
Polaroid
pole, poled, poling (stick)
  pole   poll (vote)
polemic
polemical
  polen   pollen
polenta
  poler   polar (region)
  polese   police
police, -liced, -licing
policeman, -men
policewoman, -women
policy, -cies
policyholder
  poligamous   polygamous
  poligamy   polygamy
  poliglot   polyglot
  poligon   polygon
  polinate   pollinate
  Polinesian   Polynesian
polio
poliomyelitis
  polip   polyp
polish, -ed, -ing
  polisy   policy
Politburo
polite, -ly, -ness
politick, -ed, -ing
political, -ly
politician
politicize, -cized, -cizing
politick, -ed, -ing

politics
  politision   politician
polka, -kaed, -kaing
polka dots
poll, -ed, -ing (vote)
  poll   pole (stick)
pollard, -ed, -ing
pollen
pollinate, -nated, -nating
pollination
pollster
pollutant
pollute, -luted, -luting
pollution
polo
polo shirt
  poltegist   poltergeist
poltergeist
  poltise   poultice
  poltry   poultry
  polute   pollute
  polution   pollution
polyandrous
polyandry
polychrome
polyclinic
polyester
polygamist
polygamous
polygamy
polyglot
polygon
polygraph
polyhedron, -al
polymath
polymer
polymerize, -rized, -rizing
Polynesian
polynomial
polyp
polyunsaturated
pomander
pomegranate
  pomel   pommel
Pomeranian
pommel, -ed, -ing
pomp

pom-pom
pomposity
pompous, -ly
  ponch   paunch
poncho, -chos
ponder, -ed, -ing
ponderous, -ly
  ponderus   ponderous
  ponie   pony
pontiff
pontifical, -ly
pontificate, -cated, -cating
pontoon
pony, -nies
ponytail
pooch
  poodel   poodle
poodle
pool, -ed, -ing
pooped
poor, -ly (needy)
  poor   paw (foot)
  poor   pore (skin)
  poor   pour (flow)
poorhouse
pop, popped, popping
popcorn
pope
  poper   pauper
  popet   poppet
  popie   poppy
popish, -ly
poplar (tree)
poplin
  popourri   potpourri
poppet
poppy, -pies
poppycock
populace (public)
popular, -ly (known)
  popularitey   popularity
popularity
  populase   populace
popularize, -rized, -rizing
populate, -lated, -lating
population
  populer   popular

populous (crowded)

populus	populous
popy	poppy
por	paw (foot)
por	poor (needy)
por	pore (skin)
por	pour (flow)

porcelain

porcelane	porcelain

porch

porcupine

pore (skin)

pore	paw (foot)
pore	poor (needy)
pore	pour (flow)
poridge	porridge

pork

porker

porkpie hat

porkupine	porcupine
pornografy	pornography

pornographer

pornographic

pornography

porosity

porous

porphyry, -ries

porpoise, -poises

porpus	porpoise
porrage	porridge

porridge

porselin	porcelain
porsion	portion

port

portable, -ability

portal

portant	portent
portel	portal

portend, -ed, -ing (foreshadow)

portent (omen)

portentous

porter

portfolio, -lios

porthole

portible	portable

portico, -coes, -cos

portion, -ed, -ing (share)

portion	potion (drink)

portionless, -liness

portly, -lier, -liest

portmanteau, -teaus, -teaux

portrait

portraitist

portraiture

portrat	portrait

portray, -ed, -ing

portrayal

porus	porous
posative	positive
poschure	posture

pose, posed, posing

poser (pose)

posesion	possession
posess	possess
posessive	possessive

poseur (fake)

posey	posy

posh, -ly

posibility	possibility
posible	possible
posision	position

position

positive, -ly, -ness

pospone	postpone
possable	possible

posse

possess, -ed, -ing

possesser	possessor

possession

possessive, -ly, -ness

possessor

possible, -bly

possibility, -ties

possum

post, -ed, -ing

postage

postage stamp

postal

postal service

postcard

postdate, -dated, -dating

poster

posterier	posterior

posterior, -ly

posterity
postern
postgraduate
posthaste
posthumous, -ly
   posthumus   posthumous
posthypnotic
   postige   postage
post-impressionist
postman
postmark
postmaster
postmeridian (adjective)
post meridiem (adverb)
postmortem
post office
postoperative
postpaid
postpartum
postpone, -poned, -poning
postponement
postscript
postulant
postulate, -lated, -lating
   postumus   posthumous
posture, -tured, -turing
postwar
posy, -sies
pot, potted, potting
potable
potash
   potasium   potassium
potassium
potato, -toes
potbellied
potbelly, -lies
potency
   potensial   potential
   potensy   potency
potent
potentate
potential, -ly
potentiality, -ties
   poter   potter
   potery   pottery
pothole
potion (drink)

   potion   portion (share)
potluck
potpie
potpourri
potshot
pottage
potter, -ed, -ing
pottery
pouch, pouches
poulterer
poultice, -ticed, -ticing
   poultise   poultice
poultry (birds)
   poultry   paltry (petty)
pounce, pounced, pouncing
pound, -ed, -ing
poundage
pour, -ed, -ing
   pour   poor (needy)
   pour   pore (skin)
pout, -ed, -ing
poverty
poverty-stricken
   powch   pouch
powder, -ed, -ing
powdery
power, -ed, -ing
powerboat
powerful, -ly
powerhouse
powerless, -ly
   pownce   pounce
   pownd   pound
   powt   pout
powwow, -wowed, -wowing
pox
practicable, -ibility
practical, -ly
practicality
practice, -ticed, -ticing
   practicible   practicable
   practisioner practitioner
practitioner
pragmatic, -ally
pragmatism
pragmatist
   prairey   prairie

prairie
praise, praised, praising
praiseworthy, -thily
prance, pranced, prancing
prank
prankster
   pranse   prance
   prarey   prairie
   prase   praise
prate, prated, prating
   pratel   prattle
prattle, -tled, -tling
prawn
pray, -ed, -ing (beg)
   pray   prey (hunt)
prayer
prayer book
preach, -ed, -ing
preacher
preamble
preamplifier
   prean   preen
prearrange, -ranged, -ranging, -ment
precancerous
precarious, -ly, -ness
precaution
precautionary
precede, -ceded, -ceding (before)
   precede   proceed (ahead)
precedence
precedent (law)
   precedent   president (head)
precept
   precepter   preceptor
preceptor
   prech   preach
   precice   precise
precinct
precious, -ly, -ness
   precipatation   precipitation
precipice
   precipise   precipice
precipitancy
precipitate, -tated, -tating
precipitation

precipitous, -ly
   precipitus   precipitous
precis (summary)
precise, -ly, -ness (exact)
precision
preclude, -cluded, -cluding
precocious, -ly
precocity
preconceived
   preconcieved   preconceived
preconception
   preconseived   preconceived
   preconseption   preconception
   precosious   precocious
precondition
precook
precursor
   predater   predator
predator
predatory
predawn
predecease, -ceased, -ceasing
predecessor
   predesessor   predecessor
predesignate, -nated, -nating
predestination
predestine, -tined, -tining
predetermination
predetermine, -mined, -mining
predicament
predicate, -cated, -cating
predicative, -ly
predict, -ed, -ing
predictable, -bly
   predicter   predictor
predictibility
   predictible   predictable
prediction
predictor
predilection
   predililction   predilection
predispose, -posed, -posing
predisposition
   preditor   predator
predominance
predominant, -ly
predominate, -ated, -ating

preeminence
preeminent, -ly
preempt, -ed, -ing
preen, -ed, -ing
preestablish, -ed, -ing
preexist, -ed, -ing
preexistent
prefabricate, -cated, -cating
prefabrication
preface, -faced, -facing
prefatory, -rily
prefect
prefer, -ferred, -ferring (choose)
  prefer   proffer (offer)
preferable, -bly
preference
  preferense   preference
  preferensial   preferential
preferential
preferment
  prefice   preface
prefight
  prefiks   prefix
prefix
preflight
pregnancy, -cies
  pregnansy   pregnancy
pregnant
preharden
preheat, -ed, -ing
prehensile
prehistoric, -al, -ally
prehistory
prehuman
preignition
preindustrial
prejudge, -judged, -judging
prejudgment
prejudice, -diced
prejudicial
  prejudise   prejudice
  prejudisial   prejudicial
prelate
prelaunch
preliminary, -aries
prelude, -luded, -luding
premarital

premature, -ly
premedical
premeditate, -ted, -ting
premeditation
premenstrual
premier (chief)
premiere (first performance)
premiere, -miered, -miering
premises
premium
premix, -ed, -ing
  premonision   premonition
premonition
premonitory
  prempt   preempt
prenatal
  prene   preen
prenuptial
preoccupation
preoccupy, -pied, -pying
preoperative
prep, -ped, -ping
prepackage, -aged, -aging
preparation
preparatory
prepare, -pared, -paring
preparedness
prepay, -paid, -paying
prepayment
preplan, -ned, -ning
preponderance
preponderant, -ly
preposition (grammar)
  preposition   proposition
              (offer)
prepossess, -ed, -ing
preposterous, -ly
Pre-Raphaelite
prerecord, -ed, -ing
pre-Reformation
preregister, -ed, -ing
  prerekwisit   prerequisite
pre-Renaissance
prerequisite (necessary)
  prerequisite   perquisite
              (profit)
prerogative

pres	press
presage, -saged, -saging	
preschool	
prescience	
prescribe, -scribed, -scribing (direct)	
prescribe	proscribe (condemn)
prescription (direction)	
prescription	proscription (condemnation)
prescriptive, -ly	
presence	
present, -ly	
presentable, -bly	
presentation	
present-day	
presentiment (foreboding)	
presentment (presentation)	
presept	precept
preservation	
preservative	
preserve, -served, -serving	
preset, preset, presetting	
presherize	pressurize
preshrunk	
preshure	pressure
preside, -sided, -siding	
presidency	
presidensial	presidential
presidensy	presidency
president (head)	
president	precedent (law)
presidential	
presige	presage
presinct	precinct
presious	precious
presipice	precipice
presipitate	precipitate
presipitus	precipitous
presise	precise
presoak	
press, -ed, -ing	
pressman, -men	
pressroom	
pressure, -sured, -suring	
pressurization	
pressurize, -rized, -rizing	

prest	priest
prestege	prestige
presthood	priesthood
prestige	
prestigious, -ly	
prestigus	prestigious
presto	
presume, -sumed, -suming	
presumption	
presumptuous, -ly	
presumshun	presumption
presumtuus	presumptuous
presuppose, -posed, -posing	
pretax	
preteen	
pretend, -ed, -ing	
pretender	
pretense	
pretension	
pretention	pretension
pretentious, -ly, -ness	
preternatural, -ly	
pretest	
pretex	pretext
pretext	
pretsel	pretzel
pretty, -tier, -tiest	
pretty, -tily, -tiness	
prety	pretty
pretzel	
prevail, -ed, -ing	
prevale	prevail
prevalence	
prevalense	prevalence
prevalent, -ly	
prevaricate, -cated, -cating	
prevarication	
prevension	prevention
prevent, -ed, -ing	
preventable, -bly	
preventative, -ly	
preventible	preventable
prevention	
preventive	
preview, -ed, -ing	
previous, -ly	
prewar	

prey, -ed, -ing (hunt)
  prey   pray (beg)
  pri   pry
price, priced, pricing
priceless, -ly
prick, -ed, -ing
  prickel   prickle
prickle, -led, -ling
prickliness
prickly, -lier, -liest
pride, prided, priding
  prie   pry
  prier   prior
  priery   priory
priest
priestess
priesthood
priestly, -lier, -liest, -liness
prig
priggish, -ness
prim, primmer, primmest
prim, -ly, -ness
prima ballerina
primacy
prima donna
prima facie
primary, -ries
primate, -tial
prime, primed, -ming
primer
primeval
primitive, -ly
primogenitor
primogeniture
primordial, -ly
  primray   primary
primp, -ed, -ing
primrose
prince, princes (male)
princely, -liness
princess, -es (female)
principal (head)
  principal   principle (law)
principality, -ties
principally
principle (law)
  principle   principal (head)

  princley   princely
  prinse   prince
  prinsess   princess
  prinsipal   principal
  prinsipality   principality
print, -ed, -ing
printer
printout
prior
priority, -ties
priory, -ries
  prise   price
  prisem   prism
  prisen   prison
prism
prismatic, -ally
prison
prisoner
  prisonnor   prisoner
prissy, -sier, -siest, -siness
  pristeen   pristine
pristine
privacy
  privasy   privacy
private, -ly, -ness
privateer
privation
  privelage   privilege
privet
  privie   privy
privilege, -leged, -leging
  privite   private
privy, -vies
prize, prized, prizing
prizefight
prizewinner
  prizm   prism
proabortion
proadministration
probability, -ties
probable, -ly
probate, -bated, -bating
probation
probationer
probe, probed, probing
  probibility   probability
  probible   probable

probity
problem
problematic, -ally
proboscis, -cises, -cides
probusiness
procapitalist
procedural
procedure
proceed, -ed, -ing
  procesion   procession
process, -ed, -ing
procession
processional
processor, processer
proclaim, -ed, -ing
proclamation
  proclaym   proclaim
procommunist
procrastinate, -nated, -nating
  procrastinater   procrastinator
procrastination
procrastinator
procreate, -ated, -ating
procreation
procreator
proctor
procurable
procure, -cured, -curing
procurer
  procurible   procurable
procuress
prod, prodded, prodding
prodigal, -ly
prodigality
prodigious, -ly
  prodigus   prodigious
prodigy, -gies
  producable   producible
produce, -duced, -ducing
producer
producible
  producktion   production
product
production
productive, -ly
productivity
  produse   produce

  produser   producer
profane, -faned, -faning
profanely
profanity, -ties
  profecy   prophecy (noun)
  profecy   prophesy (verb)
  profer   proffer
  profesional   professional
  profeser   professor
profess, -ed, -ing
professional, -ly
professionalism
professor
professorial
  profet   profit (gain)
  profet   prophet (seer)
proffer, -ed, -ing (offer)
  proffer   prefer (choose)
proficiency, -cies
proficient, -ly
profile, -filed, -filing
  profishency   proficiency
  profishent   proficient
profit, -ed, -ing (gain)
  profit   prophet (leader)
profitable, -bly
profiteer, -ed, -ing
profitless
profligacy
profligate, -ly
pro forma
profound, -ly
  profownd   profound
profundity, -ties
profuse, -ly
profusion
progenitor
progeny, -nies
prognosis, -noses
prognostic
prognosticate, -cated, -cating
prognostication
program, -med, -ming or -mmed, -mming
programable, programmable

programmer, programer
progress, -ed, -ing
progression
progressive, -ly, -ness
  prohibision — prohibition
prohibit, -ed, -ing
prohibition
prohibitive, -ly
proindustry
prointegration
  projecktion — projection
project, -ed, -ing
  projecter — projector
projectile
projection
projectionist
projector
  proksimate — proximate
  proksy — proxy
prolapse, -lapsed, -lapsing
proletarian
proletariat
proliferate, -rated, -rating
prolific, -ally
prologue, prolog
prolong, -ed, -ing
prom
promenade, -naded, -nading
promilitary
prominence
  prominense — prominence
prominent, -ly
promiscuity, -ties
  promiscuos — promiscuous
promiscuous, -ly, -ness
promise, -mised, -mising
promissory
promontory, -ries
  promontry — promontory
promote, -ed, -ing
promoter
promotion
  promp — prompt
prompt, -ed, -ing
prompt, -ly, -ness
prompter
  promptor — prompter

promulgate, -gated, -gating
promulgation
promulgator
prone
prong, -ed
pronoun
pronounce, -nounced, -nouncing
pronounceable
pronouncement
  pronown — pronoun
  pronownse — pronounce
pronto
pronunciation
  prood — prude
proof, -ed, -ing
proofread, -read, -reading
proofreader
  proon — prune
  proove — prove
prop, propped, propping
propaganda
propagate, -gated, -gating
  propagater — propagator
propagation
propagator
propane
propel, -pelled, -pelling
propellant, propellent
propeller
propensity, -ties
proper, -ly, -ness
property, -ties
prophecy, cies (noun)
prophesy, -sied, -sying (verb)
prophet
prophetess
prophetic, -ical, -ically (predictive)
  prophetic — pathetic (inadequate)
  prophilactic — prophylactic
prophylactic
  propisiate — propitiate
  propisious — propitious
propitiate, -ated, -ating
propitious, -ly
propman
  propoganda — propaganda

proponent
proportion
proportional, -ly
proportionate, -ly
proposal
propose, -posed, -posing
proposer
  proposision   proposition
proposition (offer)
  proposition   preposition
                (grammar)
propound, -ed, -ing
  propownd   propound
proprietary
  proprieter   proprietor
proprietor
propriety, -ties
propulsion
pro rata
prorogue, -rogued, -roguing
prosaic, -ally
proscenium, -niums, -nia
proscribe, -scribed, -scribing
(condemn)
  proscribe   prescribe
                (direct)
proscription (condemnation)
  proscription   prescription
                (direction)
prose
prosecute, -cuted, -cuting (law)
  prosecute   persecute
                (harass)
prosecution
prosecutor
  prosedure   procedure
  proseed   proceed
  proselite   proselyte
proselyte, -lyted, -lyting
proselytize, -tized, -tizing
  prosess   process
  prosicute   prosecute
  prosilitize   proselytize
prosody
  prosparity   prosperity
prospect, -ed, -ing
prospective, -ly (future)

  prospective   perspective
                (view)
prospector
prospectus
prosper, -ed, -ing
prosperity, -ties
prosperous, -ly
  prosperus   prosperous
prostate gland
prosthesis, -ses
prosthetic, -ally
prostitute, -tuted, -tuting
prostitution
prostrate, -trated, -trating
prostration
protagonist
protean
  protecktion   protection
protect, -ed, -ing
protection
protectionist
protective, -ly, -ness
protector
protectorate
  proteen   protein
protégé (male)
protégée (female)
protein
protest, -ed, -ing
Protestant
Protestantism
protestation
protocol
proton
protoplasm, -ic, -al, -atic
  protipe   prototype
prototype
protozoa, -n
protract, -ed, -ing
protractor
  protrood   protrude
  protroosion   protrusion
protrude, -ruded, -ruding
protrusion
protuberance
protruberant, -ly
proud, -ly

prounion
provable
prove, proved, proven, proving
provender
proverb
proverbial, -ly
provide, -vided, -viding
providence
  providense   providence
provident, -ly
providential, -ly
provider
province
provincial, -ly
  provintial   provincial
provision
provisional, -ly
proviso
  provison   provision
provocation
provocative, -ly
provoke, -voked, -voking
provost
prow
prowar
  prowd   proud
prowar
prowess
prowl, -ed, -ing
prowler
proximate, -ly
proximity
proxy, proxies
  prozaic   prosaic
prude, -ish, -ishly, -ishness
prudence
  prudense   prudence
prudent, -ly
prudential
prudish, -ly
prune, pruned, pruning
prurience
prurient
Prussian
pry, pried, prying
psalm
psalmist

pseudo
pseudoaristocratic
pseudoartistic
pseudobiographical
pseudointellectual
pseudonym
pseudoscientific
psych, -ed, -ing (outwit)
psyche (mind)
psychedelic, -ally
psychiatric
psychiatrist
psychiatry
psychic, -al, -ally
psycho
psychoacting
psychoanalysis
psychoanalyst
psychoanalyze, -lyzed, -lyzing
psychodrama
psychogenic
psychological, -ly
psychologist
psychology, -gies
psychoneurosis, -ses
psychopath
psychopathic
psychopathology
psychosexual
psychosis, -ses
psychosomatic, -ally
psychotherapist
pschotherapy
psychotic, -ally

> For psyco- words, look under **psycho-**.

  psykey   psyche
  psykic   psychic
ptomaine
puberty, -tal
pubes
pubescence
pubescent
pubic
pubis
  publesher   publisher

public, -ly
publican
publication
publicist
publicity
publicize, -cized, -cizing
publish, -ed, -ing
publisher
  publisity   publicity
  publisize   publicize
puce
puck
pucker, -ed, -ing (fold)
  puddel   puddle
pudding
puddle, -dled, -dling
pudgy, -ier, -iest
  puding   pudding
puerile, -ly
puerility, -ties
puff, -ed, -ing
puffin
puffy, -fier, -fiest, -finess
  pufy   puffy
pugilism
pugilist
pugilistic
pugnacious, -ly
pugnacity
  pugnasity   pugnacity
pukka
pulchritude
pulchritudinous
  pulie   pulley
  pulkritude   pulchritude
pull, -ed, -ing
pullet
pulley, -leys
pullout
pullover
pulmonary
  pulmonry   pulmonary
pulp, -ed, -ing
pulpit
pulpwood
pulpy
pulsar

pulsate, -ated, -ating
  pulsater   pulsator
pulsation
pulsator
pulse, pulsed, pulsing
  pulser   pulsar
pulverize, -rized, -rizing
puma
pumice
  pumise   pumice
  pumkin   pumpkin
pummel, -ed, -ing
pump, -ed, -ing
pump-action
pumpernickel
pumpkin
pun, punned, punning
  punative   punitive
punch, -ed, -ing
punch-drunk
puncher
punchy
punctilious, -ly, -ness
  puntilius   punctilious
punctual, -ly
punctuality
punctuate, -ated, -ating
punctuation
puncture, -tured, -turing
pundit
pungency
pungent, -ly
  punie   puny
punish, -ed, -ing
punishable
  punishible   punishable
punishment
punitive
  pungensy   pungency
  punjent   pungent
punk
punster
punt, -ed, -ing
punter
puny, -nier, -niest
puny, -nily, -niness
pup, pupped, pupping

pupet	puppet	purulence		
pupie	puppy	purulent		
pupil		purvay	purvey	
puppet		purvey, -ed, -ing		
puppeteer		purveyor		
puppy, -pies		pus		
pur annum	per annum	puse	puce	
puray	purée	push, -ed, -ing		
purceive	perceive	push-button		
purchase, -chased, -chasing		pushcart		
purdah		pusher		
pure, purer, purest, pureness, purely		pushover		
pure-blooded		pushup		
purebred		pushy, -ier, -iest		
purée, -réed, -réeing		pusillanimity		
purgative		pusillanimous		
purgatory		pussy		
purge, purged, purging		pussycat		
purifie	purify	pussyfoot		
purify, -fied, -fying		pussy willow		
purile	puerile	put, put, putting		
purist		putative		
Puritan		putdown		
puritanical		put-on		
puritanism		putout		
puritie	purity	puter	pewter	
purity		putrefaction		
purje	purge	putrefy, -fied, -fying		
purjery	perjury	putrescence		
purl, -ed, -ing (knit)		putrescent		
purl	pearl (gem)	putrid, -ness		
purloin, -ed, -ing		putrify	putrefy	
purple, -pled, -pling		putt, -ed, -ing		
purport, -ed, -ing		putter		
purportedly		puttie	putty	
purpose		putty, -ties		
purposeful, -ly, -ness		putty, puttied, puttying		
purposeless		put-up		
purpul	purple	put upon		
purr, -ed, -ing		puzel	puzzle	
purse, pursed, -sing		puzzle, -zled, -zling		
purser		pye	pi (Greek letter)	
pursuant, -ly				
pursue, -sued, -suing		pye	pie (food)	
pursuer		pygmy, -mies		
pursuit		pylon		
pursute	pursuit	pyramid		

pyramidal
pyre
Pyrex
   pyric   Pyrrhic victory
pyrotechnics
Pyrrhic victory
Pythagorean
python
pyx
   pyxie   pixie (fairy)
   pyxie   pixy (fairy)

Qq

quack, -ed, -ing
quackery, -eries
quad
   quadrangel   quadrangle
quadrangle
quadrant
   quadrafonic   quadraphonic
quadraphonic, -ally
quadrasonic
quadratic
   quadril   quadrille
quadrille
quadrillion
quadriplegia
quadriplegic
quadruped
quadrupedal
   quadrupel   quadruple
quadruple, -pled, -pling
quadruplet
quaff, quaffed, quaffing
quagmire
quail
quaint, -ly, -ness
quake, quaked, quaking
Quaker
qualification
   qualifi   qualify
qualified
qualifier
qualify, -fied, -fying
qualitative, -ly
quality, -ties
qualm
quandary, -ries
   quandry   quandary
   quanity   quantity
   quantifi   quantify

quantifiable
quantification
quantify, -fied, -fying
quantitative, -ly
quantity, -ties
quantum
quarantine, -tined, -tining
   quarel   quarrel
   quarey   quarry
quark
   quarm   qualm
quarrel, -ed, -ing
quarreler
quarrelsome
quarry, -ries
quarry, -ried, -rying
quart, quarts
quarter
quarterback
quarterdeck
quarter horse
   quarterize   cauterize
quarterly
quartermaster
quartet
quarto, -tos
quartz (rock)
   quartz   quarts
                      (measures)
quasar
quash, -ed, -ing
quasi
quatercentenary
quatrain
quaver, -ed, -ing
quay (wharf)
   quay   key (lock)
   que   cue (billiards)
queasy, -sier, -siest
queasy, -ily, -ness
Quebec
queen, -ly, -liness
Queen-size, -sized
queer, -ly, -ness
quell, -ed, -ing
quench, -ed, -ing
quenchable

quenchless
  queralous   querulous
  querie   query
querulous, -ly, -ness
  querulus   querulous
query, -ries
query, -ried, -rying
  quesion   question
quest
question, -ed, -ing
questionable, -bly, -ableness,
-ability
  questionair   questionnaire
questionnaire
  queston   question
quibble, -bled, -bling
quibbler
  quibel   quibble
  quich   quiche
quiche
quick, -ly, -ness
quicken
quick-freeze, -froze, -frozen,
-freezing
quickie
quicklime
quicksand
quicksilver
quickstep
quick-tempered
quick-witted
quid pro quo
quiescence
quiescent, -ness
  quiesense   quiescence
quiet, -ly, -ness (silent)
  quiet   quit (stop)
  quiet   quite (rather)
quill
quilt
quilted
quince
quincentenary
quinine
  quinse   quince
quinsy
  quintesense   quintessence

quintessence
quintessential
quintet
  quintupel   quintuple
quintuple, -pled, -pling
quintuplet
quip, quipped, quipping
quire (paper)
  quire   choir (sing)
quirk
  quish   quiche
  cuisine   cuisine
quit, quit or quitted, quitting (stop)
  quit   quiet (silent)
  quit   quite (rather)
quite (rather)
  quite   quiet (silent)
  quite   quit (stop)
quits
quitter
quiver, -ed, -ing
quixotic, -ally
quiz, quizzes
quiz, quizzed, quizzing
quizmaster
quizzical, -ly, -ness
quoit
quorum
  quosient   quotient

> For other **quo-** words, look
> under **qua-**.

quota (amount)
quotable
quotation
quote, quoted, quoting (price)
quotient

Rr

rabbel   rabble
rabbi, -bis
rabbinical
rabbit (animal)
rabble, -bled, -bling
rabble-rouser
rabed   rabid
rabi   rabbi
rabid, -ly, -ness, -idity (furious)
rabies
rabit   rabbit
raccoon
race, raced, racing
racecorse   racecourse
racecourse
racehorse
racer
racetrack
raceway
racial, -ly
racialism
racialist
racism
racist
rack (shelf)
rack   wrack (wreck)
rack and pinion
racket, racquet (sports)
racket (noise)
racketeer
rackit   racket
raconter   raconteur
raconteur
racy, -cier, -ciest, -cily, -ciness
radar
radarscope
rade   raid
radeo   radio

radial, -ly
radialogy   radiology
radiance
radianse   radiance
radiant, -ly
radiate, -ated, -ating
radiater   radiator
radiation
radiator
radical, -ly, -ness (drastic)
radical   radicle (root)
radicalism
radicel   radical
radicalize, -ized, -izing
radicalization
radicle (root)
radicle   radical (drastic)
radiel   radial
radio, -dioed, -dioing
radioactive
radioactivity
radio astronomy
radiocarbon
radiogenic
radiografy   radiography
radiogram
radiograph, -ed, -ing
radiographic, -ally
radiographology
radioisotope
radiologist
radiology
radioman, -men
radiometer
radiometric, -ically
radiometry
radiophone
radioscopy, -scopic
radiosonde
radiotelegraph, -ic
radiotelegram
radiotelephone, -phonic
radiotelephony
radiotherapy
radiotherapist
radish
radium

radius, radii, radiuses
radon
raffia
raffish, -ly, -ness
raffle, -led, -ling
raft
rafter
rag, ragged, ragging
ragamuffin
rag bag
rag doll
rage, raged, raging
ragged, -ly, -ness
raglan
ragout
rag picker
ragtime
ragweed
raid, -ed, -ing
rail, -ed, -ing
railing
raillery, -ries
railroad
railway
raiment
rain, -ed, -ing (water)
   rain   reign (rule)
   rain   rein (bridle)
rainbow
raincoat
raindrop
rainfall
rainforest
rainmaker
rainmaking
rainspout
rainstorm
rainwater
rainy, -ier, -iest
raise, raised, raising (lift)
   raise   rays (beams)
   raise   raze (destroy)
   riasen   raisin
raisin
raison d' être
   raje   rage
rake, raked, raking

rakish, -ly, -ness
   rakket   racket
   rale   rail
   ralie   rally
rally, -lies
rally, -lied, -lying
ram, rammed, ramming
   rambel   ramble
ramble, -bled, -bling
rambler
rambunctious, -ness
ramie
ramification
ramify, -fied, -fying
ramp
rampage, -paged, -paging
rampant, -ly
rampart
ramrod
   ramshackel   ramshackle
ramshackle
ranch
rancher
rancid
rancidity
rancor
rancorous, -ly
   rancur   rancor
   rancurus   rancorous
random, -ly
randy, -ier, -iest, -iness
   rane   rain (water)
   rane   reign (rule)
   rane   rein (bridle)
range, ranged, ranging
range finder
rangeland
ranger
   rangle   wrangle
rank, -ed, -ing
rank, -ly, -ness
ranking
rankle, -kled, -kling
ransack, -ed, -ing
   ransid   rancid
ransom, -ed, -ing
   ransome   ransom

ransum	ransom
rant, -ed, -ing	
rap, rapped, rapping (strike)	
rap	wrap (cover)
rapacious, -ly, -ness	
rapacity	
rapasious	rapacious
rapasity	rapacity
rapcher	rapture
rape, raped, raping	
rapid, -ly, -ness	
rapidity	
rapier	
rapine	
rapist	
rapport	
rapprochement	
rapsody	rhapsody
rapt (engrossed)	
rapt	wrapped (cover)
rapture	
rapturous, -ly	
rapturus	rapturous
rare, rarer, rarest, -ly, -ness (unusual)	
rare	rear (care)
rarefacktion	rarefaction
rarefaction	
rarefy, -fied, -fying	
raring	
rarity, -ties	
rarly	rarely
rasbery	raspberry
rascal, -ly	
rascality, -ties	
rase	race (run)
rase	raise (lift)
rase	raze (destroy)
rash, -ly, -ness	
rasher	
rashio	ratio
rasial	racial
rasialist	racialist
rasin	raisin
rasionalize	rationalize
rasism	racism
rasist	racist
raskal	rascal
rasp, -ed, -ing	
raspberry, -ries	
rat, ratted, ratting	
ratchet	
rate, rated, rating	
rateo	ratio
rath	wrath
rather	
rathskeller	
ratification	
ratify, -fied, -fying	
ratio, -tios	
ration, -ed, -ing	
rational, -ly (sane)	
rationale (statement)	
rationalism	
rationalist	
rationalistic, -ally	
rationality, -ties	
rationalization	
rationalize, -lized, -lizing	
ratle	rattle
rat race	
ratskeller	rathskeller
rattan	
rattle, -tled, -tling	
rattlesnake	
rattletrap	
ratty, -tier, -tiest	
raucous, -ly, -ness	
raucus	raucous
ravage, -aged, -aging	
ravager	
rave, raved, raving	
ravel, -ed, -ing	
raven	
ravene	ravine
ravenous, -ly, -ness	
ravige	ravage
ravine	
ravioli	
ravish, -ed, -ing	
ravishing	
raw (uncooked)	
raw	roar (noise)

rawcus	raucous	readjourn, -ed, -ing	
rawhide		readjournment	
ray		readjust, -ed, -ing	
rayon		readmission	
rays (beams)		readmit, -mitted, -mitting	
rays	raise (lift)	readmittance	
rays	raze (destroy)	readout	
raze, razed, razing (destroy)		ready, readied, readying	
raze	raise (lift)	ready, readier, readiest	
raze	rays (beams)	ready-made	
razer	razor	ready-to-wear	
razor		reaf	reef
razzbery	raspberry	reaffirm, -ed, -ing	
razorback, -backed		reaffirmation	
razzle-dazzle		reagent	
razzmatazz		reak	reek (smell)
reabsorb, -ed, -ing		reak	wreak (inflict)
reabsorption		real, -ly (true)	
reaccelerate, -ted, -ting		real	reel (wind)
reacclimate, -ted, -ting		realign, -ed, -ing	
reach, -ed, -ing		realignment	
reacktion	reaction	realism	
reacquaint, -ed, -ing		realist	
reacquaintance		realistic, -ally	
reacquire, -quired, -quiring		reality, -ties (fact)	
reacquisition		realization	
react, -ed, -ing		realize, -lized, -lizing	
reactant		reallocate, -ted, -ting	
reaction		reallocation	
reactionary		realm	
reactivate, -ted, -ting		realter	realtor
reactive, -ly		Realtor	
reactivity		realty (real estate)	
reactor		ream, reamed, reaming	
read, read, reading (book)		reamer	
read	red (color)	reap, -ed, -ing	
read	reed (plant)	reaper	
readability		reappear, -ed, -ing	
readable, -bly, -ness		reappearance	
readapt, -ed, -ing		reapplication	
readaption		reapply, -plied, -plying	
readdress, -ed, -ing		reappoint, -ed, -ing	
reader		reappointment	
readership		reapportion, -ed, -ing	
readible	readable	reapportionment	
readily, -iness		reappraisal	
reading (adj.)		reappraise, -ed, -ing	

rear (back)	rebuild, -built, -building
rear, -ed, -ing (care)	rebuke, -buked, -buking
rear rare (unusual)	rebus
rear gard rear guard	rebut, -butted, -butting
rear guard	rebutal rebuttal
rearm, -ed, -ing	rebuttal
rearmament	recalcitrance
rearmost	recalcitrant
rearrange, -ranged, -ranging	recall, -ed, -ing
rearrest, -ed, -ing	recant, -ed, -ing
rear-view mirror	recantation
rearward	recap, -ped, -ping
reason, -ed, -ing	recapitulate, -lated, -lating
reasonable, -bly, -ness, -ability	recapitulation
reasonible reasonable	recapture, -tured, -turing
reassembel reassemble	recast, -ed, -ing
reassemble, -bled, -bling	recede, -ceded, -ceding
reassembly, -blies	receipt (acknowledgement)
reassert, -ed, -ing	receit receipt
reassertion	receivable, -ability
reassess, -ed, -ing	receive, -ceived, -ceiving
reassessment	receiver
reassign, -ed, -ing	receivership
reassignment	recency
reassurance	recent, -ly, -ness (new)
reassure, -sured, -suring	recent resent (hurt)
reassuringly	recepe recipe
reath wreath	receptacel receptacle
reawake, -woke or waked, -waking	receptacle
reawaken	reception
rebaptism	receptionist
rebaptize, -tized, -tizing	receptive, -ly, -ness, -tivity
rebate, -bated, -bating	receptor
rebel, -belled, -belling	recernize recognize
rebelion rebellion	recess, -ed, -ing
rebellion	recession, -al
rebellious, -ly, -ness	recessive
rebild rebuild	rech retch (vomit)
rebill, -ed, -ing	rech wretch (victim)
rebirth	rechart, -ed, -ing
reboil, -ed, -ing	recheck, -ed, -ing
reborn	rechristen, -ed, -ing
rebound, -ed, -ing	recidivism
rebownd rebound	recidivist
rebroadcast, -ed, -ing	reciept receipt
rebudget, -ed, -ing	recieve receive
rebuff, -ed, -ing	recipe (cook)

recipient
reciprocal, -ly
reciprocate, -cated, -cating
reciprocation
reciprocity
   reciprosity   reciprocity
recital
recitation
recite, -cited, -citing
   reck   wreck (destroy)
   reckage   wreckage
reckless, -ly, -ness
reckon, -ed, -ing
   reckord   record
   recktify   rectify
reclaim, -ed, -ing
reclaimable
reclamation
reclassify, -fied, -fying
reclean, -ed, -ing
recline, -clined, -clining
reclothe, -clothed or -clad, -clothing
recluse
recoat, -ed, -ing
   recognision   recognition
recognition
recognizable, -bly
recognize, -nized, -nizing
   recognizible   recognizable
recoil, -ed, -ing
   recolection   recollection
recollect, -ed, -ing
recollection
recombinant
recombine, -bined, -bining
recommence, -ed, -ing
recommencement
recommend, -ed, -ing
recommendable
recommendation
recompense, -ed, -ing
recommission, -ed, -ing
reconcile, -ciled, -ciling
reconciliable
reconciliation
recondensation
recondense, -sed, -sing

recondite, -ly, -ness
recondition, -ed, -ing
reconfirmation
reconfirm, -ed, -ing
reconnaissance
reconnect, -ed, -ing
reconnoiter, -ed, -ing
reconsideration
reconsider, -ed, -ing
reconsign, -ed, -ing
reconsignment
   reconsile   reconcile
   reconsiliation   reconciliation
reconsolidate, -ted, -ting
reconstruct, -ed, -ing
reconstruction
reconstructive
recook, -ed, -ing
   recoop   recoup
recopy, -copied, -copying
record, -ed, -ing
record-breaking
recorder
recording
   recorse   recourse
recount, -ed, -ing
recoup, -ed, -ing
recourse
re-cover, -ed, -ing (again)
recover, -ed, -ing
recoverable
recovery, -eries
   recownt   recount
recreant, -ly
recreate, -ted, -ting
re-create, -ted, -ting (again)
recreation, -al
recriminate, -nated, -nating
recrimination
recriminatory
recriticize, -cized, -cizing
recross, -ed, -ing
recrown, -ed, -ing
recruit, -ed, -ing
recruiter
recruitment
   recrute   recruit

rectangel rectangle	redeployment
rectangle	redeposit, -ed, -ing
rectangular, -ly	redesign, -ed, -ing
rectifiable	redevelop, -ed, -ing
rectification	redevelopment
rectifier	red-handed
rectify, -fied, -fying	red head
rectilinear, -ly	red-hot
rectilinier rectilinear	redie ready
rectitude	redigest, -ed, -ing
rector	redirect, -ed, -ing
rectory, -ries	redirection
rectum, -tums, -ta	rediscover, -ed, -ing
recumbency	rediscovery, -ies
recumbensy recumbency	redissolve, -solved, -solving
recumbent	redistribute, -buted, -buting
recuperate, -rated, -rating	redistribution
recuperation	redistrict, -ed, -ing
recuperative	redo, -did, -done, -doing
recur, -curred, -curring	redolence
recurrence	redolent, -ly
recurrense recurrence	redouble, -led, -ling
recurrent, -ly	redoubtable, -bly
recycel recycle	redound, -ed, -ing
recyclable	redoutible redoubtable
recycle, -cycled, -cycling	redraw, -drew, -drawn, -drawing
recyclible recyclable	redress, -ed, -ing
red, redder, reddest (color)	reduce, -duced, -ducing
red read (book)	reducer
red-blooded, -ness	reducible
redbreast	reducktion reduction
redbrest redbreast	reduction
redden, -ed, -ing	reductive
reddish	redundancy, -cies
reddy ready	redundansy redundancy
redecorate, -ted, -ting	redundant, -ly
redeem, -ed, -ing	reduplicate, -cated, -cating
redeemable, -ably	reduplication
redeemer	redwood
redefine, -fined, -fining	redye -ed, -ing
redefinition	reed (plant)
redemption	reed read (book)
redemptive	reedit, -ed, -ing
redemtion redemption	reeducate, -ted, -ting
reden redden	reedy, -reedier, reediest
redeploi redeploy	reef, -ed, -ing
redeploy, -ed, -ing	reefer

reek, -ed, -ing (smell)
   reek   wreak (inflict)
   reek   wreck (destroy)
reel, -ed, -ing (wind)
   reel   real (true)
reelect, -ed, -ing
reelection
reembark, -ed, -ing
reembody, -bodied, -bodying
reemerge, -merged, -merging
reemergence
reemphasize, -ed, -ing
reemploy, -ed, -ing
reemployment
reenact, -ed, -ing
reenactment
reengage, -gaged, -gaging
reenlist, -ed, -ing
reenlistment
reentry, -tries
   reep   reap
reequip, -quipped -quipping
reerect, -ed, -ing
reestimate, -mated, -mating
reestimation
reevaluate, -ted, -ting
reevaluation
reexperience, -enced, -encing
reexport, -ed, -ing
refashion, -ed, -ing
refasten, -ed, -ing
refectory, -ies
refer, -ferred, -ferring
referable
referee, -reed, -reeing
reference
   referense   reference
referendum, -dums, -da
referent
referral
refill, -ed, -ing
refillable
refilter, -ed, -ing
refinance, -nanced, -nancing
refine, -fined, -fining
refinement
refinery, -ries

refinish, -ed, -ing
refit, -fitted, -fitting
   reflecktion   reflection
reflect, -ed, -ing
reflection
reflective, -ly
reflector
   refleks   reflex
reflex, -ive, -ively, -iveness
refloat, -ed, -ing
reflower, -ed, -ing
refold, -ed, -ing
reform, -ed, -ing
re-form (again)
reformation
re-formation
reformatory, -ries
reformer
refract, -ed, -ing
   refracktion   refraction
refraction
refractive, -ly, -ness
refractor
refractory, -rily, -riness
refracture, -tured, -turing
refrain, -ed, -ing
reframe, -framed, -framing
refreeze, -froze, -frozen, -freezing
   refrence   reference
refresh, -ed, -ing
refresher
refreshment
refrigerant
refrigerate, -rated, -rating
   refrigerater   refrigerator
refrigeration
refrigerator
refuel, -ed, -ing
refuge
refugee
refulgence
refulgent
refund, -ed, -ing
refundable
refurbish, -ed, -ing
refurnish, -ed, -ing
refusal

refuse, -fused, -fusing
refutable
refutation
refute, -futed, -futing
regain, -ed, -ing
regal, -ly (royal)
regale, -galed, -galing (feast)
regalement
regalia
  regane — regain
regard, -ed, -ing
regardless, -ly
regatta
  regeme — regime
regency, -cies
regenerate, -rated, -rating
regeneration
regenerative
regent
regerminate, -ted, -ting
regermination
reggae
regicide
regime
regimen
regiment
regimental
regimentation
region
regional, -ly
regionalism
register, -ed, -ing
registrar
registration
registry, -tries
  regon — region
  regresion — regression
regress, -ed, -ing
regression
regressive
regret, -gretted, -gretting
  regretable — regrettable
regretful, -ly
regrettable, -bly
regrow, -grew, -grown, -growing
regrowth
  regulation — regulation

  reguard — regard
regular, -ly
regularity
regulate, -lated, -lating
  regulater — regulator
regulation
regulator
regulatory
  reguler — regular
regurgitate, -tated, -tating
rehabilitate, -tated, -tating
rehabilitation
rehash, -ed, -ing
rehearsal
rehearse, -hearsed, -hearsing
reheat, -ed, -ing
  reherse — rehearse
rehire, -hired, -hiring
reign, -ed, -ing (rule)
  reign — rain (water)
  reign — rein (bridle)
reignite, -ted, -ting
reimburse, -bursed, -bursing
reimbursement
reimprison, -ed, -ing
rein, -ed, -ing (bridle)
  rein — rain (water)
  rein — reign (rule)
reincarnate, -ted, -ting
reincarnation
reincorporate, -ted, -ting
reindeer, -deer
reinduct, -ed, -ing
reinduction
reinfect, -ed, -ing
reinfection
reinfest, -ed, -ing
reinforce, -forced, -forcing
reinforcement
reinsert, -ed, -ing
reinsertion
reinstate, -stated, -stating
reinsure, -sured, -suring
reinterpret, -ted, -ting
reinterpretation
reintroduce, -ed, -ing
reintroduction

reinvest, -ed, -ing
reinvestment
reinvigorate, -ted, -ting
reinvolve, -volved, -volving
reinvolvement
reissue, -sued, -suing
reiterate, -rated, -rating
reiteration
reiterative, -ly
  rejecktion   rejection
reject, -ed, -ing
rejection
  rejeme   regime
  rejister   register
rejoice, -joiced, -joicing
rejoin, -ed, -ing
rejoinder
  rejoise   rejoice
  rejoovenate   rejuvenate
rejuvenate, -nated, -nating
rejuvenation
rekindle, -led, -ling
  rekord   record

> For **rekw-** words, look
> under **requ-**.

relabel, -beled, -beling
  relaks   relax
relapse, -lapsed, -lapsing
relate, -lated, -lating
relation
relationship
relative, -ly, -ness
relativity
relax, -ed, -ing
relaxant
relaxation
relay, -ed, -ing
relearn, -ed, -ing
release, -leased, -leasing
relegate, -gated, -gating
relegation
  releif   relief
relent, -ed, -ing
relentless, -ly, -ness
  relese   release
relevance

relevancy
  relevanse   relevance
relevant (pertinent)
  relevant   reverent
                 (respectful)
  releve   relieve
  reli   rely
  reliabel   reliable
reliable, -bly, -ableness
reliability
reliance
reliant
relic
relicense, -censed, -censing
relief
relieve, -lieved, -lieving
relight, -lighted or -lit, -lighting
religion
religious, -ly, -ness
  religon   religion
  religos   religious
  relinkwish   relinquish
reline, -lined, -lining
relinquish, -ed, -ing
relinquisher
relinquishment
relish, -ed, -ing
relishable
relive, -lived, -living
  relm   realm
reload, -ed, -ing
relocate, -ted, -ting
relocation
reluctance
  reluctanse   reluctance
reluctant, -ly
rely, relied, relying
remain, -ed, -ing
remake, remade, remaking
remainder
remains
remake, -made, -making
remand, -ed, -ing
remanufacture, -tured, -turing
remark, -ed, -ing
remarkable, -bly, -ness
remarriage

remarry, -ied, -rying
rematch, -ed, -ing
remeasure, -ed, -ing
remeasurement
remedial, -ly
remedy, -dies
remedy, -died, -dying
remember, -ed, -ing
rememberable
remembrance
  remembranse — remembrance
remind, -ed, -ing
reminder
reminisce, -nisced, -niscing
reminiscence
reminiscent, -ly
  reminisense — reminiscence
  reminisent — reminiscent
  reminiss — reminisce
  remision — remission
remiss, -ly, -ness
remission
remit, -mitted, -mitting
remittance
remnant
remodel, -ed, -ing
remonstrance
remonstrant, -ly
remonstrate, -trated, -trating
remonstrative
  remooval — removal
  remoove — remove
remorse
remorseful, -ly, -less
remote, remoter, remotest
remote, -ly, -ness
remount, -ed, -ing
removable
removal
remove, -moved, -moving
remunerate, -rated, -rating
remuneration
remunerative, -ly, -ness
  ren — wren
Renaissance
renal
rename, -named, -naming

  rench — wrench
rend, rent, rending (tear)
render, -ed, -ing
rendezvous, -voused, -vousing
rendition
renegade
renege, reneged, reneging
renegotiable
renegotiate, -ted, -ting
renegotiation
renew, -ed, -ing
renewable
renominate, -ted, -ting
renomination
renounce, -nounced, -nouncing
renovate, -vated, -vating
  renovater — renovator
renovation
renovator
renown
renowned
rent, -ed, -ing
rentable
rental
  rentel — rental
rent-free
  renue — renew
renumber, -ed, -ing
renunciation
reoccupy, -pied, -pying
reoccur, -curred, -curring
reoccurence
reopen, -ed, -ing
reorder, -ed, -ing
reorganization
reorganize, -nized, -nizing
repack, -ed, -ing
repackage, -aged, -aging
repaint, -ed, -ing
repair, -ed, -ing
repairable
repairer
repairman
reparation
repartee
repast
repatriate, -ated, -ating

repatriation
repave, -paved, -paving
repay, -paid, -paying
repayable
repeal, -ed, -ing
repeat, -ed, -ing
repeatable
repeated, -ly
repeater
repel, -pelled, -pelling
repellent, repellant, -ly
repent, -ed, -ing
repentance
repentanse   repentance
repentant
repercusion   repercussion
repercussive
repertoire
repertory, -ries
repetisious   repetitious
repetition
repetitious, -ly, -ness
rephrase, -phrased, -phrasing
repitition   repetition
replacable
replace, -placed, -placing
replacement
replan, -planned, -planning
replant, -ed, -ing
replay, -played, -playing
replenish, -ed, -ing
replenishment
replete, -ness
repletion
replica
replicate, -ted, -ting
replication
reply, -plies
reply, -plied, -plying
repopulate, -ted, -ting
report, -ed, -ing
reportable
reportage
reportedly
reporter
repose, -posed, -posing
repository, -tories

repositry   repository
repossesion   repossession
repossess, -ed, -ing
repossession
reprehend, -ed, -ing
reprehensible, -bly
reprehension
reprehention   reprehension
represent, -ed, -ing
representation
representational
representative, -ly, -ness
represion   repression
repress, -ed, -ing
repressable   repressible
repression
repressive, -ly
reprice, -priced, -pricing
reprieve, -prieved, -prieving
reprimand, -ed, -ing
reprint, -ed, -ing
reprisal
reprizal   reprisal
reproach, -ed, -ing
reproachable, -bly
reproachful, -ly, -ness
reproachingly
reprobate, -bated, -bating
reprobation
reproch   reproach
reproduce, -duced, -ducing
reproducer
reproducible
reproducktion   reproduction
reproduction
reproductive
reproof, -ed, -ing
reprove, -proved, -proving
reptile
reptilian
republic
republican
republicanism
republish, -ed, -ing
repudiate, -ated, -ating
repudiation
repudiator

repugnance
  repugnanse   repugnance
repugnant, -ly
repulse, -pulsed, -pulsing
repulsion
repulsive, -ly, -ness
reputable, -bly
reputation
repute, -puted, -puting
reputibility
  reputible   reputable
request, -ed, -ing
Requiem, requiem
  requierment   requirement
require, -quired, -quiring
requirement
  requisision   requisition
requisite, -ly
requisition
  rerite   rewrite
  reritten   rewritten
  rerote   rewrote
requisitioner
requite, -quitted, -quitting
reread, -read, -reading
rerun, -ran, -run, -running
resalable
rescind, -ed, -ing
rescue, -cued, -cuing
rescuer
reseal, -ed, -ing
resealable
research, -ed, -ing
researcher
  reseat   receipt
  resede   recede
reseed, -ed, -ing
  reseipt   receipt
resell, -sold, -selling
  resembal   resemble
resemble, -bled, -bling
resent, -ed, -ing (hurt)
  resent   recent (new)
resentful, -ly
resentment
  reseptacle   receptacle
  reseption   reception

  reseptive   receptive
  reserch   research
reservation
reserve, -served, -serving
reserved, -ly, -ness
reservoir
  resess   recess
  resession   recession
reset, -set, -setting
resettle, -tled, -tling
resettlement
  reseve   receive
  resevoir   reservoir
reshape, -shaped, -shaping
resharpen, -ed, -ing
reshuffle, -fled, -fling
reside, -sided, -siding
residence
  residensial   residential
residency
resident
residential, -ly
  residivision   recidivism
residual, -ly
residuary
residue
resign, -ed, -ing
resigned, -ly
resignation
resilience
resiliency
resilient, -ly
resin
  resind   rescind
  resine   resign
resinous
  resinus   resinous
  resipe   recipe
  resipient   recipient
  resiprocal   reciprocal
  resiprosity   reciprocity
resist, -ed, -ing
reister
resistance
  resitation   recitation
resistor
  resite   recite

resistible
resistless
resole, -soled, -soling
resolute, -ly, -ness
resolution
resolvable
resolve, -solved, -solving
resonance
resonant, -ly
resonate, -nated, -nating
resonator
 resorce   resource
resorption
resort, -ed, -ing
resound, -ed, -ing
resource
resourceful, -ly, -ness
respect, -ed, -ing
respectability, -ties
respectable, -bly
respectful, -ly, -ness
 repectible   respectable
respective, -ly
respiration
respirator
respiratory
respite
resplendence
resplendent, -ly
 responce   response
respond, -ed, -ing
respondent
response
responsibility, -ties
responsible, -bly, -bliness
responsive, -ly, -ness
rest, -ed, -ing (sleep)
 rest   wrest (grab)
 restaration   restoration
restaurant
restauteur
 resterant   restaurant
restful, -ly, -ness
 restitusion   restitution
restitution
restive, -ly, -ness
 restle   wrestle

 restler   wrestler
restless, -ly, -ness
restoration
restorative
restorable
restore, -stored, -storing
restorer
restrain, -ed, -ing
restrainable
restrainer
restraint
restrengthen, -ed, -ing
 restricktion   restriction
restrict, -ed, -ing
restriction
restrictive, -ly, -ness
restring, -strung, -stringing
restructure, -tured, -turing
restudy, -studied, -studying
restuff, -ed, -ing
restyle, -styled, -styling
resubmission
resubmit, -mitted, -mitting
resubscribe, -scribed, -scribing
resubscription
result, -ed, -ing
resultant
 resumay   résumé, resume (review)
résumé resume (review)
resume, -sumed, -suming (take up)
resumption
resupply, -supplied, -supplying
resurgence
resurgent
resurrect, -ed, -ing
resurrection
resuscitate, -tated, -tating
resuscitation
resuscitator
 resusitation   resuscitation
retail, -ed, -ing
retain, -ed, -ing
retainer
retake, -took, -taken, -taking
retaliate, -ated, -ating
retaliation

retard, -ed, -ing
retardant
retardation
reteach, retaught, reteaching
retch, -ed, -ing (vomit)
   retch   wretch (victim)
retell, retold, retelling
retention
retentive, -ly, -ness
retest, -ed, -ing
rethink, -thought, -thinking
reticence
reticent, -ly
retina, -nas, -nae
   retinew   retinue
retinue
retire, -tired, -tiring
retiree
retirement
   retisent   reticent
retitle, -titled, -titling
   retoric   rhetoric
   retorical   rhetorical
retort, -ed, -ing
retouch, -ed, -ing
retracable
retrace, -traced, -tracing
retract, -ed, -ing
retractable
retrain, -ed, -ing
retrainable
retranslate, -ted, -ting
retransmit, -mitted, -mitting
   retrase   retrace
retread, -treaded, -treading
retreat, -ed, -ing
   retred   retread
   retreive   retrieve
retrench, -ed, -ing
retrenchment
   retribusion   retribution
retribution
retributive
retrieve, -trieved, -trieving
retrievable
retrieval
retriever

retroactive, -ly
retrograde, -graded, -grading
   retrogresion   retrogression
retrogress, -ed, -ing
retrogression
retrogressive
retrorocket
retrospect
retrospective, -ly
retry, -tried, -trying
return, -ed, -ing
returnable
retype, -typed, -typing
reunion
reunite, -nited, -niting
reusable
reuse, -used, -using
rev, revved, revving
   revalie   reveille
revaluation
revalue, -ued, -uing
   revalueation   revaluation
revamp, -ed, -ing
reveal, -ed, -ing
reveille (bugle call)
revel, -ed, -ing
revelation
   revelant   relevant
reveler
revelry, -ries (festivity)
   revenew   revenue
revenge, -venged, -venging
revengeful
revenue
reverberate, -ated, -ating
reverberation
reverberator
revere, -vered, -vering (respect)
reverence, -enced, -encing
reverend (minister)
   reverense   reverence
reverent, -ly (respectful)
   reverent   relevent
                              (pertinent)
reverie, revery (daydream)
reversal
reverse, -versed, -versing

reversibility
reversible
reversion
revert, -ed, -ing
~~revertable~~ revertible
revertible
review, -ed, -ing (survey)
~~review~~ revue (theater)
revile, -viled, -viling
revisable
revise, -vised, -vising
revision
revitalize, -lized, -lizing
revitalization
revival
revivalism
revive, -vived, -viving
revocable
revocation
revoke, -voked, -voking
revolt, -ed, -ing
revolution
revolutionary, -ries
revolutionize, -nized, -nizing
revolve, -volved, -volving
revolver
revue (theater)
~~revue~~ review (survey)
revulsion
reward, -ed, -ing
rewarm, -ed, -ing
rewash, -ed, -ing
reweave, -wove, -woven, -weaving
rewed, -wedded, -wed, -wedding
reweigh, -ed, -ing
rewind, -wound, -winding
rewire, -ed, -ing
reword, -ed, -ing
rework, -ed, -ing
rewrite, -wrote, -written, -writing
rezone, -zoned, -zoning

| For rez- words, |
| look under **res-**. |

rhapsodical, -ly
rhapsodize, -dized, -dizing
rhapsody, -dies

rheologic, -al
rheology
rhesus
rhetoric
rhetorical, -ly
rhetorician
rheumatic
rheumatism
rheumatoid arthritis
rhinestone
rhino, -nos, -no
rhinoceros, -roses, -ros
rhizome
rhododendron
rhomboid
rhombus, -buses, -bi
rhubarb
rhyme, rhymed, rhyming (verse)
~~rhyme~~ rime (frost)
rhythm (beat)
rhythmical, -ly
rib, ribbed, ribbing
ribald
ribaldry
ribbon
riboflavin
ribonucleic
ribose
ribosome
rice
rich, -ly, -ness
riches
Richter scale
rick, -ed, -ing
rickets
rickety
rickshaw, ricksha
~~rickshore~~ rickshaw
ricochet, -ed, -ing
rid, rid or ridded, ridding
~~ridance~~ riddance
riddance
riddle, -dled, -dling
ride, rode, ridden, riding
rider
riderless
ridership

ridge, ridged, ridging
ridicule, -culed, -culing
ridiculous, -ly, -ness

ridiculus	ridiculous
ridle	riddle
rie	rye (grain)
rie	wry (askew)

Riesling
rife, -ly, -ness

| rifel | rifle |

riffraff
rifle, -fled, -fling
rifleman, -men

| rifrigerator | refrigrator |

rift
rig, rigged, rigging

| riggle | wriggle |

right, -ed, -ing (correct)

right	rite (ceremony)
right	wright (worker)
right	write (inscribe)

right-angled
righteous, -ly, -ness
rightful, -ly, -ness
right-hand
right-handed, -ly, -ness
rightism
rightist
rightly
right-minded
rightness
right-to-work
right wing
rigid, -ly, -ness
rigidity
rigmarole
rigor
rigorous, -ly

| rigorus | rigorous |

rile, riled, riling
rim, rimmed, rimming (edge)
rime, -y, -ed (frost)

| rime | rhyme (verse) |

rimless
rind
ring, ringed, ringing (surround)
ring, rang, rung, ringing (bell)

| ring | wring (squeeze) |

ringer (bell)

| ringer | wringer (squeezer) |

ringleader
ringlet
ringmaster
ringside
ringtailed
ringworm
rink
rinky-dink
rinse, rinsed, rinsing
riot, -ed, -ing
riotous, -ly, -ness

| riotus | riotous |

rip, ripped, ripping
rip cord
ripe, riper, ripest
ripe, -ly, -ness
ripen, -ed, -ing
rip off
riposte, riposted, riposting

| rippel | ripple |

ripper
ripple, -pled, -pling

> If the word is not under **ri-**
> look under **re-**.

rip-roaring
riptide
rise, rose, risen, rising
risk, -ed, -ing

| riskay | risqué |

riskily, -iness
risky, -kier, -kiest
risotto, -tos
risqué

| rist | wrist |
| rit | writ |

rite (ceremony)

rite	right (correct)
rite	write (inscribe)
riter	writer
rithe	writhe
ritten	written

ritual, -ly

ritualistic, -al, -ally
ritualism
ritualist
ritzy, -ier, -iest
rival, -ed, -ing
rivalry, -ries
river
riverbank
riverbed
riverboat
riverside
rivet, -ed, -ing
rivulet

ro   roe (fish)
ro   row (boat)
roach, -ches
road (street)

road   rode (did ride)
roadbed
roadblock
roadhouse
road map
roadrunner
roadside
road test
roadway
roadwork
roar, -ed, -ing (noise)

roar   raw (uncooked)
roast, -ed, -ing

roaster   rooster (bird)
roaster   roster (list)
roaster (oven)
rob, robbed, robbing
robber
robbery, -ries
robe, robed, robing

robery   robbery
robin
robot
robust, -ly, -ness
rock, -ed, -ing
rock-bottom
rock candy
rocker
rocket, -ed, -ing
rocketry

rock garden
rocking chair
rocking horse
rock-'n'-roll, rock'n'roll
rocky
rococo
rod

rodayo   rodeo
rode (did ride)

rode   road (street)
rodent
rodeo, -deos

rodio   rodeo
roe (fish)

roe   row (boat)
roge   rogue
rogish   roguish
rogue, rogued, roguing
roguery
roguish, -ly, -ness
role, rôle (character)
roll, -ed, -ing (turn)
rollback
roll bar
roll call
roller
roller coaster
roller-skate, -skated, -skating
rolling pin
rollick, -ed, -ing
rollmop
roll-on
rollover
roll-top desk
roly-poly
Roman Catholic
romance, -manced, -mancing
Romanesque
romantic, -ly
romanticism
romanticist
romanticize, -cized, -cizing

rombus   rhombus
rome   roam
romp, -ed, -ing
rompers
rondo, -dos

rong — wrong
roo — rue (regret)
roodiment — rudiment
roof, roofs
roofer
roofing
roofless
rooftop
rooful — rueful
rooge — rouge
rooin — ruin
rooinous — ruinous
rook, -ed, -ing
rookery, -ries
rookie
rool — rule
roolet — roulette
room, -ed, -ing
roomatism — rheumatism
roomer (tenant)
roomer — rumor (talk)
room service
roomy, -mier, -miest
roon — ruin
roopee — rupee
rooral — rural
roose — ruse
roost, -ed, -ing
rooster (bird)
rooster — roaster (oven)
rooster — roster (list)
root, -ed, -ing (plant)
root — route (way)
rootless
rootlet
rootstock
rope, roped, roping
ror — roar (noise)
ror — raw (uncooked)
rort — wrought (work)
rosary, -ries
rosay — rosé (wine)
rose (flower)
rosé (wine)
rosella
rosebud
rosebush

rose-colored
rosemary
rosery — rosary
roset — rosette
rosette
rosewood
rosie — rosy
rosily, -iness
rost — roast
roster, -ed, -ing (list)
roster — roaster (oven)
roster — rooster (bird)
rostrum, -trums, -tra
rosy, rosier, rosiest
rot, rotted, rotting
rotary
rotate, -tated, -tating
rotation
rote (routine)
rote — wrote (did write)
roten — rotten
roter — rotor
roth — wrath
rotisserie
rotor
rotten, -ly, -ness
rotund, -ly, -ness
rotundity
roudy — rowdy
rouge, rouged, rouging
rough, -ly, -ness (coarse)
rough — ruff (collar)
roughage
rough-and-ready
rough-and-tumble
rough-cut
roughen, -ed, -ing
roughhouse, -housed, -housing
roughshod
roulet — roulette
roulette, -letted, -letting
round, -ed, -ing
roundabout
roundish
roundly
round-shouldered

roundup
roundworm
rouse, roused, rousing
roustabout
rout, routed, routing (defeat)
route (way)
   route   root (plant)
   routeen   routine
routine
rove, roved, roving
rover
row, -ed, -ing (boat)
   row   roe (fish)
rowboat
   rowdie   rowdy
rowdily, -iness
rowdy, -dier, -diest
rowel, -ed, -ing
   rownd   round
   rowse   rouse
   rowt   rout
royal, -ly
royalist
royalty, -ties
rub, rubbed, rubbing
   rubbel   rubble
rubber
rubberize, -ed, -ing
rubbish, -y
rubble
rubella
   ruber   rubber
rubicund
   rubie   ruby
   rubish   rubbish
rubric
ruby, -bies
ruck, -ed, -ing
rucksack
   rucktion   ruction
ruckus
ruction
rudder
ruddy, -dier, -diest
rude, ruder, rudest (rough)
   rude   rued (regret)
rudely, -ness

rudeness
   ruder   rudder
rudimentary
rudiments
   rudy   ruddy
rue, rued, ruing (regret)
   rued   rude (impolite)
rueful, -ly, -ness (pity)
ruff (collar)
   ruff   rough (coarse)
   ruffel   ruffle
   ruffen   roughen
ruffian
ruffle, -fled, -fling (annoy)
   rufian   ruffian
   rufige   roughage
   ruful   rueful
rug
rugby
rugged, -ly, -ness
ruin, -ed, -ing (destroy)
   ruin   rune (letter)
ruination
ruinous, -ly, -ness
   ruinus   ruinous
rule, ruled, ruling
ruler
rum
   rumatism rheumatism
rumba
   rumbel   rumnble
rumble, -bled, -bling
   rumige   rummage
ruminant
ruminate, -nated, -nating
rummage, -maged, -maging
rumor, -ed, -ing (talk)
   rumor   roomer (tenant)
rump
   rumpel   rumple
rumple, -pled, -pling
rumpus
run, ran, run, running
runabout
runaround
runaway
rundown

run-down
rune (letter)
  rune   ruin (destroy)
rung (did ring, step)
  rung   wrung
                (squeezed)
run-in
runner
runner-up
runny, -nier, -niest
runoff
run-of-the-mill
run-on
runt
runway
  rupcher   rupture
rupee
rupture, -tured, -turing
rural, -ly
ruse
rush, -ed, -ing
  Rushan   Russian
  rusit   russet
rusk
russet
Russian
rust, -ed, -ing
rustic, -ally
rusticate, -cated, -cating
rustication
rusticator
rusticity, -ties
rustle, -tled, -tling
rustless
rustproof
rusty, -tier, -tiest
rut, rutted, rutting
ruthless, -ly, -ness
  rutine   routine
rye (grain)
  rye   wry (askew)
  ryme   rhyme
  rythm   rhythm

Ss

Sabath	Sabbath
sabattical	sabbatical
Sabbath	
sabbatical	
sabel	sable
saber	
Sabin vaccine	
sable	
sabot	
sabotage, -taged, -taging	
saboteur	
sabra (Israeli)	
sac	sack (bag)
sacarin	saccharin
saccharin	
sacerdotal, -ly	
sachay	sachet
sachel	satchel
sachet	
sack, -ed, -ing	
sackarin	saccharin
sackcloth	
sacrament	
sacramental, -ly	
sacred, -ly, -ness	
sacrement	sacrament
sacrifice, -ficed, -ficing	
sacrificial, -ly	
sacrifise	sacrifice
sacrifisial	sacrificial
sacriledge	sacrilege
sacrilege	
sacrilegious, -ly	
sacrilige	sacrilege
sacriligus	sacrilegious
sacrosanct	
sad, sadder, saddest	
sadden, -ed, -ing	

saddle, saddled, saddling	
saddlebacked	
saddlebag	
saddlecloth	
saddler	
saddlery, -ries	
saden	sadden
sadler	saddler
sadlery	saddlery
sadism	
sadist	
sadistic, -ally	
sadul	saddle
safari, -ris	
safe, safer, safest	
safe-cracker	
safe-deposit	
safegard	safeguard
safeguard	
safekeeping	
safely, -ness	
safety, -ties	
saffire	sapphire
saffron	
safire	sapphire
safron	saffron
safty	safety
sag, sagged, sagging	
saga	
sagacious, -ly	
sagacity, -ties	
sagaysious	sagacious
sagasity	sagacity
sage, sager, sagest	
sagebrush	
Sagittarius	
sago	
said	
sail (boat)	
sail	sale (sold)
sailsman	salesman
sailboat	
sailcloth	
sailer	sailor
sailor	
sailplane	
saint, -ly, -liness	

sainted		salmonella	
sainthood		salon	
sake		saloobrius	salubrious
sakred	sacred	saloon	
Sakson	Saxon	saloot	salute
saksophone	saxophone	salow	sallow
salaam		salt, -ed, -ing	
salability		saltcellar	
salable		saltery	psaltery
salacious, -ly, -ness		saltseller	saltcellar
salad		saltwater	
salamander		salty, -ier, iest	
salami		salubrious, -ly	
salamy	salami	salubrius	salubrious
salaried		salutary	
salary, -ries (wage)		salutation	
salary	celery (food)	salute, -luted, -luting	
salasious	salacious	salution	solution
sale (sold)		salvagable	
sale	sail (boat)	salvage, -vaged, -vaging (save)	
saleability		salvage	selvage (edge)
salene	saline	salvager	
salesclerk		salve, salved, salving	
salesgirl		salver	
saleslady, -dies		salvo, -vos, -voes	
salesman, -men		samantic	semantic
salesmanship		samba	
salesperson, -people		same, -ness	
saleswoman, -women		samon	salmon
salience		samovar	
saliense	salience	Samoyed	
salient, -ly		sampan	
saline		sampel	sample
salinity		sample, -pled, -pling	
saliva		sampler	
salivary		samurai	
salivate, -vated, -vating		samuri	samurai
salivation		sanatarium	sanitarium
sallow, -ness		sanitory	sanity (mental health)
sallowish			
sally, -lies		sanatorium, -toriums, -toria	
sally, -lied, -lying		sanatation	sanitation
salm	psalm	sancktion	sanction
		sanctification	
		sanctify, -fied, -fying	
For all other sall- words, look under sal-.		sanctimonious, -ly, -ness	
		sanctimonius	sanctimonious
salmon			

sanction, -ed, -ing
sanctity, -ties
sanctuary, -ries
sanctum, -tums, -ta
sand, -ed, -ing
sand castle
sand dollar
sand dune
sandal
sandalwood
sandbag, -bagged, -bagging
sandbank
sandbar
sandblast, -ed, -ing
sandbox
sandman
  sandle   sandal
sandpaper, -ed, -ing
sandpiper
sandstone
  sandwhich   sandwich
sandwich, -wiches
  sandwitch   sandwich
sandy, -ier, -iest
sane, saner, sanest (not mad)
  sane   seine (net)
sanely, -ness
  sanety   sanity
sang
sangfroid
sanguinary
sanguine
  sangwin   sanguine
sanitarium, -tariums, -taria
sanitary (clean)
sanitation
  sanitorium   sanatorium
sanity (mental health)
sank

> For all other sank- words,
> look under sanct-.

Sanskrit
Santa Claus
  Santa Klaus   Santa Claus
sap, sapped, sapping
  saper   sapper

sapience
sapient, -ly
sapling
sapper
sapphire
  sappling   sapling
sapwood
sarcasm
sarcastic, -ally
  sarcofagus   sarcophagus
sarcophagus, -gi, -guses
  sardeen   sardine
sardine, -dines
sardonic, -ally
  sargent   sergeant
sari, saree
sarong
sarsaparilla
sartorial, -ly
  sary   sari
  saserdotal   sacerdotal
sash
sashay (trip)
  sashay   sachet (bag)
  sashiate   satiate
sashimi
sassafras
Satan (devil)
Satanic
satanical, -ly
Satanism
Satanist
satchel
sate, sated, sating
sateen (cotton)
satellite
  Saten   Satan (devil)
  saten   sateen (cotton)
  saten   satin (silk)
  Saterday   Saturday
  satiabel   satiable
satiable, -ly
satiate, -ated, -ating
satiation
satin (silk)
satinwood
satire (sarcasm)

satire	satyr (mythology)	saver	savor (taste)
		savier	savior (saint)
satiric		savige	savage
satirical, -ly		savigery	savagery
satirist		savigry	savagery
satirize, -rized, -rizing		saving	
satisfacktion	satisfaction	savior (saint)	
satisfaction		savoir faire	
satisfactorily		savory, -vories (noun)	
satisfactory		savory, -riness (adj.)	
satisfactry	satisfactory	savor, -ed, -ing (taste)	
satisfiabel	satisfiable	savor	saver (keeper)
satisfy, -fied, -fying		savoy	
saturate, -rated, -rating		savvy	
saturation		saw, sawed, sawing (cut)	
Saturday		saw	soar (rise)
Saturn (planet)		saw	sore (hurt)
saturn	sauterne (wine)	sawcer	saucer
saturnine		sawcey	saucy
satyr (mythology)		sawdid	sordid
satyr	satire (sarcasm)	sawdust	
sauce (liquid)		sawfish	
sauce	source (origin)	sawfly, -flies	
saucepan		sawhorse	
saucer		sawmill	
saucerer	sorcerer	sawna	sauna
saucery	sorcery	sawnter	saunter
saucily, -ciness		saws	sauce (liquid)
sauciness		saws	source (origin)
saucy, -cier, -ciest		sawser	saucer
sauerkraut		sawsey	saucy
sauna		saw-toothed	
saunter, -ed, -ing		saxofone	saxophone
saurian		saxofonist	saxophonist
sausage		Saxon	
sausy	saucy	saxophone	
sauté, -téed, -téeing		saxophonist	
sauterne (wine)		say, said, saying	
sauturn	sauterne	sayance	séance
savage, savaged, savaging		say-so	
savagely		scab, scabbed, scabbing	
savagery, -ries		scabbard	
savana	savanna	scabees	scabies
savanna		scabies	
savant		scabious	
save, saved, saving		scabrous	
saver (keeper)		scaffold	

scaffolding
scalawag
scald, -ed, -ing (burn)
   scald   scold (chide)
scale, scaled, scaling
   scaliwag   scalawag
scallop, -ed, -ing
scalp, -ed, -ing
scalpel
scaly, -ier, -iest
   scalple   scalpel
scam
scamp
scamper, -ed, -ing
scan, scanned, scanning
   scancion   scansion
scandal
scandalize, -lized, -lizing
scandalmonger
scandalous, -ly
scanner
scansion
scant
scanty, scantier, scantiest
scanty, -ier, -iest
scanty, -tily, -tiness
scapegoat
scapula, -lae, -las
scar, scarred, scarring
scarab
scarce, scarcer, scarcest
scarcely, -ness
scarcity, -ties
scare, scared, scaring
scarecrow
scaredycat
scaremonger
scarf, scarfs, scarves
scarify, -fied, -fying
scarlet
scarp
   scarsity   scarcity
scary, scarier, scariest, -iness
scat, -ted, -ting
   scate   skate
scathing, -ly
scatter, -ed, -ing

scatterbrain, -ed
scavenge, -venged, -venging
scavenger
   sceme   scheme
scenario, -narios
scene (view)
   scene   seen (to see)
scenery, -neries
scenic, -ally
scent (perfume)
   scent   cent (coin)
   scent   sent (to send)
scepter
   scerge   scourge
   scermish   skirmish
schedule, -uled, -uling
schematic, -ally
scheme, schemed, scheming
schemer
schism
schismatic
   schizofrenia   schizophrenia
schizoid
schizophrenia
schizophrenic
schlep, schlepped, schlepping
schlock
schmaltz
schmooze, schmoozed, -moozing
schnapps
schnook
scholar
scholarly
scholarship
scholastic, -ally
scholasticism
school, -ed, -ing
schoolbag
schoolbook
schoolboy
schoolchild, -children
schoolgirl
schoolhouse
schoolmarm
schoolmaster
schoolmate
schoolmistress, -tresses

schoolroom
schoolteacher
schooner
sciatic
sciatica
science
scientific, -ally
scientist
sci-fi
scimitar
scintillate, -lated, -lating
scion
scissors

  scitsofrenia   schizophrenia
sclerosis, -ses
scoff, -ed, -ing

  scolar   scholar
  scolarship   scholarship
  scolastic   scholastic
scold, -ed, -ing (chide)

  scold   scald (burn)
scone

  scool   school
scoop, -ed, -ing
scoot, -ed, -ing
scooter
scope
scorch, -ed, -ing
scorcher
score, scored, scoring
scoreboard
scorecard
scoreless
scorer
scorn, -ed, -ing
scornful, -ly, -ness
Scorpio
scorpion

  scorpiun   scorpion
Scotch
scotch, -ed, -ing
scot-free
Scotsman, -men
Scotswoman, -women
Scottish

  scoundral   scoundrel
scoundrel

scour, -ed, -ing (scratch)

  scour   scow (barge)
scourge, scourged, scourging
scout, -ed, -ing
scow (barge)

  scow   scour (scratch)
scowl, -ed, -ing

  scowndrel   scoundrel
  scowt   scout
  scrabbel   scrabble
scrabble, -bled, -bling
scraggly, -glier, -gliest
scraggy, -gier, -giest
scram, scrammed, scramming

  scrambel   scramble
scramble, -bled, -bling
scrap, scrapped, scrapping
scrapbook
scrape, scraped, scraping
scraper
scrappily
scrappy, -pier, -piest

  scrapy   scrappy
scratch, -ed, -ing
scrawl, -ed, -ing
scrawny, -nier, -niest
scream, -ed, -ing
screamer
scree
screech, -ed, -ing
screed

  screem   scream
screen, -ed, -ing
screenplay
screw, -ed, -ing
screwball
screwdriver

  screwtinize   scrutinize
screwy, screwier, screwiest

  scribbel   scribble
scribble, -bled, -bling (write)
scribbler
scribe, scribed, scribing
scrim

  scrimage   scrimmage
scrimmage, -maged, -maging
scrimp, -ed, -ing

scrip (receipt)
  scripchere   scripture
script (handwriting)
scriptural, -ly
scripture
scrofula
scroll
  scroo   screw
  scrotem   scrotum
scrotum, -ta, -tums
scrounge, scrounged, scrounging
scrounger
  scrownge   scrounge
scrub, scrubbed, scrubbing
scrubber
scrubby, -bier, -biest
cruff
scruff, -ily, -iness
scruffy, scruffier, scruffiest
  scrumage   scrummage
scrumptious, -ly, -ness
  scrumsious   scrumptious
scrunch, -ed, -ing
  scrupel   scruple
scruple, -pled, -pling
scrupulosity
scrupulous, -ly, -ness
scrutinize, -nized, -nizing
scrutiny, -nies
  scuad   squad
scuba
scud, scudded, scudding
scuff, -ed, -ing
scuffle, -fled, -fling
  scufel   scuffle
  scul   scull (row)
  scul   skull (head)
  sculery   scullery
scull, -ed, -ing (row)
  scull   skull (head)
scullery, -leries
scullion
  scullon   scullion
  sculpchere   sculpture
sculpt, -ed, -ing
  sculpter   sculptor
sculptor (carver)

sculptress
sculptural, -ly
sculpture, -tured, -turing (carving)
scum
scummy, -mier, -miest
  scunk   skunk
scurf
  scurge   scourge
  scurie   scurry
  scurilous   scurrilous
scurrilous, -ly
scurry, -ries
scurvy, -ried, -rying
  scurvey   scurvy
scurvy, -vier, -viest
  scury   scurry
  scuttel   scuttle
scuttle, -tled, -tling
scuttlebutt
scythe, scythed, scything

> If the word is not under sc-
> look under **sk-**.

sea (ocean)
  sea   see (look)
sea anemone
seaboard
sea-borne
seacoast
seafarer
seafaring
seafood
seafront
seagoing
seagull
sea horse
seal, -ed, -ing
sealant
sealer
sea level
sealing (close)
  sealing   ceiling (roof)
seam, -ed, -ing (join)
  seam   seem (appear)
seaman, -men (sailors)
seamanship
  seamen   semen (seed)

seamless
seamstress
seamy -mier, -miest
   sean   scene (view)
   sean   seen (see)
séance
   seanse   séance
seaplane
seaport
sear, -ed, -ing (burn)
   sear   seer (prophet)
search, -ed, -ing
searcher
searchlight
search warrant
sea shell
seashore
seasick, -ness
seaside
season, -ed, -ing
seasonable, -bly
seasonal, -ly
seat, -ed, -ing
seawall
seaward
seawater
seaway
seaweed
seaworthiness
seaworthy
sebaceous
   sebaseous   sebaceous
secateurs
secede, -ceded, -ceding (withdraw)
   secede   succeed (win)
   secesion   secession
secession
   secktion   section
seclude, -cluded, -cluding
seclusion
   secluson   seclusion
second, -ed, -ing
secondary, -arily
secondary boycott
secondary education
second-class
second-degree

secondhand
secondly
second-rate
   secondry   secondary
seconds
secondstory
   secratarial   secretarial
   secratery   secretary
secrecy, -cies
   secresion   secretion
   secresy   secrecy
secret, -ly
secretarial
secretariat
secretary, -ries
secrete, -creted, -creting
secretion
secretive, -ly, -ness
   secretry   secretary
sect
   sectar   sector
sectarian
sectarianism
section
sectional, -ly
sector
secular, -ly
secularism
secularist
secure, -cured, -curing
securely
security, -ties
   sed   said
   sedament   sediment
sedan
   sedar   cedar
sedate, -dated, -dating
sedation
sedative
sedentary, -tariness
   sedentery   sedentary
sedge
sediment
sedimentary
sedimentation
   sedimentery   sedimentary
sedition

seditious
  seditive — sedative
seduce, -duced, -ducing
seducer
  seducktion — seduction
seduction
seductive, -ly, -ness
sedulous, -ly, -ness
  sedulus — sedulous
see, saw, seen, seeing (look)
  see — sea (ocean)
seed, seeded, seeding (plant)
  seed — cede (yield)
seediness
seedless
seedling
seedy, seedier, seediest
  seefarer — seafarer
  seefood — seafood
  seege — siege
  seegull — seagull
seek, sought, seeking
  seel — seal
  seelant — sealant
  seeler — sealer
  see level — sea level
  seeling — ceiling (roof)
  seeling — sealing (close)
seem, -ed, -ing (appear)
  seem — seam (join)
  seeman — seaman (sailor)
seemly, -lier, -liest
  seemstress — seamstress
  seemy — seamy
seen (see)
  seen — scene (view)
  seenery — scenery
  seenic — scenic
  seenile — senile
seep, -ed, -ing
seepage
  seepige — seepage
  seequel — sequel
seer (prophet)
  seer — sear (burn)
seersucker

seesaw, -ed, -ing
  seese — cease
  seesfire — cease-fire
  seeshore — seashore
  seeson — season
  seet — seat
seethe, seethed, seething
  seeweed — seaweed
  seeze — seize
  seezure — seizure
  sege — sedge
segment
segmentation
  segmint — segment
segregate, -gated, -gating
segregation
segregationist
  seige — siege
seine (net)
  seine — sane (not mad)
  seismagraf — seismograph
seismic, -al, -ally
seismogram
seismograph
seismologist
seismology
seize, seized, seizing (grab)
  seize — cease (stop)
seizure
  sekond — second
  sekrete — secrete
  seks — sex
  seksion — section
  sekstant — sextant
  seksual — sexual
  seksy — sexy
  sekt — sect
  sektor — sector
  sekular — secular
  sekure — secure
  sekwel — sequel
  sekwense — sequence
  sekwin — sequin
  Selcius — Celsius
seldom
  selebrate — celebrate
  selebrity — celebrity

select, -ed, -ing
　selecter　　　　　selector
selection
selective, -ly, -ness
selectivity
selector
　seler　　　　　　cellar (room)
　seler　　　　　　seller (goods)
　selerity　　　　　celerity
　selery　　　　　celery (food)
　selery　　　　　salary (wage)
　selestial　　　　celestial
self, selves
self-abandonment
self-addressed
self-adjusting
self-administered
self-advancement
self-aggrandizement
self-appointed
self-assertive
self-assurance
self-awareness
self-centered, -ly, -ness
self-cleaning
self-composed
self-confessed
self-confidence
self-confident
self-conscious, -ly, -ness
self-contained
self-control, -trolled
self-defeating
self-defense
self-denial
self-destruct, -ive
self-destruction
self-determination
self-doubt
self-educated
self-employed
self-employment
self-esteem
self-evident
self-examination
self-explanatory
self-expression

self-fertilization
self-fulfiling
self-fulfillment
self-governing
self-government
self-governing
self-help
self-image
　self-imidge　　　self-image
self-importance
self-important, -ly
self-imposed
self-improvement
self-induced
self-indulgence
self-indulgent
self-interest
selfish, -ly, -ness
selfishness
selfless, -ly, -ness
self-made
self-opinionated
self-pity
self-pollination
self-portrait
self-possessed
self-possession
self-preservation
self-proclaimed
self-protection
self-realization
self-reliance
self-reliant
self-reproach
self-respect
self-righteous, -ly, -ness
self-rising
self-rule
self-sacrifice
self-satisfaction
self-satisfied
self-sealing
self-service
self-serving
self-starter
self-sufficient
self-supporting

self-sustaining
self-taught
self-willed
self-winding

selibacy	celibacy
selibat	celibate
selibrate	celebrate

sell, sold, selling (goods)

sell	cell (prison)

seller (goods)

seller	cellar (room)
sellofane	cellophane
sellophane	cellophane

sellout

sellullar	cellular
selluloid	celluloid
sellulose	cellulose
sellvage	salvage (save)
sellvedge	selvage (edge)
Selsius	Celsius
selular	cellular
seluloid	celluloid
selulose	cellulose

selvage (edge)

selvedge	salvage (save)
semafor	semaphore

semantic
semaphore, -phored, -phoring
semblance

semblanse	semblance

semen (seed)

semen	seamen (sailors)

semester
semiannual
semiarid
semiautomatic, -tically

semicercle	semicircle

semicircle
semicircular
semicolon
semiconductor
semiconscious, -ness
semidetached
semifinal
semifinalist
semimonthly

seminal, -ly
seminar
seminary, -aries
semipermeable
semiprecious
semiprivate
semipro
semiprofessional
semiskilled
semisoft
semisweet
Semite

semitery	cemetery

Semitic
semitone
semitrailer
semiweekly
semolina

sena	senna
senario	scenario
senat	senate

senate

senater	senator

senator
senatorial
send, sent, sending
sender
sendoff
senile

senilitey	senility

senility
senior
seniority, -ties
senna

sennator	senator
senotaf	cenotaph
sensability	sensibility
sensable	sensible

sensation
sensational, -ly
sensationalism
sensationalist

sensatize	sensitize

sensationalize, -ized, -izing
sense, sensed, sensing (feeling)

sense	cents (coins)

senseless, -ly, -ness

senser	censer (incense)	sentrey	sentry
senser	censor (remove)	sentrifugal	centrifugal
senser	sensor (device)	sentifuge	centrifuge
senshual	sensual	sentripetal	centripetal
senshure	censure (condemn)	sentry, -tries	
		sentuple	centuple
sensible, -bly		senturion	centurion
sensibility, -ties		sentury	century
sensitivity, -ties		senyor	senior
sensitize, -tized, -tizing		sepal	
sensor (device)		separable, -bly	
sensor	censer (incense)	separible	separable
sensor	censor (remove)	separate, -rated, -rating	
sensor	censure (condemn)	separate, -ly, -ness	
		separation	
sensorey	sensory	separationist	
sensorious	censorious	separator	
sensory		seperable	separable
sensual, -ly, -ness		seperate	separate
sensualist		seperater	separator
sensualitey	sensuality	seperation	separation
sensuality, -ties		sephalitis	cephalitis
sensuous, -ly, -ness		sepia	
sensus	census	sepsis	
sent (to send)		September	
sent	cent (money)	septer	scepter
sent	scent (perfume)	septet	
sentenary	centenary	septic	
sentence, -tenced, -tencing		septicemia	
sentennial	centennial	septuagenarian	
sentensious	sententious	septum	
sententious, -ly, -ness		septuplet	
senter	center	sepulcher	
sentient, -ly		sepulchral, -ly	
Sentigrade	Centigrade	sepulchrel	sepulchral
sentigram	centigram	sepulker	sepulcher
sentiment		sequel	
sentimental, -ly		sequence	
sentimentalism		sequense	sequence
sentimentalist		sequensial	sequential
sentimentality, -ties		sequential, -ly	
sentimeter	centimeter	sequester, -ed, -ing	
sentinel, -ed, -ing		sequestration	
sentipede	centipede	sequin	
sentor	centaur	ser	sir
sentral	central	seraf	seraph
sentralize	centralize	serafic	seraphic

seramic	ceramic	serplice	surplice (gown)
seranade	serenade	serplus	surplus (extra)
serch	search	serprise	surprise
seremony	ceremony	serrate, -rated, -rating	
seraph, -aphs, -aphim		serration	
seraphic, -ally		sertain	certain
serch	search	sertainty	certainty
sere (dry)		sertax	surtax
sere	sear (burn)	sertifiable	certifiable
serebrul	cerebral	sertificate	certificate
sereen	serene	sertify	certify
serees	series	sertitude	certitude
serenade, -naded, -nading		serum, sera, serums	
serendipity		servant	
serene, -ly, -ness		servay	survey
serenitey	serenity	servaylanse	surveillance
serenity, -ties		serve, served, serving	
seres	series	server	
sereze	cerise	servical	cervical
serf (slave)		service, -viced, -vicing	
serf	surf (sea)	serviceability	
serfdom		serviceable, -bly, -ness	
serge (cloth)		serviceman, -men	
serge	surge (rush)	servicewoman, -women	
sergeant		serviks	cervix
serial, -ly (part)		servile, -ly	
serial	cereal (grain)	servility	
serialization		servitude	
serialize, -lized, -lizing		servival	survival
seribelum	cerebellum	servive	survive
seribral	cerebral	serviver	survivor
seribrum	cerebrum	servix	cervix
series		sesame	
serif		sese	cease
serimonial	ceremonial	seseed	secede
serimonius	ceremonious	seseless	ceaseless
serimony	ceremony	sesession	secession
serious, -ly, -ness		seson	season
serjent	sergeant	sesonal	seasonal
serloin	sirloin	sesonible	seasonable
serly	surly	sesquicentenary, -ries	
sermise	surmise	sessation	cessation
sermon		session (period)	
sermount	surmount	session	cession (yield)
sername	surname	sesspool	cesspool
serpent		set, set, setting	
serpentine		setback	

setee	settee	sexton	
seter	setter	sextuplet	
setle	settle	sexual, -ly	
settee		sexuality	
setteler	settler	sexy, sexier, sexiest	
settelment	settlement	sexy, sexily, sexiness	
setter		sezarian	Caesarian
settle, -tled, -tling		sfere	sphere
settlement		sfericul	sperical
settler		sferoid	spheroid
set-up		sfincter	sphincter
seudo	pseudo	sfinx	sphinx
seudonim	pseudonym	sha	Shah
sevanth	seventh	shabby, -bier, -biest	
sevarel	several	shabby, -ily, -iness	
sevear	severe	shaby	shabby
seven		shack	
seventeen		shackel	shackle
seventeenth		shackle, -led, -ling	
seventh		shaddow	shadow
seventieth		shade, shaded, shading	
seventy, -ties		shadow, -ed, -ing	
seventyeth	seventieth	shadowy	
sever, -ed, -ing (cut)		shady, -dier, -diest	
several, -ly		shaft	
severance		shag	
severanse	severance	shagginess	
severe, -verer, -verest (strict)		shaggy, -gier, -giest	
severely		shagrin	chagrin
severity, -ties		shagy	shaggy
sew, sewed, sewn, sewing (stitch)		Shah	
sew	sow (plant)	shak	shack
sewage		shakable	
sewer (drain)		shake, shook, shaken, shaking	
sewer (stitcher)		shakeable	
sewer	sower (planter)	shakedown	
sewerage		shaker	
sewige	sewage	Shakespearian	
sex, -ed, -ing		shakeup	
sexiness		shakey	shaky
sexism		shakily	
sexist		shakiness	
sexless, -ly, -ness		shaky, shakier, shakiest	
sexpot		shal	shall
sex-starved		shalay	chalet
sextant		shale	
sextet, sextette		shalet	chalet

shall (will)
   shall   shell (cover)
shallot
shallow, -ly, -ness
shallowness
sham, shammed, shamming
(pretend)
shamble, -bled, -bling
shambles
shame, shamed, shaming
(disgrace)
shamefaced, -ly, -ness
shameful, -ly, -ness
shameless, -ly, -ness
   shampane   champagne
shampoo, -ed, -ing
shamrock
   shamy   chamois
   shandeleer   chandelier
shanghai, -haied, -haiing
shank
shan't (shall not)
   shant   shan't
shantung
shanty, -ties
shapable
shape, shaped, shaping
shapeable
shapeliness
shapely, -lier, -liest
   shaperon   chaperon
   sharade   charade
shard
share, shared, sharing
sharecropper
sharecropping
shareholder
shark
sharkskin
sharp, -ly, -ness
sharpen, -ed, -ing
sharpener
sharper
sharpness
sharpshooter
   shasee   chassis
   shater   shatter

   shatow   chateau
shatter, -ed, -ing
shave, shaved, shaven, shaving
shaver
shawl
she
sheaf, sheaves
shear, sheared, shorn, shearing
(cut)
   shear   sheer (thin)
shearer
shearwater
sheath, sheaths
sheathe, sheathed, sheathing
sheave
shed, shed, shedding
   shedule   schedule
   sheef   sheaf
   sheek   chic
              (fashionable)
   sheek   sheik (ruler)
sheen
sheep, sheep
sheep-dip
sheepdog
sheepish, -ly
sheepishness
sheep-run
sheepskin
sheer, -ed, -ing (swerve)
sheer (thin)
   sheer   shear (cut)
sheet, -ed, -ing
   shef   chef
sheik (ruler)
   sheik   chic
              (fashionable)
   sheik   shake (move)
   sheild   shield
shekel
   shel   shell
   shelac   shellac
shelf, shelves
   shelfish   shellfish
shell, -ed, -ing (cover)
she'll (she will)
   shell   she'll

shellac, -lacked, -lacking		shipmate	
shellfish, -fishes, -fish		shipment	
shell shock		shipreck	shipwreck
shelter, -ed, -ing		shipright	shipwright
shelve, shelved, shelving		shipshape	
shenanigans		shipwreck, -ed, -ing	
sheperd	shepherd	shipwright	
shepherd, -ed, -ing		shipyard	
shepherdess		shirk, -ed, -ing	
sherbet		shirker	
sherie	sherry	shirr, -ed, -ing	
sherry, -ries		shirt	
sheth	sheath	shirtless	
sheves	sheaves	shish kebab	
shevron	chevron	shivalrous	chivalrous
shibboleth		shivalry	chivalry
shic	chic	shiver, -ed, -ing	
	(fashionable)	shivery	
shic	sheik (ruler)	shnaps	schnapps
shiek	sheik	shoal, -ed, -ing	
shield, -ed, -ing		shock, -ed, -ing	
shiffon	chiffon	shocker	
shift, -ed, -ing		shod	
shiftiness		shoddily	
shiftless, -ly, -ness		shoddiness	
shifty, -tier, -tiest		shoddy, -dier, -diest	
shiling	shilling	shoe, shoes	
shillac	shellac	shoe, shod, shoeing (footwear)	
shillelagh, shillalah		shoe	shoo (scare)
shilling		shoehorn	
shimer	shimmer	shoelace	
shimmer, -ed, -ing		shoemaker	
shimmery		shoeshine	
shimmy, -mies		shoestring	
shimmy, -mied, -mying		shoetree	
shin, shinned, shinning		shofer	chauffeur
shindig		sholder	shoulder
shine, shone, shined, shining		shole	shoal
shiner		shoo, -ed, -ing (scare)	
shingel	shingle	shoo	shoe (footwear)
shingle, -gled, -gling		shood	should
shingles		shoe-in	
shiny, shinier, shiniest		shoot, shot, shooting (gun)	
ship, shipped, shipping		shoot	chute (channel)
shipboard		shooter	
shipbuilder		shop, shopped, shopping	
shipload		shopkeeper	

shoplift, -ed, -ing
shoplifter
shoptalk
shopworn
shore, shored, shoring (sea)
   shore   sure (certain)
   shorely   surely
   shorety   surety
shorebird
shoreline
shoreward
shorn
short, -ly, -ness
shortage
shortbread
   shortbred   shortbread
shortcake
shortchange, -changed, -changing
short-circuit, -ed, -ing
shortcoming
shortcut
   shortedge   shortage
shorten, -ed, -ing
shortfall
shorthand
shorthanded
short-lived
short-order
shorts
shortsighted
   shortsited   shortsighted
short-sleeved
shortstop
short-tempered
short-term
shortwave
short-winded
shot
shotgun
shot put
shot putter
should
shoulder, -ed, -ing
shoulder blade
shoulder-high
shouldn't
shout, -ed, -ing

shove, -ed, -ing
shovel, -ed, -ing
shoveler
   shovinism   chauvinism
   shovinist   chauvinist
show, showed, shown, showing
showboat
showcase
showdown
shower
showery
showman, -men
showmanship
showoff
showpiece
showplace
showroom
show-stopper
   showt   shout
showy, showier, showiest
showy, -ily, -iness
shrank
shrapnel
shred, shredded, shredding
shredder
   shreek   shriek
shrew
shrewd, -ly, -ness
shrewish, -ly
shriek, -ed, -ing
shrike
shrill
shrimp
shrine
shrink, shrank, shrunk, shrinking
shrinkage
shrinkable
   shrinkedge   shrinkage
shrivel, -ed, -ing
   shroo   shrew
   shrood   shrewd
shroud
   shrowd   shroud
shrub
shrubbery, -ies
shrug, shrugged, shrugging
shrunk

shudder, -ed, -ing
shuffel — shuffle
shuffle, -fled, -fling
shulder — shoulder
shun, shunned, shunning
shunter
shurbet — sherbert
shurk — shirk
shurt — shirt
shush, -ed, -ing
shut, shut, shutting
shutdown
shuter — shutter
shuteye
shutout
shuttel — shuttle
shuttelcock — shuttlecock
shutter
shutterbug
shuttle, -tled, -tling
shuttlecock
shuve — shove
shuvel — shovel
shy, shied, shying
shy, shyer, shyest
shy, -ly, -ness
shyster
sianide — cyanide
siatic — sciatic
sibernetics — cybernetics
sibilant, -ly
sibling
sic (thus)
sicamore — sycamore
sicedelic — psychedelic
siciatry — psychiatry
sicick — psychic
sick (ill)
sickbed
sickel — sickle
sicken, -ed, -ing
sickle
sickliness
sickly, -lier, -liest
siclamate — cyclamate

siclamen — cyclamen
sicle — cycle
siclic — cyclic
siclist — cyclist
siclone — cyclone
siclotron — cyclotron
sicoanalize — psychoanalyze
sicological — psychological
sicology — psychology
sicopant — sycophant
sicopath — psychopath
sicosis — psychosis
sicosomatic — psychosomatic
sicotherapist — psychotherapist
sicotic — psychotic
side, sided, siding
sidearm
sideboard
sidebord — sideboard
sideburns
sidecar
sidekick
sidelight
sideline
sidelite — sidelight
sider — cider
sidesaddle
sideshow
sidesplitting
sidestep, -stepped, -stepping
sidestroke
sideswipe, -swiped, -swiping
sidetrack, -ed, -ing
sidel — sidle
sidewalk
sidewall
sideways
sidle, -dled, -dling
siduce — seduce
sie — sigh
siege, sieged, sieging
sienna
sience — science
siense — science
sientific — scientific
sientist — scientist
sierra

siesta
sieve, sieved, sieving
  sieze   seize
  sifer   cypher
  sifilis   syphilis
  sifon   syphon
sift, -ed, -ing
  sigar   cigar
  sigarette   cigarette
sigh, -ed, -ing
sight, -ed, -ing (view)
  sight   cite (quote)
  sight   site (place)
sightless, -ly, -ness
sightly, -lier, -liest
sightseeing
sightseer
sigma
sign, -ed, -ing (mark)
  sign   sine (math)
signal, -ed, -ing
signatory, -ries
signature
  signefy   signify
  signel   signal
signet (ring)
  signet   cygnet (swan)
significance
  significanse   significance
significant, -ly
signification
  signifie   signify
signify, -fied, -fying
signpost
  sikedelic   psychedelic
  sikey   psyche
Sikh
  sikiatrist   psychiatrist
  sikiatry   psychiatry
  sikick   psychic
  siksty   sixty
  silable   syllable
  silabus   syllabus
silage
silence, silenced, silencing
silencer
  silense   silence

silent, -ly
  silestial   celestial
  silf   sylph
silhouette, -etted, -etting
silica
silicon (element)
silicone (synthetic)
silicosis
  silie   silly
  silige   silage
  silinder   cylinder
  silindrical   cylindrical
silk
silken
silkiness
silkscreen
silkworm
silky, -kier, -kiest
sill
  sillable   syllable
silliness
silly, -lier, -liest
silo, -los
  silogism   syllogism
silt, -ed, -ing
  siluette   silhouette
silver, -ed, -ing
  silverey   silvery
silverfish, -fish, -fishes
silver-plate, -ted, -ting
silversmith
silvery
  sily   silly
  simbiosis   symbiosis
  simbiotic   symbiotic
  simbol   cymbal (music)
  simbol   symbol (sign)
  simbolical   symbolical
  simbolism   symbolism
  simbolize   symbolize
  siment   cement
  simer   simmer
  simetry   symmetry
  simfoney   symphony
simian
similar, -ly
similarity, -ties

simile
  similer — similar
simmer, -ed, -ing
  simmetry — symmetry
  simpathetic — sympathetic
  simpathize — sympathize
  simpathy — sympathy
  simpel — simple
  simpelton — simpleton
simper, -ed, -ing
simple, -pler, -plest
simple-minded
simpleton
simplicity, -ties
simplification
simplify, -fied, -fying
  simplisty — simplicity
simplistic, -ally
simply
  simposium — symposium
  simptom — symptom
  simptomatic — symptomatic
simulate, -lated, -lating
  simulater — simulator
simulation
simulator
simultaneous, -ly, -ness
  simultanious — simultaneous
sin, sinned, sinning
  sinagog — synagog
  sinagogue — synagogue
  sinamon — cinnamon
since
sincere, -cerer, -cerest
sincerely
sincerity, -ties
  sincronize — synchronize
sine (math)
  sine — sign (mark)
sinecure
  sinema — cinema
  sinepost — signpost
sinew
sinewy
sinful, -ly, -ness
sing, sang, sung, singing
singe, singed, singeing

  singel — single
singer
single, -gled, -gling
single-handed
single-minded
single-space, -spaced, -spacing
singsong
singular, -ly
singularity, -ties
  singuler — singular
  sinic — cynic
  sinical — cynical
  sinema — cinema
  sinisism — cynicism
sinister, -ly
sink, sank, sunk or sunken, sinking
sinker
sinkhole
sinless
  sinod — synod
  sinonim — synonym
  sinonimus — synonymous
  sinopsis — synopsis
  sinoptic — synoptic
  sinoshure — cynosure
  sinse — since
  sinsere — sincere
  sinserity — sincerity
  sintax — syntax
  sinthesis — synthesis
  sinthesize — synthesize
  sinthetic — synthetic
  sinue — sinew
  sinuos — sinuous
sinuous, -ly
sinus, -nuses
sinusitis
Sioux, Sioux
sip, sipped, sipping
  sipher — cipher
siphon, -ed, -ing
  sipress — cypress
sir
  sirca — circa
  sircharge — surcharge
sire, sired, siring
siren

siringe	syringe	sivility	civility
sirloin		sivilization	civilization
sirosis	cirrhosis	sivilize	civilize
sirup	syrup	six	
sirus	cirrus	sixfold	
sisal		six-gun	
sise	size	six-pack	
sism	schism	six-shooter	
sismic	seismic	sixteen	
sismograf	seismograph	sixteenth	
sismologist	seismologist	sixth, -ly	
sissers	scissors	sixtieth	
sissy, sissies		sixty, -ties	
sist	cyst	sixtyeth	sixtieth
sistem	system	sizable, -bly	
sistematic	systematic	size, sized, sizing	
sistematize	systematize	sizemic	seismic
sister		sizers	scissors
sisterhood		sizle	sizzle
sister-in-law, sisters-in-law		sizzle, -zled, -zling	
sisterly		sizzler	
sistern	cistern	skane	skein
sit, sat, sitting		skate, skated, skating	
sitadel	citadel	skateboard	
sitar		skater	
sitation	citation	skathing	scathing
sitcom		skedule	schedule
site, sited, siting (place)		skee	ski
site	cite (state)	skeem	scheme
site	sight (view)	skein	
sitely	sightly	skeletal	
siteseeing	sightseeing	skeletel	skeletal
siteseer	sightseer	skeleton	
sithe	scythe	skematic	schematic
sither	zither	skeme	scheme
sit-in		skeptic	
sitizen	citizen	skeptical	
sitric	citric	skepticism	
sitrus	citrus	skermish	skirmish
sitter		skert	skirt
situate, -ated, -ating		sketch, -ed, -ing	
situation		sketcher	
sity	city	sketchbook	
sive	sieve	sketchily	
sivere	severe	sketchiness	
sivic	civic	sketchy, sketchier, sketchiest	
sivilian	civilian	skew, -ed, -ing	

skewer
ski, skis, ski
ski, -ed, -ing
skid, skidded, skidding
skier
skiff

skil	skill
skilet	skillet
skilite	skylight

skill
skilled
skillet
skillful, -ly, -ness
skim, skimmed, skimming
skimp, -ed, -ing
skimpily
skimpiness
skimpy, skimpier, skimpiest
skin, skinned, skinning
skin-deep
skin-dive, -dove, -diving
skin diver
skin diving

skiney	skinny

skinflint
skinny, -nier, -niest
skinny-dip, -dipped, -dipping
skintight
skip, skipped, skipping

skiper	skipper

ski pole
skipper
skirmish
skirt, -ed, -ing

skiscraper	skyscraper

skit

skitsofrenia	schizophrenia
skittel	skittle

skittish, -ly, -ness
skivvy
skua

skue	skew

skulk, -ed, -ing
skull (head)

skull	scull (row)

skullcap
skunk

> For all **skw-** words,
> look under **squ-**.

sky
sky-blue
skycap
sky-dive, -dived, -diving
skydiver
sky-high
skyjack, -ed, -ing
skyjacker
skylark
skylight
skyline
skyrocket
skyscraper
skyward

> If the word is not under **sk-**
> look under **sc-**.

slab
slack, -ly, -ness
slacken, -ed, -ing
slacks
slag
slain
slake, slaked, slaking
slalom
slam, slammed, slamming
slander, -ed, -ing
slanderer
slanderous, -ly

slane	slain

slang
slangy, -giness
slant, -ed, -ing
slap, slapped, slapping
slapdash
slaphappy
slapstick
slash, -ed, -ing
slasher
slat
slate, slated, slating
slather, -ed, -ing
slattern, -ly
slaughter, -ed, -ing
slaughterhouse
Slav
Slavic

slave, slaved, slaving
slaver
slavish, -ly, -ness
slavery
  slawter   slaughter
slay, slew, slain, slaying (kill)
  slay   sleigh (sled)
sleazy, -zier, -ziest
sled
sledge
sledgehammer
sleek, -ly, -ness
sleep, slept, sleeping
sleeper
sleepily
sleepiness
sleepless, -ly, -ness
sleepwalker
sleepy, sleepier, sleepiest
sleepyhead
sleet, -ed, -ing
sleeve
sleeved
sleeveless
  slege   sledge
sleigh (sled)
sleight (skill)
  sleight   slight (small)
slender, -ly, -ness
slept
sleuth
slew
  sli   sly
slice, sliced, slicing
slick, -ly, -ness
slide, slid, sliding
slight, -ly (small)
  slight   sleight (skill)
slim, slimmed, slimming
slim, slimmer, slimmest
slime, slimily, sliminess
slimy, slimier, slimiest
sling, slung, slinging
slink, slunk, slinking
slinky, slinkier, slinkiest
slip, slipped, slipping
  sliper   slipper

slipcover
slipknot
  slipnot   slipknot
slip-on
slippage
slipper
slippery, -perier, -periest
slipshod
slip stitch
slipstream
slipway
  slise   slice
slit, slit, slitting
  slite   slight
slither, -ed, -ing
sliver
  slo   sloe (fruit)
  slo   slow (not fast)
slob
slobber, -ed, -ing
slobbery
sloe (fruit)
  sloe   slow (not fast)
slog, slogged, slogging
slogan
sloop
  sloose   sluice
  slooth   sleuth
slop, slopped, slopping
slope, sloped, sloping
  slopily   sloppily
sloppiness
sloppily
sloppy, -pier, -piest
  slopy   sloppy
slosh, -ed, -ing
slot, slotted, slotting
sloth
slothful, -ly, -ness
slouch, -ed, -ing
slough (shed)
sloven, -ly
slovenliness
slow, -ed, -ing (not fast)
  slow   sloe (fruit)
  slow   slough (shed)
  slowch   slouch

slow motion
slowpoke
sludge
sludgy
  slue   slew
  sluff   slough (shed)
sluggard
sluggardly
sluggish, -ly, -ness
sluice, sluiced, sluicing
slum, slummed, slumming
slumber, -ed, -ing
slump, -ed, -ing
slung
slunk
slur, slurred, slurring
  slurie   slurry
slurp, -ed, -ing
slurry
slush, -iness
slushy
slut
sluttish, -ly
sly, slyer, slyest
sly, -ly, -ness
smack, -ed, -ing
smacker
small
small-minded
smallpox
small-scale
small-time
smart, -ed, -ing
smart, -ly, -ness
smart, smarter, smartest
smart alec
smarten, -ed, -ing
smash, -ed, -ing
smasher
smattering
smear, -ed, -ing
  smeer   smear
smell, smelled, smelling
smelly, smellier, smelliest
smelter
smidgen, smidgin
smile, smiled, smiling

smirch, -ed, -ing
smirk, -ed, -ing
smite, smote, smiting
smith
smithereens
  smithey   smithy
smithy, smithies
smitten
smock, -ed, -ing
smog
smoggy, smoggier, smoggiest
  smogy   smoggy
smoke, smoked, smoking
smokehouse
smokeless
smoker
smokescreen
smokestack
smoky, smokier, smokiest
smolder
smooch, -ed, -ing
smooth, -ed, -ing
smooth, -ly, -ness
smorgasbord
smother, -ed, -ing
smoulder, -ed, -ing
smudge, smudged, smudging
smug, smugger, smuggest
smug, -ly, -ness
  smuge   smudge
  smuggel   smuggle
smuggle, smuggled, smuggling
smuggler
  smurch   smirch
  smurk   smirk
smut
  smuther   smother
smutty, smuttier, smuttiest
  smuty   smutty
  snach   snatch
snack, -ed, -ing
  snaffel   snaffle
snaffle
snag, snagged, snagging
snail
  snair   share
snake, snaked, snaking

snake bite
snaky
  snale — snail
snap, snapped, snapping
snapdragon
  snaper — snapper
snapper
snappy, -pier, -piest
snappy, -pily, -piness
snapshot
  snapy — snappy
snare, snared, snaring
snarl, -ed, -ing
snatch, -ed, -ing
snazzy, zier, -ziest
sneak, -ed, -ing
sneaker
  sneek — sneak
  sneeker — sneaker
sneer, -ed, -ing
sneeze, sneezed, sneezing
snicker, -ed, -ing
snide
  snif — sniff
  snifel — sniffle
sniff, -ed, -ing
sniffle, -fled, -fling (sniff)
  sniger — snigger
snigger, -ed, -ing
snip, snipped, snipping (cut)
snipe, sniped, sniping (shoot)
sniper
  snipet — snippet
snippet
snitch, -ed, -ing
snivel, -ed, -ing (cry)
  snivle — snivel
snob
  snoball — snowball
snobbery
snobbish, -ly, -ness
snood
snooker
snookered
snoop, -ed, -ing
snoopy
snooze, snoozed, snoozing

snore, snored, snoring
snorkel
  snorkle — snorkel
snort, -ed, -ing
snot
snout
snow, -ed, -ing
snowball
snowbank
snow-blind
snowbound
snow-capped
snowdrift
  snowey — snowy
snowfall
snowflake
snow job
snow line
snowman, -men
snowmobile
snowplow
snowshoe, -shoed, -shoeing
snowstorm
snowsuit
snow-white
  snowt — snout
snowy, snowier, snowiest
snub, snubbed, snubbing
snuff, -ed, -ing
snuffle, -fled, -fling
snug, snugger, snuggest
snuggle, -gled, -gling
so (in this way)
  so — sew (stitch)
  so — sow (pig, plant)
soak, -ed, -ing
so-and-so
soap, -ed, -ing
soapbox
soap opera
  soappy — soapy
soapstone
soapsuds
soapy, soapier, soapiest
soar, -ed, -ing (fly)
  soar — sore (hurt)
sob, sobbed, sobbing

sober, -ed, -ing
sober, -ly, -ness
sobriety
  sobrikay — sobriquet
sobriquet
  socable — sociable
soccer
  sociabel — sociable
sociability
sociable, -bly
social, -ly
socialism
socialist
socialistic, -ally
socialite
socialization
socialize, -lized, -lizing
society, -ties
socio-economic, -ally
  sociol — social
sociologist
sociology
sock, -ed, -ing
  socker — soccer
socket
  sockit — socket
sockeye salmon
sod, -ded, -ding
soda
soda water
sodden, -ly, -ness
  soden — sodden
sodium
sodomy
sofa
  sofar — sofa
  sofen — soften
  sofism — sophism
  sofist — sophist
  sofisticate — sophisticate
  sofistication — sophistication
  sofistry — sophistry
soft, -ly, -ness
softball
soft-boiled
soft-cover
soften, -ed, -ing

soft-headed
soft-hearted
soft-pedal, -ed, -ing
soft-shell-crab
soft-soap
soft-spoken
software
  softwear — software
soggily
sogginess
soggy, -gier, -giest
  sogy — soggy
soil, -ed, -ing
  soiray — soiree, soirée
soiree, soirée
  sojern — sojourn
sojourn, -ed, -ing
  soke — soak
solace, -aced, -acing
solar
  solareum — solarium
solarium
  solass — solace
  solatude — solitude
sold
solder, -ed, -ing (fuse)
soldier, -ed, -ing (army)
soldierly
sole (shoe, one)
  sole — soul (spirit)
solecism
  soled — solid
  soleful — soulful
  solem — solemn
solemn, -ly, -ness
solemnization
solemnize, -nized, -nizing
solemnity, -ties
solenoid
  soler — solar
  solesism — solecism
  soletary — solitary
sol-fa (sing)
  solger — soldier
solicit, -ed, -ing
  soliciter — solicitor
solicitation

solicitor
solicitous, -ly, -ness
solicitude
   solicitus — solicitous
solid, -ly, -ness
solidarity, -ties
   solidifi — solidify
solidification
solidify, -fied, -fying
solid-state
   solilokwy — soliloquy
soliloquy, -quies
   solisit — solicit
   solisitor — solicitor
   solisitus — solicitous
solitaire
solitary, -taries
solitude
   soljer — soldier

> For soll- words,
> look under sol-.

solo, -los
soloist
solstice
   solstiss — solstice
   solubel — soluble
solubility, -ties
soluble, -bly
   solushun — solution
solution
solvable
solve, solved, solving
solvency
   solvensy — solvency
solvent
somber, -ly
   sombraro — sombrero
sombrero
some (few)
   some — sum (total)
somebody, -bodies
someday
somehow
someone (some person)
some one (one of several)
someplace

   somersalt — somersault
somersault
something
sometime
someway
somewhat
somewhere
somnambulism
somnolence
   somnolense — somnolence
son (boy)
   son — sun (star)
sonar
sonata
   soner — sonar
song
songbird
songfest
songster
songstress
sonic
son-in-law, sons-in-law
sonnet
sonny, -nies
sonorous, -ly
   sonorus — sonorous
   soo — sue
   soocher — suture
   soocrose — sucrose
   sooet — suet
   sooflay — souffle
soon
   soop — soup
soot (chimney)
   soot — suit (clothes)
sooth (truth)
soothe, soothed, soothing (calm)
soothsayer
   soovenir — souvenir
sop, sopped, sopping
   sope — soap
   sophestry — sophistry
sophism
sophist
sophisticate, -cated, -cating
sophistication
sophistry, -ries

soporific, -ally

sopping

soppy, -pier, -piest

soprano, -pranos, -prani

sorbet

  sorcary — sorcery

  sorce — sauce (liquid)

  sorce — source (origin)

sorcerer

sorceress

sorcery, -ceries

  sord — sword

sordid, -ly, -ness

  sordust — sawdust

sore, sorer, sorest (hurt)

  sore — saw (cut)

  sore — soar (rise)

sorehead

  sorel — sorrel

  sorey — sorry

sorghum

  sorgum — sorghum

  sorie — sorry

  sorna — sauna

  sornter — saunter

sorority, -ties

  sorow — sorrow

sorrel

sorrow

sorrowful, -ly

sorry, -rier, -riest

sort (type)

  sort — sought (looked)

  sortee — sortie

sortie

  sosage — sausage

  sosiable — sociable

  sosial — social

  sosialize — socialize

  sosiety — society

so-so

sot

  soto vochay — sotto voce

sotto voce

soufflé

sough, -ed, -ing (rustling sound)

  sough — sow (pig)

sought (looked)

soul (spirit)

  soul — sole (shoe, one)

sound, -ed, -ing

sound, -ly, -ness

sound barrier

sound board

soundless

soundproof

soundtrack

soup

sour, -ed, -ing

sourball

source (origin)

  source — sauce (liquid)

sourdough

souse, soused, sousing

south

southbound

southeast

southeaster, -ly

southeastern

southeastward

southerly

southern

southerner

southernmost

southward, -ly

southwest

southwester, -ly

southwestern

southwestward

souvenir

souvlaki

sovereign

sovereignty, -ties

  soverin — sovereign

soviet

sow, sowed, sowing (pig, plant)

  sow — sew (stitch)

sown (planted)

  sown — sewn (stitched)

  sownd — sound

  sowr — sour

  sowth — south

soy

spa

space, spaced, spacing
space bar
space-craft
spaced-out
spaceflight
spaceman, -men
space shuttle
spaceship
spacesuit
   spacific   specific
spacious, -ly
spade, spaded, spading
spadework
   spagetti   spaghetti
spaghetti (plural noun)
span, spanned, spanning
   spaner   spanner
spangle, -gled, -gling
   spanial   spaniel
Spaniard
spaniel
spank, -ed, -ing
spanner
spar, sparred, sparring (fight)
spare, spared, sparing (extra)
spark, -ed, -ing
sparkle, -kled, -kling
sparkler
   sparow   sparrow
sparrow
sparrow hawk
sparse, sparser, sparsest
sparsity
Spartan
   spase   space
   spasious   spacious
spasm
spasmodic, -ally
spastic, -ally
spat (did spit)
   spatal   spatial
spate (sudden)
spatial, -ly
spatter, -ed, -ing
spatula
spawn, -ed, -ing
spay, -ed, -ing

speak, spoke, spoken, speaking
speakeasy, -easies
speaker
spear, -ed, -ing
spearmint
spec (specification)
   spec   speck (spot)
special, -ly
specialist
speciality, -ties
specialization
specialize, -lized, -lizing
specialty, -ties
specie (coin)
species, -cies (group)
specific, -ly
specification
specify, -fied, -fying
specimen
specious, -ly, -ness
speck, -ed, -ing (spot)
   speck   spec (specification)
speckle, -kled, -kling
spectacle
spectacular, -ly
spectator
specter
   specticle   spectacle
spectrograph
spectroscope
spectrum, -tra, -trums
speculate, -lated, -lating
speculation
speculator
speech
speed, sped, speeding
speedboat
speedometer
speedway
speedy, -dier, -diest
   speek   speak
   speer   spear
   spekul   speckle
   spel   spell
spell, spelt or spelled, spelling
spellbinder

spellbinding
spellbound
spend, spent, spending
spendthrift
sperm
spern — spurn
spert — spurt
spesial — special
spesialist — specialist
spesify — specify
spesimen — specimen
spesious — specious
spew, -ed, -ing
sphere
spherical, -ly
spheroid
sphinx
spi — spy
spice, spiced, spicing
spick-and-span
spicy, spicier, spiciest
spider
spidery
spiel, -ed, -ing
spigot
spike, spiked, spiking
spill, spilled or spilt, spilling
spillage
spillige — spillage
spin, spun, spinning
spinach
spinaker — spinnaker
spinal
spindle, -dled, -dling
spin-dry, -dried, -drying
spine
spine-chilling
spineless, -ness
spinige — spinach
spinnaker
spinner
spinoff
spinster
spinsterhood
spiny, spinier, spiniest
spiral, -ed, -ing
spire

spirel — spiral
spirit, -ed, -ing
spiritless, -ly
spiritual, -ly
spiritualism
spiritualist
spirituality
spiritule — spiritual
spirituleist — spiritualist
spise — spice
spisy — spicy
spit, spat, spitting
spite, spited, spiting
spiteful, -ly, -ness
spitfire
spittel — spittle
spittle
spittoon
splash, -ed, -ing
splashboard
splashdown
splatter, -ed, -ing
splay, -ed, -ing
spleen
splendid, -ly
splendor
splice, spliced, splicing
splicer
splint
splinter, -ed, -ing
splise — splice
split, split, splitting
split-level
split-second
splurge, splurged, splurging
splutter, -ed, -ing
spoil, spoiled or spoilt, spoiling
spoilage
spoilsport
spoke
spoken
spokesperson
sponge, sponged, sponging
sponger
spongy, -gier, -giest
sponser — sponsor
sponsor, -ed, -ing

sponsorship
spontaneity
spontaneous, -ly, -ness
   sponteneity   spontaneity
spoof, -ed, -ing
spook, -ed, -ing
spool
spoon, -ed, -ing
spoonbill
spoonerism
spoon-feed, -fed, -feeding
spoonful
spoor (trail)
   spoor   spore (germ)
sporadic, -ally
spore, spored, sporing (germ)
   spore   spoor (trail)
sport, -ed, -ing
sportive, -ly
sportscast
sportscaster
sportsman, -men
sportswoman, -women
sportswriter
sportswriting
spot, spotted, spotting
spotless, -ly
spotlight, -ed, -ing
   spotlite   spotlight
spouse
spout, -ed, -ing
   spowse   spouse
   spowt   spout
sprain, -ed, -ing
   sprane   sprain
sprang
sprat
sprawl, -ed, -ing
spray, -ed, -ing
spread, spread, spreading
spread-eagle, -gled, -gling
   spred   spread
spree
   sprie   spry
sprightly, -lier, -liest
spring, sprang, sprung, springing
springboard

springbok, -boks, -bok
spring-clean, -ed, -ing
spring-loaded
springtime
springy, -gier, -giest
   sprinkel   sprinkle
sprinkle, -kled, -kling
sprinkler
sprint, -ed, -ing
sprit (pole)
sprite (elf)
sprocket
   sproose   spruce
sprout, -ed, -ing
   sprowt   sprout
spruce, spruced, sprucing
spruce, sprucer, sprucest
sprung
spry, spryer, spryest
spud
spume, spumed, spuming
spun
   spunge   sponge
spunk
spunky, spunkier, spunkiest
spur, spurred, spurring
spurious, -ly, -ness
   spurius   spurious
   spurm   sperm
spurn, -ed, -ing
spurt, -ed, -ing
sputnik
sputter, -ed, -ing
sputum, sputa
spy, spies
spy, spied, spying
squabble, -bled, -bling
   squabel   squabble
squad
squadron
squalid, -ly, -ness
squall, -ed, -ing
squalor
squander, -ed, -ing
square, squared, squaring
square, -ly, -ness
square-rigged

square-shouldered
squash, -ed, -ing
squat, squatted, squatting
squatter
squaw
squawk, -ed, -ing
squeak, -ed, -ing
squeal, -ed, -ing
squeamish, -ly
squeeze, squeezed, squeezing
squelch, -ed, -ing
squert — squirt
squib
squid, squids, squid
squiggel — squiggle
squiggle, -gled, -gling
squiggly
squint, -ed, -ing
squire, squired, squiring
squirm, -ed, -ing
squirrel
squirt, -ed, -ing
squod — squad
squodron — squadron
squolid — squalid
squonder — squander
squosh — squash
squot — squat
stab, stabbed, stabbing
stabel — stable
stability, -ties
stabilization
stabilize, -lized, -lizing
stabilizer
stable, -bled, -bling
stabul — stable
staccato
stack, -ed, -ing
stackade — stockade
stadium, -dia, -diums
staf — staff
staff, -ed, -ing
stag
stage, staged, staging
stagecoach
stage-door
stage-hand

stager — stagger
stagestruck
stagflation
stagger, -ed, -ing
stagnant
stagnate, -nated, -nating
stagnation
staid, -ly (calm)
staid — stayed (stopped)
staidium — stadium
stain, -ed, -ing
stainless, -ly
stair (step)
stair — stare (look at)
staircase
stairway
stairwell
stake, staked, staking (post)
stake — steak (meat)
stakeout
stalactite
stalagmite
stale, staled, staling
stale, staler, stalest
stalemate, -mated, -mating
stalion — stallion
stalk, -ed, -ing (hunt)
stalk — stork (bird)
stall, -ed, -ing
stallion
stalwart
stalwert — stalwart
stamen
stamena — stamina
stamer — stammer
stamina
stammer, -ed, -ing
stamp, -ed, -ing
stampede, -peded, -peding
stance
stanchion
stanchon — stanchion
stand, stood, standing
standard
standardbred
standardize, -dized, -dizing

standby
~~standerd~~   standard
stand-in
standoffish, -ly
standout
standpoint
standstill
~~stane~~   stain
stank
~~stansa~~   stanza
~~stanse~~   stance
stanza
~~stapel~~   staple
staple, -pled, -pling
stapler
star, starred, starring
starboard
~~starbord~~   starboard
starch, -ed, -ing
star-crossed
stardom
stare, stared, staring (look at)
~~stare~~   stair (step)
~~stareo~~   stereo
starfish, -fishes, -fish
stargaze, -gazed, -gazing
stargazer
stark, -ly, -ness
starlet
starlight
starling
starlit
starry, -rier, -riest
starry-eyed
star-studded
start, -ed, -ing
~~startch~~   starch
starter
startle, -tled, -tling
starvation
starve, starved, starving
stash, -ed, -ing
state, stated, stating
statehood
statehouse
stateless
stateliness

stately, -lier, -liest
statement
stateroom
statesman, -men
stateswoman, -women
static, -ally
station, -ed, -ing
stationary (still)
stationer (sells paper)
stationery (paper)
statistical, -ly
statistician
statistics
~~statistisian~~   statistician
~~stattic~~   static
statuary (statues)
statue (image)
~~statuesk~~   statuesque
statuesque
stature (height)
status (position)
status quo
statute (law)
statutory (law)
staunch
stave, staved, staving
~~stawk~~   stalk
stay, stayed, staying
stead
steadfast, -ly, -ness
steadily
steady, steadied, steadying
steady, steadier, steadiest
steak (meat)
~~steak~~   stake (post)
steal, stole, stolen, stealing (rob)
~~steal~~   steel (metal)
stealth
stealthily
stealthy, -thier, -thiest
steam, -ed, -ing
steamboat
steam engine
steamer
steamroller
steamship
~~sted~~   stead

stedfast	steadfast	stethoscope	
stedy	steady	Stetson	
steed		stevedore	
steel, -ed, -ing (metal)		stew, -ed, -ing	
steel	steal (rob)	steward	
steelwork		stewardess	
steelworker		sti	sty
steely		stich	stitch
steelyard		stick, stuck, sticking	
steep, -ed, -ing		stickball	
steepel	steeple	sticker	
steeple		stick-in-the-mud	
steeplechase		stickler	
steer, -ed, -ing		stickup	
steerable		sticky, stickier, stickiest	
steerige	steerage	stif	stiff
steersman, -men		stifel	stifle
stelth	stealth	stifen	stiffen
stem, stemmed, stemming		stiff	
stench		stiffen, -ed, -ing	
stencil, -ed, -ing		stiffener	
stenografer	stenographer	stifle, -fled, -fling	
stenografy	stenography	stigma, -mas, -mata	
stenographer		stigmatize, -tized, -tizing	
stenography		stikler	stickler
stensil	stencil	stil	still
step, stepped, stepping, (pace)		stile (steps)	
stepchild		stile	style (type)
stepladder		stiletto, -tos	
stepparent		stilish	stylish
steppe (plain)		stilist	stylist
steppingstone		still, -ed, -ing	
stereo, stereos		stillbirth	
stereophonic, -ally		stillborn	
stereotype, -typed, -typing		still life	
sterile		stilt	
sterility		stilted	
sterilization		Stilton	
sterilize, -lized, -lizing		stilus	stylus
sterilizer		stimie	stymie
sterio	stereo	stimulant	
steriofonic	stereophonic	stimulate, -lated, -lating	
steriotype	stereotype	stimulater	stimulator
sterling		stimulation	
stern, -ly, -ness		stimulator	
sternum, -nums, -na		stimulus, -li	
		sting, stung, stinging	

stinger
stingray
stingy, -gier, -giest
stink, stank or stunk, stunk,
stinking
stinker
stinkhorn
stinkpot
stint, -ed, -ing
stipel   stipple
stipend
stipple, -pled, -pling
stipulate, -lated, -lating
stipulation
stir, stirred, stirring
stir-crazy
stirling   sterling
stirrup
stirup   stirrup
stitch, -ed, -ing
stoat
stock, -ed, -ing
stockade, -aded, -ading
stockbroker
stock car
stockholder
stocking
stockman, -men
stockpile, -piled, -piling
stockpot
stockroom
stocktaking
stocky, -kier, -kiest
stockyard
stodgily
stodgy, -gier, -giest (dull)
stoical, -ly
stoicism
stoisism   stoicism
stoke, stoked, stoking
stoker
stole
stolen
stolid, -ly
stoma, stomata, matas
stomach
stomachache

stomick   stomach
stone, stoned, stoning
stone-blind
stone-broke
stone-dead
stone-deaf
stonemason
stonewall
stoneware
stony, stonier, stoniest
stood
stooge, stooged, stooging
stool
stoop, stooped, stooping
stop, stopped, stopping
stopcock
stopgap
stop light
stopover
stoppage
stopper
stopwatch
storage
store, stored, storing
storefront
storekeeper
storeroom
storie   story
storige   storage
stork (bird)
stork   stalk (hunt)
storm, -ed, -ing
stormily
stormy, -mier, -miest
story, -ries
stout, -ly, -ness
stove
stow, -ed, -ing
stowage
stowaway
stowic   stoic
stowt   stout
straddle, -dled, -dling
straf   strafe
strafe, strafed, strafing
straggle, -gled, -gling
straggler

straight (line)
straight   strait (passage)
straightaway
straight edge
straighten, -ed, -ing
straightforward, -ly, -ness
strain, -ed, -ing
strainer
strait (passage)
strait   straight (line)
straitened
straitjacket
straitlaced
strand
strane   strain
strange, stranger, strangest
strangel   strangle
strangle, -gled, -gling
strangler
stranglehold
strangulate, -lated, -lating
strangulation
strap, strapped, strapping
strapless
strata
stratagem
stratagy   strategy
strate   straight (line)
strate   strait (passage)
stratefy   stratify
strategic, -ally
strategist
strategy, -gies
stratification
stratify, -fied, -fying
stratigem   stratagem
stratosfear   stratosphere
stratosphere
stratum, strata
straw
strawberie   strawberry
strawberry, -ries
stray, -ed, -ing
streak, -ed, -ing
streaky, streakier, streakiest
stream, -ed, -ing
streamer

streamline, -lined, -lining
streek   streak
streem   stream
street
streetcar
strength
strengthen, -ed, -ing
strenuos   strenuous
strenuous, -ly, -ness
streptomycin
stress, -ed, -ing
stretch, -ed, -ing
stretchable
stretcher
stretchy, -ier, -iest
strew, strewed, strewn, strewing
striate
striation
strick   strict
stricken
stricknine   strychnine
strict, -ly, -ness
stricture
stride, strode, striding
stridence
strident, -ly
strife
strike, struck, stricken, striking
strikebound
strikebreaker
strikeout
striker
string, strung, stringing
stringency
stringensy   stringency
stringent, -ly
stringer
stringy, -gier, -giest
strip, stripped, stripping
stripe, striped, striping
stripling
stripper
striptease
strive, strove, striven or strived,
striving
strobe
stroboscope

strode
stroke, stroked, stroking
stroll, -ed, -ing
stroller
strong, -ly
strongbox
stronghold
strongman, -men
strongminded
strongpoint
strongroom
  stroo — strew
strop, stropped, stropping
strove
struck
  struckture — structure
structure, -tured, -turing
strudel
struggle, -gled, -gling
struggler
  strugle — struggle
strum, strummed, strumming
strummer
strung
strut, strutted, strutting
strychnine
  stu — stew
  stuard — steward
stub, stubbed, stubbing
stubble
stubbly
stubborn, -ly, -ness
  stuben — stubborn
stucco, -coes, -cos
stucco, -ed, -ing
stuck-up
stud, studded, studding
student
  studie — study
studied
studio, -dios
studious, -ly, -ness
  studius — studious
study, studies
study, studied, studying
  stuf — stuff
stuff, -ed, -ing

stuffy, -fier, -fiest
stuffy, -ily, -iness
  stufy — stuffy
  stuko — stucco
  stultifie — stultify
stultify, -fied, -fying
  stumbel — stumble
stumble, -bled, -bling
stumblebum
stump, -ed, -ing
stumpy, -pier, -piest
stun, stunned, stunning
stunt, -ed, -ing
stuntman, -men
  stupefie — stupefy
stupefy, -fied, -fying
stupendous, -ly
  stupendus — stupendous
stupid, -ly
stupidity, -ties
  stupify — stupefy
stupor
  sturdie — sturdy
sturdy, -dier, -diest
sturdy, -dily, -diness
  sturgen — sturgeon
sturgeon
  sturling — sterling
  sturn — stern
  stuter — stutter
stutter, -ed, -ing
stutterer
  stuward — steward
sty, sties
style (type)
  style — stile (steps)
stylish, -ly, -ness
stylist
stylistic, -ally
stymie, -mied, -mieing
styptic
  suage — sewage
suave, -ly, -ness
suavity, -ties
sub, subbed, subbing
subarctic
subatomic

subbasement
subcategory
subclass
subcomitee   subcommittee
subcommittee
subcompact, -ness
subconscious, -ly
subconshus   subconscious
subcontinent, -al
subcontract, -ed, -ing
subcontractor
subculture
subcutaneous, -ly
subdivide, -vided, -viding
subdivision
subdivison   subdivision
subdue, -dued, -duing
subeditor
suberb   suburb
suberban   suburban
subgigate   subjugate
subgroup
subheading
subjecktion   subjection
subject, -ed, -ing
subjection
subjective, -ly, -ness
subjectivity
sub judice
subjugate, -gated, -gating
subjugation
subjunctive
sublease, -leased, -leasing
sublet, -let, -letting
sublimate, -mated, -mating
sublimation
sublime, -limed, -liming
sublime, -ly, -ness
subliminal, -ly
sublimity, -ties
sublimminal   subliminal
submachine
submarine
submerge, -merged, -merging
submision   submission
submergence
submergibility

submergible
submerse, -mersed, -mersing
submersibility, -ness
submersible
submersion
submicroscopic
submission
submissive, -ly, -ness
submit, -mitted, -mitting
submolecular
submurge   submerge
subnormal, -ly
subordinate, -nated, -nating
subordination
suborn, -ed, -ing
subpena   subpoena
subplot
subpoena, -naed, -naing
subscribe, -ribed, -ribing
subscriber
subscription
subsection
subsekwent   subsequent
subsequent, -ly
subservience
subservient, -ly
subset
subside, -sided, -siding
subsidence
subsidie   subsidy
subsidize, -dized, -dizing
subsidy, -dies
subsist, -ed, -ing
subsistence
subsistense   subsistence
subsoil
subspecies
substance
substandard
substansial   substantial
substantial, -ly
substantiate, -ated, -ating
substation
substitute, -tuted, -tuting
substructure, -tured, -turing
subsume, -sumed, -suming
subsystem

subtefuge	subterfuge	sucses	success
subterfuge		sucseser	successor
subterranean		sucsesful	successful
subterraneous		sucsesion	succession
subtitel	subtitle	sucsint	succinct
subtitle, -tled, -tling		suction	
subtle, -tly		sudden, -ly, -ness	
subtlety, -ties		suds	
subtotal, -ed, -ing		sue, sued, suing	
subtracktion	subtraction	suede	
subtract, -ed, -ing		suer	sewer
subtraction		suet (meat)	
subtropical		sufer	suffer
suburb		suffer, -ed, -ing	
suburban		sufferance	
suburbanite		sufferanse	sufferance
suburbia		suffice, -ficed, -ficing	
subversion		sufficiency	
subversive, -ly		sufficient, -ly	
subvert, -ed, -ing		suffiks	suffix
subway		suffix	
subzero		suffocate, -cated, -cating	
succeed, -ed, -ing (win)		suffocation	
succeed	secede (withdraw)	suffrage	
		suffragette	
success		suffuse, -fused, -fusing	
successer	successor	suffusion	
successful, -ly		sufocate	suffocate
succession		sufocation	suffocation
successive, -ly		sufrajet	suffragette
successor		sufrance	sufferance
succinct, -ly, -ness		sufrige	suffrage
succor, -ed, -ing (aid)		sufuse	suffuse
succulence		sugar	
succulent, -ly		sugary	
succumb, -ed, -ing		sugest	suggest
such		sugestion	suggestion
such-and-such		suggest, -ed, -ing	
suchure	suture	suggestive, -ly, -ness	
suck, -ed, -ing		suicidal	
sucker (dupe)		suiside	suicide
suckle, -led, -ling		suit, -ed, -ing (clothes)	
sucktion	suction	suit	suet (meat)
suckulent	succulent	suitability	
suckum	succumb	suitable, -bly	
sucrose		suitcase	
sucsede	succeed	suite (rooms)	

suiter	suitor	sundae (ice cream)	
suitor		Sunday (day)	
sukiyaki		sun deck	
sulfur (element)		sunder, -ed, -ing	
sulfur	sol-fa (sing)	sundial	
sulfuric		sundown	
sulk, -ed, -ing		sundress	
sulky, sulkier, sulkiest		sundry, sundries	
sullage		sunfish, -fishes, -fish	
sullen, -ly, -ness		sunflower	
sully, -lied, -lying		sung	
sultan		sunglasses	
sultana		sunk	
sultrie	sultry	sunken	
sultriness		sun lamp	
sultry, -trier, -triest		sunless	
sum, summed, summing (total)		sunlight	
sum	some (few)	sunlit	
sumbody	somebody	sunny, -nier, -niest	
sumhow	somehow	sunrise	
summarine	submarine	sunroof	
summarize, -rized, -rizing		sunset	
summary, -ries (short)		sunshine	
summary	summery (warm)	sunspot	
		sunstroke	
summation		suntan	
summer		suntanned	
summerhouse		sup, supped, supping	
summerize	summarize	supena	subpoena
summertime		super	
summery (warm)		superannuate, -ated, -ating	
summery	summary (short)	superb, -ly	
		supercharge, -charged, -charging	
summit		supercilious, -ly, -ness	
summon, -ed, -ing (call)		supercool, -ed, -ing	
summons, -monses (court)		superficial, -ly	
sumo		superfisial	superficial
sump		superfluity, -ties	
sumptuous, -ly, -ness		superfluous, -ly, -ness	
sun, sunned, sunning (star)		superfosfate	superphosphate
sun	son (boy)	superheat, -ed, -ing	
sun inlaw	son-in-law	superhighway	
sunbathe, -bathed, -bathing		superhuman, -ly	
sunbather		superimpose, -posed, -posing	
sunbeam		superimposition	
sunburn, -ed, -ing		superintendent	
sunburst		superior, -ly	

superiority
superlative, -ly, -ness
superliner
superman, -men
supermarket
supernatural, -ly, -ness
supernova
supernumerary, -aries
superphosphate
superpose, -ed, -ing
superposition
superpower
supersaturate, -rated, -rating
superscribe, -scribed, -scribing
superscript
superscription
supersede, -seded, -seding
supersonic, -ally
superstar
superstition
superstitious
superstructure
supertanker
supervise, -vised, -vising
  superviser   supervisor
supervision
supervisor
supervisory
supine, -ly
  suple   supple
  suplement   supplement
  suport   support
  suposition   supposition
supper
suppertime
supplant, -ed, -ing
supple, -pler, -plest
supplement
supplementation
supplementary
suppliant
supplicant
supplicate, -ted, -ting
supplication
supplier
supply, -plied, -plying
support, -ed, -ing

supporter
supposable, -bly
suppose, -posed, -posing
supposed, -ly
  supposible   supposable
supposition
suppository, -ries
suppress, -ed, -ing
suppressible
suppression
suppressive
suppressor
suppurate, -rated, -rating
suppuration
supremacy
  supremasy   supremacy
supreme, -ly, -ness
  supres   suppress
  supreshun   suppression
  suprintend   superintend
  supul   supple
  sur   sir
surcharge, -charged, -charging
surcingle

> For other surc- words,
> look under circ-.

sure, -ly, -ness (certain)
  sure   shore (sea)
surefire
surefooted
  sureptitious   surreptitious
surety, -ties
surf, -ed, -ing (sea)
  surf   serf (slave)
surface, -faced, -facing
  surfase   surface
surfboard
  surfeet   surfeit
surfeit, -ed, -ing
surfer
surge, surged, surging
  surgen   surgeon
surgeon
surgery, -geries
surgical, -ly
  surloin   sirloin

surly, -lier, -liest	
surly	surely
surmise, -mised, -mising	
surmount, -ed, -ing	
surmountable	
surname	
surogate	surrogate
surpass, -ed, -ing	
surplice (garment)	
surplis	surplice
surplus (extra)	
surprise, -prised, -prising	
surrealism	
surrealist	
surrender, -ed, -ing	
surreptisious	surreptitious
surreptitious, -ly	
surrogate	
surround, -ed, -ing	
surtaks	surtax
surtax	
surveillance	
survey, -veys	
surveyer	surveyor
surveyor	
survival	
survive, -vived, -viving	
surviver	survivor
survivor	
susceptibility	
susceptible, -bly	
sushi	
suspect, -ed, -ing	
suspend, -ed, -ing	
suspender	
suspense, -ful	
suspension	
suspicion	
suspicious, -ly, -ness	
suspision	suspicion
sustain, -ed, -ing	
sustane	sustain
sustenance	
sustenanse	sustenance
sut	soot
sutable	suitable
sutel	subtle
suter	suitor
suthen	southern
sutlety	subtlety
suture, -tured, -turing	
swab, swabbed, swabbing	
swaddle, -dled, -dling	
swade	suede
swag	
swagger, swaggered, swaggering	
swain	
swallow, -ed, -ing	
swallow-tailed	
swam	
swamp, -ed, -ing	
swampy, -pier, -piest	
swan	
swank	
swanky, -kier, -kiest	
swap, swapped, swapping	
sware	swear
swarm, -ed, -ing	
swarthy, -thier, -thiest	
swashbuckler	
swastika	
swat, swatted, swatting	
swathe, swathed, swathing	
sway, -ed, -ing	
swear, swore, sworn, swearing	
sweat, -ed, -ing	
sweatband	
sweater	
sweat shirt	
sweatshop	
sweat suit	
sweaty, -tier, -tiest	
Swede	
sweep, swept, sweeping	
sweeper	
sweepstakes	
sweet, -ly, -ness (taste)	
sweet	suite (rooms)
sweet-and-sour	
sweetbread	
sweeten, -ed, -ing	
sweetener	
sweethart	sweetheart
sweetheart	

sweet-talk, -ed, -ing		syciatry	psychiatry
swell, swelled, swollen, swelling		sycick	psychic
swelter, -ed, -ing		syclone	cyclone
swerve, swerved, swerving		sycoanalisis	psychoanalysis
swet	sweat	sycoanalize	psychoanalyse
sweter	sweater	sycofant	sycophant
swich	switch	sycological	psychological
swift, -ly, -ness		sycologist	psychologist
swill, -ed, -ing		sycology	psychology
swim, swam, swum, swimming		sycophant	
swimmer		sycophantic, -ally	
swimsuit		sycosis	psychosis
swimwear		sycotherapist	psychotherapist
swindel	swindle	sycotherapy	psychotherapy
swindle, -dled, -dling		sycotic	psychotic
swine		syfilis	syphilis
swing, swung, swinging		sygnet	cygnet
swipe, swiped, swiping		sylable	syllable
swirl, -ed, -ing		sylf	sylph
swish, -ed, -ing		sylinder	cylinder
switch, -ed, -ing		syllabic, -ally	
switchback		syllable	
switchblade		syllabus, -buses, -bi	
switchboard		syllogism	
swivel, -ed, -ing		syllogistic, -ally	
swob	swab	syllogize, -gized, -gizing	
swollen		sylph	
swollow	swallow	sylvan	
swomp	swamp	sylvin	sylvan
swoon, -ed, -ing		symbiosis	
swoop, -ed, -ing		symbiotic	
sword		symbol (sign)	
swordy	swarthy	symbol	cymbal (music)
swordfish, -fish, -fishes		symbolic, -ally	
swordsman, -men		symbolism	
sworm	swarm	symbolist	
sworn		symbolize, -lized, -lizing	
swum		symfony	symphony
swurl	swirl	symmetrical, -ly	
swurve	swerve	symmetry, -tries (even)	
syanide	cyanide	symmetry	cemetery
sybarite			(graveyard)
sybaritic		sympathetic, -ally	
sycamore		sympathey	sympathy
sycedelic	psychedelic	sympathize, -ized, -izing	
syche	psyche	sympathizer	
syciatrist	psychiatrist	symphonic	

symphony, -nies
symposium, -siums, -sia
symptom
symptomatic
  synagog   synagogue
synagogue
  synanym   synonym
synchronization
synchronize, -nized, -nizing
synchronous, -ly
  synchronus   synchronous
syncopate, -pated, -pating
syncopation
syndicate, -cated, -cating
syndication
syndrome
  synic   cynic
  synical   cynical
synod
synodal, -ic, -ical
  synonimus   synonymous
synonym
synonymous, -ly
synopsis, -ses
synoptic, -ally
syntactical, -ly
  syntaks   syntax
syntax
synthesis, -ses
synthesize, -ized, -izing
synthesizer
synthetic, -ally
  sypher   cipher
syphilis
syphilitic
syringe, -ringed, -ringing
syrup
syrupy
system
systematic
systematical, -ly
systematization
systematize, -tized, -tizing
systemic, -ally
systole
  sythe   scythe
Szechwan

Tt

tab, tabbed, tabbing
  tabacco — tobacco
tabard
Tabasco
  tabasko — Tabasco
tabby, -bies
  tabel — table
  taberculosis — tuberculosis
table, -bled, -bling
table manners
table tennis
tableau, -leaux, -leaus
tablecloth
tablespoon
tablespoonful, -fuls
tablet
tableware
  tablit — tablet
  tablo — tableau
tabloid
taboo, tabu
taboo, -booed, -booing
tabular
tabulate, -lated, -lating
tabulation
  taby — tabby
tachometer
tacit, -ly, -ness
taciturn, -ly
tack, -ed, -ing
  tackel — tackle
  tackie — tacky
tackle, -led, -ling
tackler
  tackometer — tachometer
tacky, -kier, -kiest
taco
tact

tactful, -ly
tactic
tactical, -ly
tactician
tactics
tactile
tactless, -ly, -ness
tadpole
taffeta
  tafita — taffeta
tag, tagged, tagging
tagliatelle
tail (end)
  tail — tale (story)
tailback
tailcoat
tailgate
tailless
taillight
tailor, -ed, -ing
tailor-made
tailpiece
tailpipe
tailspin
taint, -ed, -ing
take, took, taken, taking
takeoff
take-out
takeover
  taks — tax
  taksation — taxation
  taksi — taxi
talc (powder)
  talc — talk (speak)
talcum powder
tale (story)
  tale — tail (end)
talent
talented
  talie — tally
talisman, -men
talk, -ed, -ing (speak)
  talk — talc (powder)
talkative, -ly, -ness
tall
tallboy
tallow

tally, -lies
tally, -lied, -lying
Talmud
talon
  talor   tailor
  talow   tallow
tamale
tamarind
tambourine
tame, tamed, taming
tame, tamer, tamest
tameable
tam-o'-shanter
tamper, -ed, -ing
tampon
tan, tanned, tanning
tanbark
tandem
tang
  tangable   tangible
  tangensial   tangential
tangent
tangential, -ly
tangerine
tangible, -bly
  tangel   tangle
tangle, -gled, -gling
tango, -gos
tango, -goed, -going
  tanjent   tangent
tank
tankard
tanker
tannin
tantalize, -lized, -lizing
tantamount
tantrum
tap, tapped, tapping
tap dance
tape, taped, taping
taper, -ed, -ing
tape recorder
tapestry, -tries
tapeworm
tapioca
  tapistry   tapestry
tappet

taproom
taproot
tar, tarred, tarring
tarantella (dance)
tarantula (spider)
  tardie   tardy
tardy, -dier, -diest
tardy, -ily, -iness
tare (weight)
  tare   tear (crying, rip)
  tare   tier (row)
  tare   tire (weary, wheel)
target, -ed, -ing
  targit   target
  tarie   tarry
tariff
tarmac
tarnation
tarnish, -ed, -ing
tarot
  tarow   tarot
tarpaper
tarpaulin
  tarpollin   tarpaulin
tarragon
  tarrif   tariff
tarry, -ries
tarry, -ried, -rying
tart, -ly, -ness
tartan
tartar
tartar sauce
  tarter   tartar
  tasel   tassel
  tasit   tacit
  tasiturn   taciturn
task
taskmaster
tasseled
taste, tasted, tasting
taste bud
tasteful, -ly, -ness
tasty, -tier, -tiest
tasty, -ily, -iness
  tatoo   tattoo

tattle, -led, -ling
tattletale
tattoo, -toos
tattoo, -tooed, -tooing
  taudry   tawdry
taught (did teach)
  taught   taut (not slack)
  taught   tort (law)
taunt, -ed, -ing
Taurus
taut, -ly (not slack)
  taut   tort (law)
  taut   taught (teach)
tautological, -ly
tautology, -gies
  taven   tavern
tavern
tawdry, -drier, -driest
tawdry, -ily, -iness
tawny, -nier, -niest
tax, -ed, -ing
taxable
  taxasion   taxation
taxation
tax-deductible
tax deducation
tax-exempt
taxi, taxis, taxies
taxi, taxied, taxiing or taxying
  taxible   taxable
taxicab
taxidermy
  taxie   taxi
taxonomy, -mies
taxpayer
tea (drink)
  tea   tee (golf)
teacake
teacart
teach, taught, teaching
teachable, -ably
teacher
  teachible   teachable
teach-in
teacup
teak
teakettle

teal
team, -ed, -ing (group)
  team   teem (rain)
teammate
teamster
teamwork
teapot
tear (crying)
tear, tore, torn, tearing (rip)
  tear   tare (weight)
  tear   tier (row)
tearful, -ly
tearjerker
tearoom
tease, teased, teasing
teaspoon
teat
  teath   teeth (noun)
  teathe   teethe (verb)
teatime
  tech   teach
  techer   teacher
technical, -ly, -ness
  tear   tire (weary, wheel)
technicality, -ties
technician
Technicolor
technique
technocracy
technocrat
technological, -ly
technologist
technology
  tecneek   technique
  tecnical   technical
  tecnicality   technicality
  tecnisian   technician
  tecnocrasy   technocracy
  tecnology   technology
tedious, -ly, -ness
tee, teed, teeing (golf)
  tee   tea (drink)
  teech   teach
  teek   teak
  teel   teal
teem, -ed, -ing (rain)

teem	team (group)	teliphoto	telephoto
teenager		teliscope	telescope
teens		telivise	televise
teensy-weensy		telivision	television
teeny, -nier, -niest		tell, told, telling	
teeny-bopper		teller	
teeny-weeny		telltale	
teese	tease	temerity	
tee shirt		temper, -ed, -ing	
teet	teat	tempera	
teeter, -ed, -ing		temperament	
teeth (plural of tooth)		temperamental, -ly	
teethe, teethed, teething (verb)		temperance	
teetotal		temperanse	temperance
teetotaler		temperary	temporary
Teflon		temperate, -ly	
tekneek	technique	Temperate Zone	
teknical	technical	temperature	
teknicality	technicality	tempest	
teknicolor	Technicolor	tempestuos	tempestuous
teknisian	technician	tempestuous, -ly, -ness	
teknocrasy	technocracy	template	
teknology	technology	temple	
tekst	text	templet	template
tekstile	textile	tempo, -pos	
teksture	texture	temporal, -ly	
telecast, -ed, -ing		temporarily	
telecommunications		temporary	
telefone	telephone	temporize, -rized, -rizing	
telefoto	telephoto	temprament	temperament
telegraf	telegraph	temprature	temperature
telegram		tempremental	temperamental
telegraph		tempt, -ed, -ing	
telegraphic		temptation	
telegraphist		tempter	
teleks	Telex	temptress	
telepathic		temtation	temptation
telepathist		tenable, -bly, -ness, -bility	
telepathy		tenacious, -ly, -ness	
telephone, -phoned, -phoning		tenament	tenement
telephoto lens		tenancy	
telescope, -coped, -coping		tenansy	tenancy
televise, -vised, -vising		tenant (occupant)	
television		tend, -ed, -ing	
Telex		tendency, -cies	
telifone	telephone	tendentious, -ly, -ness	
teligram	telegram	tender, -ed, -ing	

tenderfoot, -foots, -feet
tenderhearted, -ness
tenderize, -rized, -rizing
tenderloin
tenderly
tendon
tendril
tenement
tenet
tenfold
  tenis — tennis
tennis
tenon
tenor
tenpenny
tenpin
tense, tensed, tensing
tense, tenser, tensest
tense, -ly, -ness
tension
tent
tentacle
tentative, -ly, -ness
tenterhook
tenth
  tention — tension
  tenuos — tenuous
tenuous, -ly, -ness
tenure
tenured
tepee
tepid, -ly, -ness
  teracota — terra cotta
  terain — terrain
  terarium — terrarium
  terazo — terrazzo
  terban — turban
  terbid — turbid
  terbine — turbine
  terbo — turbo
  terbulent — turbulent
  terf — turf
  tergid — turgid
  terible — terrible
  terier — terrier
  terific — terrific
  terifie — terrify

  teritry — territory
  terjid — turgid
  terkey — turkey
  terkwoise — turquoise
term
termagant
  termanation — termination
terminable
terminal, -ally
terminate, -nated, -nating
termination
  terminible — terminable
terminology, -gies
terminus, -ni, -nuses
termite
  termoil — turmoil
tern (bird)
  tern — turn (move)
ternary
  ternip — turnip
  teror — terror
  terorist — terrorist
  terpentine — turpentine
  terpitude — turpitude
terrace, -raced, -racing
terra cotta
terrain
terrarium, -rariums, -raria
terrazzo
terrestrial, -ly
terrible, -bly
  terribul — terrible
terrier
terrific, -ally
terrify, -fied, -fying
territorial, -ly
territory, -ries
terror
terrorism
terrorist
terrorize, -rized, -rizing
terse, terser, tersest
tersely
tertiary, -ries
  tertle — turtle
  teselate — tessellate
  teselation — tessellation

tespoon	teaspoon		theirs (possessive)	
tess	test		theirs	there's (there is)
tessellate, -ated, -ating			theism	
tessellation			theist	
test, -ed, -ing			theistic, -ally	
testacle	testicle		theif	thief
testament			theives	thieves
testicle			theiving	thieving
testifie	testify		thematic, -ally	
testify, -fied, -fying			theme	
testimonial			themselves	
testimony, -nies			then	
testis, testes			thence	
test tube			thense	thence
test-tube baby			theocracy, -cies	
testy, -tier, -tiest			theocrasy	theocracy
tetanus			theocrat	
tête-à-tête			theodolite	
tether, -ed, -ing			theological, -ly	
tetrahedron, -drons, -dra			theologian	
Teusday	Tuesday		theology, -gies	
text			theolojian	theologian
textbook			theorem	
textile			theoretic	
textual, -ly			theoretical, -ly	
texture, -tured, -turing			theorist	
thach	thatch		theorize, -rized, -rizing	
thalidomide			theorm	theorem
than			theory, -ries	
thank, -ed, -ing			theosofie	theosophy
thankful, -ly, -ness			theosophical, -ly	
thankless, -ly, -ness			theosophist	
thanksgiving			theosophy	
Thanksgiving Day			therapeutic, -ally	
that, those			therapey	therapy
that's (that is)			therapist	
thats	that's		therapy, -pies	
thatch, -ed, -ing			therd	third
thaw, -ed, -ing			there (at that place)	
thay	they		there	their (possessive)
thealogy	theology			
theater			there	they're (they are)
theatrical, -ly				
theft			thereabouts	
their (possessive)			thereafter	
their	there (at that place)		thereby	

therefor (for that)
therefore (consequently)
  therem — theorem
therein
thereof
thereon
there's (there is)
  theres — theirs (possessive)
  theres — there's (there is)
  theretic — theoretic
  theretical — theoretical
  therey — theory
thereupon
therewith
  therist — theorist
  therize — theorize
thermal, -ly
thermodynamic, -ally
thermodynamics
thermometer
thermometrical, -ly
thermonuclear
thermoplastic
thermos
thermostat
thermostatic, -ally
  Thersday — Thursday
  therst — thirst
  thersty — thirsty
  therteen — thirteen
  therty — thirty
thesaurus, -sauruses, -sauri
these
thesis, -ses
  thesorus — thesaurus
Thespian
they'd (they had)
  theyd — they'd
they'll (they will)
  theyll — they'll
they're (they are)
  theyre — they're
  they're — their (possessive)
  they're — there (that place)

they've (they have)
  theyve — they've
  thi — thigh
thick, -ly
thicken, -ed, -ing
thickener
thicket
thick-headed
thickness
thickset
thickskinned
thief, thieves
thieve, thieved, thieving
thievish
thigh
thimble
  thime — thyme
thin, thinned, thinning
thin, thinner, thinnest
thin, -ly, -ness
thine
  thiner — thinner
thing
thingamajig
think, thought, thinking
think tank
third, -ly
third degree
  throid — thyroid
thirst, -ed, -ing
thirsty, -tier, -tiest
thirsty, -tily, -tiness
thirteen
thirteenth
  thirteith — thirtieth
  thirtie — thirty
thirtieth
thirty, -ties
this, these
  thisis — thesis
  thisle — thistle
  thisorus — thesaurus
thistle
thistledown
  thitha — thither
thither
  tho — though

thong

thor	thaw

thorax, thoraces, thoraxes
thorn
thorny, -nier, -niest
thorough, -ly, -ness (absolute)

thorough	through (pass)

thoroughbred
thoroughfare
those
thou (you)
though (but)
thought (did think)
thoughtful, -ly, -ness
thoughtless, -ly, -ness
thousand
thousandth

thout	thought
thowsand	thousand
thowt	thought

thrall
thrash, -ed, -ing
thread, -ed, -ing
threadbare
threat
threaten, -ed, -ing

thred	thread

three
three-dimensional
three-fold
three-lane
three-legged
three-ply
three-quarter
threescore
threesome
three-wheeler
thresh, -ed, -ing
threshold

thret	threat

threw (did throw)

threw	through (between)
threwout	throughout

thrice

thrift
thrifty, -tier, -tiest
thrifty, -ily, -iness
thrill, -ed, -ing
thriller
thrips, thrips

thrise	thrice

thrive, throve or thrived, thrived, thriving
thro' (through)
throat
throb, throbbed, throbbing
throe (spasm)

throe	throw (toss)

thrombosis, -oses
throne (chair)

throne	thrown (tossed)

throng, -ed, -ing

throo	threw (tossed)
throo	through (between)
throte	throat

throttle, -tled, -tling
through (pass)

through	thorough (absolute)
through	threw (tossed)

throughout
throve
throw, threw, thrown, throwing (toss)

throw	throe (spasm)

throwaway
throwback
thrown (tossed)

thrown	throne (chair)

thrum, thrummed, thrumming
thrush
thrust, thrust, thrusting
thruway
thud, thudded, thudding
thug
thuggery
thuggish

thum	thumb

thumb, -ed, -ing
thumbnail
thumbscrew

thumbtack
thump, -ed, -ing
thunder, -ed, -ing
thunderation
thunderbird
thunderbolt
thunderclap
thundercloud
thunderous, -ly
thundershower
thunderstorm
thunderstruck

thundrous	thunderous
thurer	thorough
thurerbred	thoroughbred
thurerfare	thoroughfare

For thurm- words, look
under **therm-**.

Thursday

thurst	thirst
thurteen	thirteen
thurty	thirty

thus

thwort	thwart

thwart, -ed, -ing
thyme (herb)
thyroid
tiara
tibia, tibiae, tibias
tic (twitch)
tick, -ed, -ing (sound)

tickel	tickle

ticker
ticket
tickle, -led, -ling
ticklish
ticktock

ticoon	tycoon

tidal
tidbit
tiddlywinks
tide, tided, tiding (ocean)

tide	tied (bound)
tidel	tidal
tidie	tidy

tidings

tidy, tidied, tidying
tidy, tidier, tidiest
tidy, -dily, -diness
tie, tied, tying
tie-dye, -dyed, -dying
tier (row)

tier	tare (weight)
tier	tear (crying, rip)
tier	tire
tif	tiff

tiff

tifoid	typhoid
tifoon	typhoon
tifus	typhus

tiger

tigeress	tigress
tigger	tiger

tight, -ly, -ness
tighten, -ed, -ing
tightfisted
tight-knit
tight-lipped
tightrope
tights
tightwad
tigress
tile, tiled, tiling
till, -ed, -ing
tiller
tilt, -ed, -ing
timber (wood)

timbral	timbrel

timbre (sound)
timbrel
time, timed, timing (clock)

time	thyme (plant)

timecard
timeclock
time-consuming
timekeeper
timelag
time-lapse
timeless, -ly, -ness
timely, -lier, -liest
timeout
timepiece

timer
timesaving
time share
timetable
timeworn
timid, -ly
timidity
timorous, -ly
   timorus — timorous
timpani
tin, tinned, tinning
   tinckture — tincture
tincture, -tured, -turing
tinder
tinderbox
tine
tinfoil
tinge, tinged, tingeing
tingle, tingled, tingling
   tinie — tiny
tinker, -ed, -ing
tinkle, -led, -ling
   tinkture — tincture
tinny, -nier, -niest
tinny, -nily, -niness
tinplated
tinsel
tinseled
tinsmith
tint, -ed, -ing
tiny, tinier, tiniest
tininess
tip, tipped, tipping
   tipe — type
   tipewriter — typewriter
   tipical — typical
   tipify — typify
   tipist — typist
   tipografy — typography
tipple, -led, -ling
tipsy, -sier, -siest
tipsy, -sily, -siness
tiptoe, -toed, -toeing
tiptop
tirade
   tiranical — tyrannical
   tiranize — tyrannize

   tiranous — tyrannous
   tirant — tyrant
   tirany — tyranny
tire, tired, tiring (weary)
   tire — tier (row)
tiresome, -ly, -ness
   tiresum — tiresome
'tis (it is)
   tis — 'tis (it is)
   tishoo — tissue
tissue
tit
   titaler — titular
titan
titanic
   titavation — titivation
   tite — tight
   titen — tighten
   tites — tights
tithe, tithed, tithing
titian
titillate, -lated, -lating
titillation
titivate, -vated, -vating
titivation
title, -tled, -tling (name)
titrate, -trated, -trating
titter, -ed, -ing
   tittillate — titillate
tittle (dot)
tittle-tattle, -tled, -tling
titular
to (toward)
   to — toe (foot)
   to — too (also)
   to — tow (pull)
   to — two (number)
toad
toadstool
toady, toadies
toady, toadied, toadying
toast, -ed, -ing
toaster
toastmaster
toastmistress
tobacco
tobacconist

tobaco	tobacco	tolerate, -rated, -rating	
tobogan	toboggan	toll, -ed, -ing	
toboggan		tolrable	tolerable
tobogganist		tomahawk	
tocsic	toxic	tomahork	tomahawk
tocsin (alarm)		tomaine	ptomaine
tocsin	toxin (poison)	tomarto	tomato
today		tomato, -toes	
toddle, -dled, -dling		tomb	
toddler		tomboy	
toddy, -dies		tomcat	
tode	toad	tombstone	
todler	toddler	tome	
todstool	toadstool	tomfoolery	
tody	toddy	tomorow	tomorrow
toe, toed, toeing (foot)		tomorrow	
toe	to (toward)	ton (imperial weight)	
toe	too (also)	tonal, -ly	
toe	tow (pull)	tone	
toe	two (number)	tone-deaf	
tofee	toffee	toneless, -ly	
toffee		tongs	
tofu		tongue, tongued, tonguing	
tog, togged, togging		tongue-tied	
together		tongue twister	
togetherness		tonic	
toggel	toggle	tonight	
toggle, -gled, -gling		tonite	tonight
toi	toy	tonnage	
toil, -ed, -ing		tonnige	tonnage
toilet		tonsher	tonsure
toiletrain	toilet train	tonsil	
toiletry, -tries		tonsillectomy, -mies	
toilet train		tonsillitis	
toillet	toilet	tonsure	
token		tonsured	
tokenism		too (also)	
toksic	toxic	too	to (toward)
toksin	tocsin (alarm)	too	two (number)
toksin	toxin (poison)	too	tow (pull
tol	toll	too	toe (foot)
told		took	
tole	toll	tool, -ed, -ing	
tolerable, -bly		toom	tomb
tolerance		toomstone	tombstone
toleranse	tolerance	toon	tune
tolerant, -ly		toor	tour

toot, -ed, -ing		torism	tourism
tooth, teeth		torment, -ed, -ing	
toothache		tormenter	tormentor
toothake	toothache	tormentor	
toothbrush, -brushes		torn	
toothless		tornado, -does, -dos	
toothpaste		tornament	tournament
toothpick		torney	tawny
toothsome		tornt	taunt
toothy, -thier, -thiest		torpedo, -does	
top, topped, topping		torpedo, -doed, -doing	
topas	topaz	torper	torpor
topaz		torpid, -ly	
topcoat		torpidity	
topflight		torpor	
top-heavy		torque	
topic		torrent	
topical, -ly		torrential, -ly	
topknot		torrid, -ly, -ness	
topless, -ly		torsion, -ally	
top-level		torso, -sos	
topmast		torson	torsion
topmost		tort (law)	
topnotch		tort	taught (did teach)
topografer	topographer		
topografy	topography	tort	taut (not slack)
topper		tortilla	
topple, -pled, -pling		tortoise	
top-ranking		tortoise-shell	
topsail		tortology	tautology
topside		tortuos	tortuous
topsoil		tortuous, -ly, -ness	
topsy-turvy		torture, -tured, -turing	
tor (hill)		torturer	
tor	tore (ripped)	tortus	tortoise
tor	tour (trip)	toss, tossed, tossing	
torch		tossup	
torchbearer		tost	toast
torcher	torture	tot, totted, totting	
torchlight		total, -ed, -ing	
torchlite	torchlight	totalitarian	
tore (ripped)		totalitarianism	
tore	tour (trip)	totality, -ties	
tore	tor (hill)	totalizator	
toreador		totally	
torent	torrent	tote, toted, toting	
torid	torrid	totel	total

totem		toxicity	
toter	totter	toxin (poison)	
totter, -ed, -ing		toxin	tocsin (alarm)
touch, -ed, -ing (feel)		toy, -ed, -ing	
touch-and-go		toyl	toil
touchback		toylet	toilet
touchdown		trace, traced, tracing	
touché (good point)		tracer	
touchstone		tracery, -ries	
touch-type, -typed, -typing		trachea, tracheae	
touchy, -chier, -chiest		trachoma	
tough, -ly, -ness		track, -ed, -ing (trail)	
toughen, -ed, -ing		track meet	
tough-minded		track record	
toupee		track suit	
tour, -ed, -ing (trip)		tracktion	traction
tour	tor (hill)	tract (region)	
tour	tore (ripped)	tractable, -bly	
tourism		tracter	tractor
tourist		traction	
tournament		tractor	
tournikit	tourniquet	trade, traded, trading	
tourniquet		tradein	
tousle, -sled, -sling		trademark	
tout, -ed, -ing		trader	
tow, -ed, -ing (pull)		tradesman, -men	
tow	to (toward)	tradeswoman, -women	
tow	too (also)	tradishun	tradition
tow	toe (foot)	tradition	
tow	two (number)	traditional, -ly	
toward		traduce, -duced, -ducing	
towaway zone		traducer	
tow boat		traduse	traduce
towel, -ed, -ing		traffic, -ficked, -ficking	
tower, -ed, -ing		trafficker	
towheaded		trafic	traffic
towl	towel	tragedian	
town		tragedienne	
town hall		tragedy, -dies	
townhouse		tragic	
township		tragical, -ly	
townsfolk		tragicomedy, -dies	
townspeople		trail, -ed, -ing (track)	
towring	towering	trail	trial (court)
towsl	tousle	trailblazer	
towt	tout	trailer	
toxic, -ally		train, -ed, -ing (teach)	

trainable
trainee
trainer
trainload
traipse, traipsed, traipsing
trait (feature)
traiter   traitor
traitor
traitorous
traitress
traitrous   traitorous
trajectory, -ries
trajectry   trajectory
trajedy   tragedy
trakia   trachea
traksion   traction
tram
tram car
trammel, -ed, -ing
tramp, -ed, -ing
trample, -pled, -pling
trampoline, -lined, -lining
trance
trane   train
trankwil   tranquil
trankwility   tranquillity
tranquil, -ly
tranquility
tranquilizer
transact, -ed, -ing
transacter   transactor
transaction
transactor
transceiver
transcend, -ed, -ing
transcendent
transcendental, -ally
transcontinental
transcribe, -scribed, -scribing
transcript
transducer
transe   trance
transend   transcend
transept
transfer, -ferred, -ferring
transferral
transference

transfigure, -ured, -uring
transfiks   transfix
transfix, -ed, -ing
transform, -ed, -ing
transformasion   transformation
transformation
transformer
transfuse, -fused, -fusing
transfusion
transgress, -ed, -ing
transgresser   transgressor
transgression
transgressor
transient, -ly
transision   transition
transister   transistor
transistor
transit, -sited, -siting
transition
transitional, -ly
transitory
translate, -lated, -lating
translater   translator
translation
translator
translucent, -ly
transmigrate, -grated, -grating
transmigration
transmigratory
transmishun   transmission
transmission
transmit, -mitted, -mitting
transmitter
transom
transparency, -cies
transparensy   transparency
transparent, -ly
transperant   transparent
transpire, -spired, -spiring
transplant, -ed, -ing
transplantation
transport, -ed, -ing
transporter
transportation
transpose, -posed, -posing
transsexual
transversal, -ly

transverse, -versed, -versing
transvestism
transvestite
trap, trapped, trapping
trapdoor
trapeze
trapezium, -ziums, -zia
trapezoid
trapper
trappings
    trapse   traipse
    trase   trace
trash
trashy, trashier, trashiest
    trate   trait
    trater   traitor
    traterus   traitorous
trauma, -mata, -mas
traumatic
travail, -ed, -ing (labor)
    travale   travail
travel, -ed, -ing (tour)
traveler
    travelog   travelogue
travelogue, travelog
traverse, -versed, -versing
travesty, -ties
travesty, -tied, -tying
trawl, -ed, -ing
trawler
    trawma   trauma
    trawmatic   traumatic
tray (container)
    tray   trait (feature)
treacherous, -ly, -ness
treachery, -eries
tread, trod, trodden or trod, treading
treadle, -dled, -dling
treadmill
treason
treasonable
treasonous
    treasonus   treasonous
treasure, -ured, -uring
treasurer
treasure trove

treasury, -uries
treat, -ed, -ing
treatable
treaties (agreements)
    treaties   treatise (writing)
treatise (writing)
    treatise   treaties (agreements)
treatment
treaty, -ties (agreement)
treble, -bled, -bling
    trecherus   treacherous
    trechery   treachery
    treck   trek
    tred   tread
tree
treeless
    treet   treat
    treetis   treatise
    treetment   treatment
treetop
    treety   treaty
trefoil
trek, trekked, trekking
trekker
trellis
tremble, -bled, -bling
trembly, -blier, -bliest
tremendous, -ly, -ness
    tremendus   tremendous
    tremer   tremor
tremolo, -los
tremor
tremulous, -ly, -ness
    tremulus   tremulous
trench, -ed, -ing
trenchant, -ly
trench coat
trend
trend-setter
trendy, -dier, -diest
trendy, -ily, -iness
    treo   trio
trepidation
    treson   treason
    tresure   treasure

tresury	treasury	trimaran	
trespass, -ed, -ing		trimester	
trespasser		trimeter	
tress		trimmer	
tressel	trestle	trimonthly	
trestle		trinity, -ties	
tresurer	treasurer	trinket	
tri	try	trinomial	
triad		trio, trios	
trial (court)		trip, tripped, tripping	
trial	trail (track)	tripartite	
triangel	triangle	tripe	
triangle		triple, -pled, -pling	
triangular, -ly		triplet	
tribal, -ly		triplex	
tribalism		triplicate, -cated, -cating	
tribe		tripod	
tribel	tribal	tripple	triple
tribulation		triptick	triptych
tribunal		triptych	
tribune		trise	trice
tributary, -ries		trisicle	tricycle
tribute		trite, triter, tritest	
tributry	tributary	triteness	
trice		triumf	triumph
triceps		triumph	
trick, -ed, -ing		triumphal	
trickery, -eries		triumphant, -ly	
trickle, -led, -ling		trivia	
trickster		trivial, -ly	
tricky, -kier, -kiest		triviality, -ties	
tricolor		trod	
tricycle		trodden	
trident		troff	trough
tried		trofy	trophy
triel	trial	troglodyte	
triennial, -ly		troika	
trifel	trifle	troll, -ed, -ing	
trifle, trifled, trifling		trolley, trolleys	
trifler		trollop	
trigger, -ed, -ing		trolop	trollop
trigonometrical, -ly		trombone	
trigonometry		trombonist	
trillion		troo	true
trilogy, -gies		trooant	truant
trim, trimmed, trimming		trooly	truly
trim, trimmer, trimmest		troop, -ed, -ing (soldier)	

troop	troupe (band)	trulie	truly
trooper		trump, -ed, -ing	
troos	truce	trumpery, -ries	
trooth	truth	trumpet	
troothful	truthful	trumpeter	
trophy, -phies		truncate, -cated, -cating	
tropic		truncheon	
tropical, -ly		trundle, -dled, -dling	
trorma	trauma	trunk	
trormatic	traumatic	truseau	trousseau
trot, trotted, trotting		truss, -ed, -ing	
troth		trust, -ed, -ing	
trotter		trustee	
troubadour		trusteeship	
trouble, -bled, -bling		trustful, -ly, -ness	
troublemaker		trustworthy, -thiness	
troublesome, -ly		trusty, trustier, trustiest	
troubleshooter		truth	
troublesum	troublesome	truthful, -ly, -ness	
trough		try, tries	
trounce, trounced, trouncing		try, tried, trying	
troupe (band)		tryce	trice
trousers		trycycle	tricycle
trousseau, -seaux, -seaus		trype	tripe
trout		tryst	
trowel, -ed, -ing		tryte	trite
trownce	trounce	tryumph	triumph
trowsers	trousers	tsar	
trowt	trout	tsarina	
truancy		tsarist	
truansy	truancy	T-shirt	
truant		tub	
truble	trouble	tuba (instrument)	
truce		tubby, -bier, -biest	
truck, -ed, -ing		tube	
trucker		tuber (plant)	
truckload		tuberculosis	
truculence		tuberculous	
truculent, -ly		tubular	
trudge, trudged, trudging		tuch	touch
true, truer, truest		tuchy	touchy
true-blue		tuck, -ed, -ing	
truehearted		tucker	
truf	trough	Tuesday	
truffle		tuf	tough
truge	trudge	tuffen	toughen
truism		tuffet	

tuft, -ed, -ing		turm	term	
tug, tugged, tugging		turmeric		
tugboat		turminable	terminable	
tuision	tuition	turminal	terminal	
tuition		turminate	terminate	
tuk	tuck	turminus	terminus	
tuksedo	tuxedo	turmite	termite	
tulip		turmoil		
tulle		turn, -ed, -ing (rotate)		
tumble, -bled, -bling		turn	tern (bird)	
tumbler		turnaround		
tumbleweed		turncoat		
tumer	tumor	turndown		
tumescent		turnip		
tumor		turniquet	tourniquet	
tumult		turnkey		
tumultuous, -ly		turnoff		
tuna (fish)		turnout		
tundra		turnover		
tune, tuned, tuning		turnpike		
tuneful, -ly, -ness		turnstile		
tuner (radio)		turntable		
tung	tongue	turnup	turnip	
tungsten		turpentine		
tunic		turpitude		
tunige	tonnage	turquoise		
tunnel, -ed, -ing		turret		
turban (hat)		turse	terse	
turbid, -ly, -ness		turtel	turtle	
turbine (power)		turtiary	tertiary	
turboelectric		turtle		
turbofan		turtledove		
turbojet		turtleneck		
turboprop		Tusday	Tuesday	
turbot, -bots, -bot		tusk		
turbulence		tussel	tussle	
turbulent, -ly		tussle, -sled, -sling		
tureen		tussock		
turet	turret	tutelage		
turf		tutelige	tutelage	
turgid, -ly		tuter	tutor	
turgidity		tutor		
turist	tourist	tutorial		
turjid	turgid	tutoriel	tutorial	
turkey, -keys		tutu		
Turkish		tuxedo, -dos		
turkwoise	turquoise	twaddle, -dled, -dling		

twain

twang

twangy

tweak, -ed, -ing

tweed

~~tweek~~ tweak

tweet

tweeter

tweezers

twelfth

~~twelth~~ twelfth

twelve

twentieth

twenty, -ties

twice

~~twich~~ twitch

twiddle, -dled, -dling

twig, twigged, twigging

twiggy

twilight

~~twilite~~ twilight

twill (fabric)

'twill (it will)

~~twill~~ 'twill (it will)

twin, twinned, twinning

twine, twined, twining

twinge, twinged, twinging

twinkle, -kled, -kling

twirl, -ed, -ing

twirler

twist, -ed, -ing

twister

twitch, -ed, -ing

twitcher

twitter, -ed, -ing

two (number)

~~two~~ to (toward)

~~two~~ toe (foot)

~~two~~ too (also)

~~two~~ tow (pull)

two-dimensional

two-edged

two-faced

two-fisted

twofold

two-handed

two-ply

twoseater

twosided

twosome

two step

two-time, -timed, -timing

two-tone

'twould (it would)

~~twould~~ 'twould

two-up

two-way

two-wheeler

~~twurl~~ twirl

tycoon

~~tyfoid~~ typhoid

~~tyfoon~~ typhoon

~~tyfus~~ typhus

tympanic

tympanum, -nums, -na

type, typed, typing

typecast, -cast, -casting

typeface

typescript

typeset, -set, -setting

typesetter

typewriter

typhoid

typhoon

typhus

typical, -ly

typify, -fied, -fying

typist

typographical, -ally

typography

~~tyranical~~ tyrannical

tyrannical, -ly

tyrannize, -nized, -nizing

tyranny, -nies

tyrant

~~tyrany~~ tyranny

tyro, -ros

tzar

Uu

ubikwity	ubiquity
ubiquitous, -ly	
ubiquity	
U-boat	
ubote	U-boat
uda	udder
udder (gland)	
udder	utter (speak)
ug	ugh
ugh	
uglee	ugly
ugliness	
ugly, -lier, -liest	
ugly duckling	
ukulele	
ulcer	
ulcerate, -rated, -rating	
ulceration	
ulcerous, -ly	
ullage	
ulltra	ultra
ulsa	ulcer
ulserate	ulcerate
ulseration	ulceration
ulserous	ulcerous
ultamatum	ultimatum
ulteeria	ulterior
ulterior, -ly	
ultimate, -ly	
ultimatum, -tums, -ta	
ultimit	ultimate
ultra	
ultracentrifuge	
ultraconservative	
ultrafashionable	
ultrafiche	
ultrahigh	
ultramareen	ultramarine

ultramarine	
ultramicroscope	
ultramicroscopic, -ally	
ultramodern	
ultrapure, -ly	
ultrashort	
ultrasonic, -ally	
ultrasound	
ultraviolet	
ululate, -lated, -lating	
umber	
umberella	umbrella
umbilical cord	
umbilicus, -bilici, -bilices	
umbra, -bras, -brae	
umbrage	
umbrella	
umbridge	umbrage
umpire, -pired, -piring (referee)	
umpire	empire (nations)
umpyre	umpire
umpteen	
umpteenth	
unabashed, -ly	
unabated	
unable	
unabridged	
unabsolved	
unabsorbed	
unaccented	
unaccentuated	
unacceptable, -tably	
unacclaimed	
unacclimated	
unaccommodating	
unaccompanied	
unaccomplished	
unaccountable, -bly	
unaccounted	
unaccredited	
unaccustomed	
unacknowledged	
unacorn	unicorn
unacquainted	
unacustumed	unaccustomed
unadapted	

unaddressed
unadjusted
unadorned
unadulterated
unadvertized
unadvisable
unadvised, -ly
unaffected, -ly
unaffiliated
unafraid
unaged
unaging
unaided
unakumpneed — unaccompanied
unalarmed
unalienable
unaligned
unalike
unallayed
unalleviated
unallied
unalloyed
unalphabetized
unalterable, -bly
unaltered
unambiguous, -ly
unambitious
un-American
unamplified
unamused
unamusing
unanchored
unanimated
unanimity
unanimous, -ly
unanimus — unanimous
unannounced
unanswerable
unanswered
unanticipated
unapologetic
unapparent
unappealing, -ly
unappeasable
unappeased
unappetizing
unapplicable

unapplied
unappointed
unapportioned
unappreciated
unappreciative
unapprehensive
unapproachable, -bly
unaprochible — unapproachable
unarguable
unarmed
unarmored
unarticulate, -ly
unarticulated
unartistic
unashamed, -ly
unasked
unaspiring
unassertive, -ly
unassessed
unassigned
unassailable, -bly
unassimilated
unassisted
unassuming, -ly
unattached
unattainable
unattempted
unattended
unattractive, -ly, -ness
unatural — unnatural
unauspicious, -ly
unauthenticated
unauthorized
unavailability
unavailable
unavailing, -ly
unavaleing — unavailing
unavenged
unavoidable, -bly, -bility
unawakened
unaware, -ness
unawares
unawear — unaware
unbaked
unbalance, -anced, -ancing
unbalanced
unbaptized

unbearable
unbeatable
unbeaten
unbecoming, -ly
  unbecuming   unbecoming
unbeknown
unbeknownst
  unbeleif   unbelief
  unbeleiver   unbeliever
  unbeleiving   unbelieving
unbelief
unbelievable
unbeliever
unbelieving, -ly
unbeloved
unbend, -bent or -bended, -bending
  unbenown   unbeknown
unblamed
unblinking, -ly
unblock
unblushing, -ly
unbolt, -ed, -ing
unborn
unbosom, -ed, -ing
unbounded, -ly
  unbownded   unbounded
unbreakable
  unbrideld   unbridled
unbridled
unbroken
unbuckle, -ed, -ing
unburden, -ed, -ing
unbutton
uncalled-for
uncanny, -nily
uncap, -ped, -ping
uncanceled
uncared-for
uncaring, -ly
uncarpeted
uncatalogued
uncaught
unceasing, -ly
uncelebrated
uncensored
uncensured
unceremonious, -ly

uncertain, -ly
uncertainty
uncertified
unchained
unchallenged
unchangeable
unchanged
unchanging
unchaperoned
uncharacteristic
uncharitable, -ly, -ness
uncharted
uncircumcised
uncle
unclean, -ly, -liness, -ness
unclear, -ly
uncleared
unclench, -ed, -ing
uncloak, -ed, -ing
unclog, -clogged, -clogging
unclothe, -clothed, -clothing
unclouded
uncluttered
uncoil, -ed, -ing
uncollected
uncolored
uncombined
uncomfortable, -ly
  uncomfortible   uncomfortable
uncomforted
uncomforting
uncommon, -ly
uncommunicative, -ly
  uncomon   uncommon
uncompensated
uncomplaining
uncompleted
uncomplicated
uncomplimentary
uncompounded
uncomprehending, -ly
uncompromising, -ly
unconcerned, -ly
  uncondisional   unconditional
unconditional, -ly
unconfined
unconfirmed

unconnected, -ly
unconscionable, -bly
unconscious, -ly, -ness
unconsecrated
unconsidered
   unconsionable   unconscionable
   unconsious   unconscious
unconsoled
unconsolidated
unconstitutional, -ly
unconstrained
unconstricted
unconsumed
unconsummated
uncontrollable
unconventional, -ly
unconvinced
unconvincing, -ly
uncooked
uncooperative
uncoordinated
   uncooth   uncouth
uncork
uncorrected
uncorroborated
uncorrupted
uncounted
uncouple, -led, -ling
uncouth, -ness
uncover, -ed, -ing
uncredited
uncritical, -ly
uncross, -ed, -ing
uncrowded
uncrowned
unction
unctuous, -ly
uncultivated
uncultured
   uncumftible   uncomfortable
uncurbed
uncure, -cured, -curing
uncured
uncustomary
uncut
   uncuver   uncover
undamaged

undated
undaunted
undecided
undeciperable
undeclared
undecorated
undefeated
undefended
undefined
undemanding
undemocratic, -ally
undemonstrative, -ly
undeniable, -bly
   undenyable   undeniable
undependable
under
underachieve, -chieved, -chieving
underachiever
underachievement
underage
underarm
undercarriage
   undercarridge   undercarriage
undercharge, -charged, -charging
underclassman, -men
underclothes
undercoat
undercoating
undercook
   undercote   undercoat
undercover
   undercurent   undercurrent
undercurrent
undercut, -cut, -cutting
   undercuver   undercover
underdeveloped
underdeveloping
underdevelopment
   underdevelopt   underdeveloped
underdog
underdone
   underdun   underdone
underemphasis
underemphasize, -ed, -ing
underemployed
   underestamate   underestimate
underestimate, -mated, -mating

underexpose, -exposed, -exposing
  underexposhur   underexposure
underexposure
  underexpows   underexpose
underfeed, -fed, -feeding
underfinanced
underfoot
undergo, -went, -gone, -going
undergraduate
  undergrajuate   undergraduate
  undergroth   undergrowth
underground
undergrowth
underhand
underhanded, -ly
  underite   underwrite
underlay, -laid, -laying
underlie, -lay, -lain, -lying
  underlieing   underlying
underline, -lined, -lining
underling
  underly   underlie
underlying
undermine, -mined, -mining
underneath
  underneeth   underneath
undernourish, -ed, -ing
  undernurish   undernourish
underpaid
underpants
underpass
underpay, -paid, -paying
underpin, -pinned, -pinning
underplay, -played, -playing
underpopulated
underpowered
underpriced
underprivileged
underproduce, -duced, -ducing
  underscaw   underscore
underscore, -scored, -scoring
undersea
undersecretary, -taries
undersell, -sold, -selling
undershirt
undershoot, -shot, -shooting
underside

undersigned
  undersined   undersigned
undersized
understaffed
understand, -stood, -standing
understandable, -bly
understanding
  understait   understate
understate, -stated, -stating
understatement
understood
understudy, -studied, -studying
  undertaik   undertake
  undertaiker   undertaker
undertake, -took, -taken, -taking
undertaker
undertaking
under-the-counter
under-the-table
  undertoan   undertone
  undertoe   undertow
undertone
undertow
  underware   underwear
undervalue, -ued, -uing
underwater
underwear
underweight
underwent
underworld
underwrite, -written, -writing
undescribable, -bly
undeserved
undeserving
undesigned, -ly
undesirable, -bly
  undesirible   undesirable
undestroyed
undetected
undeterminable, -ably
undetermined
undeterred
undeveloped
  undevelupt   undeveloped
  undew   undue
  undewlate   undulate
  undewly   unduly

undiagnosed
undifferentiated
undigested
undiluted
undiminished
undiplomatic, -ally
undirected
undiscerned
undiscernible, -ibly
undiscerning
undisciplined
undignified
undisclosed
undiscovered
undiscriminating, -ly
undisguised
undisputable, -ably
undisputed
undissolved
undistinguishable
undistinguished
undistorted
undistributed
undisturbed
undivided
undivulged
undo, -did, -done, -doing
undocumented
undogmatic, -ally
undomesticated
  undoo   undo
undone
undoubted, -ly
  undowted   undoubted
undreamed, -drempt
undreamed-of, undrempt-of
undress, -dressed, -dressing
undue
undulate, -lated, -lating
undulation
undulatory
unduly
  undur   under
undyed
undying
  undyou   undue
unearned

unearned income
unearth, -ed, -ing
unearthly
uneasy, -easier, -easiest
uneasy, -ily, -iness
  unecessary   unnecessary
uneaten
uneconomical
uneducated
  uneekwell   unequal
  uneesy   uneasy
  uneeven   uneven
  unekwivacal   unequivocal
unemancipated
unembarrassed
unembellished
unemotional
unemphatic
unemployable
unemployed
unemployment
unenclosed
unencumbered
unending
unenforceable
unenforced
unenlightened
unenrolled
unentered
unenterprising
unenthusiastic, -ally
unenviable, -bly
unequal, -ly
unequaled
  uneque   unique
unequipped
unequivocal, -ly
unerring, -ly
unescapable, -bly
  unesesary   unnecessary
unessential
unestablished
unethical
uneven, -ly, -ness
unexaggerated
unexcavated
unexcelled

unexcited
unexciting
unexcusable, -bly
unexcused
unexecuted
unexercised
unexpended
unexperienced
unexpired
unexplainable, -ably
unexplained
unexploded
unexploited
unexplored
unexposed
unexpressed
unextended
unextinguished
unfading
unfailing, -ly
unfair, -ly
unfaithful, -ly, -ness
 unfaling   unfailing
unfaltering, -ly
unfamiliar, -ly
unfamiliarity
 unfare   unfair
unfashionable, -ably
unfasten, -ed, -ing
unfathomable, -ably
unfathomed
unfazed
unfeasible
unfed
unfeeling, -ly
 unfemilyer   unfamiliar
unfeminine
unfenced
unfertilized
unfilled
unfiltered
unfinished
unfit, -fitted, -fitting
unflagging, -ly
unflappable, -bly
 unflappible   unflappable
unflattering

unflavored
unflinching
unfocused
unfold, -ed, -ing
 unforchinate   unfortunate
unforeseeable, -ably
unforeseen
unforgettable, -ably
unforgivable, -ably
unforgiven
unforgiving
unformed
 unforsean   unforeseen
unfortunate, -ly, -ness
unfounded
 unfowld   unfold
 unfownded   unfounded
unframed
unfreeze, unfroze, unfrozen,
unfreezing
unfrequented
unfriendly, -liness
unfrock, -ed, -ing
unfruitful, -ness
unfulfilled
unfunny
unfurl, -ed, -ing
unfurnished
ungainly, -liness
 unganely   ungainly
 ungarded   unguarded
unglued
ungodly, -liness
ungraceful, -ly
ungracious, -ly, -ness
 ungrasious   ungracious
ungraded
ungrammatical, -ly
ungrateful, -ly
ungratifying
ungrounded
unguarded
unguent
ungulate
unhappy, -pier, -piest
unhappy, -pily, -piness
unhealthy, -thier, -thiest

unhealthy, -ily, -iness
unheard-of
unheeded
unhelpful
  unhelthy   unhealthy
  unherdoff   unheard-of
unhindered
unhinge, -hinged, -hinging
  unhinj   unhinge
  unholey   unholy
unholy, -lier, -liest
  unholesum   unwholesome
unhonored
unhook, -ed, -ing
unhoped-for
uniaxial
unicameral
unicellular
  uniceluler   unicellular
unicorn
unicycle
unidentifiable
unidentified
  unidirechunal   unidirectional
  unifacation   unification
unification
uniform, -ly, -ness
uniformity, -ties
unify, -fied, -fying
  unike   unique
unilateral, -ly
unimaginable, -ably
  unimaginible   unimaginable
unimaginative
unimpeachable, -ably
  unimpeechible   unimpeachable
  unimployed   unemployed
unimportant
unimposing
unimpoverished
unimpressed
unimpressive, -ly
  unimprooved   unimproved
unimproved
uninclosed
unincumbered
unindorsed

uninfected
uninfluenced
uninformative
uninformed
uninhibited, -ly
uninspired
uninspiring
uninsurable
uninsured
unintelligent, -ly
unintelligible, -bly
unintended
unintentional, -ly
uninterested, -ly
uninteresting, -ly
uninterrupted, -ly
uninvested
uninvited
uninviting, -ly
uninvolved
union
unionist
unionization
unionize, -nized, -nizing
Union Jack
unique, -ly, -ness
unironed
  unirve   unnerve
unisex
unison
unit
Unitarian
Unitarianism
unitary
unite, united, uniting
unity, -ties
univalve
universal, -ly
universe
university, -ties
unjust, -ly, -ness
unjustifiable, -ably
unjustified
unkempt
  unkemt   unkempt
unkind, -ly, -ness
  unkined   unkind

unkle — uncle
unknowing, -ly
unknown
unlabeled
unlace, -laced, -lacing
unlatch, -ed, -ing
unlawful, -ly, -ness
unleaded
unlearned
unleash, -ed, -ing
unleavened
unleesh — unleash
unlerned — unlearned
unles — unless
unless
unlettered
unlicensed
unlike, -ness
unlikely, -lihood, -liness
unlikelyhood — unlikelihood
unlimited
unlined
unlisted
unlit
unlivable
unload, -ed, -ing
unlode — unload
unlocated
unlock, -ed, -ing
unlooked-for
unlucky, -kily, -kiness
unluckyly — unluckily
unmake, -made, -making
unmanagable — unmanageable
unmanageable, -bly
unman, -manned, -manning
unmanly, -liness
unmannerly, -liness
unmapped
unmarked
unmarred
unmarried
undmastered
unmatched
unmeasured
unmeditated
unmelodious

unmended
unmenchunable — unmentionable
unmentionable, -bly
unmerciful, -ly
unmerited
unmethodical, -ly
unmilitary
unmindful
unmistakable, -bly
unmistakeable — unmistakable
unmistaken, -ly
unmitigated
unmooved — unmoved
unmotivated
unmounted
unmoved
unnamed
unnatural, -ly, -ness
unnavigable
unnecessary, -rily, -riness
unneeded
unnegotiable
unneighborly
unnerve, -nerved, -nerving
unnesesarily — unnecessarily
unnesesary — unnecessary
unnoticable, -bly
unnoticed
unnumbered
unobjectionable
unobliged
unobliging
unobscured
unobservant
unobserved
unobstructive
unobtainable
unobtrusif — unobtrusive
unobtrusive, -ly
unoccupied
unoffending
unoffensive, -ly
unofficial, -ly
unofishel — unofficial
unopened
unopposed
unorganized

unorgenized	unorganized	unprinsipled	unprincipled
unoriginal		unprintable	
unorthodox		unprintible	unprintable
unostentatious, -ly		unprocessed	
unowned		unproclaimed	
unpack, -ed, -ing		unproductive, -ly	
unpaid		unprofeshunel	unprofessional
unpainted		unprofessional, -ly	
unpalatable, -bly		unproffessinal	unprofessional
unpalatible	unpalatable	unprofitable, -ably	
unparaleled	unparalleled	unproductive, -ly	
unparalleled		unpromising	
unpardonable, -bly		unprompted	
unparraleled	unparalleled	unpronouncable	
unpatented		unpronounced	
unpatriotic, -ally		unprotected	
unpaved		unprotective	
unpenetrable		unprotesting	
unpenetrated		unprovable	
unperceived		unproven	
unperfected		unprovided	
unpersuaded		unprovoked	
unpicked		unpublishable	
unpin, -pinned, -pinning		unpublished	
unplaced		unkwalified	unqualified
unplaised	unplaced	unqualified	
unplanned		unquenchable	
unpleased		unquenched	
unpoetic		unquestionable, -bly	
unpoised		unquestionible	unquestionable
unpolished		unravel, -ed, -ing	
unpopular, -ly		unravell	unravel
unpopularity		unreadable	
unpopuler	unpopular	unreal, -ly	
unpracticed		unrealistic, -ally	
unprecedented		unrealized	
unpredictable, -ably		unreasonable, -ably	
unpredictibility		unreasoned	
unprejudiced		unreasoning	
unpremeditated		unreceptive	
unprepared, -ness		unrecognizable	
unpresentable, -bly		unrecognized	
unpreserved		unrecommended	
unpresidented	unprecedented	unreconcilable, -bly	
unpreventable		unreconciled	
unpretentious, -ly, -ness		unrecorded	
unprincipled		unrectified	

unredeamed	unredeemed	unroll, -ed, -ing	
unredeemable		unromantic, -ally	
unredeemed		unrooly	unruly
unreel	unreal	unruffled	
unreelistic	unrealistic	unrufled	unruffled
unreesenable	unreasonable	unruled	
unrefined		unruly	
unreflecting		unsafe, -ly	
unreflective		unsaid	
unreformed		unsaif	unsafe
unregimented		unsalted	
unregistered		unsalvable	
unregulated		unsalvagable	
unrehearsed		unsanctified	
unrekwited	unrequited	unsanctioned	
unrelaited	unrelated	unsanitary (dirty)	
unrelated		unsanitary	insanitary
unrelenting, -ly			(dirty)
unrelieved	unrelieved	unsanitary	insanity
unreliable, -bly			(mental
unrelieved			disorder)
unremiting	unremitting	unsaterated	unsaturated
unremitting		unsatisfactory	
unremorseful, -ly		unsatisfied	
unrepaid		unsaturated	
unrepeatable, -bly		unsavery	unsavory
unrepeetable	unrepeatable	unsavory	
unreplaced		unscathed	
unreported		unscented	
unrepresented		unscheduled	
unrepressed		unschooled	
unrequited, -ly		unscientific, -ally	
unresentful		unscratched	
unresisting		unscrew, -ed, -ing	
unresolved		unscrupulous, -ly, -ness	
unresponsive, -ly		unskru	unscrew
unrest		unskuled	unschooled
unrestrained, -ly		unseal, -ed, -ing	
unreturned		unseasonable, -bly, -bleness	
unrevealed		unseat, -ed, -ing	
unrewarding		unseesenable	unseasonable
unrhymed		unseet	unseat
unrighteous, -ly, -ness		unsecured	
unripe		unsecurred	unsecured
unrivaled		unseemly	
unriveled	unrivaled	unseeing	
unrobe, -robed, -robing		unseen	

unsegregated
unselective, -ly
unself-conscious, -ly
unselfish, -ly, -ness
unsellfish — unselfish
unserviceable
unservisable — unserviceable
unsetled — unsettled
unsettled
unshakable, -bly
unshaped
unshaven
unsheathe, -sheathed, -sheathing
unshore — unsure
unshrinkable
unsightly
unsigned
unsitely — unsightly
unskild — unskilled
unskilled
unsnap, -snapped, -snapping
unsociability
unsociable, -bly
unsoiled
unsold
unsolicited
unsolisited — unsolicited
unsosiable — unsociable
unsophisticated
unsought
unsound, -ly, -ness
unsownd — unsound
unsparing, -ly, -ness
unspeakable, -bly
unspeekable — unspeakable
unspecific, -ally
unspecified
unspoiled
unspoyled — unspoiled
unstabel — unstable
unstable, -bly
unstained
unstamped
unstandardized
unstapled
unstarched
unstated

unsteady, -dily, -diness
unstedie — unsteady
unsterilized
unstrained
unstressed
unstructured
unstruxured — unstructured
unstudied
unstudyed — unstudied
unsubstansial — unsubstantial
unsubstantial, -ly
unsubstantiated
unsuccessful, -ly
unsuited
unsung
unsupervised
unsupported
unsuppressed
unsuppressible
unsure
unswerving
unswurving — unswerving
unsymmetrical, -ly
unsympathetic, -ally
unsystematic
untactful
untainted
untalented
untamed
untangel — untangle
untangle, -gled, -gling
untapped
untarnished
untasted
untaught
untaxed
unteachable
untempted
untenable, -bly
untested
unthankful
unthinkable, -bly
unthinkible — unthinkable
unthinking, -ly
untidie — untidy
untidiness
untidy, -died, -dying

untidy, -dier, -diest
untie, -tied, -tying
until
   untill   until
untimely
untiring, -ly
unto
   untoo   unto
untold
untouchable, -ably
   untouchible   untouchable
   untooward   untoward
untoward
untracable
untrained
untranslatable
untranslated
untraveled
untreated
untried
untrimmed
untrodden
   untroo   untrue
   untrooth   untruth
untroubled
untrue
untrustful
untrustworthy, -iness
untruth
untruthful, -ly, -ness
unturned
untutored
untwist, -ed, -ing
untypical, -ly
unusable
   unushual   unusual
unusual, -ly, -ness
unused
unutterable, -bly
   unutterible   unutterable
   unvale   unveil
unveil, -ed, -ing
unventilated
unverifiable
unversed
unvoiced
   unvoised   unvoiced

unwanted
   unwarented   unwarranted
unwarrantable, -ably
unwarranted
unwary, -ily, iness
unwashed
unwatched
unwavering
unwaxed
unwearying
unwed
   unweeldy   unwieldy
unwelcome
   unwellcum   unwelcome
unwelcomed
unwholesome, -ly, -ness
unwieldy, -iness
   unwiling   unwilling
unwilling, -ly, -ness
unwind, -wound, -winding
   unwined   unwind
unwise, -ly
unwitting, -ly
unwonted, -ly
unworkable
unworldliness
unworldly
unworn
unworried
unworthy, -ily, -iness
unwrap, -ped, -ping
unwrinkled
unwoven
unwritten
unyielding
unzip, -ped, -ping
up, upped, upping
up-and-coming
up-beat
   upbrade   upbraid
upbraid, -ed, -ing
upbringing
upcoming
upcountry
   updait   update
update, -dated, -dating
updraft

upeld — upheld
uper — upper
upend, -ed, -ing
upgrade, -graded, -grading
upgraid — upgrade
upheaval
upheeval — upheaval
upheave, -heaved, -heaving
upheld
uphill
uphold, -held, -holding
upholster, -ed, -ing
upholsterer
upholstery, -ries
upill — uphill
upkeep
upland
uplift
upold — uphold
upolster — upholster
upon
upper
upper case
upper-class
upperclassman, -men
uppercut
upper hand
upper house
uppermost
upright
uprising
uprite — upright
uproar
uproarious, -ly, -ness
uproot, -ed, -ing
uprore — uproar
upset, -set, -setting
upshot
upside-down
upstage, -staged, -staging
upstairs
upstaje — upstage
upstanding
upstate
upstream
upstroke
upsurge, -surged, -surging

upsurje — upsurge
upswept
upswing, -swung, -swinging
uptaik — uptake
uptake
uptight
uptite — uptight
up-to-date
up-too-date — up-to-date
upturn, -ed, -ing
upward, -ly, -ness
upwind
upwood — upward
uranic
uranium
Uranus (planet)
urban (town)
urbane, -ly (civilized)
urbanite
urbanity, -ties
urbanize, -nized, -nizing
urchin
urea
urear — urea
ureter
urethra, -thras, -thrae
urethral
urge, urged, urging
urgency
urgent, -ly
urinal
urinary
urinate, -nated, -nating
urination
urine
urinel — urinal
urj — urge
urjensy — urgency
urjent — urgent
urn (jug)
urn — earn (gain)
urogenital
urojenital — urogenital
urology
urolojy — urology
ursine
usabel — usable

usability
usable
usableness
usage
  usaje   usage
use, used, using
used
useful, -ly, -ness
useless, -ly, -ness
usher
usherette
usual, -ly, -ness
  ushuel   usual
  ushuelly   usually
usurp, -ed, -ing
usurpation
usurper
usury, -ries
  utalization   utilization
utensil
  utensle   utensil
uterine
uterus, uteri
utilitarian
utilitarianism
utility, -ties
utilization
utilize, -lized, -lizing
utmost
Utopia, utopia
Utopian, utopian
  utta   utter
utter, uttered, uttering (speak)
  utter   udder (gland)
utterly
uttermost
U-turn
  uttur   utter
  uturus   uterus
uvula, -las, -lae
uxorious, -ly, -ness
Uzbek
  uzually   usually

Vv

vacancy, -cies
vacansy — vacancy
vacant, -ly
vacate, -cated, -cating
vacation (holiday)
vacation — vocation (job)
vaccinate, -nated, -nating
vaccination
vaccine
vaccuum — vacuum
vacency — vacancy
vacillate, -lated, -lating
vacseen — vaccine
vacsinate — vaccinate
vacsination — vaccination
vacsine — vaccine
vacuity, -ties
vacuous, -ly, -ness
vacuum
vacuum-packed
vacuum-sealed
vacuus — vacuous
vagabond
vagary, -ries
vagarious
vagarius — vagarious
vage — vague
vagina, -nas, -nae
vaginal
vagrancy, -cies
vagransy — vagrancy
vagrant, -ly
vague, vaguer, vaguest
vaguely
vail — vale (valley)
vail — veil (cover)
vain, -ly, -ness (proud)
vain — vane (blade)

vain — vein (blood)
vainglorious
vainglorius — vainglorious
vainglory
vajina — vagina
valadation — validation
valantine — valentine
valay — valet
vale (valley)
vale — veil (cover)
valedicktion — valediction
valediction
valedictory
valedictry — valedictory
valentine
valer — valor
valerus — valorous
valese — valise
valet, -ed, -ing
valiancy
valiant, -ly
valid, -ly
validate, -dated, -dating
validation
validity, -ties
valise
valley, -leys
valor
valorous, -ly
valorus — valorous
valuable, -bly
valuation
value, -ued, -uing
valuer
valve, valved, valving
valvular
valy — valley
valyu — value
valyuble — valuable
valyuless — valueless
vamoose, -moosed, -moosing
vamp, -ed, -ing
vampire
van
vandal
vandalism
vandalize, -ed, -ing

vandle	vandal	vaudeville	
vane (blade)		vault, -ed, -ing	
vane	vain (proud)	vaunt, -ed, -ing	
vane	vein (blood)	vaze	vase
vaneer	veneer	veal	
vangard	vanguard	vector	
vanglorius	vainglorious	veel	veal
vanguard		veemense	vehemence
vanilla		veement	vehement
vanish, -ed, -ing		veer, -ed, -ing	
vanity, -ties		vegatation	vegetation
vankwish	vanquish	vegetable	
vanquish, -ed, -ing		vegetarian	
vantage		vegetarianism	
vapid, -ly		vegetate, -tated, -tating	
vapor		vegetation	
vaporize, -rized, -rizing		vegetative	
vaporizer		vegetible	vegetable
vaporous, -ly, -ness		vegtable	vegetable
variabel	variable	vehemence	
variability		vehemency	
variable, -bly		vehement, -ly	
variance		vehicle	
varianse	variance	vehicular	
variant		veicular	vehicular
variation		veil, -ed, -ing (cover)	
varicolored		veil	vale (valley)
varicose		vein (blood)	
varied		vein	vain (proud)
variegated		vein	vane (blade)
varietal, -ly		veks	vex
variety, -ties		veksatious	vexatious
various, -ly		vektor	vector
varius	various	Velcro	
varnish, -ed, -ing		veld, veldt	
vary, varied, varying (change)		vellum	
vary	very (extremely)	velocipede	
		velocity, -ties	
vascular		velour	
vase		velum	vellum
vasectomy, -mies		velt	veldt
Vaseline		velvet	
vasillate	vacillate	velveteen	
vast, -ly, -ness		velvety	
vat		venal, -ly (corruptible)	
Vatican		venal	venial (excusable)
vaudavil	vaudeville		

venality, -ties
vend, -ed, -ing
  vender   vendor
vendetta
vendor
veneer
venerability
venerable, -bly
venerate, -rated, -rating
veneration
venereal
  venerial   venereal
  venerible   venerable
Venetian blind
  venew   venue
vengeance
vengeful, -ly, -ness
  vengense   vengeance
venial, -ly (excusable)
  venial   venal
              (corruptible)
venison
venom
venomous, -ly
  venomus   venomous
venous (of veins)
  venous   Venus
              (planet)
vent, -ed, -ing
  ventalation   ventilation
ventilate, -lated, -lating
  ventilater   ventilator
ventilation
ventilator
ventral, -ly
  ventrical   ventricle
ventricle
  ventrilokwism ventriloquism
ventriloquism
ventriloquist
venture, -tured, -turing
venturer
venturesome, -ly, -ness
venturous, -ly, -ness
  venturus   venturous
venue
Venus (planet)

  venus   venous (of
              veins)
  veola   viola
veracious, -ly, -ness (honest)
  veracious   voracious
              (greedy)
veracity, -ties
veranda
  verasity   veracity
verb
verbal
verbalize, -lized, -lizing
verbally
verbatim
  verbel   verbal
verbena
verbiage
  verbige   verbiage
verbose, -ly, -ness
verbosity
verdant, -ly
verdict
verdure
verge, verged, verging
verger
  vergin   virgin
  verie   vary
verifiable, -bly
verification
  verifie   verify
verify, -fied, -fying
verily
verisimilitude
veritable, -bly
vermicelli
vermilion
vermin
verminous
vermouth
vernacular, -ly
vernal, -ly
vernier
versatile, -ly
versatility
verse, verses (poem)
  verses   versus (against)
versification

versify, -fied, -fying

version

versus (against)

   versus   verses (poems)

vertebra, -brae

vertebrate

   verteks   vertex

vertex, -tices

vertical, -ly, -ness

vertiginous, -ly

   vertiginus   vertiginous

vertigo, -goes

verve

very (extremely)

   very   vary (change)

   vesa   visa

vespers

vessel

vest, -ed, -ing

vestal

   vestibul   vestibule

vestibule

vestige

vestigial, -ly

vestment

   vestrie   vestry

vestry, -tries

   vestul   vestal

vet, vetted, vetting

   vetenary   veterinary

veteran

veterinary, -ries

veto, -toes

veto, -toed, -toing

vex, -ed, -ing

vexation

vexatious, -ly, -ness

   veza   visa

   vi   vie

via

   viabel   viable

viability

viable, -bly

viaduct

vial (tube)

   vial   vile (bad)

   vialate   violate

   vialet   violet

   vialin   violin

viand

viaticum, -ca, -cums

vibes

vibrancy

   vibransy   vibrancy

vibrant, -ly

vibrate, -brated, -brating

vibration

   vibrater   vibrator

vibrator

viburnum

vicar

vicarage

   vicarige   vicarage

vicarious, -ly, -ness

   vicarius   vicarious

vice

vice president

   vicer   vicar

viceregal, -ly

   viceroi   viceroy

viceroy

vice versa

vicinity, -ties

vicious, -ly, -ness (evil)

   vicious   viscous (thick)

vicissitude

   vicount   viscount

   victer   victor

victim

victimization

victimize, -mized, -mizing

victor

Victorian

victorious, -ly, -ness

   victorius   victorious

victory, -ries

victuals

victualer

video

video cassette

videodisc

videotape, -taped, -taping

   vidio   video

vie, vied, vying

vieing — vying
Vietnamese, -ese
view, -ed, -ing
viewer
viewfinder
viewpoint
viger — vigor
vigil
vigilance
vigilanse — vigilance
vigilant, -ly (watchful)
vigilante (law enforcer)
vignette, -gnetted, -gnetting
vigor
vigorous, -ly, -ness
vigorus — vigorous
viksen — vixen
vilafication — vilification
vilain — villain
vile, viler, vilest (bad)
vile, -ly, -ness
vile — vial (tube)
vilification
vilifie — vilify
vilifier
vilify, -fied, -fying
vilige — village
villa
village
villager
villain
villainous, -ly, -ness
villainy, -nies
villanus — villainous
vim
vinaigrette
vincible (beatable)
vincible — visible (seen)
vindicate, -cated, -cating
vindicater — vindicator
vindication
vindicator
vindictive, -ly
vine
vinegar
vinegary
vineyard

vinigar — vinegar
vinil — vinyl
vintage, -taged, -taging
vintige — vintage
vinyl
viola
violate, -lated, -lating
violator — violater
violation
violator
violence
violense — violence
violent, -ly
violet
violin
viper
viperous
viperus — viperous
virago, -goes, -gos
viral
virgin
virginal, -ly
virginity
Virgo
virile
virility, -ties
virtual, -ly
virtue
virtuos — virtuous
virtuoso
virtuous, -ly, -ness
virulence
virulense — virulence
virulent, -ly
virus, viruses
visa, -saed, -saing
visable — visible
visage
vis-à-vis
viscera
visceral
viscosity
viscount
viscountess
viscous, -ly, -ness (thick)
viscous — vicious (evil)
viscuus — viscous (thick)

vise	vice	vivisection	
vise-president	vice president	vivisectionist	
visera	viscera	vixen	
viseregal	viceregal		
viseversa	vice versa	For viz- words	
vishiate	vitiate	look under **vis-**.	
visious	vicious (evil)		
vison	vision	vocabulary, -ries	
visonary	visionary	vocal, -ly	
visibility, -ties		vocalist	
visible, -bly (seen)		vocalization	
visible	vincible (beaten)	vocalize, -lized, -lizing	
visinity	vicinity	vocation (job)	
vision		vocation	vacation (holiday)
visionary, -ries		vocational, -ly	
visionry	visionary	vociferous, -ly, -ness	
visissitude	vicissitude	vociferus	vociferous
visit, -ed, -ing		vodka	
visitant		voge	vogue
visitation		vogue	
visiter	visitor	voiage	voyage
visitor		voice, voiced, voicing	
viskosity	viscosity	voiceless, -ly, -ness	
vista		voice-over	
visual, -ly		voiceprint	
visualize, -lized, -lizing		void, -ed, -ing	
visuel	visual	voidable	
vital, -ly		voile	
vitality, -ties		voise	voice
vitamin		volatile	
vitel	vital	volatility	
vitiate, -ated, -ating		volcanic, -ally	
viticulture		volcano, -noes, -nos	
vitreous		voley	volley
vitrification		volision	volition
vitrify, -fied, -fying		volition, -al, -ally	
vitriol		volley, -leys	
vitriolic		volley, -ed, -ing	
vituperate, -rated, -rating		volleyball	
viul	vial (tube)	volt	
viul	vile (bad)	voltage	
vivacious, -ly, -ness		voltaic	
vivasious	vivacious	voltmeter	
viva voce		voluable	voluble
vivid, -ly, -ness		voluble, -bly	
vivisect, -ed, -ing		volume	
		volumetric, -ally	

voluminous, -ly, -ness
  voluminus — voluminous
voluntarily
voluntary, -taries
volunteer, -ed, -ing
  voluptuos — voluptuous
voluptuous, -ly, -ness
vomit, -ed, -ing
voodoo, -doos
voodooism
voracious, -ly, -ness (greedy)
  voracious — veracious
                (honest)
voracity
  vorasious — voracious
vortex, -texes, -tices
vortical
  vosiferus — vociferous
votary, -ries
vote, voted, voting
voter
votive, -ly
vouch, -ed, -ing
voucher
vouchsafe, -safed, -safing
vow, -ed, -ing
  vowch — vouch
  vowcher — voucher
vowel
  vowl — vowel
voyage, -aged, -aging
voyager
  voyd — void
voyeur
voyeurism
  voyse — voice
  vue — view
vulcanism
vulcanite
vulcanize, -nized, -nizing
  vulcher — vulture
vulgar, -ly, -ness
vulgarism
vulgarity, -ties
vulnerability
vulnerable, -bly
  vulnerible — vulnerable

vulpine
vulture
vulva, -vae, -vas
  vurb — verb
  vurgin — virgin
  vurtual — virtual
  vurtue — virtue
  vurtuous — virtuous
  vye — vie

wach	watch
wack	whack

wad, wadded, wadding
waddle, -dled, -dling
wade, waded, wading
wader
wadi, -dies

wadle	waddle
wafe	waif

wafer
wafery
waffle, -fled, -fling
wag, wagged, wagging
wage, waged, waging

wagen	wagon

wager
waggish, -ly, -ness
waggle, -gled, -gling
wagon
wagtail
waif
wail, -ed, -ing (cry)

wail	wale (welt)
wail	whale (mammal)

wainscot, -ed, -ing
wainwright
waist (body)

waist	waste (squander)

waistband
waistcoat
waistline
wait (stay)

wait	weight (amount)

waiter

waitey	weighty

waitress
waive, waived, waiving (forgo)

waive	wave (ocean)

waiver (law)

waiver	waver (sway)
waje	wage

wake, woke or waked, waked
  or woken, waking
wakeful, -ly, -ness
waken, -ened, -ening

waks	wax

wale, waled, waling (welt)

wale	wail (cry)
wale	whale (mammal)

walk, -ed, -ing
walkathon
walkaway
walker
walkie-talkie
walk-in
walk-on
walkout
walkover
walkup
walkway
wall
wallaby, -bies
wallboard
wallet
wallflower
wallop, -ed, -ing
wallow, -ed, -ing
wallpaper
wall-to-wall
walnut

walop	wallop
walow	wallow

walrus, -ruses

walts	waltz

waltz, -ed, -ing
wampum
wan, wanner, wannest (pale)

wan	won (win)

wand
wander, -ed, -ing (walk)

wander	wonder (think)

wanderer
wanderlust
wane, waned, waning
wangle, -gled, -gling
wangler
want, -ed, -ing
wanton, -ly, -ness (lewd)
| wanton | won ton (dough) |

war, warred, warring
| warant | warrant |
| warantee | warranty |

warble, -bled, -bling
warbler
war cry
ward
warden
wardrobe
ware (goods)
ware	wear (cover)
ware	were (was)
ware	where (place)

warehouse
| warey | wary |
| warf | wharf |

warfare
warhead
| warior | warrior |

warlike
warlock
warm, -ed, -ing (heat)
| warm | worm (animal) |

warm-blooded
warmed-over
warmhearted, -ly, -ness
warmonger
warmongering
warmth
warmup
warn, -ed, -ing (signal)
| warn | worn (tired) |

warp, -ed, -ing
warpath
warplane
warrant, -ed, -ing
warrant officer
warrantee (person)

| warrantee | warranty (guarantee) |

warrantor
warranty, -ties (guarantee)
| warranty | warrantee (person) |

warren
warrior
| warsh | wash |

warship
wart (lump)
| wart | wort (plant) |

warthog
wartime
| warves | wharves |

wary, warier, wariest (alert)
wary, -ily, -ness
| wary | weary (tired) |

was
wash, -ed, -ing
washable
wash-and-wear
washboard
washcloth
washed-out
washer
washing soda
washout
washroom
washtub
wasn't (was not)
| wasnt | wasn't |

wasp
waspish, -ly, -ness
wassail
wassailer
wastage
waste, wasted, wasting (squander)
| waste | waist (body) |

wasteful, -ly, -ness
wasteland
wastepaper
wastrel
| wat | watt (power) |
| wat | what (interrogative) |

watch, -ed, -ing

watchband
watchdog
watchful, -ly, -ness
watchmaker
watchman, -men
watchtower
watchwoman, -women
watchword

wate	wait (stay)
wate	weight (measure)

water, -ed, -ing
waterbed
water buffalo
water closet
watercolor
watercolorist
watercourse
watercraft
watercress
waterfall
waterfowl
waterfront
Watergate
water gate
water hole
watering can
watering hole
waterless
waterlily
waterline
waterlogged
Waterloo
watermark
watermelon
water pistol
water polo
waterpower
waterproof, -ed, -ing
water-rat
water-repellent
water-resistant
watershed
water ski
water-skiing
water table
watertight

watertite	watertight

water tower
waterway
waterwheel
waterworks
watery

watige	wattage

watt (power)

watt	what (interrogative)

wattage
wattle
wave, waved, waving (ocean)

wave	waive (forgo)

wave band
wave front
wavelength
waver, -ed, -ing (sway)

waver	waiver (law)

wavy, -vier, -viest
wavy, -vily, -viness
wax, waxed or waxen, waxing
waxen
waxwork
way (method)

way	weigh (amount)
way	whey (liquid)

waybill
wayfarer

wayfer	wafer

waylay, -laid, -laying
way-out
wayside
wayward, -ness

waywerd	wayward
wazn't	wasn't

we (pronoun)

we	wee (little)
wead	weed (wild plant)

weak, -ly, -ness (feeble)

weak	week (time)

weaken, -ed, -ing

weakend	weekend

weakling
weakly, -lier, -liest (feebly)

weakly	weekly (time)

weal (hurt)	
weal	wheel (disk)
weal	we'll (we will)
wealth	
wealthy, -thier, -thiest	
wealthy, -iness	
wean, -ed, -ing	
weapon	
weaponry	
wear, wore, worn, wearing (cover)	
wear	ware (goods)
wear	were (was)
wear	where (place)
wearable	
wearey	weary
wearisome, -ly, -ness	
weary, -rier, -riest (tired)	
weary, -ried, -rying (tired)	
weary	wary (alert)
weasel	
weat	wheat
weather (condition)	
weather	wether (gelding)
weather	whether (if)
weather-beten	
weatherboard	
weathercock	
weatherman, -men	
weatherproof, -ed, -ing	
weather vane	
weave, wove or weaved, weaving	
weave	we've (we have)
web, webbed, webbing	
web-footed	
wed, wedded or wed, wedding (join)	
we'd	
wed	we'd (we did, had)
Wednesday	Wednesday
wedge, wedged, wedging	
wedlock	
Wednesday	
wee, weer, weest (small)	
wee	we (pronoun)
weed, -ed, -ing (remove)	
weed (wild plant)	

weed	we'd (we did, had)
weedle	wheedle
weedy, -dier, -diest	
weedy, -ily, -iness	
weed-killer	
week (time)	
week	weak (feeble)
weekday	
weeken	weaken
weekend	
weekender	
weekling	weakling
weekly, -lies (time)	
weekly	weakly (feebly)
weel	weal (hurt)
weel	wheel (disk)
weelbarow	wheelbarrow
weeld	wield
ween	wean
weep, wept, weeping	
weeping willow	
weet	wheat
weevil	
weeze	wheeze
weft	
wege	wedge
weigh, -ed, -ing (amount)	
weigh	way (method)
weigh	whey (liquid)
weightless, -ly, -ness	
weighty, -tier, -tiest	
weighty, -tily, -tiness	
weild	wield
weir (dam)	
weird, -ly, -ness	
weja	ouija
Welch, Welsh	
welcome, -comed, -coming	
weld, -ed, -ing	
welder	
welfare	
well, better, best	
we'll (we will)	
we'll	weal (hurt)
we'll	wheel (disk)
well-acquainted	

well-advised		wer	weir (dam)
well-appointed		werd	weird
well-balanced (remove)		were (was)	
well-behaved		were	ware (goods)
well-being		were	wear (cover)
well-born		were	where (place)
well-bred		we're (we are)	
well-built		were	we're (we are)
well-connected		wereabouts	whereabouts
well-defined		wereas	whereas
well-deserved		wereby	whereby
well-developed		werefore	wherefore
well-disposed		wereof	whereof
well-founded		wereon	whereon
well-groomed		weren't (were not)	
well-grounded		werent	weren't
well-heeled		wereupon	whereupon
well-informed		werever	wherever
well-known		werewithal	wherewithal
well-liked		werewolf, -wolves	
well-loved		werey	weary
well-meaning		werisum	wearisome
well-off		werk	work

For other **werk-** words,
look under **work-**.

well-planned		werld	world

For other **werl-** words,
look under **worl-**.

well-preserved			
well-qualified		werm	worm
well-read			

For other **wer-** words,
look under **wor-**.

well-rounded		west	
well-spoken		westbound	
well-to-do		westerly, -lies	
well-traveled		western	
well-wisher		Westerner	
welsh, -ed, -ing		westernize, -nized, -nizing	
Welsh, Welch		westernmost	
welt		westward	
welter		westwardly	
welterweight		wet, wetted, wetting (soak)	
welth	wealth	wet, wetter, wettest	
wen (swelling)		wet, -ly, -ness	
wen	when (time)	wet	whet (sharpen)
wench			
wend, -ed, -ing			
wenever	whenever		
Wensday	Wednesday		
went			
wepon	weapon		
wept			

wether (gelding)
  wether   weather (rain)
  wether   whether (if)
  wetherboard   weatherboard
  wethercock   weathercock
  wethervane   weather vane
wetlands
wet suit
we've (we have)
  weve   weave (cloth)
  weve   we've (we have)
  weevel   weevil
whack, -ed, -ing
whale, whales (mammal)
whale, whaled, whaling
whaleboat
whalebone
whaler
wham, whammed, whamming
whammy, -mies
wharf, wharves, wharfs
what (interrogative)
  what   watt (energy)
whatever
whatnot
what's (what is, has, does)
whatsoever
wheat
wheat germ
wheedle, -dled, -dling
wheel (disk)
  wheel   weal (hurt)
  wheel   we'll (we will)
wheelbarrow
wheelchair
wheeler-dealer
  wheet   wheat
wheeze, wheezed, wheezing
wheezy, -zier, -ziest
whelk
whelp
when
whenever
  wheras   whereas
where (place)
  where   ware (goods)
  where   wear (cover)

where   were (was)
whereabouts
whereas
whereby
wherefore
whereof
whereon
whereupon
wherever
wherewithal
  wherl   whirl (spin)
  wherl   whorl (circle)
whet, whetted, whetting (sharpen)
  whet   wet (soak)
whether (if)
  whether   weather (condition)
  whether   wether (gelding)
whew
whey (liquid)
  whey   way (method)
  whey   weigh (amount)
which (pronoun)
  which   witch (magic)
whichever
whiff
Whig (politics)
  whig   wig (hair)
while, whiled, whiling (time)
  while   wile (trick)
whim
whimper, -ed, -ing
whimsey, -sies
whimsical, -ally
whimsicality, -ties
whimsy, -sies
whine, whined, whining (complain)
  whine   wine (grape juice)
whinny, -nies
whinny, -nied, -nying
whip, whipped, whipping
whipcord
whiplash
whippersnapper
whippet

whippoorwill
whipsaw
whir, whirred, whirring
whirl (spin)
   whirl   whorl (circle)
whirlpool
whirlwind
whisk, -ed, -ing
whisker
whiskey, whisky, -keys, -kies
   whisle   whistle
whisper, -ed, -ing
whist
whistle, -tled, -tling
whistler
whistle stop
whit (jot)
   whit   wit (humor)
white, whiter, whitest
whitebait, -bait
whitecap
white-collar
white elephant
whitefish, -fish, -fishes
white flag
White House
white lie
whitewall
whitewash
whither (where)
   whither   wither (shrivel)
whiting
whitish
whitlow
whittle, -tled, -tling
whiz, whizzed, whizzing
who
whoa (interjection)
   whoa   woe (sorrow)
who'd (who would)
   whod   who'd
whodunit
whoever
whole (all)
   whole   hole (opening)
wholehearted, -ly, -ness
whole number

wholesale, -saled, -saling
wholesome, -ly, -ness
whole-wheat
who'll (who will)
   wholl   who'll
wholly (all)
   wholly   holey (holes)
   wholly   holly (plant)
   wholly   holy (religious)
whom
   whom   womb (uterus)
whoop (cry)
   whoop   hoop (ring)
whoopee
whooping cough
whoops
whoosh
whopper
whopping
whore (prostitute)
   whore   who're (who are)
who're (who are)
   who're   whore
                (prostitute)
whorl (circle)
   whorl   whirl (spin)
whorled
who's (who is, has)
   whos   who's
   whos   whose (of
                whom)
whose (of whom)
   whose   who's (who is,
                has)
whosoever
   whur   whir
   whurl   whirl (spin)
   whurl   whorl (circle)
who've (who have)
   whove   who've
why, whys
   wich   which
                (pronoun)
   wich   witch (magic)
wick
wicked, -ly, -ness
wicker

wickerwork
wicket
wickiup
  widdow   widow
wide, wider, widest
wide, -ly, -ness
wide-angle
wide-awake
wide-eyed
widemouthed
widen, -ed, -ing
wide-open
wide-ranging
widespread
widow, -ed, -ing
widower
width
wield, -ed, -ing (brandish)
  wierd   weird
wife, wives
wig, wigged, wigging (hair)
  wig   Whig (politics)
wiggle, -gled, -gling
wiggly
wigwam
wilco
wild, -ly, -ness
wildcat, -catted, -catting
wilderness
wild-eyed
wildfire
wildfowl
wild-goose chase
wildlife
wile (trick)
  wile   while (time)
will, -ed, -ing
willful, -ly, -ness
willingness
will-o'-the-wisp
willow
willowy
willpower
willy-nilly
  wilst   whilst
wilt, wilted, wilting
wily, -lier, -liest

  wim   whim
  wimen   women

> For other wi- words,
> look under **whi-**.

wimp
wimple, -pled, -pling
win, won, winning
wince, winced, wincing
winch, winched, winching
wind, -ed, -ing (air)
wind, wound, winding (turn)
windbag
windblown
windbreak
windburn
windfall
windjammer
windlass
windless, -ly, -ness
windmill
window
window box
window dressing
window-shop, -shopped, -shopping
window shopper
windpipe
windproof
windrow
windshield
windsock
windstorm
windsurfing
wind surfer
windswept
windup
windward
windy, windier, windiest
wine, wined, wining (grape juice)
  wine   whine (complain)
wineglass
wing
winged
wingspan
wingspread
wink, -ed, -ing

winner
winnings
winnow, -ed, -ing
winsome, -ly, -ness
winsomeness
winter
wintergreen
winterize, -ized, -izing
wintertime
wintry
wip   whip

> For other wip- words,
> look under **whip-**.

wipe, wiped, wiping
wipe out
wiper
wippoorwill   whippoorwill
wire, wired, wiring
wirehaired
wireless
wirl   whirl (spin)
wirl   whorl (circle)
wirr   whir
wiry, wirier, wiriest
wisdom
wisdom tooth, -teeth
wise, wiser, wisest
wisecrack
wish, -ed, -ing
wishbone
wishful, -ly, -ness
wishy-washy
wisk   whisk

> For other wis- words,
> look under **whis-**.

wisp, -ed, -ing
wisteria
wistful, -ly, -ness
wit (humor)
wit   whit (jot)

> For other wit- words,
> look under **whit-**.

witch (magic)
witch   which

                 (pronoun)
witchcraft
witch doctor
witch hunt
with
withdraw, -drew, -drawn, -drawing
withdrawal
withdrawn
withdroo   withdrew
wither, -ed, -ing (shrivel)
wither   whither (where)
withers
withhold, -held, -holding
withholder
within
withold   withhold
without
withstand, -stood, -standing
witless, -ly, -ness
witness, -ed, -ing
witth   width
witticism
wittisism   witticism
wittle   whittle
witty, -tier, -tiest
wives
wiz   whiz
wizard
wizdom   wisdom
wizened
wizerd   wizard
wo   whoa
                 (interjection)
wo   woe (sorrow)
wobble, -bled, -bling
wod   wad
woddle   waddle
woe (sorrow)
woe   whoa
                 (interjection)
woebegone
woeful, -ly, -ness
woft   waft
woful   woeful
wok
wolf, wolves
wolfhound

wolfram	
wollet	wallet
wollop	wallop
wollow	wallow
wolves	
wom	womb
woman, women	
womanhood	
womanish	
womanize, -nized, -nizing	
womanizer	
womankind	
womanlike	
womanly, -liness	
woman's rights	
womb	
wombat	
women (plural of woman)	
women	woman
womenfolk	
won (win)	
won	one (number)
wonder, -ed, -ing (think)	
wonder	wander (walk)
wonderful, -ly, -ness	
wonderland	
wonderment	
wondrous, -ly, -ness	
wondrus	wondrous
wont (accustomed)	
wont	want (need)
wont	won't (will not)
won't (will not)	
won ton (dough)	
wonton	wanton (lewd)
woo, -ed, -ing	
wood (timber)	
wood	would (will)
woodblock	
woodcarver	
woodcarving	
woodchopper	
woodchuck	
woodcock	
woodcut	
woodcutter	
wooded	

wooden, -ly, -ness	
woodland	
wood lot	
woodman, -men	
woodpecker	
woodpile	
woodshed	
woodsman	
woodwind	
woodwork	
woody, woodier, woodiest	
woof, -ed, -ing	
woofer	
wool	
woolen	
woolf	wolf
woolgathering	
woolgrower	
woolly, -lier, -liest	
woom	womb
wooman	woman
woond	wound
woozy, -zily, -ziness	
wop	whop (hit)
wor	war
worble	warble
word, -ed, -ing	
worden	warden
wordless, -ly, -ness	
wordplay	
word processor	
wordrobe	wardrobe
wordy, -dier, -diest	
wordy, -dily, -diness	
wore	
worf	wharf
worfair	warfare
work, worked, working	
workable	
workaday	
workaholic	
workbench	
workbox	
workday	
worker	
work force	
workhorse	

workhouse
working capital
working-class, -classes
working model
workman, -men
workmanship
workout
workroom
workshop
worktable
work week

worl	whirl (spin)
worl	whorl (circle)

world (earth)

world	whirled (spun)

worldbeater
world-famous
worldliness
worldly, -lier, -liest
worldwide
worm, wormed, worming (animal)

worm	warm (heat)
wormth	warmth

wormwood
wormy, wormier, wormiest
worn (tired)

worn	warn (signal)

worn-out

worp	warp

worrier
worrisome
worry, -ries
worry, -ried, -rying
worse
worsen, -ed, -ing
worship, -ed, -ing
worshiper
worst
worsted
wort (plant)

wort	wart (lump)

worth
worthless, -ly, -ness
worthwhile
worthy, -thier, -thiest
worthy, -ily, -iness

wos	was

For other wo- words,
look under **wa-**.

would (will)

would	wood (timber)

would-be
wouldn't (would not)

wouldnt	wouldn't

wound, wounded, wounding
(injure)
wove
woven
wrack (wreck)

wrack	rack (shelf)

wraith
wrangle, -gled, -gling
wrangler
wrap, wrapped or wrapt,
wrapping (cover)

wrap	rap (strike)

wrapper
wrath
wrathful, -ly, -ness
wreak, -ed, -ing (inflict)

wreak	wreck (destroy)
wreak	reek (smell)

wreath, wreaths (flowers)
wreathe, -thed, -thing (encircle)
wreck, -ed, -ing (destroy)

wreck	wreak (inflict)
wreck	reek (smell)

wreckage
wrecker

wrek	wreck

wren
wrench, -ed, -ing
wrest, -ed, -ing (grab)

wrest	rest (sleep)

wrestle, -tled, -tling
wrestler
wretch (victim)

wretch	retch (vomit)

wretched, -ly, -ness

wri	wry

wriggle, -gled, -gling
wriggler

wriggly
   wrigle   wriggle
wring, wrung, wringing (squeeze)
   wring   ring (bell)
wringer (squeezer)
   wringer   ringer (bell)
wrinkle, -kled, -kling
wrist
wristband
wristlet
wristwatch
writ
write, wrote, written, writing
(inscribe)
   write   right (correct)
   write   rite (ceremony)
writeoff
writer
writhe, writhed, writhing
written
wrong
wrongdoing
wrongful, -ly, -ness
wroth
wrought (work)
wrought iron
wrung (squeezed)
   wrung   rung (did ring,
                          step)
wry, wryer, wryest or wrier, wriest
(askew)
   wry   rye (grain)
   wun   one (number)
   wun   won (win)
   wunce   once
   wunder   wonder
   wunse   once
   wur   whir
   wurl   whirl (spin)
   wurl   whorl (circle)
   wurld   world
   wurm   worm
   wurry   worry
   wurse   worse
   wurship   worship

x-axis
X chromosome
x-coordinate
   X cromosome   X chromosome
   xenofobia   xenophobia
xenolith
xenophobe
xenophobia
xenophobic
   xerograf   xerograph
   xerografic   xerographic
   xerografy   xerography
xerograph
xerographic
xerography
   xeroks   Xerox
Xerox
Xmas
x-rated
x-ray, x ray, X-ray
x-ray, x ray, X-ray, -ed, -ing
x-ray tube
   x-rey   x-ray
xylem
   xylofone   xylophone
   xylograf   xylograph
   xylografer   xylographer
   xylografic   xylographic
   xylografy   xylography
xylograph
xylographer
xylographic
xylography
xyloid
xylophagous
xylophone
xylophonic
xylophonist

Yy

y	why
yacht	
yachting	
yack	yak
yaht	yacht
yak, yakked, yakking	
yam	
yamaka	yarmulke
yank, -ed, -ing (pull)	
Yank (American)	
Yankee	
yap, yapped, yapping	
yard	
yardage	
yardarm	
yardbird	
yardstick	
yarmulke	
yarn, -ed, -ing	
yaw, -ed, -ing (move)	
yaw	yore (long ago)
yaw	your (pronoun)
yaw	you're (you are)
yawl	
yawn, -ed, -ing	
yaws (disease)	
yaws	yours (pronoun)
y-axis	
yay	yea
Y chromosome	
Y cromosome	Y chromosome
ye	
yea	
yeah	
yeald	yield
year	
yearbook	

year-end	
yearling	
yearlong	
yearly	
yearn, -ed, -ing	
year-round	
yeast	
yeasty, yeastier, yeastiest	
yeasty, -ily, -iness	
yeeld	yield
yeer	year
yeest	yeast
veild	yield
yell, -ed, -ing	
yellow	
yellowbellied	
yellowish	
yellow pages	
yelow	yellow
yelowish	yellowish
yelp, -ed, -ing	
yen	
yeoman, -men	
yern	yearn
yerself	yourself
yes, yeses	
yesman, -men	
yesterday	
yesteryear	
yestirday	yesterday
yet	
yeti	
yety	yeti
yew (tree)	
yew	ewe (sheep)
yew	you (pronoun)
yewse	use
yewsual	usual
yewsuul	usual

> For other ye- words,
> look under **u-**.

Yiddish
yield, -ed, -ing
yin and yang
yippee
yodel, -ed, -ing

yodeler
  yodle — yodel
yoga
  yogert — yoghurt
  yogert — yogurt
yoghurt, yogurt
yogi, -gis
yoke, yoked, yoking (frame)
  yoke — yolk (egg)
yokel
  yokle — yokel
yolk (egg)
  yolk — yoke (frame)
  yoman — yeoman
Yom Kippur
  yon — yawn
yonder
yore (long ago)
  yore — yaw (move)
  yore — your (pronoun)
  yore — you're (you are)
  yors — yours
  yot — yacht
you (pronoun)
  you — ewe (sheep)
  you — yew (tree)
you'd (you would)
  youd — you'd
you'll (you will)
  you'll — yule (Christmas)
  youll — you'll
young
youngster
your (pronoun)
  your — yaw (move)
  your — yore (long ago)
  your — you're (you are)
you're (you are)
  youre — you're
yours
  your's — yours
yourself, -selves
youth, youths
  youthanasia — euthanasia
youthful, -ly, -ness
you've (you have)

  youve — you've
yowl, -ed, -ing
yo-yo, -yos
yuan
yucca
yule (Christmas)
  yule — you'll (you will)
yummy, yummier, yummiest
  yung — young
  yungster — youngster
  yurn — yearn
  yuse — use
  yuscful — useful
  yusual — usual
  yutensil — utensil
  yuterine — uterine
  yuterus — uterus
  yuth — youth
  yutilise — utilize
  yutopia — Utopia, utopia

> For other yu- words,
> look under u-.

Zz

zabaglione
zany, -nier, -niest
zap, zapped, zapping
  zar   czar
  zar   tsar
  zar   tzar
  Zavier   Xavier
zeal
zealot
zealotry
zealous, -ly
zebra
zebu
  zeel   zeal
  zefer   zephyr
  zelot   zealot
  zelous   zealous
Zen
zenith
zenithal
  zenofobia   xenophobia
  zenophobia   xenophobia
  zepher   zephyr
zephyr
  zeplen   zeppelin
Zeppelin, zeppelin
  zercon   zircon
zero, -ros, -roes
zero, -roed, -roing
  zeroks   Xerox
zero population growth
  zerox   Xerox
zest
zestful, -ly, -ness
  zigote   zygote
zigzag, -zagged, -zagging
zilch
zillion

  zilofone   xylophone
  zilophone   xylophone
zinc
zing
  zink   zinc
zinnia
Zion
Zionism
Zionist
zip, zipped, zipping
zip code
zipper
zippy, -pier, -piest
zircon
zirconium
  ziro   zero
zither
zodiac
zodiacal
zombie
  zomby   zombie
zone, zoned, zoning
zonked
zoo
  zoochini   zucchini
  zoologey   zoology
zoological, -ly
zoologist
zoology, -gies
zoom, -ed, -ing
zoomorphism
zoophyte
zooplankton
zoophore
zoot suit
zucchini, zucchini, zucchinis
Zulu, -lus, -lu
Zuñi, -ñis, -ñi
zwieback
zygote
  zylophone   xylophone

> Look under **x-** if the
> word is not under **z-**.